Economic Lessons from China's Forty Years of Reform and Opening-up

David Daokui Li
Editor

Economic Lessons from China's Forty Years of Reform and Opening-up

清華大學出版社
TSINGHUA UNIVERSITY PRESS

Springer

Editor
David Daokui Li
An Academic Center for Chinese Economic Practice and Thinking
Tsinghua University
Beijing, China

ISBN 978-981-33-4522-5 ISBN 978-981-33-4520-1 (eBook)
https://doi.org/10.1007/978-981-33-4520-1

Jointly published with Tsinghua University Press
The print edition is not for sale in China Mainland. Customers from China Mainland please order the print book from: Tsinghua University Press

This Springer imprint is published by the registered company Springer Nature Singapore Pte Ltd.
The registered company address is: 152 Beach Road, #21-01/04 Gateway East, Singapore 189721, Singapore

Preface

In this report, we demonstrate that the past 40 years of China's economic reform and opening up represent the greatest magnitude of economic growth in history. These 40 years are unique in comparison with other episodes of rapid economic growth, including the British Industrial Revolution; the US economic emergence following the Civil War; Japanese economic growth after the Meiji restoration; German economic development following unification; and the economic take-off of the Four Tigers. The most unique aspect of China's economic growth is that it began under extremely tight government political control. Because of the uniqueness of the Chinese experience, we argue that China's rapid growth serves as an invaluable laboratory for understanding the relationship between the government and the economy.

Based on field visits, extensive and intensive interviews, and literature surveys, we argue that there are five general lessons for a rapidly growing economy that can be taken from China's economic reform and opening up, all pertaining to the relationship between the government and the economy. First, local governments should be incentivized to assist with the rapid entry and development of enterprises. Second, local governments should also be incentivized to facilitate rapid land conversion from agricultural to non-agricultural. Third, financial deepening is vital—that is, inducing households to hold an increasing number of financial assets in the local currency. Financial deepening is essential for converting savings into investments. This requires financial stability, which is crucial. Fourth, learning through opening up is the key to endogenous economic growth. In fact, the fundamental benefit of opening up is learning rather than enjoying a comparative advantage. Comparative advantage alone can often trap the economy at a low level of development. The fifth and final lesson from China is that the central government must proactively manage the macroeconomy. The rationale for this is that enterprises compete with each other in games of industrial organization. Therefore, we often find too many enterprises entering the same industry and then becoming reluctant to exit from a crowded market. In order to resolve this problem, proactive measures including market-oriented means, administrative orders, and reform measures should be implemented.

The primary lesson from China's past 40 years of reform and opening up is that proper incentives and behavior of the government, at both a local and central level, are important for economic growth. China has conducted reforms along these lines, and as a result, the government has essentially played the role of a "helping hand" for economic growth. However, China's economic system is far from perfect and many reforms are still needed.

Beijing, China
2020

David Daokui Li

Research Team

David Daokui Li, Keaobo Li, Gangming Yuan, Hongling Wang, Meixin Guo, Bing Li, Lin Lu, Lin Fu, Ming Feng, Xiang Xu, Jinjian Shi, Xingye Jin, Shaobo Long, Hongyu Zhao, Sijia Hu, Dapeng Chen, Yusha Li, Di Zhou, Chi Zhang, Yifan Chen, Xushuo Wang, Peng Zhou, He Zhang, Kangyi Liu, Kun Lang

Contents

Introduction

David Daokui Li

Among the many significant 40 year periods in history, China's past four decades stand out. Over this span, China's share of global GDP has risen from 4.9% to 18.2%. In comparison, during the 40 years of British Industrial Revolution, Britain's share of global GDP increased from 3.8% to 5.9%. During the 40 years following the American Civil War, the US share of global GDP increased from 7.9% to 17.3%. During the 40 years after the Japanese Meiji Restoration and the 40 years following World War II, Japan's GDP share increased from 2.3% to 2.6% and from 3.3% to 8.9%, respectively. Finally, during the 40 years of rapid growth among the Asian Tigers (Hong Kong China, South Korea, Singapore, and Taiwan China) from 1960 to 2000, their share of GDP increased from 0.7% to 3.5%. Thus, in terms of magnitude, China's past 40 years represent the single greatest leap of economic growth in history.

The past 40 years are also special to China because they represent the country's greatest global economic revival in nearly five centuries. According to a study by Broadberry, Fu, Guan, Jin, and Li, China's share of the world's GDP, when at its peak around the year 1600, was 34.6%. However, this share subsequently experienced a decline, which accelerated starting in 1820 when other countries began to industrialize. By 1978, at the beginning of reform and opening up, China's GDP share stood at 4.9%. Now, after 40 years, China's share of world GDP has reached 18.2%.

Why is it important to take stock of the economic knowledge acquired from the past 40 years of China's reform? After all, despite the impressive growth of the Chinese economy, 40 years is still a comparatively brief time in history. The first reason is rather obvious: for China's own sake. China did many things right on its journey to produce the largest amount of economic growth in history, but it also did many things wrong. Thus, many aspects of the Chinese economy still require further reform and restructuring. Therefore, it is essential for Chinese economists as well

D. D. Li (✉)
An Academic Center for Chinese Economic Practice and Thinking (ACCEPT), Tsinghua University, Beijing, China
e-mail: daviddaokuili@126.com

D. D. Li (eds.), *Economic Lessons from China's Forty Years of Reform and Opening-up*, https://doi.org/10.1007/978-981-33-4520-1_1

as economists with an interest in the Chinese economy to study economic lessons from the past 40 years. Economists outside China should also be interested in the Chinese economy, given that it has already become the world's second-largest and contributes the greatest amount to global growth.

The second reason why we should study economic lessons from the past 40 years is that China's economic growth is unique in comparison with other 40-year periods. The single-most unique feature is that it began in a tightly controlled economy under a very powerful government, although the Chinese economy was not a centrally planned economy like the former Soviet Union. Starting from a tightly controlled economy, China has been adjusting its relationship between the government and the economy over the past 40 years. This process, of course, is unique. Knowledge is often gained through special cases, which provide more insights than uniform and repeated events. In the Chinese case, the relationship between the government and the economy is the area from which economists can most likely gain valuable insights potentially relevant to other economies.

The third reason why it is crucial to take stock of the economic lessons from China's past 40 years of reform is that a growing number of emerging market economies have taken an interest in China's experience of rapid economic growth. World leaders are trying to identify and understand the Chinese policies and institutions from which they can learn. There are many special kinds of Chinese political and economic arrangements that cannot be duplicated in other countries, yet there are numerous general lessons to be gleaned from China's experience.

China's past rapid economic growth can be explained in many ways. The most general and perhaps the most famous analysis came from Deng Xiaoping, who from the very beginning of the reform continually said that China should "emancipate the mind" and "seek truth from facts." That is to say, China should experiment in whichever ways necessary to find the most appropriate institutions and policies for economic success. This, of course, is the most fundamental lesson from China's economic reform.

The second approach to understanding China's economic success is to rely on existing wisdom from economics textbooks. That is, for example, to argue that China correctly placed significant emphasis on education and, even before the reform era, provided girls with the same educational opportunities and priorities as boys. Within this approach, some analysts argue that China was successful because it implemented the protection of property rights and privatized state-owned enterprises, while others say that China relied on playing up its comparative advantage through international trade. Each of these points is grounded in truth—indeed, China has made progress in all of these areas.

Yet another approach to explaining China's economic success is to go deeper and examine the specific institutional factors behind China's growth, such as the details of gradualist reform [1–6]. Research has demonstrated how China's local governments have consistently been incentivized to experiment, especially because pre-reform China was decentralized, with each province functioning as an independent and self-contained unit. From these locally initiated experiments, the central government has been able to identify the most successful ones. An example of this can also be seen in the Soviet Union, where the economy was vertically integrated, with each region specializing in a few lines of production. Another line of research argues that China's success is due to the neutral decision-making of the Chinese Communist Party, which is free from the control of interest groups. Each of these points provides effective analyses of China's institutional setup.

In our report, we take a different approach. We inquire: Are there general economic textbook principles that we can learn from China's economic reform and opening up? Are there common principles of rapid economic growth that were also at play in other economies during periods such as the British Industrial Revolution, the US economic emergence following the Civil War, and Japanese economic growth after the Meiji Restoration and World War II—principles that might have been forgotten or ignored? Are there general economic principles at the policy level that other countries can learn or duplicate? These are the questions we attempt to address in this report.

In order to answer these questions, the Academic Center for Chinese Economic Practice and Thinking of Tsinghua University formed a research team consisting of faculty members from Tsinghua University as well as research fellows and Ph.D. students. Because we believe that it is essential to obtain first-hand and detailed knowledge from the grassroots level, we made several field visits to representative areas of China. One such field visit was to the province of Jiangsu, which has the highest per capita GDP and the second-largest economy among Chinese provinces. We visited two cities in Jiangsu: one on the northern section of the Yangtze River and another on the southern section, which is traditionally more dynamic and enterprising. We also visited "China's Detroit," the city of Shenyang, which suffered tremendous pains from China's opening up. Shenyang was the industrial capital of China and received the most Soviet Union industrial support in the 1950 s. At one time, there were 1,400 state-owned enterprises under the municipal government of Shenyang—today, only 26 survive. In addition to these field visits, we interviewed dozens of officials in the central government who experienced and participated in the process of reform and opening up, including officials retired from or active in the National Development and Reform Commission, the Ministry of Finance, the Central Bank, the Chinese Banking and Insurance Regulatory Commission, the Ministry of Urban and Housing Development, and the Ministry of Natural Resources, as well as other entities. They provided significant insights into the process of decision-making reform. In addition, we also examined a monumental number of documents written by policymakers, including speeches of senior leaders such as Chen Yun, Deng Xiaoping, Jiang Zemin, Zhu Rongji, and Xi Jinping.

There are two important caveats we would like to express before summarizing our findings. First, by no means do we claim or believe that China's economic reform has been a complete success. Indeed, there are many aspects of China's economic system that require further reform. We also acknowledge that Chinese decision-makers made incorrect decisions in many areas. The purpose of our exercise is to determine what China did correctly and which steps China still needs to take in order to improve and progress. For example, in our study of opening up, we concluded that in the past decade, China has not continued opening up as the policy originally intended and that the process of opening up should have been more rapid. As a result of recent decisive moves by senior Chinese leaders, the pace of reform and the re-opening process have finally increased. The second caveat is that we attempt to refrain from ideological labeling and the ongoing political disputes between China and some Western nations. We do our best to remain in the domain of economics and to understand and explain the general principles behind China's economic reform and opening up.

We summarize the five basic lessons from China's 40 years of reform and opening up below.

First, in order to have rapid economic growth, it is necessary to facilitate the fast entry and development of new firms. Furthermore, in order for new firms to start up, there must be a positive market and business environment. However, market imperfections often exist, and local governments hold the key to resolving such imperfections. Local governments must be pro-business, and in order to facilitate this, government officials need to be incentivized. For rapid growth to occur, they must support and assist new enterprises in the resolution of any issues including the use of land, hiring labor, and clearing licenses. Even in the United States, new businesses encounter issues such as those involving highly skilled labor through immigration—issues which must be resolved through the relaxation of immigration policies. For example, in Silicon Valley, high housing prices, which in turn increase labor costs, are another issue requiring resolution by local governments. The key lesson from China is that local government officials must be incentivized to help new local businesses, and incentives in the Chinese case can come both in political and economic forms. Political incentives emanate from the fact that the promotion of local government officials is based increasingly on local economic performance in comparison with peer governments. In the Chinese case, economic incentives are also important for local government officials because only prosperous local enterprises can provide tax revenues to governments—especially in the early days, during which local governments are able to return much of the new tax revenue. Thus, local governments compete with their peers in supporting new enterprises, often establishing industrial parks to help attract business investments. Officials managing the industrial parks are highly incentivized since their pay is linked to the amount of tax revenue they generate.

The second lesson from China is that rapid land conversion is a key component of rapid economic growth. This is a lesson that is grossly ignored by modern economics. Before a business grows, it must use land which is already occupied. Thus, the conversion of the rights of land use from one economic agent to another is the key.

This process is often tremendously costly because of the expensive nature of Coasian bargaining. In the Chinese case, local governments are incentivized and have the authority to accelerate the process. Over the course of land conversion, most of the land for China's economic growth—whether through industrial parks or real estate developers—came directly from local governments. This land was either auctioned off by local governments to developers for housing projects or directly awarded to industrial enterprises at a low fee. The rapid land conversion facilitated by this process has been crucial for the rapid entry of new enterprises. We also see evidence for this phenomenon during the early days of the British Industrial Revolution, during which the government helped industrialists eliminate the commons and forced farmers to work in industry. However, in modern economics, the availability of land is rarely mentioned and implicitly assumed.

The third general economic lesson is that "financial deepening" and financial stability are essential for economic growth. Financial deepening refers to the phenomenon that occurs when households are comfortable enough and willing to hold an increasing amount of their wealth in financial assets, such that the growth in financial assets can outpace economic growth. Financial deepening is essential for investment in the real economy because it allows household savings to be transformed into investments via the financial sector. Otherwise, individual savers would be forced to find investors who could potentially be uninformed about what to do with the investments. In the Chinese case, the volume of financial assets has increased to about four times the GDP. As a general rule, the financial sector must be reasonably stable in order to cultivate financial deepening. Otherwise, households will not be willing to hold financial assets, and will instead rely on banks or other financial institutions. Furthermore, financial deepening must be conducted in the local currency. This way, local enterprises can borrow domestically rather than from foreign countries—a potential source of financial instability. In order to maintain financial stability, the central government must be very proactive in dealing with any potential financial risks, especially those associated with commercial banks, as commercial banks attract a large number of small investors. When investors lose their confidence, it can easily become an epidemic. In the Chinese case, the central government has imposed severe punishments (including the death penalty) on those accused or suspected of behavior undermining the banking sector. On the other hand, the government has been relatively relaxed regarding the Chinese stock market—in this sector, no such sentences have been imposed for fraudulent behavior.

The fourth economic lesson from China is that learning through opening up is vital in order for the economy to grow endogenously rather than relying heavily on foreign capital and technologies. All economic agents, ranging from entrepreneurs and workers to the government, must learn. Moreover, the most effective mechanism for learning is opening up. Opening up certainly creates opportunities to boost comparative advantage, but comparative advantage alone is not sufficient, as it may trap the economy in low value-added activities. Rather, learning is the most fundamental benefit of opening up. There are numerous examples demonstrating that opening up to advanced market economies enabled Chinese economic agents to learn new business models, management techniques, and market development strategies. However, opening up also carries risks, and the government must absorb the resulting shocks. During its opening up process, China had problems similar to Detroit, but the central and local governments have worked hard to compensate by helping to retrain unemployed workers in the outdated industries and assisting municipal governments in attracting new businesses to create tax revenue. Unemployment is an area in which opening up should be carefully managed.

China's opening up was often in conflict with the principle of comparative advantage, but nevertheless proved to be successful. For example, the Chinese automobile industry was developed as early as the 1980 s even though China's comparative advantage at this time was to export labor-intensive products and import passenger cars, rather than to develop a domestic automobile industry for local consumption. China attracted a German auto firm to form a joint venture and required it to gradually increase its number of locally sourced components. The entire industry of automobile parts began to thrive as automobile factories helped local parts suppliers produce parts. Following this, related industries began to take off. Again, learning is the key—it is the most fundamental benefit of opening up and is the foundation for economic upgrading. In comparison with comparative advantage, this has not been emphasized enough in economics textbooks. In US economic history, comparative advantage was not at play at all during the industrialization process. During the Civil War, the North opposed free trade. The North wanted to develop its own textile industry instead of sending US cotton to the UK. The UK subsequently blocked technology transfer to the United States by prohibiting textile workers from working there. However, a young British textile engineer named Samuel Slater memorized details of the textile machines and went to the United States to help establish America's industrial textile industry. The British regarded Slater as a traitor, but US President Andrew Jackson dubbed him the father of the American Industrial Revolution.

The fifth and final lesson from China's 40 years of opening up is that the central government must proactively manage the macroeconomy during rapid economic growth, which inevitably creates macroeconomic shocks. Sometimes the economy becomes too hot, while at other times it becomes too cold. In the Chinese case, we found that there tends to be intense competition among enterprises during the upswing of the macroeconomic cycle. Most enterprises decide to gamble and expand production because if they can reach the top of the industry, their market powers will be secured. However, if they fail to reach the top, they will suffer severe losses. It is rational for new enterprises to gamble because the expected return is extremely high. As enterprises rush to increase their production capacity, the result is an excess in both investment and production capacity. On the other hand, when the macroeconomy is slow, the incumbent industries are reluctant to exit. This is because if they can survive while waiting for others to leave the market, they will be able to generate profits because their prices will recover. This is like the war of attrition in game theory, where equilibrium creates an outcome of delayed adjustment.

Both the equilibria of the "rush to the top" and the "war of attrition" are rational from the perspective of individual investors or enterprises. However, from the perspective of the economy as a whole, they are not socially efficient because the process of adjustment takes too long. In the Chinese case, the central government has always been active in managing the macroeconomy. When the economy is cool, the government forces unprofitable enterprises with redundant production capacity to exit by providing subsidies to help absorb unemployment. When the economy is running hot, new projects are prohibited and the government instructs banks to cut down on loans to industries. In addition, the central government utilizes multiple measures, including market-oriented measures such as fiscal policy and monetary policy, administrative mandates, and reform measures to deal with macroeconomic cycles. Reform measures during the Asian financial crisis, for example, included measures to kick-start the housing market—which grew from almost nothing 20 years ago into the world's largest—and also to help universities expand enrollment.

Overall, the main lesson from China's past 40 years of reform and opening up is that proper incentives for and behavior of the central and local governments are important for economic growth. Often in economics, one assumes the role of the government and labels it as either benevolent or evil. The reality is far more complicated. The incentives and behavior of the government regarding the economy are critical issues requiring careful study. In the Chinese case, the government has been a helping hand in facilitating market growth. In previous episodes of rapid growth, other governments have also played a crucial role. Take, for example, the UK Industrial Revolution, when the government converted village commons into industrial plants and therefore induced farmers to work in factories. The historical role of governments in cases like these tends to be overlooked by modern economics.

The remainder of this report is organized in the following manner: Part one examines lessons regarding the rapid entry of new firms. Part two details lessons on the topic of rapid land conversion and the growth and cultivation of the real estate market. Part three explores financial deepening and financial stability. Part four considers opening up as an instrument for accelerating learning and therefore endogenous economic growth. Part five delves into proactive macroeconomic management.

References

1. Maskin, E., & Xu, C. (2001). Soft budget constraint theories: From centralization to the market. *Economics of Transition, 9*(1), 1–27.
2. Lau, L. J., Qian, Y., & Roland, G. (2000). reform without losers: an interpretation of China's dual-track approach to transition. *Journal of Political Economy, 108*(1), 120–143.
3. Bai, C. E., Li, D. D., Tao, Z., & Wang, Y. (1999). A multi-task theory of the state enterprise *Reform. In Journal of Comparative Economics.*
4. Li, D. D. (1998). Changing incentives of the chinese bureaucracy. *The American Economic Review, 88*(2), 393–397.
5. Qian, Y., & Xu, C. (1993). Why China's economic reforms differ: The m-form hierarchy and entry/expansion of the non -state sector. *Economics of Transition, 1*(2), 135–170.
6. Berglöf, E., & Roland, G. (1997). Soft budget constraints and credit crunches in financial transition. *European Economic Review, 41*(3–5), 807–817.

Rapid Entry and Development of Enterprises

David Daokui Li, Keaobo Li, Xingye Jin, Hongling Wang, Xiang Xu, and Kun Lang

Abstract Governmental assistance in the rapid entry and development of enterprises has been a direct impetus for the rapid economic growth of China. The development and success of enterprises depend greatly on the role of the "visible hand" of local governments. Governments at all levels, especially at the local level, can guide the coordinated development of both upstream and downstream industries by continuously helping new enterprises solve practical problems in terms of land, labor, and transportation coordination. Based on the aforementioned basic facts and history of enterprise entry and development, we arrive at the following two economic conclusions: first, during the process of reform and opening up, incentives for governments to cultivate and assist enterprises were of utmost importance for enterprise entry and development; second, since local governments were subject to a certain amount of blindness and limitation, they occasionally made some irrational decisions in the process of assisting enterprises with their entry and development. A corresponding restrictive system should be put in place to regulate local governments' behavior as they help with enterprise entry and development.

D. D. Li (✉) · K. Li · H. Wang
An Academic Center for Chinese Economic Practice and Thinking (ACCEPT), Tsinghua University, Beijing, China
e-mail: daviddaokuili@126.com

K. Li
e-mail: likeaobo@126.com

H. Wang
e-mail: hlwang@cass.org.cn

X. Jin · X. Xu
Central University of Finance and Economics, Beijing, China
e-mail: starjinxy@126.com

X. Xu
e-mail: seanxuxiang@126.com

K. Lang
School of Economics and Management, Tsinghua University, Beijing, China
e-mail: langkunprc@gmail.com

D. D. Li (eds.), *Economic Lessons from China's Forty Years of Reform and Opening-up*, https://doi.org/10.1007/978-981-33-4520-1_2

Keywords Rapid entry · Governmental assistance · Coordinated development

1 Stylized Facts

Governmental assistance in the rapid entry and development of enterprises has been a direct impetus for the rapid economic growth of China ever since the inception of the drive for reform and opening up. The development and success of enterprises depend greatly on the role of the "visible hand" of local governments. Governments at all levels, especially at the local level, can guide the coordinated development of both upstream and downstream industries by continuously helping new enterprises solve practical problems in terms of land, labor, and transportation coordination. However, excessive governmental assistance to new enterprises may also bring about some side effects, including overlapping investment, overcapacity, and corruption, which can be improved by regulating governmental incentives in the medium to long term.

1.1 Rapid Entry and Development of Enterprises Is the Driving Force of the Chinese Economy

The most important lesson from China's 40-year process of economic reform and opening up is that governments at all levels, especially local governments, should give continuous assistance and support to new enterprises in order to facilitate their rapid entry, development, and success. New enterprises represent new social production demand and resident consumption demand, as well as new production capacity and a new form of production organization after economic development is improved. Well-developed new enterprises can generate remarkable upstream and downstream effects as well as industrial agglomeration, drive the rapid development of local economies, and create substantial tax revenues and employment opportunities. Therefore, it is clear that the rapid entry and development of enterprises has been a direct impetus for the rapid economic development of China since the inception of the reform and opening up policy (Chart 1).

One important piece of evidence that China's economic development has been directly driven by the rapid entry and development of enterprises is the contribution made to China's economic development by those enterprises established after 1978—the commencement of China's reform and opening up drive. For example, of the top 100 enterprises in the machinery industry announced by CMEMA and GlobalManufacturer.com each year for the past six years, enterprises established after the inception of reform and opening up account for about half of the top 100 enterprises. Furthermore, these new enterprises have an average ranking significantly higher than that of the enterprises established prior to the initiation of reform and opening up, fully illustrating the role of new enterprises in promoting the development of the

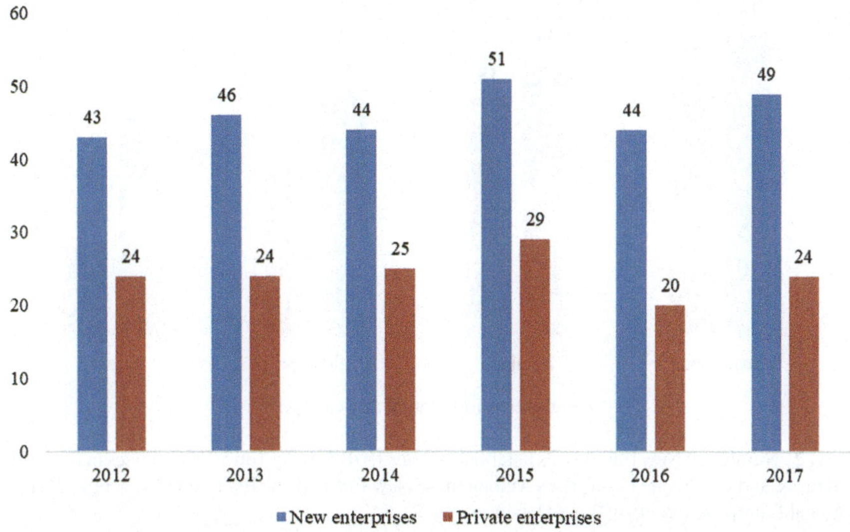

Chart 1 Number of New Enterprises Established after 1978 Among Top 100 Machinery Industry Enterprises, and Private Enterprises Among These New Enterprises. *Source* China Machinery Enterprise Management Association (CMEMA)

Chinese economy. In addition, in most years, more than half of these new enterprises named for their outstanding contributions to China's industrial development are private enterprises. **This proves that the Chinese government's facilitation of the rapid entry and development of enterprises is undiscriminating. Chinese local governments simply attract and help entrepreneurs rather than focusing on industrial policies. Furthermore, they don't favor state-owned enterprises over private ones or domestic businesses over foreign ones. The development of both private and state-owned enterprises would be impossible without the support and assistance of the government at all levels.**

The rapid entry and development of enterprises largely determines the development status of regional economies. Chart 2 shows the number of new enterprises established after the inception of reform and opening up among the top 50 enterprises in four provinces—namely Guangdong, Zhejiang, Heilongjiang, and Gansu—in the year of 2017 and the number of private enterprises among these new enterprises (excluding branches of large national enterprises). As can be seen from Chart 2, economically developed provinces have more new enterprises and private enterprises than less economically developed provinces, **suggesting that the rapid entry and development of enterprises can explain the difference in economic development between regions to a great extent.**

The third piece of strong evidence for the importance of the rapid entry and development of enterprises is the significant contributions they have made to China's economic growth. The new enterprises established after 1978 make up nearly all of the existing small and medium-sized enterprises. Table 1 shows the rates of contribution

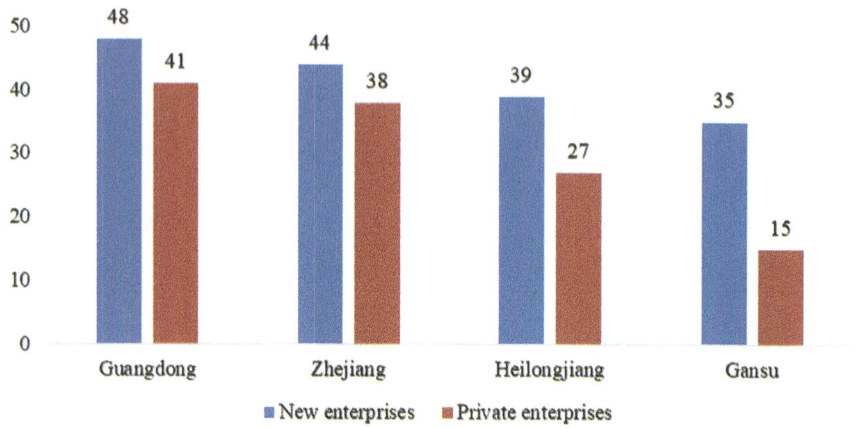

Chart 2 Number of New Enterprises Established after 1978 Among Top 50 Enterprises in Different Provinces, and the Private Enterprises Among these New Enterprises (Excluding Branches of Large National Enterprises) *Source* Wind Database

Table 1 Rates of Contribution by SMEs to Economic Growth

Province	Rate of contribution	Year
Guangdong	55%	2017
Fujian	~70%	2017
Henan	50%	2017
Shandong	65%	2015
Zhejiang	81.61%	2004–2008
Hubei	53%	2006
Hunan	42.4%	2011

Source Public Data

made by SMEs to economic growth in some provinces at the last available point in time. From the table, it can be seen that in the provinces with data, SMEs have made very important contributions to economic growth in their respective regions. Furthermore, the rates of contribution by new enterprises to economic growth are in reality much higher than reflected in the data—their contributions extend far beyond economic growth. Whether from the perspective of employment creation, upstream and downstream industry support, or social welfare, private enterprises have served as the backbone of China's economic development since the initiation of reform and opening up.

In addition to the three pieces of evidence previously specified, international experience also shows that governmental support for the development of new enterprises largely determines the soundness of a country's long-term economic development. In the 1980s, the Soviet Union and some Eastern European countries—all socialist countries like China—were faced with a choice between heavy and light industry and between old enterprises and new ones. These countries chose heavy industry and old enterprises, and thus input significant policy and social resources to save the old enterprises and give priority to the development of heavy industry. In the Soviet Union, for example, at the plenary session of the CPSU in April 1985, the then-supreme leader of the Soviet Union, Mikhail Gorbachev, proposed that economic leverage be used to actively support heavy industry—particularly, the pre-existing machine-building industry. He developed the twelfth five-year plan of the Soviet Union accordingly, but such attempts to revitalize old enterprises proved unsuccessful, resulting in the further expansion of the Soviet Union's budget deficit and an aggravated shortage of consumer goods. This exacerbated the worsening economic condition of the Soviet Union, and to a certain extent, sped up its collapse.

Joseph Alois Schumpeter stated that development is a qualitative spontaneous breakthrough inherent in economic life, and this spontaneous breakthrough comes from innovation, which is, in turn, a fundamental driving force for economic development. Innovation is the process of continuously destroying the old structure and creating a new one; more simply, it is the process of creative destruction wherein innovative and dynamic enterprises can thrive. During this process, old enterprises are eliminated in droves as new enterprises emerge, thus facilitating the optimized combination of production factors and promoting steady economic development. Each burst of large-scale innovation weeds out old technology and production systems, building new ones in their place. This theory can be applied to government economic policies **because new enterprises are better able to seize limited market opportunities, are subject to fewer restrictions in terms of enterprise transformation, and are free of various "burdens" unavoidable for old enterprises. Therefore, in order to promote local economic development and upgrade production systems to the fullest extent, governments at all levels should allocate limited planning, administrative, and financial resources to the rapid entry and development of enterprises. Such governmental support is independent from a country's political system and ideology, and is therefore largely universally applicable**.

Even in the United States, which advocates economic liberalism, governments at all levels—especially state governments—spare no effort to help establish and develop new enterprises. At the end of 2014, Tesla, an electric vehicle maker courted by many states, eventually decided to locate its Gigafactory in Nevada. The state was able to win Tesla's favor mainly through a new low tax policy. In order to attract Tesla to Nevada, in addition to individual income tax and corporate income tax reliefs, the state also released a series of tax preference policies, including refundable credit for employment creation and investment, sales tax relief, and property tax relief. Beyond Tesla, many other major US technology companies have received various subsidies from their respective state governments. For example, the parent company of Google has received a total of USD762 million in US governmental subsidies since 2000. Tesla has received over USD3.5 billion in subsidies since its establishment in 2007.

The incentives provided by various levels of the US government to facilitate the rapid entry and development of enterprises are not limited to domestic American enterprises. For example, Wisconsin and iPhone OEM Foxconn Technology Group signed an agreement in which the Wisconsin State Government agreed to provide

Foxconn with up to USD3 billion (later increased to USD3.1 billion) of income and sales tax relief over the course of 15 years, while Foxconn was expected to bring 13,000 high-paying jobs and USD10 billion of investment capital to the state. Wisconsin's governor called the deal a "golden opportunity" and a "change" for the state of Wisconsin. In another instance of international collaboration with a state government, Chinese pharmaceutical company Aland negotiated with Arkansas on its plan to build a plant in the state. The Arkansas State Government agreed that if Aland could offer 400 jobs, the state government would grant one square kilometer of land and assist with the plant's construction. Such examples of governmental assistance in the rapid entry and development of enterprises (including foreign enterprises) have not been uncommon in the 40-year process of China's reform and opening up.

1.2 Governments, Especially Local Governments, Have Strong Incentives to Help New Enterprises Form and Develop

Over the 40 years since the beginning of reform and opening up, the Chinese government at all levels has promoted the rapid entry and development of enterprises on a level that far exceeds the scope of industrial policy in the traditional sense. In this process of continuous exploration, the government at all levels has taken active measures to create conditions conducive to the rapid entry and development of enterprises, proactively carry out close interactions with market players, create a healthy and effective competition environment, and provide support at the key nodes of enterprise development. The government has accumulated valuable experiences through these practices, and has made the best use of circumstances to create a positive feedback loop in the national economy. From these experiences, we have identified two major ways in which the Chinese government facilitates the rapid entry and development of enterprises: namely, by creating a good business environment to actively attract investment and by helping enterprises restructure and upgrade in order to achieve institutional innovation.

(a) **Creating a good business environment to actively attract investment**

The government uses its "visible hand" to create a good business environment conducive to the entry and development of new enterprises. To accomplish this, the government develops appropriate macro and regional strategic plans and helps enterprises obtain the necessary factors of production.

As for local governments, they can play a regulating role in the overall economic layout planning and adjustment of cities and create favorable conditions for the rapid entry and development of enterprises. One prominent case is the "Industrial Relocation and Re-planning Program" of Tiexi District, Shenyang.

At the beginning of 2002, Tiexi District of Shenyang—often referred to as the "Oriental Ruhr"—fell into serious developmental difficulty. Many large state-owned enterprises in the district were struggling, leading to massive lay-offs of industrial workers. In actuality, the seeds of trouble were sown at the end of the 20th century, when the tide of market-oriented reform was surging high across the whole country but enterprises in Tiexi District remained predominantly public, with exclusively industrial economic structures. The state-owned economy and collective economy made up 99% of the total economy, and the industrial economy accounted for over 90%. Reform became imperative as some long-standing state-owned enterprises, such as Shenyang Explosion-proof Equipment Factory, Shenyang Tractor Factory, and Shenyang Smelter and Refinery of Nonferrous Metals declared bankruptcy one after another. Under the joint planning and unified support of various levels of government in Shenyang, more than 240 enterprises based in Tiexi District were successively relocated to the Shenyang Economic and Technological Development Zone. During this process, the demolished portion of Tiexi District reached 5.95 million square meters, and most of this newly vacant land was used to develop the service industry. Throughout the relocation process, the government acted not only as the commander but also as the super developer. It gave reasonable subsidies to the relocated enterprises according to their circumstances, with the difference in land price reaching RMB26 billion. Subsequently, the Tiexi District Government carried out reasonable planning, urged relocated enterprises to engage in equipment upgrading and technological transformation, revitalized decaying state-owned enterprises and land resources, and introduced a new development mechanism.

In contrast with Shenyang, the American city of Detroit, which is also regarded as an old industrial base, made a different choice when responding to external impact. In the 1970s and 1980s, as a huge number of Japanese cars were exported to the United States, Detroit—widely known as the "Motor City" of the country—was hit hard. There was a mass exodus of automakers and auto parts manufacturers from the city. Faced with external pressure, the City of Detroit Government did not take effective actions to support the rapid entry and development of enterprises, but instead increased its support for existing big enterprises (automakers such as Ford, GM, and Chrysler). This course of action failed to reverse the trend of continuous decline in Detroit's economy. From 1970 to 1980, the unemployment rate surged from 5.7% to 11.7% and remained as high as 8.9% even into 1990. In December 2013, the City of Detroit Government officially declared bankruptcy, and Detroit's economy continues to decline due to lack of new activity.

In addition to efforts by local governments, higher levels of government can also support enterprises at the macropolicy level. One example of this is the growth of Geely Automobile. In 2003, Xi Jinping—currently General Secretary of the CPC Central Committee and then acting as the Secretary of the CPC Zhejiang Provincial Committee—took the time to visit Geely's Linhai Automobile Base shortly after he took office. After listening to reports from Geely Group's Chairman Li Shufu and CEO Xu Gang, Mr. Xi affirmed the achievements of Geely Automobile and praised the company for its efforts in talent cultivation, technological innovation, and independent development, as well as its strategic goal of "making good cars affordable for ordinary people." Mr. Xi pointed out, "If we do not offer vigorous support to enterprises like Geely, who else will deserve our support? As the only automobile enterprise in Zhejiang Province, it is truly an incredible feat that Geely has become a '3 + 6 member'[1] amid the fierce competition in the Chinese market. In the future, we will continue to enhance the policy support for national automobile enterprises and create a desirable investment environment for private enterprises."[2]

While developing macroplanning for the rapid entry and development of enterprises, the Chinese government also uses a variety of means to help enterprises overcome shortages and problems in various production factors including land and labor. In the days after the establishment of the BMW Brilliance joint venture in Shenyang, Liaoning Province, BMW exercised strict control over the enterprise, controlled the purchasing, and recruited employees through standardized tests. In our survey, a senior leader told us "even a note written by the mayor will not get you into BMW!" In addition, BMW proposed detailed and strict requirements for the land used to build the plant. In order to guarantee the flat land required, the Shenyang Municipal Government used administrative means and fiscal expenditures to remove hilltops, level the land, and add traffic lights in the proposed areas. They also built an exclusive railway and provided commuting bus lines for the new plant, and issued land, tax, and other related certificates and licenses for the expansion of the plant within merely one day, providing holistic support to BMW. Since 2005, BMW Brilliance has been the largest taxpayer in Shenyang for 12 straight years, has directly created more than 10,000 jobs, and has driven the development of local upstream and downstream industries on an equivalent scale. According to the data, in the year 2016, the automobile and parts industry in Shenyang produced an output of RMB201.86 billion and manufactured 1.061 million complete vehicles. Over the next 3 years, Shenyang will continue its efforts to develop new energy vehicles and reinforce the auto parts industry. The company will also accelerate the construction of several major projects, with the aim of increasing the production capacity of new energy vehicles to 200,000 by 2020 and building an automobile and parts industry cluster in Shenyang valued at RMB300 billion. One example of a company drawn to the area by BMW Brilliance is Shenyang Minghua Mould & Plastic Technology Co., Ltd. Its parent company is Jiangnan Mould & Plastic Technology Co., Ltd. located in Jiangyin, Jiangsu Province, which set up a production plant in Shenyang in order to provide better ancillary services to BMW Brilliance. The company covers a floor area of 95,000 square meters and currently employs more than 700 employees. It owns world-class spraying line equipment and specializes in the development, production, and sale of bumpers, with an annual production capacity of 600,000 sets.

Another way that local governments can assist enterprises is to help them address employment difficulties. In Dongguan, Guangdong Province, manufacturing enterprises tend to face serious labor shortages after Spring Festival. In order to solve this problem, the Dongguan Human Resource Bureau built a unified recruitment platform to meet enterprises' labor demands, alleviate recruitment pressure after the

[1]"3 + 6" refers to the big 3 private car companies and the big 6 state-owned enterprises in China's automotive industry.

[2]Xi Jinping: who else will deserve our support other than Geely? [EB/OL]. http://people.com.cn/GB/jinji/222/2174/2956/20030108/904079.html.

Spring Festival, and provide talent support. Specifically, the platform established recruitment points in several regions under the jurisdiction of Dongguan to carry out recruitment activities at fixed locations for a sustained period of time, released recruitment information via both online and offline channels, arranged for enterprises to recruit workers from other provinces and cities, and discussed labor issues with relevant departments in other regions with a relatively sufficient manufacturing workforce. Following Dongguan's example, many other local governments in Guangdong Province have adopted similar models for recruitment.

Local governments also provide enterprises with numerous preferential policies covering tax benefits, administrative approval, and talent training. Take, for example, the Jingjiang City Government. First, in terms of **preferential tax policies,** it has adopted the dynamic assessment approach rather than the traditional "one size fits all" approach. Specifically, the local government bases its measurement standard on dynamic indicators such as annual sales or tax contributions, and provides some preferential and incentive policies to those top-ranking enterprises. The aim is to motivate enterprises to drive local economic development and thus generate higher tax revenue for the future development of the region. Second, in terms of the **reform of the administrative approval system**, in order to encourage the listing of enterprises, the Jingjiang City Government specially formed a listing office. The listing office serves to create a competitive environment where local enterprises can grow bigger and stronger, and it also provides information assistance and guidance on approval procedure issues met by enterprises during the listing process. Another noteworthy local government contribution in this regard is the Jiangyin City Government's "approval waiter" system, which facilitates the administrative approval process of enterprises. Third, **in terms of talent training**, local governments provide learning and training opportunities for enterprises to build their human capital. Again, take the Jiangyin City Government for example: back in the 1990s, the government led entrepreneurs on an exercise to inspect the operation and development model of Huawei.

(b) **Helping enterprises restructure and upgrade**

In order to ensure the sound development of enterprises and bring vitality to the local economy, local governments aim to create a good business environment and also make full use of their resources to help enterprises restructure and upgrade. To illustrate this type of assistance, we will enumerate five cases: Jiangyin Mould & Plastic Technology, Jiangsu Asian Star Anchor Chain, Northeast Pharm, Chengxing Group, and Henan Agriculture Investment Group.

Jiangyin Mould & Plastic Technology was established in 1988. It is a Chinese high-end exterior automotive parts system service supplier and is included in the list of the top 500 Chinese manufacturing enterprises. The company is primarily engaged in the development, production, and sale of bumpers and other auto parts, plastic products, molds, and high-tech molded plastic products. It has an annual production capacity of more than 3 million sets of bumpers and plays an important role in the economic development of the city of Jiangyin. However, the company was not always so successful—at a key stage in its development, it lacked the foreign exchange necessary to purchase equipment. In order to help Jiangyin Mould & Plastic Technology purchase equipment and expand the market, the Jiangyin City Government boldly used the city's foreign exchange quota to provide a guarantee for the enterprise, helping it obtain a bank loan of USD2.53 million to purchase imported German equipment. In addition, leaders of the Jiangyin City Government actively recommended market opportunities to the company, escorted its leaders to Shanghai to meet the then-leaders of the Shanghai Municipal Economic and Trade Commission and Shanghai Volkswagen, and created desirable opportunities to expand its market share.

Jiangsu Asian Star Anchor Chain faced a major adjustment of tax policy in 2007, with the export rebate rate dropping from 18% to 5%, putting the enterprise under enormous pressure of profit decline. To help the company survive, leaders of the local government contacted the Tax Policy Department of the Ministry of Finance. Asian Star Anchor Chain explained its importance and high value-added in the industry and provided a strong basis for governmental policy adjustments. In January 2008, the Ministry of Finance, the Ministry of Commerce, and the State Administration of Taxation issued a *Notice on the Application of Tax Rebate Policies to Old Long-term Trading Contracts*, requiring the application of the original tax rebate policies to the long-term export contracts signed prior to July 1, 2007, thus ensuring the steady development of Asian Star Anchor Chain.

The mixed-ownership reform of Northeast Pharm from 2000 to 2010 is an excellent example of proper government assistance in the critical period of enterprise development. Initially, the local government granted fiscal funds of RMB870 million for the relocation of the company's old factory, but this was far from sufficient. In 2017, the Shenyang Municipal Government resubmitted its plan to introduce a strategic investor. In 2018, the government made a policy breakthrough, deciding that the strategic investor could become the largest shareholder. Under the guidance of this policy, Northeast Pharm decided to introduce Fangda Group as the largest shareholder with a share of 26%. They also allowed Fangda Group to dispatch two executive directors and recommend two independent directors. In this mixed-ownership reform, Shenyang managed to break first-tier enterprise restrictions through indirect shareholding by an industrial investment fund and create a favorable environment for enterprise development.

Chengxing Group is the first technology-supported enterprise in Suzhou and has been bolstered by the generous support of the local government for its listing. For example, "to send the documents before the Jiangsu Provincial Party Committee started a meeting, the Jiangyin Government would hold a meeting until 10:00 pm, send someone to deliver the documents to Yixing for a signature, and then go to Nanjing before dawn to wait at the door of the office of the executive provincial leader so that the documents could be signed at 7:45 before the provincial party committee held a meeting to approve the transaction." "Jiangyin government leaders would contact and recommend the enterprise to the leaders of Yixing as well as provincial leaders." In 2001, in order to change the pattern of factory managers seizing profits while leaving the enterprise to bear losses, Jiangyin proposed enterprise restructuring for Chengxing Group. However, due to the significant amount of funds required for this, Chengxing Group was not motivated to follow through. As a solution, the city granted RMB24 million toward the restructuring initiative, the employees raised 30% of the required funds, and the remaining amount was given as a loan to be repaid within five years. In this way, the government provided direct financial support for the successful restructuring of Chengxing Group.

In addition to direct financial support, the government can also utilize innovative means to assist enterprises. Since its establishment, Henan Agriculture Investment Group Co., Ltd. has always stuck to its orientation as "a specialized large-scale agriculture investment group with full-fledged investment and financing functions in the field of governmental agriculture investment, and a comprehensive investment and financing service provider led by the provincial party committee and the provincial government for building a large modern agricultural province." Currently, it has evolved into a large agriculture investment holding group with complete functions and an investment capacity of over RMB200 billion. In line with the principles of "governmental guidance, social participation, professional management, and market-oriented operation," Henan Province adopted the method of "converting directness into indirectness, free into paid, and funds into capital" within the enterprise. That is to say, **the government provides fiscal funds and makes use of the power of the company to pool decentralized funds, convert funds into capital, and transform administration into market regulation. This strategy makes use of funds in a centralized way, guides and levers social capital, and introduces central enterprises, substantial financial capital, and well-known institutions from other provinces to the agriculture of Henan Province. This process will eventually change the previous administrative allocation of fiscal funds, reducing the direct allocation of resources by the government, and realize the transformation of government functions**. While attracting social capital, this approach has also helped facilitate the guiding and amplifying functions of fiscal funds. Henan Agriculture Investment Group has already established 45.20 billion in funds, levered 82.05 billion in social capital, and amplified fiscal funds by 7.73 times.

Industrial funds can support enterprises through market-based means, improve their financing capabilities, regulate their operations and management, help them introduce strategic resources, and effectively enhance the endogenous impetus and quality of enterprise development. At the same time, companies can select and invest in projects according to market-oriented standards and exit these projects at the proper time. This strategy has the ability to both assist enterprises and achieve capital appreciation. For example, in 2017, the Comprehensive Agricultural Development Fund brought an additional RMB600 million of social investment to its enterprises. Furthermore, after investing in Sunwood Lvyuan, the fund drove a direct investment of RMB70 million from other social capital, effectively promoting the supply chain construction and rapid development of the enterprise. In addition, the Agricultural Development Corporation views investment in leading enterprises as the key to driving the industry. The corporation thus comprehensively applies a variety of investment and financing means and gives priority support to industry-leading enterprises in such sectors as planting and processing, cotton spinning, and manufacturing. The company has also built a group-wide collaboration platform and mechanism for integrating resources to make investments in major projects.

Take the development of Lotus Flower Gourmet Powder, for example. Beginning in 2004, the company began to have difficulties in its operations and faced the risk of collapse. Tens of thousands of employees were on the verge of unemployment, leading to social instability. During 2004–2006, according to the provincial government's requirements for aiding Lotus Flower Gourmet Powder, Henan Agriculture Investment Group dispatched personnel and injected funds into the company, carrying out several all-round bailout measures. The aim was to give full play to the role of the government as an investor, protect the enterprise brand, and maintain the company's steady development. To an extent, Henan Agriculture Investment Group bought into Lotus Flower Gourmet Powder during the most difficult time of the company's development, provided it with substantial financial support to avoid bankruptcy, and ensured the stable operation of the enterprise through asset restructuring and reorganization, thus successfully playing its role as a policy-oriented investment company.

1.3 Side Effects of Overzealous Government

On the whole, governmental assistance through the "visible hand" in the rapid entry and development of enterprises has played a direct role in driving the economic growth of China. **However, we must acknowledge that excessive government intervention in economic development has also in some instances caused irrational decision-making, ineffective allocation of resources, market distortions, and other side effects on economic development.** Of these side effects, the three most prominent ones are excessive investment, overcapacity, and corruption.

First, we will address excessive investment and overcapacity. During the process of regional economic development planning and deciding which industries and enterprises to support, local governments often base their important judgments on the macroeconomic hot spots and policy orientation of the time, giving less consideration to whether other regions at the same level will select the same industries and development strategies. At the national level, this is reflected in the repeated construction of and excessive investment in the same industry or similar enterprises (mostly industrial enterprises) in different regions, resulting in problems of overcapacity and high industrial concentration in the entire macroeconomy. For example, China currently has over 1,400 steel enterprises, with more than 40 in each province on average. After the overcapacity cut commenced in 2016, the current output of

China's steel industry is still approaching 800 million tons, accounting for over 40% of the global steel output, with a capacity utilization rate of 77%. Meanwhile, China now has a total of 2,143 automobile manufacturers (almost every one of the 34 provinces, municipalities, and autonomous regions has an automobile enterprise of its own), more than half of all the provinces and municipalities have some electrolytic aluminum enterprises, and the national electrolytic aluminum output accounts for 56% of the global output. This is in contrast with a capacity utilization rate of merely 75%. From the perspective of the overall economy, such overlapping investments are relatively inefficient. The resulting low industrial concentration could give rise to wasted resources, slow technological advancement, and many other problems.

Another side effect of excessive governmental intervention is the potential for corruption. The overall support that a local government can give to new enterprises is relatively limited, but the number of new enterprises and entrepreneurs wishing to enter the local market is huge. Therefore, while the local government is creating the business environment and choosing new enterprises to provide with various kinds of support and assistance, even if it aims to help new enterprises and promote local economic development, a certain degree of corruption and power rent-seeking will inevitably arise. **What must be emphasized is that corruption in China is different from corruption in countries like India and Russia in that, due to political and economic incentives, local governments are much more concerned about local economic development. Leaders of local governments are truly motivated to improve the local economic development level, and thus corruption might to some extent affect, but not completely distort local governments' support for new enterprises. Therefore, corruption in China has a comparatively smaller effect on economic development.**

2 Historical Overview

In order to better understand the contribution of the government to the rapid entry and development of enterprises during reform and opening up, we will review five historical stages that have had a significant influence on enterprise entry over the past 40 years: **(1) A sudden emergence of township and village enterprises (TVEs) from 1984 to 1994; (2) privatization of TVEs from 1995 to 2002; (3) the reform of state-owned enterprises (SOEs) through "grasping the large and letting go of the small" from 1998 to 2000; (4) active investment promotion by all levels of government from 1992 to 2012; and (5) business environment improvement through "streamlining administration, delegating powers, strengthening regulation, and improving services" from 2013 to the present.** We review this process through data, policies, and leaders' speeches in conjunction with a large number of cases.

2.1 The Sudden Emergence of Township and Village Enterprises (TVEs) from 1984 to 1994

In the 1980s, a host of township and village enterprises (TVEs) emerged in China's rural areas and played a significant role in driving regional and national economic development. In the Yangtze River Delta and Pearl River Delta regions, TVEs accounted for one-third of local GDP during this time. In the 1990s, TVEs accounted for one-third of foreign exchange earned through export on a national scale.

The predecessors of township and village enterprises were commune- and brigade-run enterprises, which were collectively owned enterprises established before reform and opening up. Following the process of rural reform begun in 1978, much rural labor was freed from the shackles of land. In order to assimilate rural labor, increase collective income, improve the livelihood of commune members, and speed up China's industrial development, the Third Plenary Session of the 11th Central Committee of the CPC proposed "a large push in the development of commune- and brigade-run enterprises" in 1978. In July 1979, the State Council issued the *Provisions of the State Council on Several Issues Concerning the Development of Commune- and Brigade-Run Enterprises (Draft for Trial Implementation)*, which required the departments of planning, capital construction, transportation, science and technology, and others to actively support the development of commune- and brigade-run enterprises, including through preferential tax policies.[3] From 1978 to 1983, the number of employees at commune- and brigade-run enterprises increased from 28.21 million to 32.35 million and their output value increased from RMB49.3 billion to RMB101.7 billion.[4]

From 1984 to 1988, township and village enterprises reached their first peak of development. In 1984, *Document No.4 of the CPC Central Committee*[5] officially renamed "commune- and brigade-run enterprises" as "township and village enterprises." TVEs were regarded as "an important approach to help farmers achieve common prosperity as well as an important source of national fiscal revenue." Thus, the government and agencies at all levels were required to support the development of TVEs.[6] The document stated, "we (governments) should focus on supporting

---

[3]According to the document "All walks of life must make it an important task to support the development of commune- and brigade-run enterprises, develop plans and put forth measures to contribute to the great development of commune- and brigade-run enterprises." "Commune- and brigade-run enterprises are subject to income tax at the proportionate tax rate of 20%." For details, please refer to the PKU Law website, 1979: Provisions of the State Council on Several Issues Concerning the Development of Commune and Brigade Run Enterprises (Draft for Trial Implementation), http://pkulaw.cn/fulltext_form.aspx?Gid=555&Db=chl [2018-11-15].

[4]Zhang et al. [1].

[5]The full name of the document is Notice of the CPC Central Committee and the State Council on Forwarding the Report of the Ministry of Agriculture, Animal Husbandry and Fishery and Ministerial Party Group on Creating a New Situation for Commune and Brigade Run Enterprises.

[6]According to the document "The party committees and governments at all levels should actively guide the development direction of township enterprises, and manage them according to relevant

the survival and development of TVEs, and only in this way can we increase fiscal revenue steadily and persistently in the long run." Subsequently, additional favorable policies for TVEs were also established in *Document No.1 of the CPC Central Committee in 1985, Document No.1 of the CPC Central Committee in 1986, and Document No.5 of the CPC Central Committee in 1987.*

During this period, different TVE development models emerged, such as the "Su'nan Model," "Wenzhou Model," and "Pearl River Model." The "Su'nan Model" was proposed by sociologist Fei Xiaotong at the end of 1983 in the article *Re-exploring Small Towns,* written after his survey into the Su'nan region (consisting of Suzhou, Wuxi, and Changzhou). Fei defined the "Su'nan model" as "a rural economic development path focused on developing industry and the collective economy, market regulation, and the direct leadership of county and township governments." Its main organizational characteristic was that township governments would organize land, capital, labor, and other production factors and designate capable individuals to act as enterprise leaders. Professor Jean C. Oi of Stanford University, after investigating the development history of TVEs in the Su'nan region, generalized this practice of direct governmental participation in economic operation and intervention in enterprise activities as the "Local State Corporatism" model. She believed that in this model, local governments took on many characteristics of business corporations, with officials acting as the equivalent of a board of directors.[7] At the initial stage of the transition from planned economy to market economy, this approach, where local governments directly mobilized and organized production, could organize various production factors rapidly at a low cost, thus greatly accelerating the progress of enterprises' access to the market (Charts 3 and 4).

In this period, TVEs across the country developed rapidly. In 1987, the output value of township and village enterprises surpassed agricultural output value for the first time. Deng Xiaoping, in a meeting with foreign guests, said that "our largest unexpected gain has been the development of TVEs."[8] By 1988, the number of

---

national policies to enable them to develop soundly. We should treat township enterprises and state-owned enterprises equally and give them necessary support…the planning, materials, finance, banking and transportation departments at all levels should create accounts for commune- and brigade-run ente rprises and give guidance and support to them." For details, please refer to the China Law Edu website, 1984: *Notice of the CPC Central Committee and the State Council on Forwarding the Report of the Ministry of Agriculture, Animal Husbandry and Fishery and Ministerial Party Group on Creating a New Situation for Commune and Brigade Run Enterprises,* www.chinalawedu.com/falvfagui/fg22016/275.shtml [2018-11-15].

[7]According to Professor Jean C. Oi "Local government has taken on many characteristics of a business corporation, with officials acting as the equivalent of a board of directors." "By local state corporatism I refer to the workings of a local government that coordinates enterprises in its territory as if it were a diversified business corporation." For details, please refer to Oi, J. (1992). Fiscal Reform and the Economic Foundations of Local State Corporatism in China. World Politics, 45(1), 99-126. doi: 10.2307/2010520. "Village, township, and county make up the local corporate state directly responsible for the dramatic growth of rural enterprises in China." For details, please refer to Oi, Jean C. Rural China Takes Off: Institutional Foundations of Economic Reform. Berkeley: University of California Press, 1999. http://ark.cdlib.org/ark:/13030/ft8j49p1hv/.

[8]Li et al. [2].

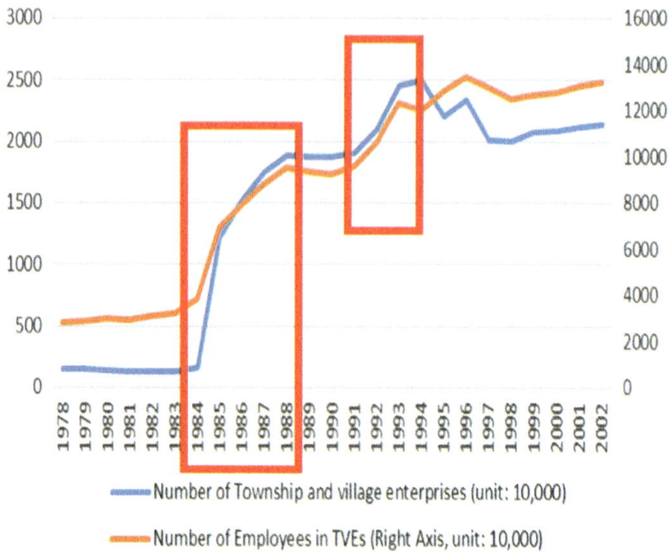

Chart 3 Number of Township and Village Enterprises and Number of Their Employees during 1978–2002 (unit: 10,000)

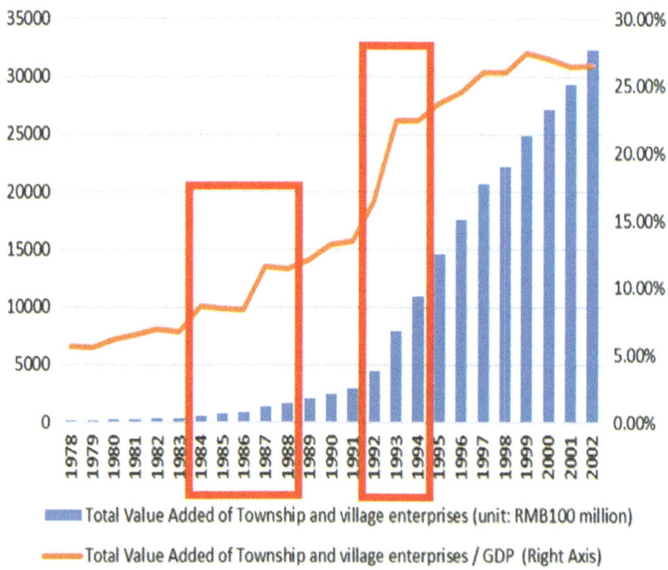

Chart 4 Total Value-Added of Township and Village Enterprises and Proportion in GDP during 1978–2002 (unit: RMB100 million)

township and village enterprises had reached 18.88 million, they employed 95.46 million people, and they generated a total revenue of RMB42.33 billion. From 1984 to 1988, the number of township and village enterprises rose by 52.8%, the number of employees by 20.8%, and the total revenue by 58.4%, all on an average annual basis.[9] Numerous industry-leading enterprises were established during this period, including Huaxi Village (known as China's richest village), Chengxing Group (China's largest fine phosphorous chemical manufacturer), Jiangyin Mould Plastics Group (China's largest bumper manufacturer), Fasten Group (China's largest metal products manufacturer), Jiangsu Sunshine Group (China's largest worsted textile enterprise), Shenda Enterprise Group (China's largest flexible plastic packaging base), and more.

From 1989 to 1991, township and village enterprises entered a three-year period of improvement and rectification. During this period, the government restricted loans to TVEs, reduced tax preferences, cut down on the scale of capital construction, and closed down enterprises with poor economic efficiency as well as serious pollution output.

After Deng Xiaoping's Southern Tour Speeches in 1992, township and village enterprises embraced their second peak of development. During this period, the central government promulgated a series of policies in support of the development of TVEs, such as *Document No.19 of the State Council (1992)* and *Document No.10 of the State Council (1993)*. These documents emphasized the important role of TVEs in economic growth and declared that "governments at all levels and their agencies should actively serve the development of TVEs while providing services to large and medium-sized state-owned enterprises…tax departments should apply preferential tax policies to TVEs in central and western China and foster tax sources by growing township and village enterprises."[10] With the help of these policies, a desirable external environment coupled with improved internal management enabled the rapid development of TVEs. From 1992 to 1994, the total output value of TVEs increased by 1.4 times, their net profit increased by 1.3 times, the profit per RMB100 of fixed-assets increased by 48.6%, the profit per RMB100 of capital increased by 25%, the working capital occupied per RMB100 of operating revenue declined by 16.8%, and per capita profit and tax more than doubled.[11]

---

[9]National Bureau of Statistics, 1999: *A Sudden Emergence of the Township and Village Enterprises*, http://www.stats.gov.cn/ztjc/ztfx/xzg50nxlfxbg/200206/t20020605_35964.html [2018-11-14].

[10]Ministry of Commerce of People's Republic of China, 1993: *Decision of the State Council on Accelerating the Development of Township Enterprises in Central and Western China*, http://www.mofcom.gov.cn/article/b/bf/200207/20020700031377.shtml [2018-11-14].

[11]National Bureau of Statistics, 1999: *A Sudden Emergence of the Township and Village Enterprises*, http://www.stats.gov.cn/ztjc/ztfx/xzg50nxlfxbg/200206/t20020605_35964.html [2018-1-14].

2.2 *Privatization of TVEs from 1995 to 2002*

At the early stage of China's transition from a planned economy to a market economy, the government-dominated development model of township and village enterprises did speed up the entry and development of TVEs. However, beginning in mid to late 1990s, as opening up deepened and the Asian Financial Crisis took its toll, many TVEs were struggling to survive. Thus, it was necessary for the government to loosen its control over the enterprises. Lu Yongjun, the former Deputy Director of the Bureau of Township and Village Enterprises in the Ministry of Agriculture described the situation at the time as follows: "due to unclear property rights and integration of government and enterprise functions, TVEs had an apparent lack of competitiveness in terms of decision-making mechanisms, employment mechanisms, operation mechanisms, distribution mechanisms, and market resilience compared with foreign enterprises and individual private enterprises. Therefore, at that time, some enterprises had too much debt, and some others even suffered losses or went bankrupt. To get out of trouble, the only choice left was to fundamentally reform TVEs."[12]

The mid to late 1990s witnessed the inauguration of a government-led privatization reform of TVEs. Under this reform, a large number of enterprises originally owned by the government were sold to individuals in various arrangements. Although some regions had already begun their attempts to privatize TVEs back in 1984, privatization really began to progress quickly and on a large scale beginning in 1997. On March 11, 1997, the *Notice of the CPC Central Committee and the State Council on Forwarding the Ministry of Agriculture's Report on the Situations of China's Township and Village Enterprises and Future Reform and Development Opinions* was released, which gave top priority to the ownership reform (Chart 5).

There were three privatization models for TVEs: the shareholding system for large enterprises, the joint stock cooperative system for small and medium enterprises, and restructuring by means of leasing, auction, conglomeration, mergers, or bankruptcy for small and loss-making enterprises. According to statistics from the Ministry of Agriculture, **by 2006, 95% of the 1.68 million township collective enterprises across the country underwent privatization, wherein 200,000 were converted into joint stock enterprises and joint stock cooperative enterprises, and 1.39 million were converted into individual and private enterprises.**

Take the Su'nan region, for example: before the mid-1990s, the TVEs in the region were predominantly collective enterprises. In 1995, the employees and value-added of private individual enterprises accounted for merely 11.02% and 4.01% of those of TVEs, respectively. In contrast, collective enterprises, accounting for a higher proportion of the total, were faced with general losses and high debts. For instance, in Jiangyin (a county-level city in the Su'nan region), 70% of the 30 large-sized collective enterprises in the city went bankrupt, mobilizing the local government to enact ownership reform. As the central government gradually liberalized its policies on the

[12] Sina Finance News, 2007: Full History of Township Enterprises, http://finance.sina.com.cn/g/20070424/13483534098.shtml [2018-11-14].

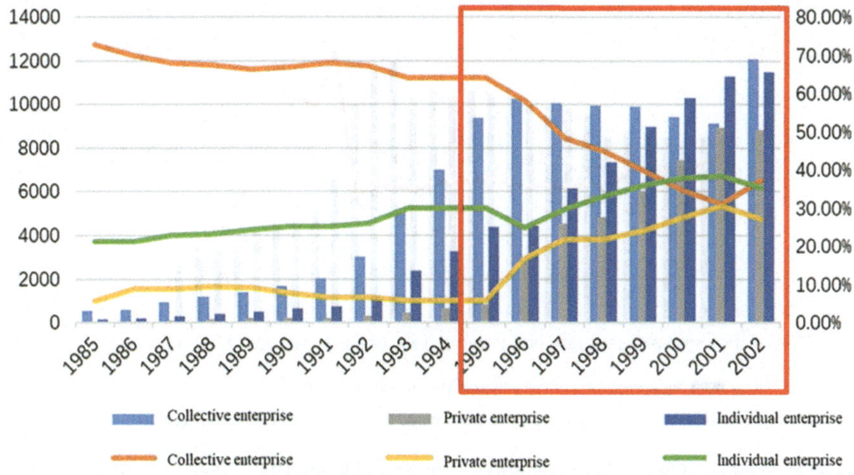

Chart 5 Value-Added of Various TVEs and Their Proportion during 1985–2002 (unit: RMB100 million) *Source* China's Township and Village Enterprises Yearbook 1978–2002

private economy, local governments also streamlined their approval procedures to encourage the entry of private individual enterprises into the market and help collective enterprises carry out ownership reform. A host of subsequent industry leaders, such as Hongdou Group, Mold Plastics Group, and Chengxing Group completed their ownership reforms during this period. By the end of 2001, the ownership structure of TVEs in the Su'nan region had changed dramatically: private individual enterprises accounted for about 92.65% of all enterprises, their employees accounted for 64.91%, and their value-added stood at 54.39%.

2.3 *The Reform of State-Owned Enterprises by "Grasping the Large and Letting Go of the Small" from 1998 to 2000*

Before the start of reform and opening up, the government uniformly issued plans, arranged employment, and allocated resources to SOEs under the planned economy system. Therefore, SOEs had no autonomy in management and had been operating inefficiently for a long time before 1993, when the central government proposed the plan to build a socialist market economy system.[13] At this time, many SOEs struggled to survive in the face of competition from foreign enterprises and TVEs. In 1997, almost one-third of state-owned enterprises suffered losses, while one-third made a profit, and the remaining third could barely make ends meet. The outbreak of the Asian financial crisis in the same year further exacerbated the problems of SOEs.

[13] According to the Report of the Third Plenary Session of Fourteenth CPC Central Committee.

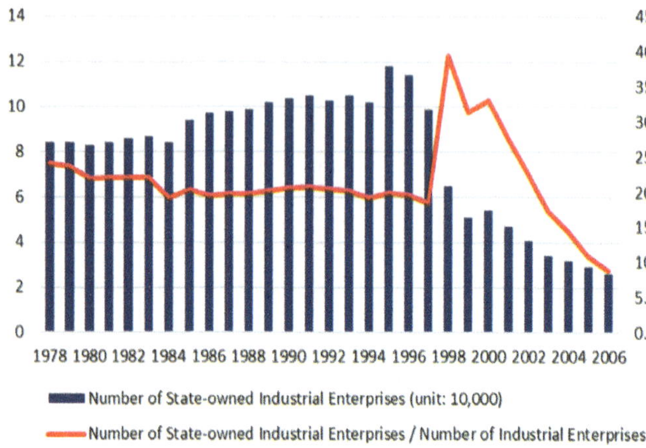

Chart.6 Number of State-Owned Industrial Enterprises During 1978–2006 (unit: 10,000) *Source* China Statistics for 55 Years and China Statistical Yearbook 2006 and 2007

Under these circumstances, on March 19, 1998, the then newly elected Premier of the State Council, Zhu Rongji, said, "we should use three years or so to get most of the loss-making large and medium-sized SOEs out of trouble and establish a modern enterprise system." Thus began the "three-year bailout of SOEs." During this period, "grasping the large and letting go of the small" became the basic guiding principle of SOE reform. This principle stipulated that concentrated efforts should be made to gain control over a host of large-sized SOEs, while small and medium-sized SOEs should be liberalized. This was mainly done by taking a series of policy measures such as debt-to-equity swaps, interest subsidies for technological transformations, and policy-based closure and bankruptcy. The main purpose for the reform was to lighten the burdens on enterprises, promote technological advancement and industrial upgrading, and encourage "survival of the fittest" for SOEs (Charts 6 and 7).

From 1998 to 2002, breakthroughs were made in three aspects of SOE reform: (1) more than one million small and medium-sized SOEs were restructured and removed from the public ownership system; (2) through policy-based closure and bankruptcy of distressed large and medium-sized SOEs, more than 5,000 distressed enterprises exited the market; (3) through the reemployment centre and basic security line policies, nearly 30 million laid-off workers were resettled, thus establishing a mechanism for SOE employee turnover.

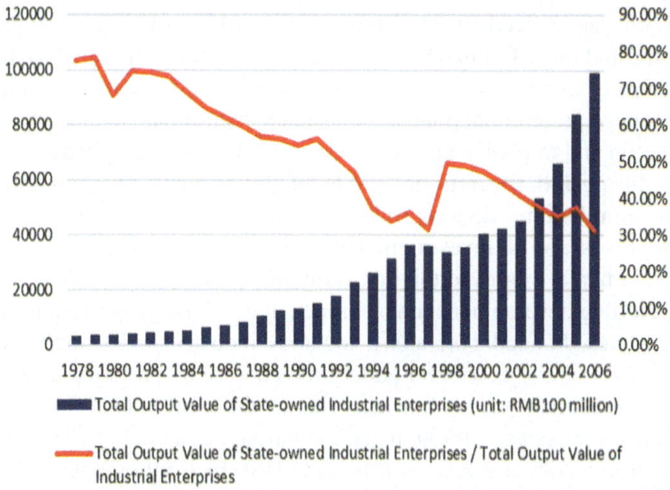

Chart 7 Total Output Value of State-Owned Industrial Enterprises During 1978–2006 (unit: RMB100 million) *Source* China Statistics for 55 Years and China Statistical Yearbook 2006 and 2007

2.4 Active Investment Promotion by All Levels of Government from 1992 to 2012

The period from 1978 to 1992 represented the initial exploration stage of investment promotion in China. During this period, China mainly accepted FDI (especially from Hong Kong, Macao, and Taiwan) on a small scale, and investments were concentrated in several special economic zones and open coastal port cities. Local governments were generally skeptical of investment promotion.

The period from 1992 to 2002 represented the stage of rapid advancement in China's investment promotion. At this stage, local governments gradually replaced the central government as the main force in investment promotion. This was mainly due to the tax system reform, which gave local governments greater economic management authority and thus also confronted them with greater fiscal pressure, creating the motivation mechanism for local governments to promote local economic development. Due to the incentives of both political and economic benefits, investment promotion became a priority for local governments. Some local governments even regarded investment promotion as a "top leadership project,"[14] arranged for governmental officials to participate in investment promotion seminars

[14]People's website, 2018: *What is the secret of investment promotion? 13 district party committee secretaries and district mayors tell stories about investment promotion*, http://hb.people.com.cn/n2/2017/0217/c194063-29727829.html [2018-11-14]. Tieling city news, 2018: *Investment Promotion Achievements by Tieling*, http://www.tielingcn.com/2018/0614/226037.shtml [2018-11-14]. Yining city news, 2018: *Investment Promotion Achievements by Yining*, http://www.sohu.com/a/257487807_183787 [2018-11-14].

and workshops, announced investment promotion achievements in newspapers on a regular basis, and directly linked the amount of investment attracted to the income and promotion of cadres. Some governments established various kinds of economic parks, introduced preferential policies, and set up institutions specifically to manage the formulation and implementation of investment promotion policies.

During this period, the national and local governments promoted investment mainly by establishing various industrial development parks and economic parks, and the scale of investment rose sharply in these areas. In 1984, the central governmental approved the first economic park. By 2002, there were 5,000 of them, including development zones, hi-tech industrial development parks, export processing zones, bonded port areas, logistics industry parks, higher education parks, and more. These economic parks utilized various preferential policies and led regional investment promotion activities in different fields. Take the Suzhou Industrial Park, for example: through 2002, it introduced a total of 105 foreign enterprises, with foreign direct investments totaling USD16.1 billion and the total output value of the park reaching RMB25.2 billion. In 2002, China's actual use of foreign direct investment was USD52.7 billion, 12 times that of 1991 (Chart 8).

After 2003, China's investment promotion efforts proceeded to the stage of optimization and adjustment. During the previous stage, local governments scrambled to attract investors with more tax rebates and lower land prices, resulting in vicious competition, overlapping investment, and wasted resources, among other problems. In response to these problems, the State Council issued the *Notice of the General Office of the State Council on Straightening and Rectifying Land Use in Construction of Various Development Zones* in 2003, which began to straighten out and rectify the different kinds of economic parks. The policy reduced the number of economic parks to 2,065 and the total planned area to 14,000 square meters, with the aim of guiding local governments to attach greater importance to the quality and efficiency of investment projects given the limited land supply.

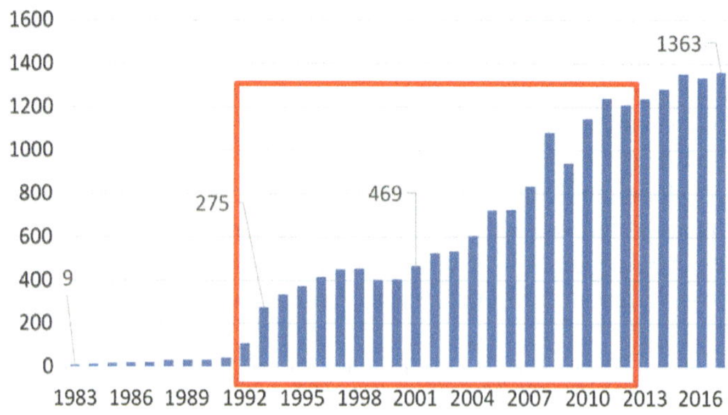

Chart 8 Amount of Foreign Investment Actually Used by China During 1983–2017 (Unit: USD100 million) *Source* The Ministry of Commerce

To this day, investment promotion is still an important part of the overall mission of local governments. However, in contrast with the extensive investment promotion pattern before, local governments today pay more attention to the investment per acre, GDP per acre, and tax per acre of projects when attracting investments, and attach greater importance to the quality and efficiency of the projects introduced. At the same time, the focus of investment promotion has also shifted from foreign investment to a combination of domestic and foreign investments, and from secondary industry investments to tertiary and primary industry investments. Also, the carriers of investment promotion are not limited to various economic parks. Some new investment promotion models have arisen, such as investment promotion in industrial chains, enterprise-led investment promotion, and public–private partnerships (PPP).

2.5 Business Environment Improvement by "Streamlining Administration, Delegating Powers, Strengthening Regulation, and Improving Services" from 2013 to Present

Since 2013, in response to the "Fang Guan Fu" Reforms (literally meaning streamlining administration, delegating powers, strengthening regulation, and improving services), governments at all levels have taken measures to become more service-oriented and to improve the business environment. Furthermore, China also established 12 pilot free trade zones in several provinces and municipalities including Shanghai, Guangdong, and Hainan, granted these areas greater autonomy over reforms, and promoted a series of administrative streamlining and power delegation measures, such as "negative list management," "separation of certificates from business licenses," and "one code for one license," in the zones on a pilot basis.

Remarkable achievements have been made in the five years since the reforms were initiated: (1) administrative approval items have been drastically reduced—departments under the State Council have cumulatively cancelled and delegated 618 administrative approval items and completely eliminated non-administrative licensing approval items; **(2) taxes and fees have been sharply reduced**—the government gradually expanded the scope of the initiative to replace business taxes with VAT and cancelled, terminated, or exempted more than 1,100 administrative service fees at the central and provincial government levels, cumulatively releasing market players from burdens of over RMB3 trillion; **(3) a large number of new market players emerged**—over these five years, the number of various market players has increased by nearly 80% and now exceeds 100 million, including more than 31 million enterprises, with many individual businesses also developing toward enterprises[15]; **(4) the business environment was greatly improved**; according to the *Ease of Doing Business Index* issued by the World Bank, China was ranked 46th among the 190 economies in the world in 2019, up by 32 places compared with the previous year.

The behaviors and interests of local governments have also changed during this time. As Premier Li Keqiang said at the meeting of the State Council held on January 3, 2018: "In recent years, when I have visited provinces, I have found that more and more officials are not just focusing on serving a few enterprises, but rather they are trying to improve the local business environment."

3 Economic Analysis

Based on the aforementioned basic facts and history of enterprise entry and development, we arrive at the following two economic conclusions: first, during the process of reform and opening up, incentives for governments to cultivate and assist enterprises were of utmost importance for enterprise entry and development; second, since local governments were subject to a certain amount of blindness and limitation, they occasionally made some irrational decisions in the process of assisting enterprises with their entry and development. Therefore, we can see that a corresponding restrictive system should be put in place to regulate local governments' behavior as they help with enterprise entry and development.

3.1 The Incentives of Local Governments Are Critical

The incentives offered to governments for cultivating and helping enterprises have a direct bearing on government behavior and its results during the process of enterprise entry and development. **After summarizing the process of enterprise entry and development history in the 40 years of China's reform and opening up, we believe that political and economic incentives are two important dimensions through which local governments can promote enterprise entry and development. Specifically, political incentives are directly linked to the promotion of officials, while economic incentives are directly linked to taxation. Both types of incentives exert a significant effect on enterprise entry and development.**

[15]The State Council, 2018: *Speech by Li Keqiang at the national video and telephone conference themed on deepening "delegation of powers, regulation and service" reform and transforming government functions*, http://www.gov.cn/xinwen/2018-07/12/content_5305966.htm [2018-11-14].

(a) **Political incentives motivate local governments to offer help for enterprise entry and development**

Political incentives for governments to help with enterprise entry and development are derived from local government officials' continuous pursuit of promotions. The wider scope of power and higher sense of personal achievement that accompany a promotion usually motivate officials to do their utmost to keep their positions, and even to scramble for all possible promotion opportunities. This is a common theme among local officials. **It is on this basis that local government officials' actions are often guided by promotion appraisal indicators. Officials also strategize on how to stand out on their appraisals and win a competitive edge.** Since reform and opening up, political achievement—i.e. local GDP growth—has been a key factor for the promotion of local officials. Therefore, **it has become a priority for local governments to take initiative and assist with enterprise entry and development.**

(i) **Political competition through the "political tournament" is an important factor driving local governments to help enterprises.**

Since the early 1980s, the selection and promotion standards for local officials in China have shifted from purely political indicators to economic performance indicators. This shift is highlighted in the importance of local GDP growth, which is counted as a key political achievement in the promotion scheme of local officials, and is thus enthusiastically pursued. **According to the evaluation of various measurable indicators, local officials scramble for victories with the aim of getting promoted, level by level, starting with the grassroots level.** According to the promotion tournament model of local officials built by Professor Zhou Li'an, local officials are promoted to higher positions if they can outcompete their peer regions in GDP growth.[16] **Therefore, in order to obtain an advantage in the political tournament, local governments often make every effort to help with enterprise entry and development.**

The case is very different in the United States, where the most important motivation for local governments to help with enterprise entry and development is the prospect of victory in the next election. For instance, in order to keep local sports clubs, US municipal governments often spend a great deal of money subsidizing baseball fields, football fields, basketball courts, and ice hockey arenas. In addition, great efforts are made to solve local unemployment problems. In September 2017, Amazon announced a plan to select a city in North America as its second headquarters and to invest USD5 billion in this city, providing more than 50,000 jobs. Shortly after the announcement, numerous North American cities offered bids in the hopes of wooing Amazon, including some well-known cities like Boston, Washington DC, Atlanta, Dallas, and Denver. These cities offered various preferential policies—for example,

[16] *The Incentive and Cooperation of Government Officials in the Political Tournaments: An Interpretation of the Prolonged Local Protectionism and Duplicative Investments in China* [J] by Zhou Li'an. Economic Research, 2004(06):33–40.

the Governor of New Jersey said that if Amazon chose a city in the state to establish its second headquarters, the company would be granted USD5 billion in tax benefits over the next 10 years.[17]

(ii) **The government provides macroeconomic regulation in the overall economic planning and adjustments of cities**

Under particular circumstances, through macroeconomic regulation, the government can make corresponding deployments and adjustments in the overall economic planning of cities to help them out of trouble and revive or reshape their development. To an extent, this practice serves as one of the sources of competitive edge available to local governments in the political tournament, and therefore is an important political incentive. At the same time, governments can also take the overall economic development plan of a city as the starting point and create a new impetus for enterprise development. Compared with enterprises, the government is able to plan the direction of development for the urban economy using a more macroscopic perspective, and thus provide guidance and serve as a beacon for enterprise development. **While assisting in enterprise development, governments further sharpen their competitive edge in the political tournament. For example, in the enterprise restructuring of Jiangsu Province, local governments gave substantial assistance to enterprises in terms of funds and land.**

The macroeconomic regulatory role of governments in the deployment and adjustment of cities' overall economic planning is particularly apparent in northeast China. In this region, the most representative case is the **industrial relocation and re-planning program of Tiexi District**, as detailed in Section I. The rejuvenation of Tiexi District was highly affirmed by the central government. In a visit to Tiexi District, then General Secretary Hu Jintao encouraged the people of Tiexi to overcome their challenges and forge a Chinese-style path of rejuvenation for old industrial bases. On June 9, 2007, the NDRC and the Northeast Rejuvenation Office of the State Council granted Shenyang the title of "Tiexi Old Industrial Base Adjustment and Reconstruction & Equipment Manufacturing Development Demonstration Area." For Tiexi District, this meant that the country recognized the results of its old industrial base adjustment and reconstruction project and its equipment manufacturing development program over the past 5 years, marking the beginning of a new era.[18] **To some extent, the affirmation of the central government can serve as an important political incentive for the local government and urge it to provide further assistance for enterprise entry and development.**

---

[17]*Amazon to build its second headquarters, and these American cities are nearly crazy to canvas it!* https://baijiahao.baidu.com/s?id=1581421217844812515&wfr=spider&for=pc.

[18]news.hexun.com article at http://news.hexun.com/2009-07-14/119593001.html.

(b) Economic incentives promote mutual benefit and win–win situations for governments and enterprises

Economic incentives for local governments to assist in enterprise entry and development are directly linked to taxes. On one hand, taxes have a bearing on the ability of local governments to obtain resources that they can utilize independently to advance various policies; on the other hand, when the economic development of a region is in good condition and attracts abundant taxes, the income of government officials may see improvement accordingly. This mechanism of linking taxes to the income of officials often has a strong economic incentive effect on local governments and is one of the most important reasons why they try their best to help with enterprise entry and development. Professor Qian Yingyi argues that evidence for this phenomenon can be seen in the 1980s, when the delegation of powers from the central government to local governments and the implementation of the tax-contracting system had a notable effect on the behavior of local governments and the local economies under their jurisdiction. The tax-contracting system, while intensifying local protectionism and resulting in the decline of central fiscal revenue, granted local governments an extremely high marginal fiscal retention rate. Empirical research has found that **during the era of the financial contract system, the higher the rate of marginal financial retention, the more financial incentives there were for local governments to help and support local firms.** This is in stark contrast to the case of Russia in the 1990s, where local fiscal revenue had no relationship with local economic development, so local governments received no economic incentives for developing the regional economy or for assisting with enterprise entry and development.[19]

In terms of China's tax revenue and the structure of sources, the entire indirect tax revenue plus other local taxes with obvious indirect tax characteristics accounts for more than 70% of total tax revenue. In contrast, revenue from direct taxes such as corporate income taxes and individual income taxes accounts for merely 26.2%. Of the total tax revenue in 2013, the revenue from taxes paid by state-owned enterprises, collective enterprises, joint stock cooperative enterprises, joint stock companies, private enterprises, and other types of enterprises accounted for 90%. On the whole, **in China's current tax system structure, over 70% of tax revenue comes from indirect taxes, and over 90% comes from firms.**[20] In this structure, **taxes from enterprises bind local governments to firms.** Unlike China, western countries like the United States depend more heavily on personal taxes. Judging from the composition of the US federal government's fiscal revenue, individual income taxes have always accounted for a high proportion. In most years, individual income taxes in the United States account for more than 45% of federal fiscal revenue. Even when calculated as a proportion of total fiscal revenue in the entire country, individual income taxes contribute more than 30% of revenue—the highest percentage

---

[19] Qian Yingyi. *Understanding Modern Economics* at https://www.douban.com/note/369127038/.

[20] *The Future Direction of China's Tax Structure Reform* at http://tax.rednet.cn/c/2017/06/16/4325716.htm.

among various taxes. Conversely, individual income taxes in China account for a very low proportion of central and local fiscal revenues—so low, in fact, that it is almost negligible.[21] Therefore, we can see that **the United States and other western countries rely more heavily on individual taxes, while China is more dependent on enterprise taxes. This distinction is significant because the economic incentives arising from taxes can motivate local governments to promote enterprise entry and development.**

Of course, the fulfillment of tax objectives is not merely the result of the unilateral efforts by governments or enterprises. Rather, success rests on the government's ability to provide a high-quality environment for enterprise entry and development, monitor the development dynamics of enterprises, and achieve mutual benefit and win–win arrangements with enterprises.

(i) **Linking the income of government officials to taxes is an important economic incentive**

When the income of government officials is directly linked to the taxes derived from enterprises, governments are deeply motivated to help with enterprise entry and development. Development zones are a good example of this. In the period after reform and opening up, due to the economic efficiency and rapid progress of development zones, governments invested heavily in their success. They assigned special personnel to the zones and set up an innovative special administrative structure of management committees, with the income of officials in these committees dependent on tax revenue from incoming firms. It was this model that drove governments to create environments conducive to enterprise entry through various means and to initiate a variety of preferential policies aimed at promoting enterprise entry and development. Development zones even offer one-on-one services to help firms with problems, including tax preparation, inspection and quarantine, employment, etc. The electronic information industry provides especially strong incentives for government assistance because it generates a large amount of tax revenue and only requires a small management committee, thus resulting in significant income for committee members.

(ii) **Governments endeavor to help with enterprise entry and development and achieve mutual benefit with enterprises**

The economic incentives for local governments to assist in enterprise entry and development are largely derived from taxes, which in turn have a direct correlation with the development status of enterprises. When the development status of enterprises is good, they can bring more taxes to local governments, obtain more resources, and further ensure the smooth progress of work. Therefore, **motivated**

---

[21] Comparison between Tax Structure and Tax Burden in China and the United States at http://www.sohu.com/a/124772907_126158.

by economic incentives, local governments will vigorously encourage enterprise development and spare no effort to guide the coordinated development of upstream and downstream industries to achieve mutual benefit and win–win arrangements.

A good example of this is the establishment and development of BMW Brilliance in Shenyang, which was a result of the local government's efforts to guide the coordinated development of upstream and downstream industries and achieve mutual benefit with the enterprise. The Shenyang Municipal Government's vigorous efforts to introduce BMW to the area have played a significant role in propelling local economic development. **First, BMW Brilliance has strongly driven Shenyang's fiscal revenue, with the company contributing nearly RMB20 billion of the city's total tax revenue of over RMB60 billion**. Second, the location of Brilliance BMW in Shenyang has **also promoted the coordinated development of relevant upstream and downstream enterprises, thus further increasing the fiscal revenue of the city.**

While making efforts to guide the coordinated development of upstream and downstream industries, local governments tend to provide some **preferential policies, such as tax preferences, administrative approval conveniences** (e.g., Jingjiang's reward policy and Jiangyin's "approval waiter" system), and the **provision of learning and training opportunities** to build enterprises' human capital. **Local governments make the best use of their circumstances to help with enterprise entry and development, which in turn allows them to strive for more financial support for the smooth advancement of their own policies.**

The establishment and entry of new enterprises serves as an important impetus for regional development. Whether developed countries like the United States or rising developing countries, all governments can develop their local economies by granting appropriate preferential policies and effective guidance to attract enterprises with development potential.

Governmental assistance and guidance for enterprises are not limited to the initial stage of attraction. In the subsequent process of enterprise development, especially at key turning points, governments should also provide adequate support. The previously discussed development of Mould & Plastic Technology, Asian Star Anchor Chain, Northeast Pharm, and Chengxing Group could not have thrived without the attention and support of local governments. Here, we again harken back to the words of Xi Jinping, current General Secretary and the then Secretary of the CPC Zhejiang Provincial Committee: "If we do not offer vigorous support to enterprises like Geely, who else will deserve our support?" These words are a direct reflection of the Chinese government's concern with enterprise development. The government has placed so much stress on the development of Geely because **the automobile industry has the ability to drive for the rapid growth of the local economy due to its high rate of return and large-scale effects. The case of Geely also reflects the policy favor and strong support given to private enterprises by the Zhejiang Provincial Party Committee and provincial government.**

Driven by economic incentives, governments usually try their best to offer help to enterprises and pay close attention to their development dynamics. In addition to the aforementioned preferential policies and guidance in the coordinated development of upstream and downstream industries, there are many other **innovative models**. For example, in line with the principles of "governmental guidance, social participation, professional management, and market-oriented operation," Henan Province has adopted the method of "converting directness into indirectness, free into paid, and funds into capital." Under this model, the government has managed to enhance the endogenous impetus of enterprises and improve their efficiency and industrial level by supporting strong enterprises and helping weaker ones and by allowing the benefits of government assistance to fan outwards. **This has generated tax revenue for the local government and created economic incentives for helping enterprises.**

With the goal of spurring mutual benefits and win–win arrangements, the US government has also adopted the same practice. For example, Wisconsin and iPhone OEM Foxconn Technology Group signed an agreement in which the Wisconsin State Government agreed to provide Foxconn with up to USD3 billion of income and sales tax relief over the next 15 years, while Foxconn pledged to bring 13,000 high-paying jobs and USD10 billion of investment capital to the state.

3.2 There Must Be Restraints on Local Government Behavior

Over the 40 years of China's reform and opening up, governments at all levels have used various means to support enterprise entry and development. On the whole, governmental assistance in enterprise entry has played a direct role in driving the economic growth of China through the government's "visible hand." However, for various reasons, **local governments can be subject to blindness and other limitations, which can give rise to a series of problems. Therefore, an appropriate restrictive system should be established to regulate the behavior of local governments as they assist with enterprise entry and development.**

Specifically speaking, in the process of local governments' decision-making, they often give inadequate consideration as to whether other regions at the same level will select similar industries and development planning strategies. This is because they are primarily concerned with the economic development of the regions under their jurisdiction and are prone to base their important judgments on the macroeconomic hot spots and policy orientation of the time. Moreover, as they compare themselves with surrounding provinces and municipalities, local governments often demonstrate herd behavior and focus on projects offering immediate returns or industries with present policy support. Coupled with the aforementioned corruption problem, local governments sometimes demonstrate power rent-seeking and make decisions favorable only for themselves. Under the combined effects of these factors, local governments tend to engage in overlapping or inefficient investments, resulting in overcapacity and many other problems. At the same time, motivated by political or economic incentives, local governments often rely on preferential policies to build up their competitive edge and attract new enterprises, resulting in vicious competition among the local governments of different regions.

With this in mind, it is clear that **on one hand, it is necessary to build a unified and well-established market system to reasonably allocate and manage products and funds via the market force, and it is also necessary to restrict the behaviors of local governments through the market force with the aim of avoiding vicious competition, excessive investment, and other relevant problems. On the other hand, it is crucial to effectively respond to "overzealous" local governments via central macroeconomic regulation.** Because the central government possesses some natural advantages over local governments—including a greater understanding of the big picture by virtue of more information—macroeconomic regulation from the central government is essential. For instance, in response to general losses and serious overcapacity in the textile industry in the late 1990s, Premier Zhu Rongji initiated an overcapacity cut program in the state-owned enterprises of the textile industry. By 2000, the entire industry managed to turn profitable again, laying a sound foundation for the industrial upgrading and revitalization of the textile industry. **Beyond macroeconomic regulation, measures should also be taken to effectively respond to the current corruption and "disguised corruption" problems.** At present, in addition to some corruption and power rent-seeking in local governments with regard to their development planning strategies, allocation of administrative resources, and selection of enterprises to receive various kinds of support, some other problems have arisen, including neglect of duties and lazy administration. With strengthening efforts to implement the "eight-point austerity rules" of the CPC Central Committee and deepening efforts to eliminate corruption and build a clean government, governments at all levels have begun to demonstrate fear and reluctance to take action. This disguised corruption will likewise have a negative effect on local development. Therefore, it is necessary to take appropriate actions to eliminate corruption and disguised corruption in local governments. **Of course, legal constraints are also essential for regulating the behaviors of local governments with regard to their assistance in enterprise entry and development.** It is necessary to build a well-designed legal system, repair the relations between the government and the market, and prevent an excess, absence, or dislocation of government authority in macroeconomic regulation. In this way, we can effectively solve the problems of non-local administration and enforcement, and thus promote the sound development of the economy.

References

1. Zhang, S. et al. (1996). *Research on the Coordinated Economic and Social Development of Urban and Rural Areas in China.*
2. Li, B. et al. (2004). *Report on China's Agriculture, Rural Areas and Farmers.*

Rapid Land Conversion

David Daokui Li, Sijia Hu, Bing Li, Hongyu Zhao, Yifan Chen, and He Zhang

Abstract This section analyzes the role land conversion plays in economic activities. Land conversion was a key issue in classical political economy, but modern economics has not paid enough attention to this. While the process of industrialization, urbanization, and the development of the real estate market is highly dependent upon the conversion of agricultural land into non-agricultural use, land conversion and the Coasian negotiations can be very costly. China's experiences indicate that government can play an active role in the conversion of land usage, by helping reduce the transaction costs of land conversion. In addition, there needs to be top-down overall planning of land usage, including urban planning.

Keywords Land conversion · Government behavior · Urbanization · Urban planning

D. D. Li (✉) · B. Li · H. Zhao
Academic Center for Chinese Economic Practice and Thinking (ACCEPT), Tsinghua University, Beijing, China
e-mail: daviddaokuili@126.com

B. Li
e-mail: libing@sem.tsinghua.edu.cn

H. Zhao
e-mail: zhaohongyuthu@126.com

S. Hu
Central University of Finance and Economics, Beijing, China
e-mail: husj2019@cufe.edu.cn

Y. Chen · H. Zhang
School of Economics and Management, Tsinghua University, Beijing, China
e-mail: chenyf.15@sem.tsinghua.edu.cn

H. Zhang
e-mail: zhangherdfz@163.com

D. D. Li (eds.), *Economic Lessons from China's Forty Years of Reform and Opening-up*, https://doi.org/10.1007/978-981-33-4520-1_3

Table 1 Estimation of real estate market value

	Zillow[a] (US)	Savills[b] (UK)	CCWE[c]
China		2016: 39.4 trillion	2017: 36.5–39 trillion
USA	2017: 31.8 trillion	2016: 34.1 trillion	

[a]Zillow Research [2]
[b]Tostevin [3]
[c]As published by the National Bureau of Statistics, the per capita housing areas of the entire population, urban residents, and rural residents were 40.8 m^2, 36.6 m^2, and 45.8 m^2, respectively, in 2016. In the same year, China's urban and rural permanent populations were 813.47 million and 576.61 million, respectively. Urban: the average selling price of residential commercial housing was 7203.00 RMB/m^2 in 2016, and accordingly we estimated a total real estate market value of 215 trillion RMB. Rural: the rural residential construction cost for completion was 866.69 RMB/m^2 in 2016, and accordingly we estimated a total real estate market value between 26 and 30 trillion RMB. With the urban estimation plus rural estimation as well as the growing rate of the housing prices between 2016 and 2017, the total market value of the whole country was estimated to be USD36.5–39 trillion
Source Forecast by institutions and calculated by ACCEPT

1 Stylized Facts

In 1998, the Ninth National People's Congress (NPC) of the PRC announced that it would deepen the reform of the urban housing system and suggested real estate as a new engine for China's economic growth. Subsequently, the Chinese government began to gradually abolish the welfare-oriented public housing distribution system and implement a market-oriented housing policy in its place. Since this housing reform, the real estate market in China has been developing for 20 years.

1. **The Chinese real estate market has grown from the scratch into the world's largest within 20 years, with rapid land conversion as the key factor**

The beginning of housing reform in 1998 unleashed the growth momentum of China's real estate market, building it up from nothing into the largest capital market in China. **Data indicates that the total value of China's real estate market was about RMB280 trillion (USD39 trillion) in 2017 (exceeding total GDP by 300%), while that of the United States was USD31.8 trillion for the same period**. Furthermore, the average housing prices in large Chinese cities are higher than those in the United States. Take the housing prices in July 2016, for example: Shenzhen (USD7768/m^2), Beijing (USD6836/m^2), and Shanghai (USD6446/m^2) ranked as the top three most expensive cities for housing among large cities in China and the United States, while San Francisco (USD4888/m^2) and Los Angeles (USD4023/m^2) ranked fourth and fifth, respectively (Table 1).[1]

Over the past two decades, the real estate industry has rapidly developed into the backbone of the Chinese economy. **From 1998 to 2017, the scale of the real estate market continuously increased from RMB343.45 billion to RMB5.38,507**

[1]Terrazas [1].

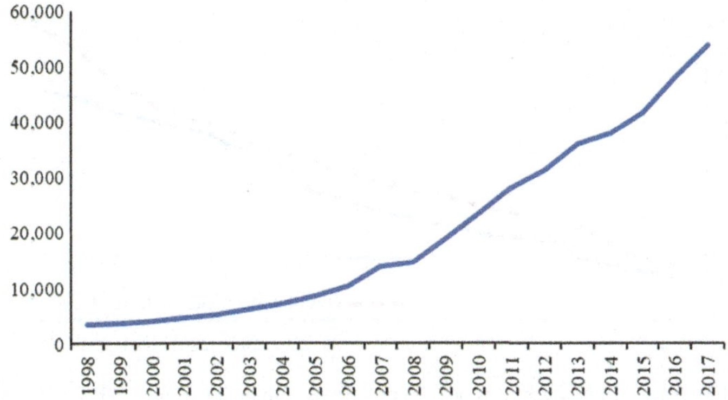

Chart 1 Total output value of China's real estate (Unit: RMB100 Million). *Source* Wind database

trillion, multiplying in size by 14.6 times and growing an average of 15.6% per year. Meanwhile, the proportion of the real estate market as a percentage of GDP steadily increased from 4.03% in 1998 to 6.51% in 2017, reflecting the leading role of real estate in the national economy.[2] Furthermore, besides the real estate industry itself, we should also consider the impact of its upstream (e.g., cement, glass, steel, etc.) and downstream (e.g., home appliances, building materials, decoration, etc.) industries (Chart 1).

2. **Households' housing consumption has been fundamentally enhanced**

Before reform and opening up, China used a welfare-oriented public housing distribution system within the context of the planned economy, in which housing for residents was uniformly distributed through workplaces. Although the system was able to meet basic housing demands, insufficient investment in housing construction led to small living spaces, poor living conditions, and a growing shortage of housing supply, which suppressed housing demand for many years. Since the implementation of reform and opening up, the Chinese government has attached great importance to housing and has continuously reformed the housing system. The 1988 "Monetization of Housing Distribution" was the most important turning point of this reform, when the Chinese government abolished the welfare-oriented public housing distribution system and officially established the real estate market. Led by the Chinese government and driven by the market, the real estate industry has rapidly developed since then. Housing supply has skyrocketed, housing quality has continuously improved, and living standards have fundamentally risen.

The figure below shows historical changes in China's per capita housing area. **In 1978, urban and rural per capita housing areas were only 6.7 and 8.1 m^2, respectively. Over the past 40 years of reform and opening up, with the continuous development of the real estate market, the per capita housing area in China has increased year by year. In 2017, urban and rural per capita housing areas**

[2]Source: National Bureau of Statistics: http://data.stats.gov.cn/easyquery.htm?cn=C01.

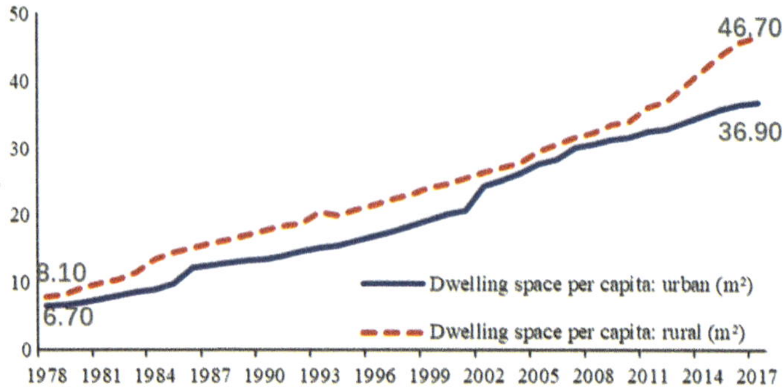

Chart 2 China's dwelling conditions have been largely enhanced. *Source* NBS of China

reached 36.9 and 46.7 m^2, respectively. These changes reflect a significant overall improvement in quality of life over the past 40 years. For example, people moved out of their tube-shaped apartments where several generations lived together and into spacious and beautiful homes where they could enjoy more comfortable lives. Compared with developed countries, China is still behind the United States in terms of per capita housing area, but far surpasses Japan and South Korea in this regard and is on par with the UK and France. According to *Modern Housing Economy* by Guan Ke, since the 1990s, the per capita housing areas of the USA, UK, Germany, and Japan have been 61.3, 36.6, 35.5, and 31 m^2, respectively.[3] As these countries completed their urbanization earlier, their real estate markets have already reached maturity. Overall, China's housing conditions have greatly improved since reform and opening up, and are gradually catching up with developed countries (Chart 2).

After the establishment of the real estate market, sales trends in commercial housing also began to indicate rapid growth. According to data issued by the National Bureau of Statistics, Chinese commercial housing sales reached RMB9.906417 trillion in 2016, a 24-fold increase compared with RMB402.115 billion in 2001. Furthermore, the area of commercial housing property sold in 2016 reached 1.375 billion sqm, about six times that of 199 million sqm in 2001. Although we must also consider the effects of real estate speculation, these skyrocketing sales trends nevertheless reflect an improvement in housing quality and living standards.

The rapid development of the real estate industry has not only improved housing quality, but has also promoted the development of urban infrastructure and generated a series of achievements in Chinese urbanization. **At the beginning of reform and opening up, China's urbanization rate was only 18%. After four decades of steady development, this rate increased to 57% by 2016**—still 20% less than most developed countries (e.g., the corresponding rates of the USA, UK, and Germany were 82%, 83%, and 77%, respectively). Many new economic growth points have emerged through the processes of migration and urbanization, making important contributions to economic development since the implementation of reform and opening up (Chart 3).

[3]Guan [4].

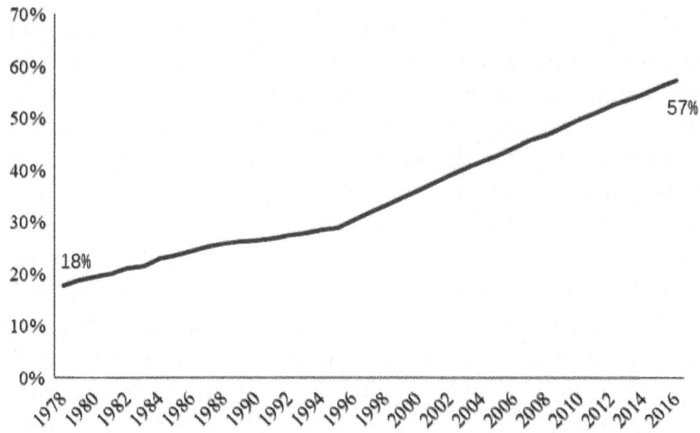

Chart 3 Urbanization rate of China. *Source* NBS of China

3. **Problems arise: High housing prices and housing inequality**

Although the development of the real estate market has greatly improved people's living standards, it has also been plagued by serious problems such as high prices and uneven distribution of housing resources. Since 2013, China's steady rise in housing prices has attracted broad attention. According to the year-on-year changes in the housing sale price index issued by the National Bureau of Statistics, the rise in housing prices was particularly notable in 2016 and 2017. Moreover, from May 2016 to February 2017, the year-on-year growth rate of the sale price index for newly constructed houses held steadily at 20%, while that of second-hand houses was more than 30%.

In our investigation of the real estate market's development via the annual growth rate of average commercial housing prices, we have found that soaring housing prices are not only a recent phenomenon, but have occurred many times in the past. For instance, the average housing prices increased by 19, 25, and 11% in 2004, 2009, and 2016, respectively, thus exceeding the growth rate of urban residents' per capita disposable income. This has led to uneven housing distribution, as young people in need of homes cannot afford the high housing prices, and therefore often have to rent a house or make a living in another city. Additionally, high housing prices have led to capital speculation as well as housing speculation, causing Chinese society to deviate from the position that "housing is to be used for living".

Often, housing prices are so much higher than incomes in Chinese cities that many residents are unable to afford houses. According to the *Report on Housing Price-to-Income Ratios in 35 Key Cities in China in 2017* issued by China Real Estate Newspaper,[4] the housing price-to-income ratios of all 35 key cities in China are higher than the reasonable range of three to six, which is a widely used international standard (Changsha has the lowest ratio among the 35 cities, with a ratio of 6.67).

[4]See http://www.sohu.com/a/225313656_99961827.

The ratios of the top five cities (Shenzhen, Sanya, Shanghai, Beijing, and Xiamen) are all higher than 20, and Shenzhen ranks first with a ratio of 39.64. **According to the international housing price-to-income ratios of 2018**[5] **issued by NUMBEO Global Database, in the first half of 2018, the ratio in mainland China was 27.17, and 46.89 in Hong Kong. On the whole, China's ratio has jumped to the second highest in the world**. For comparison, ratios in Japan, France, the UK, Germany, and the United States are 11.16, 11.51, 8.89, 8.48, and 3.44, respectively—far lower than China's. Furthermore, China's major cities dominate the top of the housing price-to-income rankings. Beijing (44.34), Shanghai (44), Shenzhen (39.86), and Guangzhou (23.10) rank third, fourth, fifth, and eleventh in the world, respectively, while Hong Kong (46.89) ranks second. Among developed countries, London is known as an internationally renowned city with high housing prices, but its housing price-to-income ratio is 20.58, far lower than that of Beijing, Shanghai, and Shenzhen. Moreover, the ratios of other international metropolises such as New York, Tokyo, Paris, and Berlin are 11.93, 12.97, 18.51, and 10.38, respectively. To sum up, the ratios in Beijing, Shanghai, and Shenzhen are several times higher than in other foreign cities. For this reason, residents in the aforementioned Chinese cities are faced with intense financial pressure as they seek to purchase homes.

Generally speaking, China's real estate market has made remarkable contributions to the development of the economy, but has also created many difficulties. Thus, it is important for various levels of government, enterprises, and academia to carefully summarize the experiences and lessons learned over the course of the real estate market's development so as to strive for a better path forward.

2 Historical Overview

1. Evolution of China's Land Policy

Since the implementation of reform and opening up, China's land system has undergone several changes. **In 1982**, the Constitution officially stated for the first time that "urban land shall belong to the state," thus laying the foundation for the development of a government-adjusted real estate market.

Beginning in 1987, due to the demands of reform and opening up, the land system began to change into a system of compensated land transfer based on agreements. After reform and opening up, the demand for land by foreign and private enterprises created a system of paid land use. As a pioneer in this field, Shenzhen first implemented the system of paid use of state-owned land in 1987, and in April 1988, the provision that "land use rights may be transferred in accordance with the law" was included in the Chinese Constitution. In this way, land ownership was separated from land use rights, and the system of paid land use was established through the legal transfer of land use rights. Later, the provision that "market mechanisms shall

[5] See https://www.numbeo.com/property-investment/rankings_by_country.jsp.

be introduced into the land supply mechanism through the collection of land use fees, paid transfer of land use rights, and other forms" was enacted via the Land Administration Law in December 1988.

The enaction of national laws and regulations on land use rights promoted the formation of a compensated land transfer system during this period. **In 1990**, the State Council adopted the Interim Regulations on the Assignment and Transfer of Urban State-owned Land Use Rights, which clearly stipulated that the land use rights of state-owned land may be transferred through "agreement, bidding, and auction" as well as other market transactions. The land transfer system established on the basis of these regulations began to play a role in the utilization and efficiency of land resources.

The most important tasks during this historical period were to define and clarify land property rights, specifically by distinguishing land use rights from ownership. For example, the Interim Measures for the Administration of Allocated Land Use Rights adopted in 1992 introduced new norms for the traditional administrative approval of land, the Urban Real Estate Management Law of the People's Republic of China adopted in 1994 added detailed provisions on the acquisition of urban land use rights, the transfer of land use rights, and the transfer of real estate mortgages, and the Guarantee Law of the People's Republic of China adopted in 1995 allowed state land use rights to be used as collateral. The land supply system during this period was unsound and possessed a large institutional loophole, which resulted in some harmful phenomena such as land-buying binges by developers, illegal land supplies, low-cost transfers, land occupation, wasted resources, rent-seeking, and popular speculation in the early 1990s.

Since 1999, with the advancement of housing reform, China has further established a local government-led land supply system as well as a bidding, auction, and listing system for usage rights transfer. In April 2001, the Notice on Strengthening the Administration of State-Owned Land Assets issued by the State Council stipulated that six basic systems should be established to manage the land market: a unified supply system for market construction land, a system for total control of construction land, a system for land use rights transactions within the market, a system for benchmark land price updating and publication, a public inquiry system for land registration, and an internal review system for collective decision-making. Driven by the central government, 1300 or more urban land acquisition and reserve institutions were established nationwide by the end of 2003.[6] Today, most cities have land reserve institutions and open markets for land.

2. The History of China's Real Estate Market

Looking back on the past 38 years of real estate development in China, we can see that the real estate market has been a pillar industry and the object of long-term mechanism regulation ever since its early development. The real estate market has undergone several stages of evolution, with the government adopting different positioning and development ideas at each stage. Over the course of this process, a regulatory tool

[6] Lang [5].

based on monetary, credit, tax, and land control policies was gradually formed. The eight development stages can be summarized as follows.

Before reform and opening up: There was a serious shortage of housing during this period. In urban areas, the government settled housing problems by implementing a system for welfare-oriented public housing distribution and low-rent public housing. In this system, the government and work units were responsible for investment, construction, distribution, management, and maintenance of housing. Housing was distributed via a top-down system and was regarded as a typical welfare product. In the countryside, the Draft Amendments to the Regulations of Rural People's Communes were adopted, which established the property model of rural homesteads (one house and two systems, private houses on public land) and confirmed that rural homesteads were property of the commune, and thus could not be bought or sold by members, but houses built on the land could be rented or sold. In this period, the systems for collective ownership of rural homesteads and farmers' free access to use rights were essentially formed.

From 1980 to 1998: The earliest stage of the real estate market. Housing commercialization was first officially presented in 1980, thus promoting China's housing and land reform and allowing the real estate market to begin its first round of development. In 1988, Hainan Province was established, and a large number of young people went there to establish real estate enterprises, including Vanke, Greenland, Wantong, and others. The State Council also carried out housing reform in 24 provinces in 1991, tremendously catalyzing the real estate market. Although the government subsequently introduced a number of policies to curb the development of real estate and prevent the bursting of the real estate bubble, this stage laid the foundation for housing commercialization.

From 1998 to 2002: Development brought about by housing reform. Affected by the Asian financial crisis in 1998, the State Council issued the *Notice on Further Deepening Urban Housing Reform and Accelerating Housing Construction* to stimulate domestic demand. In this way, the government began to establish the urban housing commercialization system, under which people could buy houses with property rights.[7] This move established the housing market as a new source of economic growth and laid a foundation for housing system reform. Subsequently, supporting policies such as bank credit and land management were introduced. With the introduction of a housing credit policy, buyers could purchase a house with a down payment, and the housing provident fund system was also implemented. A system for bidding, auction, and listing transfer of operating land was also established. At this stage, driven by real estate investment, GDP increased by 1.2%. Moreover, the increase rate of housing prices during this time was <5%, allowing China to achieve steady growth in the real estate market.

[7] China's housing system provides that the land ownership shall be different from housing. Housing ownership is permanent and without time limit, while the period of land ownership varies according to the nature of the land (70 years for housing; 50 years for industry, science, education, culture, and health; 40 years for tourism and business). In addition, housing property can be renewed automatically.

From 2002 to 2007: Real estate became a pillar industry. In August 2003, the State Council issued the Notice on Promoting the Sustainable and Healthy Development of the Real Estate Market, which posited that "real estate has become a pillar industry of the national economy" for the first time. In 2003, investment in national property development projects grew by more than 30%, demonstrating overheated development. Therefore, in order to promote the sustainable and healthy development of the real estate market, the government formulated appropriate policies involving strict land management, control of real estate development, and an increase in the down payment ratio of high-end commodity houses and villas. However, housing prices continued to rise due to the suppression of supply. As the proportion of urbanization increased, demand for housing was further released. In March 2005, the State Council issued a document to stress the importance of stabilizing housing prices. This was the first year of macroeconomic regulation and control in China's real estate market. In terms of housing supply, housing of 90 m^2 or under was required to account for 70% of the total development area. Moreover, the government implemented a financial policy to increase the down payment ratio as well as a land policy that established a strict process for land approval. At this stage, despite the intensive implementation of policies to adjust the real estate market, housing prices continued to climb.

From 2008 to 2009: The real estate stimulus policy was implemented once more. Affected by the 2008 international financial crisis, in order to stabilize economic development and stimulate real estate consumption, the State Council issued Several Opinions on the Promotion of Healthy Development of the Real Estate Market, which regarded real estate as an important pillar industry and positively supported the development of the real estate market. In terms of credit, the People's Bank of China issued the Notice on Expanding the Float-down Amplitude of Loan Interest Rates of Personal Commodity Houses and Other Relevant Issues to increase credit support for self-occupied and renovated housing, lower the down payment ratio, and provide discounts on loan interest rates to make monetary policy accommodative. Meanwhile, the government granted tax preferences: the Ministry of Finance issued the Notice on Adjustment of Taxes Policies in Real Estate Transactions, reducing the business tax and cutting the deed tax to 1%. At this stage, the stimulus policy had obvious effects, and housing prices maintained a stable development trend.

From 2010 to 2013: The excessive rise in housing prices was curbed. At the end of 2009, the State Council promulgated "Four Measures" to comprehensively utilize land, finance, taxation, and other means to curb the excessive rise in housing prices. In April 2010, the State Council issued the Notice on Resolutely Curbing the Excessive Rise in Housing Prices in Some Cities, which announced the adoption of purchase restriction policy for the first time, increased the down payment ratio to 30%, and restored the exemption period of the business tax from 2 to 5 years. At this stage, housing prices were generally curbed.

From 2014 to September 2016: Excess urban real estate inventory was cut to stimulate the market again. Through the process of "cutting excess urban real estate inventory" to achieve shifts in economic growth, real estate once again became an important engine for driving economic development. In September 2014, the Central Bank and the China Banking Regulatory Commission issued the Notice on Further

Conducting Housing Financial Services, which adjusted the housing loan policy. For second-home loans, the bank switched from a policy of "receiving and refinancing" to "recognizing and not refinancing." The down payment ratio for first homes was reduced to 30%, and buyers were granted a preferential interest rate on first-home loans (30% off). Real estate destocking was proposed at the Central Economic Work Conference in December 2015, and housing prices skyrocketed at this stage.

Since September 2016: A long-term real estate mechanism has been established. Due to skyrocketing housing prices, the Political Bureau emphasized in July 2016 that major efforts should be made to "suppress asset price bubbles." From September 30 to October 6, 2016, real estate policies were intensively introduced in various regions, and 16 cities, including Beijing, Tianjin, and Shenzhen successively issued real estate regulation policies. In December 2016, the Central Economic Work Conference proposed for the first time that "housing should be used for living, not for speculation." In February 2017, the Central Secretary laid out "A Study on the Long-Term Mechanism of Real Estate and Basic Institutional Arrangements" for the first time, marking the transition of China's real estate market from short-term regulation to a long-term mechanism and housing system. As stressed in the 19th Party Congress Report, "we will move faster to put in place a housing system that ensures supply through multiple sources, provides housing support through multiple channels, and encourages both housing purchase and renting." With the implementation of a series of policies such as "restricted purchases, restricted loans, restricted sales, price limits, limited land auctions, and restricted transformation of commercial land into residential land," the real estate market's overheating has been suppressed. The "restricted sales" policy is a particularly innovative policy in this round of regulation. The policy of "encouraging both housing purchase and renting" was proposed as the core component of the housing system, and joint-property housing as an innovative system has been piloted in first-tier cities such as Beijing and Shanghai. In this stage, the government has started to explore the establishment of the housing system and is focused on further developing the long-term mechanism, which has figured prominently in China's real estate regulation and control. It has also provided a point of reference for the development of real estate in other countries.

3 Economic Analysis

1. **Land conversion is too important to be ignored by modern economics**

Land conversion was a key issue in classical political economy. Early in the era of the industrial revolution, economists such as Smith and Riccardo discussed land conversion at length. However, modern economics has not paid an equivalent amount of attention to this issue. As major developed countries have entered the post-industrial stage, discussions of land conversion have nearly disappeared from mainstream economics textbooks. Modern economics assumes that as long as property rights are defined, land conversion will be carried out through Coasian bargaining. **However, the cost of Coasian bargaining can be astonishingly high, which makes land conversion very costly**. The processes of industrialization, urbanization, and development of the real estate market are highly dependent on the conversion of agricultural land for non-agricultural use. The government, as an administrator of economic activities' geographical distribution, plays an essential role in directing the process of land conversion.

First, the conversion from agricultural to non-agricultural land affects the urbanization process. When agricultural land cannot be successfully converted, the processes of urbanization and industrialization are hindered. Second, the specific use of urban construction land seriously affects the economic activities of a region. The conversion from industrial to commercial and residential land will directly affect local economic development. Finally, the construction and distribution of public works and infrastructure, including public transport, are closely related to the allocation of land.

We take India and Brazil as examples to demonstrate the negative impact of laissez-faire land policies on economic development. India established the feudal private ownership of land during its colonial period, and since its independence, it has never been able to thoroughly reform this system. A large amount of land is concentrated in the hands of landlords, which is a major obstacle to India's industrial development and urbanization. On the topic of urbanization, both India and China had urbanization rates of less than 30% in 1978, with India ahead of China by five percentage points. However, India's urbanization rate held at only 33% in 2017, far lower than China. From the perspective of industrial structure, the share of primary industry in China's GDP has fallen to 8%, and China has begun to transform and upgrade to secondary and tertiary industries. India, on the other hand, has a greater dependence on agriculture, and the proportion of its industry in GDP is still below 30% (Charts 4 and 5).

Brazil's development has been different from India's, but it is another state in which lack of government intervention in the allocation of land resources has exerted adverse effects on the economy. Brazil's land system evolved from the large manor

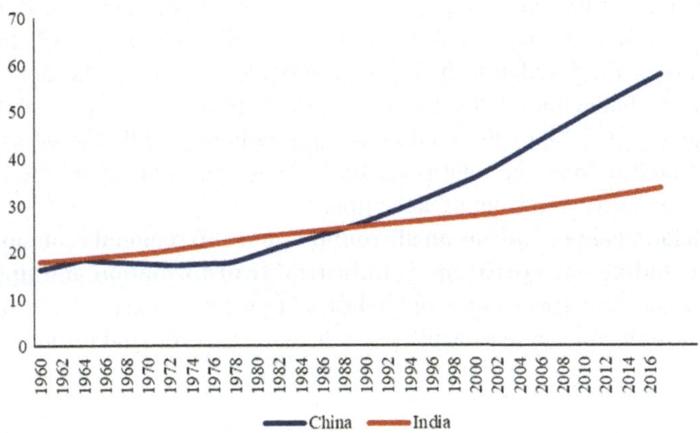

Chart 4 Urbanization rates of China and India. *Source* WDI

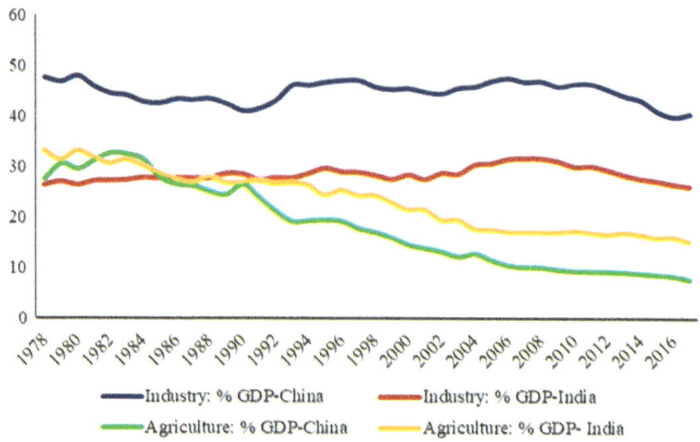

Chart 5 GDP composition of China and India. *Source* WDI

system of Latin American colonialism. At the end of the nineteenth century, Brazil began modernizing, but the degree of land concentration not only failed to decrease, but increased instead. By the 1950s,[8] 78% of farmers in Brazil still had no land. In contrast, the large manors had an extensive scale of operations with an average operating area of 2000 km^2. In 2003, manors with more than 2000 ha accounted for 0.8% of the country's farmers, but 31.6% of total land.[9] Under this arrangement, Brazil's urbanization has experienced abnormal development. As a large number of landless farmers rushed into cities, Brazil completed its urbanization in the 1980s, and its urbanization rate rose to 84.2% in 2005. However, the formal housing market has limited capacity, and the poor rural labor force that has migrated to cities lacks the ability to buy houses. For these reasons, constraints on both supply and demand have hindered Brazil's urban economy from launching effectively. This has led to growing slums, which have spread across all large and medium-sized cities in Brazil. According to the 2000 census, there were 3905 slums in Brazil, an increase of 717 from 1991. During the same year, the urban area of Rio de Janeiro had a population of 5.85 million, among which more than 1.5 million lived in 513 slums. The Rocinha slum, with a population of more than 300,000, is known as the largest slum in Latin America. In the mid-1970s, the population working in Brazil's manufacturing field accounted for 20% of the total working population, while the urban population represented 61% of the total population. These phenomena are the results of industrialization divorced from urbanization.[10]

Second, land conversion has an all-round impact on regional economic development, including enterprise entry, industrial transformation and upgrading, etc. Furthermore, enterprise entry and industrial transformation are more successful when the government can reasonably guide the allocation of land resources.

[8]Han et al. [6].

[9]Li and Wang [7].

[10]Zheng [8].

This is well demonstrated by the case of the "Industrial Relocation and Re-planning Program" (i.e., the partial relocation of enterprises from Tiexi District to the Economic and Technological Development Zone). In 2002, the reform of state-owned enterprises in Tiexi District faced many difficulties. For example, the asset/liability ratio of more than 1100 state-owned enterprises was over 90%, and half of the area's 300,000 industrial workers were on the verge of unemployment. To address the situation, the Tiexi District government proposed the "Industrial Relocation and Re-planning Program," which successfully revitalized the old industrial area through rational land development and utilization. The Tiexi District government allocated land resources to those in need through the conversion of industrial land—where the city-center enterprises were located—into commercial land. At the same time, the district government used the income from land price differences to carry out urban environment construction in the old city and to reestablish the factories of relocated enterprises in the western development zone.

By 2005, Tiexi District had basically weathered the difficulties of state-owned reform. Of the income of RMB14 billion from land exchange, RMB5 billion was used to resolve the historical legacy of state-owned enterprises, RMB5.5 billion to support the new establishment and development of enterprises moving west, RMB3.5 billion to reconstruct the center of the old city, and RMB3 billion to repay debts and resettle 150,000 workers. Tiexi District's 2002 dilemma of state-owned enterprise reform indicates that some land resources in the district had been unreasonably allocated. On one hand, the old city was unable to provide industrial enterprises with the ingredients necessary for further industrial development, resulting in numerous developmental difficulties. On the other hand, the old city was home to a large population and significant economic demand, which appealed greatly to commercial development investors, but the investors were not able to enter the old city due to the planning at the time. The Tiexi District government's bold transformation of land use patterns in the area was in line with demands for the rational distribution of resources, and has thus successfully repaid the reform costs of state-owned enterprises, allowed for industrial transformation of the old city, and spurred construction of a new development zone.

2. Government can play an active role in the conversion of land usage

The development experience of China's real estate market over the past two decades indicates that regardless of land ownership, the government can play an active role in the conversion of land usage.

First, local governments should be incentivized to help reduce the transaction costs of land conversion. In China, local governments rather than real estate agents are directly involved in negotiations with the users of agricultural land, thus greatly accelerating the conversion process from agricultural to non-agricultural usage. The government is uniquely equipped to play this role for two reasons. First, the government's ability to coordinate and negotiate is far greater than that of a single developer. The government can also collectively negotiate with land users in relevant districts, which improves the feasibility of the total conversion of land use patterns in the area. Second, government negotiations are more flexible than those with solo developers.

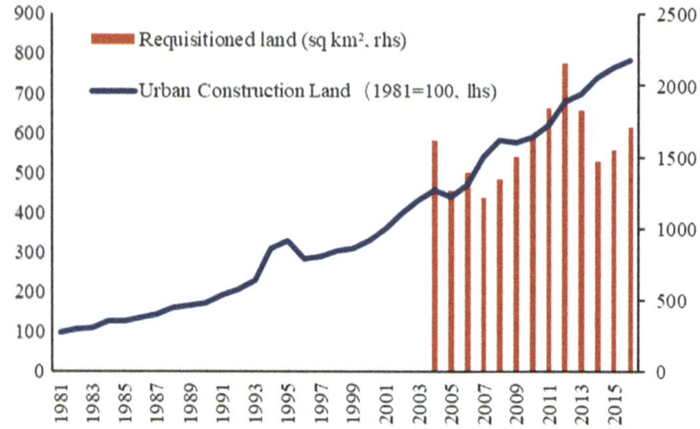

Chart 6 Expansion of urban construction land in China. *Source* NBS of China

In addition to cash compensation, the government can also access comprehensive resources to provide non-cash compensation, such as employment settlements, thus significantly reducing negotiation costs.

Beyond this, the Chinese government has also closely tracked the least cultivated land areas over the course of agricultural to non-agricultural land conversion. The government has paid close attention to changes in cultivated land areas and strictly implemented a bottom line of 1.8 billion μ (120 million ha) to provide a greater guarantee for China's food security.

Since reform and opening up, China's urban construction land areas have risen rapidly. The beginning of housing reform policy and the real estate market in 1998 have also promoted the urbanization process. The national urban construction land area was only 6720 km^2 in 1981, and by 2016 it had reached 52,671.3 km^2 (Charts 6 and 7).

Second, there should be top-down overall planning for land usage, including urban planning, regardless of land ownership. In China, the land and resource authorities, as well as urban planning organs, make an overall plan for land use distribution patterns. In the United States and Europe, despite the private ownership of land, relevant government authorities still manage land use patterns. There are development planning departments at various levels of the US government:[11] the federal government is responsible for conducting national development planning and adjustment, while local governments at the city and county levels directly participate in specific urban planning. Every 20 years, local urban planning departments issue *Guidelines for Urban Master Planning and Development* to lay out the objectives and locations of residential, commercial, and industrial land. Based on the guidelines, the planning department of each community specially determines the detailed construction objectives of each sub-district, including land use, transportation, and public service facilities. Moreover, the US urban planning commission sets

[11] Shi and Xu [9].

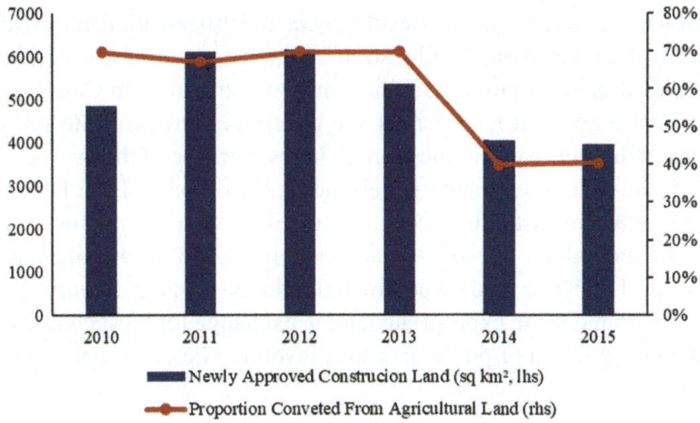

Chart 7 Land conversion in China. *Source* NBS of China, Ministry of Natural Resources, ACCEPT calculation

forth requirements on the stories, floor area ratio, and even appearances for certain areas. For example, when Trump planned to build a Trump Tower[12] in New York, he conducted a long-term negotiation and communication with the local urban planning committee in order to build a tall building with a floor area ratio of 21.6 among lower building complexes, and finally obtained the affirmative votes of the commission through media and other multi-party operations. Furthermore, in the preparation for the Trump International Building in Chicago, a tug-of-war with the local urban planning committee was also carried out due to public transportation problems. These examples indicate that the United States government is very strict with the management of land use. In Germany,[13] the Urban Development and Research Department publishes the urban construction plan in a legal form, providing for the possible usage of all development projects. The management scope of the construction plan covers whether a certain residential area is allowed to build partial offices or industrial buildings, and stipulates that no buildings may be constructed within the scope of the land allocated to public facilities and roads.[14]

After the Second World War, with the guidance of the United States and the cooperation of each relevant government, Japan, South Korea, and Chinese Taiwan implemented the policy of compensated land use to reform feudal land ownership and reduce the concentration of and monopoly on agricultural land. The US government also became involved in land use planning within its own borders to solve problems like overcrowding and poor sanitation, which were common before the nineteenth century. Zoning regulations were adopted in New York State in 1916, and by 1926, all states in the United States had adopted their own zoning regulations to plan and guide land use patterns.[15]

---

[12]Schwartz and Trump [10].

[13]Wang et al. [11].

[14]Wang [12].

[15]Sun [13].

In addition to regional economic development and urbanization, the government's direct or indirect guidance on the allocation of land resources also contributes to the construction of important public facilities and infrastructure. In China, urban land is owned by the state, so it is easier for the government to carry out infrastructure construction, including roads. In the United States, because of the private ownership of land, both the federal and state governments own a part of the land needed to carry out important infrastructure construction. Take San Diego, for example: the land owned by the federal government accounts for 27.7% of the city, and the state government, 27.1%.[16] For land owned by individuals, *eminent domain* also ensures that the US government can expropriate land in exchange for "just compensation" to carry out the construction of public facilities involving defense, water conservancy, and transportation.[17]

3. **Local governments should be incentivized to mitigate the social problems of a free real estate market**

After two decades of development, China's real estate market has significantly improved the living conditions of residents and become China's largest asset market. Although the government's guidance on land resources has promoted economic development, the government still needs to further improve the rational regulation of the real estate market to solve the many problems that continue to face Chinese real estate.

The first of these problems is that Chinese local governments are presented with more incentives to build industrial parks than housing, leading to high housing prices. Chinese local governments are encouraged to promote economic development by guiding the allocation of land resources. In addition, the long-term tax revenue generated by attracting investment is far higher than the fiscal revenue brought by one-time land transfer (taking into account the compensation for demolition and other issues, the government can actually receive limited income from the transfer of land), so the Chinese government gives priority to increasing the proportion of industrial land when delineating land usage. Under the local land transfer system in pursuit of economic growth, the proportion of industrial and commercial land within urban areas remains at a high level, creating a shortage of residential land. While this arrangement has greatly promoted the rapid development of China's economy, such development has come at a high price—massive land consumption and expensive residential property. The proportion of residential land in relation to total newly added land each year is <30%, and the proportion of newly added residential land supply in first-tier cities is kept at 20% or lower. In fact, China International Capital Corporation released a report on the supply potential of China's construction land at the beginning of 2010,[18] which indicated that compared to China's residential land to total urban land ratio of 30%, other major countries and cities demonstrate

[16]Shi and Xu [14].

[17]Bao [15].

[18]CICC-100112: *Real Estate-Land is not scarce, so we will analyze the construction land supply potential in China.*

much higher percentages: 76% in Japan, 42.4% in New York, 62.5% in Seoul, and 46.7% in London. Thus, we can see that the reason urban housing prices have been rising so rapidly and remaining so high in Chinese cities is a lack of residential land supply (Charts 8 and 9).

The second major problem is that despite the overall rapid development of the real estate market and the increase in per capita housing area, the distribution of housing resources is seriously imbalanced. China's low- and middle-income populations are unable to afford housing due to the continuous rise in housing prices. This phenomenon is particularly serious in large cities such as Beijing. China's urbanization will encounter similar challenges to Brazil's if this contradiction cannot be effectively alleviated.

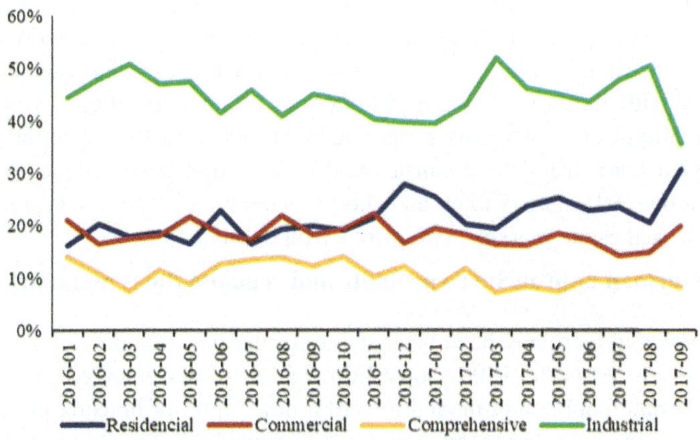

Chart 8 Proportion of land supplied—usage (monthly). *Source* NBS of China, Wind

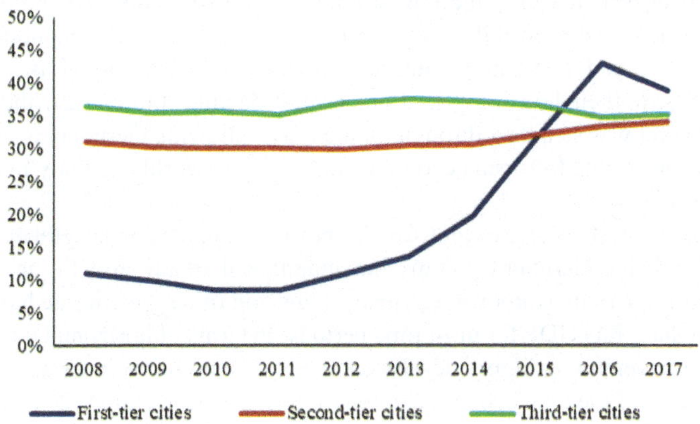

Chart 9 Proportion of residential land in total supply. *Source* NBS of China, Wind

The third major problem is that the government's stronger negotiation abilities in the process of converting land from agricultural to non-agricultural damages the interests of agricultural landowners. China's provisions on compensation for demolition and settlement of "nail houses"[19] have been constantly improved, but they still need to be further clarified. In addition, the government should have different ideas for guiding land use patterns at different stages of economic development. At present, as urbanization has progressed, China has been reforming its policies on agricultural land expropriation, and developers in some regions have begun to negotiate directly with farmers.

Since its inception, the Chinese real estate market has served the dual purposes of promoting economic development and improving residential standards. Over the past two decades, the overall positioning of the real estate market has leaned notably more toward its economic function. For example, one purpose of the 1998 housing reform was to cope with the Asian financial crisis. China also made major efforts to develop and invest in the real estate market in response to the global financial crisis of 2008. Faced with the above problems, China's real estate market began to experience a transformation from a primarily economic function to a focus on people's welfare. China should learn from the countries and regions that better attend to people's welfare via the real estate market, and should maintain a proper balance as it shifts between the real estate market's two primary functions.

(a) **The German approach: To promote and regulate the rental market**

Housing prices in Germany have been stable for the past decade, not experiencing any fluctuations. After the 1990s, most European countries emerged from the burst of the real estate bubble and moved toward a new round of housing price growth, while housing prices in Germany "remained unmoved." In the seven to eight years preceding the 2008 economic crisis, the price-to-income ratio in the UK, France, and the United States continued to expand, rising by an average of 30%. The German ratio, however, was not only the lowest among these four countries, but remained extremely stable and even fell slightly in many years. During the economic crisis, the UK, France, and the United States all experienced the bursting of the real estate bubble and saw their housing prices enter stark decline. In contrast, the German housing market was steadfast throughout the crisis, allowing Germany to contribute to the recovery of the European economy and even the world economy in the years that followed.

Over the past 10 years, except for the negative impact of the global financial crisis in 2009, the German economy has maintained steady growth, and national income has increased. Moreover, Germany's housing price growth rate has been far lower than that of its GDP for most time periods. In terms of horizontal comparison, the German economy is highly developed, and its economic volume accounted for about one-fifth of the total economic output of the European Union (28 countries) in 2007. During the same time period, housing prices in Germany were miraculously

[19]A "nail house" refers to a home whose resident refuses to leave to make way for real estate development.

far lower than that of its European peers. In 2007, the aggregate GDP of Germany, the UK, and France represented about one half of the EU economy, but the average price of commercial houses in Germany was EUR5907/m^2, far lower than in the UK (EUR23,932/m^2) and France (EUR12,796/m^2). In short, Germany has created a "miracle" of stable housing prices for many years while concurrently maintaining stable economic growth. This is extremely rare—we should learn from the experience of Germany.

An important reason why German housing prices are stable is that Germany has a well-established leasing market and imposes strict tenancy control to fully protect tenants' rights and interests. About 60% of the population in Germany lives in rented houses, and the remaining 40% have their own homes. The rental rate is as high as 82% in big cities such as Berlin, Hamburg, and Frankfurt as well as their surrounding regions. At present, government-subsidized housing and market-based rental housing represent about 8 and 92% of the rental housing market in Germany, respectively.[20] The German government imposes strict rent control on both government-subsidized rental housing and market-based private leasing markets, namely through the implementation of the rental price guidance system. Local governments and industry associations prepare a list of rental prices according to different locations, housing structures, and qualities, and propose rental guidance prices in line with the market conditions of various regions as a reference for contracts between leasers and the lessees. The government also promulgates corresponding laws and regulations to ensure the implementation of guidance prices. If the rent for a new contract exceeds 20% of the rent of a house with the same quality and in the same district, it will be deemed "extra high rent." In such cases, tenants can open a lawsuit in accordance with the *Economic Crimes Act*, demanding that the rent be reduced to a reasonable level, resulting in a fine of up to 100,000 German marks for the landlord. If the rent fixed by the landlord exceeds 50% of the guidance price, it will be deemed as "excessive profit on rent" and the landlord can be sentenced to up to 3 years in prison.[21] Furthermore, landlords shall not raise the price arbitrarily once the housing contract is in effect. If the rent increases by more than 15% within 3 years, it will also be regarded as "extra high rent" and the landlord will be subject to punishment in accordance with the law. Moreover, landlords cannot terminate tenancy agreements at will. Generally speaking, the terms of tenancy agreements are indefinite in Germany. Unless the tenant fails to fulfill their obligations as specified in the agreement, the landlord may terminate the agreement only after providing a reasonable explanation and notifying the tenant at least 9 months in advance.

Second, Germany implements a strict house pricing mechanism to directly guarantee the stability of housing prices. Housing prices in Germany are determined by independent property appraisers, whose prices are legally binding—all real estate transactions are obliged to comply with their guidance prices, and transaction prices must float within a reasonable range. According to the *Economic Crimes Act*, if a real

[20] Yi [16].

[21] He and Teng [17].

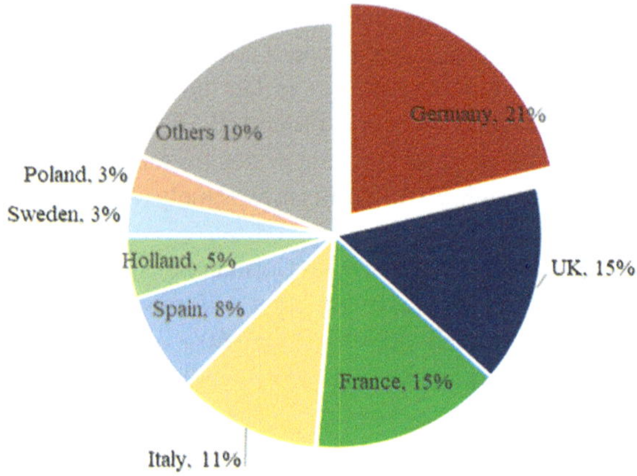

Chart 10 Proportion of GDP for major EU countries in 2017. *Source* IMF and EuroStat

estate developer sells a house at a price higher than 20% of the independently determined reasonable price, then it will be deemed an "excessive housing price," and if the developer fails to immediately reduce the price to the reasonable range, then the seller will be fined up to EUR50,000. If a real estate developer fixes a housing price at 50% higher than the guidance price, they will be deemed as committing "excessive profit of housing prices," and can be sentenced to up to three years in prison while also facing huge fines (Chart 10).[22]

Third, Germany focuses on strengthening the social attributes of housing while weakening its financial attributes. The German government has clarified in its Constitution that the basic functions of the state and the government are to guarantee the living conditions of residents, and that housing should function as a consumer product to meet the needs of citizens rather than an investment product. To realize this vision, the government provides a stable amount of social welfare housing each year to meet the housing needs of low-income groups in the form of in-kind subsidies. Furthermore, the German government also grants monetary housing subsidies for residents to rent and purchase homes nationwide. Speculation in the real estate market is also severely restricted by the corresponding tax system. The property tax in Germany mainly includes two aspects: the property holding tax (property tax) and the transaction tax.[23] The former is levied on residential houses each year, and is calculated as follows. The tax rate determined by the federal government is 0.26–0.60% of the housing appraisal price, then local governments multiply the above ratio by the local coefficient, yielding a final tax rate generally between 0.98 and 2.84%. An individual's first self-owned home is subject to a lower tax rate, while those holding several homes are subject to higher property taxes. As for the transaction tax, German law provides that housing that has undergone a transaction within the past 10 years shall be subject to a 3.5% transfer fee, a 1–5% assessment fee, a 25% capital gain tax, and a personal income tax with a progressive tax rate. The transaction tax does not apply to homes held for longer than 10 years. If a house held for <7 years is

[22] Ye [18].

[23] Wang [19].

transferred, it may be subject to a comprehensive tax rate of up to 50%. Through this tax system, the German government has greatly increased the cost of real estate speculation.

Fourth, in addition to economic policy factors, the stability of German housing prices is also attributed to certain historical and political causes. Until the second half of the nineteenth century, Germany was historically divided. During this time, hundreds of independent states contributed to unique historical conditions, and Germany was not allowed to concentrate resources on the development of its capital. To this day, Germany maintains some feudalist characteristics of its past. Each state has independent economic and cultural autonomy, and resources are not excessively concentrated in the capital, forming a balanced urban model. Although Germany does not possess any large-scale cities with populations over 10 million, it is home to many small and strong world-class cities such as Frankfurt and Munich, which to a certain extent are able to avoid the objective pressure of high housing prices. However, with the acceleration of the domestic economy, the improvement of the employment market, and the shortage of existing homes in recent years, some major cities in Germany have been faced with a rapid rise in housing prices. Currently, Germany is researching the possibility of tax incentives to grant tax preferences for the construction of ordinary new homes, increase housing supplies, and "cool down" the housing market.

China can learn a lot from Germany's stable real estate market: first, we should decentralize the functions of large cities to alleviate the pressure on urban populations. At present, China's high housing price problem is particularly prominent in first-tier and quasi-first-tier cities. These cities have concentrated populations and heavy traffic, so their limited land supplies will inevitably lead to objectively problematic high housing prices. In the future, we should carry out functional zoning of large cities and gradually drain their populations to second- and third-tier cities, alleviating the excessive pressure on large cities and also promoting the balanced development of all regions and cities. Second, we should imitate Germany's guidance price system to guide buyers to form rational and reasonable housing rent expectations. Over the past 10 years, housing prices have continued to rise, while other investment channels remain limited. Many people still regard housing as the most important investment channel for wealth growth and have a speculative mentality, hoping to realize rapid wealth appreciation through housing transactions. This is clearly demonstrated by the fact that over the past two years, people have often waited in line overnight at sales offices to buy housing in second- and third-tier cities. Many speculators expect that the housing markets in these cities will replicate the history of the rapid rise in housing prices in first-tier cities such as Beijing, Shanghai, Guangzhou, and Shenzhen. In this environment, it is important to implement a guidance system like Germany's to guide people to form reasonable expectations for the real estate market and to emphasize that "housing is to be used for living, not speculating." In this vein, we should also severely crack down on speculation, increase the capital gain tax on real estate transfer transactions completed within a short period of time, and implement a property holding tax on idle housing, thus encouraging owners to rent their otherwise idle homes and increase the supply of the rental market.

(b) **The Singaporean and Hong Kong approach: Public housing provided by the government**

Singapore is a city-state with a small land area and a dense population of about 7300 people per m^2. Although it is one of the world's top three most crowded countries, it has managed to successfully implement a "Home Ownership Scheme" and reach a home ownership rate of 90.7%—the second highest in the world.[24] The Singaporean government has primarily solved the country's housing problem through the development and provision of low-rent and low-cost housing known as "Housing and Development Board (HDB) Flats." The country functions on a dual-tract system consisting of the public HDB flats as the first tract and private housing as the second.

According to the Housing and Development Board (HDB) of Singapore, by March 2017, about 82% of the country's population lived in government-constructed HDB flats, while the remaining 3% of low-income families rented HDB flats from the government. There are strict requirements for purchasing and applying for these HDB flats. Only Singaporean citizens can purchase new ones, while permanent residents can only buy second-hand HDB flats. Besides HDB flats, the remaining 18% of the housing system is made up of private housing. Buyers of private housing mainly include high-income Singaporeans, permanent residents, and foreign investors.

Singapore's existing housing system, which is dominated by HDB flats and supplemented by private housing, did not come into being overnight. Following Singaporean independence, the government's housing policy underwent five stages of development. The general trend was to move HDB flats from rented to owned properties, and after the rate of residential home ownership reached a certain level of stability, to develop a diversified residential market. Early on in Singapore's autonomy, the government promulgated the *Housing Development Law* in 1960[25] to establish the Housing Development Board (HDB) and build low-standard, small-sized houses on a large scale, so as to meet the housing rental demand of low- and middle-income people. Subsequently, in order to enhance the national identity of citizens, the government began to encourage low- and middle-income groups to purchase HDB flats in installments, gradually increasing the home ownership rate. In 1964, the Singaporean government issued the "Home Ownership Scheme" to further encourage home ownership, and in 1968, the *Central Provident Fund (Amendment) Act* was introduced to allow home buyers to use the Central Provident Fund for the purchase of public HDB flats. Since the 1970s, the scope of individuals to which public HDB flats are provided has gradually expanded from low-income to middle-income groups. By 1975, 47% of the country's population lived in HDB flats. After the problem of the housing shortage for low- and middle-income residents was basically solved, the government began to focus on improving the quality of HDB flats, increasing the types of housing units, and developing high-rise and high-density housing. Around the 1980s, the public housing market entered a mature period, the supply of HDB flats became saturated, the number of new homes was significantly

---

[24]Wikipedia https://en.wikipedia.org/wiki/List_of_countries_by_home_ownership_rate.

[25]China Report Network [20].

reduced each year, and the resale transactions of HDB flats gradually increased. The rate of home ownership reached about 90% in 1990, and the proportion of people living in HDB flats peaked at about 87%. Since the 1990s, the housing security function of small-sized HDB flats has been fully utilized, and the supply of HDB flats has become dominated by large-sized units (four or five bedrooms). With the improvement of income levels and the development of globalization, the demands of private housing for high-income residents, permanent residents, and foreigners have been growing. As such, the government has begun to give policy support to the private residential market and promote its gradual development. The proportion of the population living in HDB flats has also begun to decline, from 87% in 1990 to 82% in 2017.

Singapore's public HDB flats are characterized by government subsidies for construction, adequate supply, and stable prices. The Singaporean government is the only seller of new HDB flats and fully controls their pricing power to maintain a stable low growth rate. Singaporean law also provides very strict and clear rules on applying for public HDB flats, including clear income restrictions for purchasing new public flats.[26] People with a monthly household income exceeding the upper limit can only apply to purchase HDB flats on the secondhand market. Furthermore, each family is only allowed to purchase one flat. If a family wants to purchase a second flat, they must first sell their current one and then buy the desired flat from the secondhand market at a rate that will be higher than if it was purchased new. Furthermore, HDB flat applicants are required by law to be Singaporean citizens or permanent residents. Finally, in addition to managing the construction and supply of HDB flats, the government has implemented a clear and reasonable system for HDB flat distribution and adopted a purchase and rent subsidy policy to increase the home ownership rate. For example, the government requires that rent payments generally account for 4–15% of household income,[27] far lower than market-based rent prices. As for purchasing, the government has set the principle that 90% of families should be able to afford a three-bedroom flat and 70% of families should be able to afford a four-bedroom home. Thus, the HDB provides corresponding purchase price concessions for different types of HDB flats. The smaller the size, the higher the discount. For example, the discounts for three- and four-bedroom HDB flats are 44% and 33%, respectively. In addition, the government has directly granted housing purchase and rent payment subsidies to some eligible groups, such as first-time married buyers, single Singaporean citizens, and low- and middle-income populations (Chart 11).

Singapore has perfected its established HDB flats system. Objectively limited by the extremely low per-capita land occupation rate, it has realized its "Home Ownership Scheme" and has become a world leader in home ownership rate. The following valuable lessons can be drawn from Singapore's experience.

First, the government should directly participate in the supply and management of the housing market. Although Singapore implements a market economy, its housing

[26]Zhang [21].

[27]Li et al. [22].

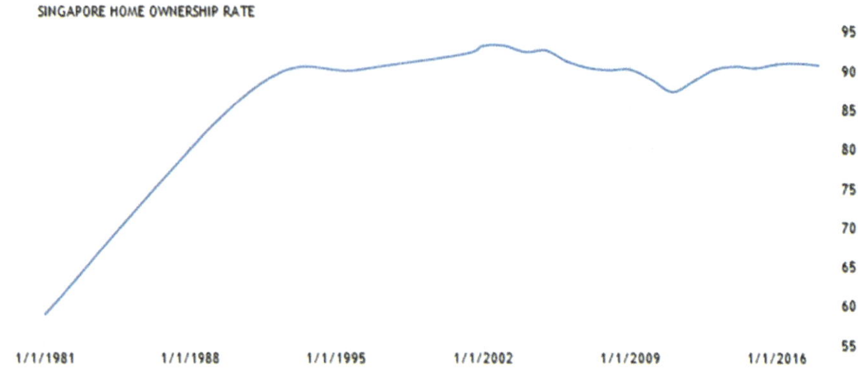

Chart 11 Ratio of homeowner households in Singapore. *Source* Trading economics, Singapore statistics

construction and distribution do not rely entirely on market forces. Rather, the government establishes and guides the housing market through the affordable HDB flats system. This is done via a special administrative management agency—the Housing and Development Board—which conducts the centralized planning, construction, distribution, and management of housing. Additionally, the government has further worked toward solving Singapore's housing problem by establishing a financial support system, including the corresponding provident fund system, and promulgating appropriate laws and regulations to guarantee the normal and smooth operation of the HDB flats program. Thus, we can see that an effective housing system requires cooperation and coordination between the government and market.

Second, the government should establish an effective land supply mechanism. The Singaporean government has implemented a mandatory land acquisition policy and forced the expropriation of private land for construction through legislation. Due to its extremely scarce land resources, Singapore has become one of the few countries in the world to include residential, commercial, and industrial land in the scope of government land acquisition.[28] At present, the total land area controlled by the Singaporean government accounts for about 90% of the national land area. Therefore, the Singapore government has sufficient capacity to effectively regulate land supply and provide the necessary land for HDB flats in a timely manner.[29] The land market is closely related to the real estate market. To regulate and manage the real estate market, we should first reorganize the relationship between the government and the land market in order to secure a stable real estate market via a sound land market.

Third, the government should improve the provident fund system. Singapore's provident fund savings are an important source of financial support for the construction of HDB flats and also serve as a financial guarantee for the individuals who purchase them. Singapore implements a comprehensive central provident fund

[28]Liu [23].

[29]Xie [24].

system involving pension, housing, medical care, insurance, education, and other uses. This system consists of an ordinary, medical, and special account. The ordinary account can be used to purchase a house, and is essentially a mandatory savings plan. Each employee is required to pay 20% of their salary into their individual account, while their employer is required to pay 17% of the employee's salary into the account.[30] The provident fund paid by the individual and employer is uniformly collected, managed, and operated by the Central Provident Fund Board (CPFB). After retaining enough for member withdrawals, the CPFB transfers about 80% of the provident fund to the Central Government through the purchase of government bonds, and the government then uses these funds to build and subsidize the public HDB flats through allocation and loans. The provident fund is also one source of funds that residents can use to buy a house. According to the *Central Provident Fund (Amendment) Act* promulgated in 1968, members of the Central Provident Fund may use their provident fund deposits to directly pay for part of an HDB flat. Subsequently, the government adopted a more liberal policy which stated that members could use their provident fund deposits to purchase an HDB flat in full. In certain circumstances, through the provident fund, price preference, and housing subsidies, Singaporean citizens can even purchase a home with zero down payment, thus greatly improving residents' ability to buy homes.[31] China can learn from the success of the Singaporean system. In accordance with these lessons, we should improve the provident fund system to increase home affordability, guide the flow of domestic provident funds into the construction of government-subsidized housing, and also attract other insurance funds to contribute to the construction of government-subsidized housing in order to ensure adequate funding for public affordable housing construction.

References

1. Terrazas, A. (2017). Viewed from Beijing, even silicon valley housing looks affordable. Retrieved April 12, 2017, from https://www.zillow.com/research/china-united-states-housing-costs-14795.
2. Zillow Research. (2017). Total value of all US homes: $31.8 trillion. How big is that? Retrieved December 28, 2017, fromhttps://www.zillow.com/research/total-value-homes-31-8-trillion-17763/.
3. Tostevin, P. The 10 most valuable real estate markets in the world. Retrieved from https://www.savills.com/blog/article/219340/international-property/the-10-most-valuable-real-estate-markets-in-the-world.aspx.
4. Guan, K. (2002). *Modern housing economy*. China Building Industrial Press.
5. Lang, C. (2007). *Land reserve evaluation and research*. Doctoral dissertation, Tongji University.
6. Han, J., Cui, C., & Zhao, Y. (2005). Slum issues in the process of urbanization in Brazil and its implications for China. China Development Reservation, No. 06.
7. Li, R., & Wang, C. (2006). Urbanization in Brazil and its implication for China-compared with China's urbanization. *Journal of Yanbian University (Social Science Edition)* (2).

[30] The payment will gradually decrease after the employee turns 50.

[31] Bao [25].

8. Zheng, X. (2011). Land problems in the process of industrialization and urbanization—A case study of Brazil. Productivity Research, No. 1.
9. Shi, J., & Xu, L. (2004). Discussion on the U.S. urban planning system: A case study of San Diego County. *Foreign Urban Planning* (4).
10. Schwartz, T., & Trump, D. *Trump autobiography* (pp. 112–113).
11. Wang, T., Jiang, Y., & Yang, C. (2009). German urban planning and construction, urban development research, No. 6.
12. Wang, X. (2005). Germany: Statement and cases of urban planning public participation system. Beijing Planning and Construction, No. 6.
13. Sun, S. (1999). Urban planning system of the United States. Urban Planning, No. 7.
14. Shi, J., & Xu, L. (2004). Discussion on urban planning system of the United States: A case study of San Diego County. Foreign Urban Planning, No. 4.
15. Bao, D. (2004). How the United States prevents the abuse of demolition privileges. China Real Estate Information, No. 2.
16. Yi, Y. (2015). Housing renting: A choice of most Germans–Germany's perfect housing renting system. China Construction, No. 6.
17. He, F., & Teng, X. (2017). Reference and enlightenment from control on german residence renting and preparation of rent system. Price Theory and Practice, No. 3.
18. Ye, C. (2017, July 14). Long-term regulation–How do we imitate the "New German Model?". Retrieved from https://www.sohu.com/a/157172867_617246.
19. Wang, J. (2012). Experience in German housing prices regulation and its enlightenment for China. Price Theory and Practice, No. 2.
20. China Report Network. (2017, October 16). Analysis of China's real estate market status and research report on investment development trend. Retrieved from http://market.chinabaogao.com/fangchan/10162a4N2017.html.
21. Zhang, H. (2018). Singapore's HDB flats system. Zhejiang Economics, No. 1.
22. Li, J., Li, W., Li, Z., & Xue, D. (2012). Study and reference of Singapore's affordable housing policy. International Urban Planning, No. 4.
23. Liu, A. (2005). Measures of intensive land use in Singapore and its development trends. Science and Technology Management of State Land and Resources, No. 4.
24. Xie, B. (2015). *Success and implication of Singapore's HDB flats policy-and discussion of enlightenment for China's affordable housing policy*. China Administration, No. 5.
25. Bao, Z. (2005). See importance of regulating housing prices from the experience of Singapore and Germany. China Real Estate Information, No. 7.

Financial Deepening and Financial Stability

David Daokui Li, Jinjian Shi, Dapeng Chen, Lin Lu, Xushuo Wang, and Kangyi Liu

Abstract The cultivation and regulation of the financial system has been a key component of the Chinese economy's reform and opening-up process over the past 40 years. In this section, we will focus on some stylized facts and provide a brief history of the cultivation and regulation of the financial system over the past 40 years of reform and opening-up before summarizing some economic lessons we can learn from this process. Our main argument is that the steady progress of local-currency-based financial deepening is essential for fast investment in the real economy and channeling savings into investment. However, financial deepening is based on financial stability, which requires the government to proactively monitor and mitigate financial risk.

Keywords Financial system · Financial deepening · Financial stability · Financial risk

---

D. D. Li (✉) · D. Chen · L. Lu
An Academic Center for Chinese Economic Practice and Thinking (ACCEPT), Tsinghua University, Beijing, China
e-mail: daviddaokuili@126.com

D. Chen
e-mail: Derekdapengchen@gmail.com

L. Lu
e-mail: lulin@sem.tsinghua.edu.cn

J. Shi
China Institute of Finance and Capital Markets,China Securities Regulatory Commission (CSRC), Beijing, China
e-mail: shijinj@csrc.gov.cn

X. Wang
Bank of China, Beijing, China
e-mail: wangxushuo@bankofchina.com

K. Liu
INSEAD, Fontainebleau, France
e-mail: kangyi.liu@insead.edu

D. D. Li (eds.), *Economic Lessons from China's Forty Years of Reform and Opening-up*, https://doi.org/10.1007/978-981-33-4520-1_4

1 Stylized Facts

1.1 Achievement 1: The Chinese Economy Has Managed to Avoid a Financial Crisis During the Past 40 Years

First, it is necessary to define the concept of a "financial crisis." Academia tends to categorize financial crises into different types such as currency exchange crises, hyperinflation, international balance risks, debt crises, and banking crises [1–3]. Specific criteria for identifying these phenomena include quantitative index and critical events. For quantitative index, for instance, Frankel and Rose [4] define a currency crisis as an event that occurs when the exchange rate depreciation in a particular year exceeds 25% and is at least 10% higher than the previous year. Reinhart and Rogoff [2] define a currency crisis as occurring when the exchange rate depreciation in a particular year exceeds 15%. For critical events, for instance, the bankruptcy of Lehman Brothers in 2008 is often regarded as the symbol of the outbreak of the 2008 global financial crisis.

According to this literature, we may argue that the Chinese economy has managed to avoid financial crisis during the past 40 years.

First, regarding the currency exchange rate, during 1980–1994, China implemented the "dual-track" exchange rate system in which the official exchange rate and adjusted market exchange rate coexisted. During this period, the exchange rate fluctuated drastically, which reflected the government's subjective will and active adjustment. In 1994, the foreign exchange management system was greatly altered, and China made it clear that the ultimate objective of RMB reform was free exchange. The official exchange rate and adjusted market exchange rate were unified, and the RMB became unofficially pegged to the US dollar. The exchange rate of 1 US dollar to RMB rose quickly from ~5.8 to ~8.7. After that, the exchange rate remained basically stable. Following the "811" exchange rate reform in 2015, the RMB began to depreciate but the maximum year-over-year monthly depreciation rate was merely ~7.5%. **Thus, we can say that there has been no currency exchange crisis since the start of China's reform and opening-up**.

Second, in terms of inflation, Reinhart and Rogoff [2] define hyperinflation as an annualized inflation rate exceeding 40% based on their studies of inflation problems in economies after the Second World War. **Although China previously experienced some periods of high inflation, peak inflation (month over month) was below 30% and was quickly controlled. Thus, no inflation crisis occurred**.

Third, as for the balance of payments, according to the definition given by Forbes and Warnock [5], the combined growth of capital inflow in the most recent four quarters must be below the average value by two standard deviations to be deemed as a sign of the "sudden stop" of capital inflow. According to data detailing China's international balance of payments (1998–2018) (In the CEIC database, quarterly data on China's international balance of payments has used "non-reserve financial account" to measure capital inflows since 1998), **China has not experienced a "sudden stop" of capital inflows**.

Fourth, in terms of a foreign debt crisis, the proportion of China's total foreign debts concerning GDP is not high (the peak value is 17%), and there has been no sovereign debt crisis or systematic corporate foreign debt default. In terms of domestic debt risk, although China's rising macroeconomic leverage (especially local government debt and non-financial corporate debt) has recently attracted much attention, China has addressed its debt crises fairly well within the past 40 years of reform and opening-up. For instance, China cleared up "chain debts" among enterprises in 1991. Around 2000, China disposed of bad assets of national commercial banks (chiefly enterprise loans). **In 2017, China effectively resolved accumulated risks of local government debts, and thus successfully avoided bankruptcy of local governments and systematic bankruptcy of enterprises and financial institutions**.

Fifth, in terms of a banking crisis, although there were times when the risks of individual banks flared up (e.g., the 1998 run on Hainan Development Bank), and in 1995–1997 some people argued that "the Chinese banking system is technically bankrupt" (the NPL ratio of banks exceeded 20% or even reached 40%, and their capital adequacy ratio was negative); on the whole, **the Chinese government has maintained the stability of its banking system. This is exemplified by the fact that the government helped national commercial banks strip off their bad assets and go public during 2005–2010**.

It is noted that there are disagreements in the literature with respect to whether a "stock market crash" (a collapse in stock indexes within a short period) is treated as a "financial crisis." Researchers like Friedman and Schwartz [6] and Eichengreen and Bordo [3] tend to define a financial crisis from the perspective of "real economic effects" instead of "nominal effects" and pay particular attention to bank crises and currency crises. Samuelson (1966) once sarcastically commented that Wall Street indexes predicted nine out of the last five recessions [7]. Schwartz [8] argues that pure stock market decline or property price decline can only be seen as a "pseudo crisis." However, scholars like Aliber and Kindleberger [9] maintain that the scope of the definition of a financial crisis should be broader and include collapse in asset price. Reinhart and Rogoff [2] introduce Kindleberger's concept into a systematic analysis of financial crises and use the method provided by Barro and Ursúa [10] to define a "stock market crash," i.e., cumulative, multi-year inflation-adjusted real returns that were –0.25 or less. However, Reinhart and Rogoff [2] do not shed much light on the analysis of a "pure stock market crash" (e.g., the dot.com bubble burst in the United States in 2001).

Based on the definition given by Barro and Ursua (2009), the period of Chinese stock market crashes were: 1993–1995 (−72.7%), 2001–2005 (−58.4%), 2008 (−68.5%), 2010–2011 (−34.2%), and 2018 (−24.5% in the first 10 months).[1]

[1]It is noted that the reason why the 2015 "stock market crash" is not included here is that the literature including Barro and Ursúa [10] emphasizes that a stock market crash means "a long period of decline" instead of a "short period of fluctuations" of the stock market. In 2015, the Chinese stock market experienced a period of "sharp growth" before declining. The stock market generally exhibited a rising trend in the whole year.

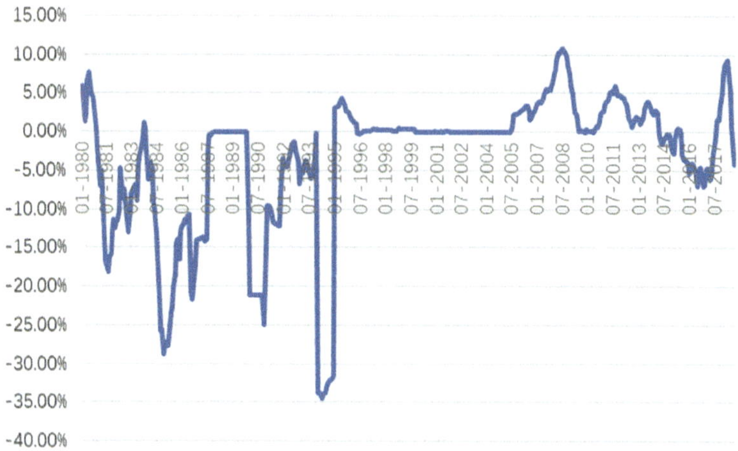

Chart 1 Fluctuations in the exchange rate of RMB against USD (on a YoY basis). *Source* CEIC database

As we will further explore later on in this report, one of the biggest problems facing the Chinese stock market is its limited function for rewarding investors. The limited impact of stock market crises on real economic activities is mainly reflected in the following two aspects: first, stocks are not a major investment target of residents. At present, the total market capitalization of the entire stock market is less than RMB50 trillion. In contrast, the balance of residents' deposits is ~RMB65 trillion, the balance of bonds exceeds RMB50 trillion, the balance of financial products exceeds RMB30 trillion, and the total market capitalization of the real estate market is ~RMB280 trillion.[2] Second, stock financing is not a major financing method for Chinese enterprises, and share price plays a limited role in corporate investment. As discovered by Wang et al. [11], due to the limited information provided by stock prices, corporate investment is not significantly influenced by fluctuations in the market capitalization of relevant companies. In this sense, we are more inclined to adopt the reasoning of Eichengreen and Bordo [3] and define a financial crisis from the perspective of real economic effects. **None of the previous "crashes" of the Chinese stock market led to systematic business failures, bankruptcy of financial institutions, or a serious decline in residents' living standards. Thus, we do not qualify such crashes as the occurrence of a financial crisis** (Charts 1, 2, 3 and 4).

Transitional economies tend to be hit by a financial crisis after a certain period of high-speed growth. In history, the Japanese economy grew rapidly after the Meiji Restoration and "profited a lot from war" via export trade during the First World War. Later on, Japan fell into an economic downturn and the "Showa Financial Crisis" broke out. Similarly, the South Korean economy began to take off in the 1960s, but

[2]The total market capitalization of the Chinese real estate market is ~RMB280 trillion based on our forecast on China's real estate sector.

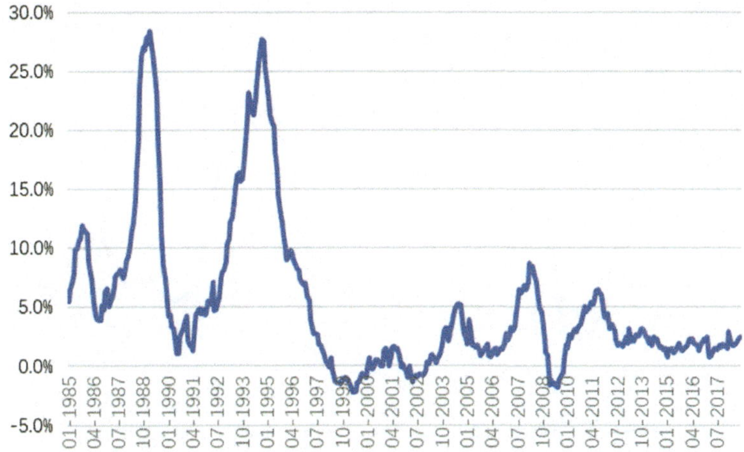

Chart 2 Inflation (consumer price index growth, monthly, YoY). *Source* CEIC database

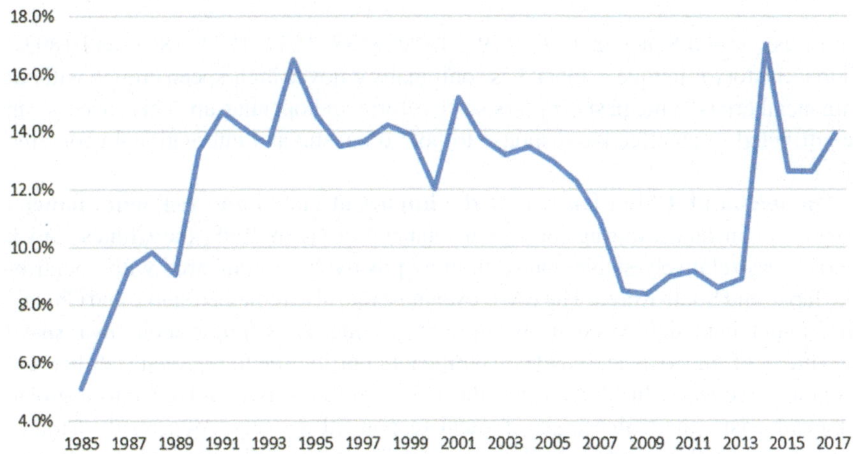

Chart 3 The ratio of China's foreign debts to Its GDP. *Source* CEIC database

was hit hard during the 1998 Asian financial crisis and had to resort to the help of the International Monetary Fund (IMF). In the 1930–1980s, Latin American countries adopted import substitution industrialization and their economies continued to grow. However, their foreign debts also increased dramatically during this time, and their economies suffered from successive debt crises, such as the Latin American debt crisis in 1982, the Mexican financial crisis in 1994, and the Brazilian financial crisis in 1999. Even the United States was frequently hit by financial crises during its early developmental stages. Financial panic (bank failures, economic recessions) broke

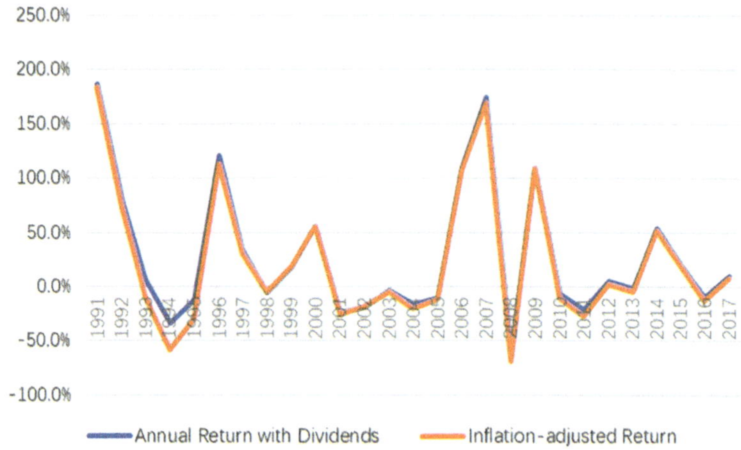

Chart 4 Annual Return of the Chinese Stock Market (composite A-shares market, tradable market value-weighted). *Source* CSMAR database, CEIC database, Authors' calculation

out in the United States in 1792, 1797, 1819, 1837, 1857, 1873, 1884, and 1893.[3] China's history is unique in that it has continually enjoyed high-speed growth without a financial crisis in the past 40 years since reform and opening-up. This success can be attributed to an effective response to both domestic and international economic threats.

On one hand, China fended off the impact of global and regional financial crises. For instance, during the Asian financial crisis in 1998, the Chinese stock market was relatively stable and even grew positively as compared with countries like Japan and South Korea. The RMB exchange rate also remained stable and China's GDP maintained high-speed growth during this time. The Chinese economy resisted the spread of the crisis and made a significant contribution to regional stability and economic recovery. In 2008, when the US subprime crisis evolved into a global financial crisis, the Chinese government responded actively. As a result, China's economic growth stayed at a relatively high level and real estate prices fell only slightly before recovering quickly.

On the other hand, China tried to avoid financial crises of its own. For example, at the end of the 1990s, the problem of domestic banks' non-performing loans began to intensify, and the Chinese government intervened in time. Thanks to concerted efforts by departments such as the State Economic and Trade Commission, the People's Bank of China (PBOC) and the Ministry of Finance, banks stripped off their non-performing assets, which were transferred into the four newly established asset management companies. The successful reinvigoration of those banks prevented the outbreak of a potential financial crisis. If China had also fallen into a financial crisis

[3]https://en.wikipedia.org/wiki/List_of_banking_crises.

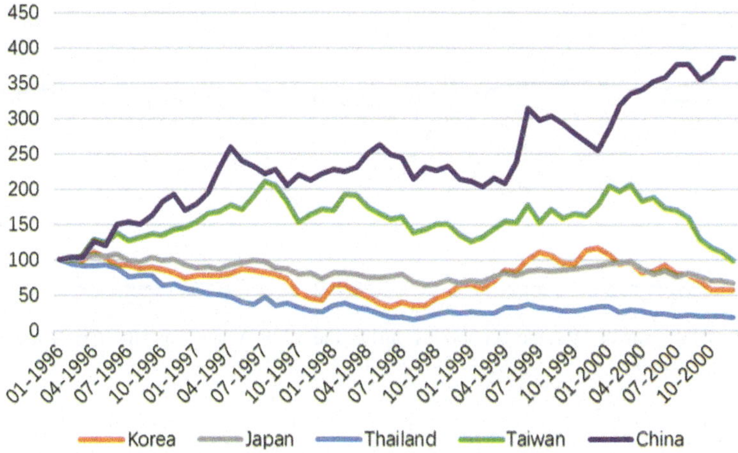

Chart 5 The trend of stock indexes in some economies during the 1998 Asian Financial Crisis (January 1996 = 100). *Source* CEIC database

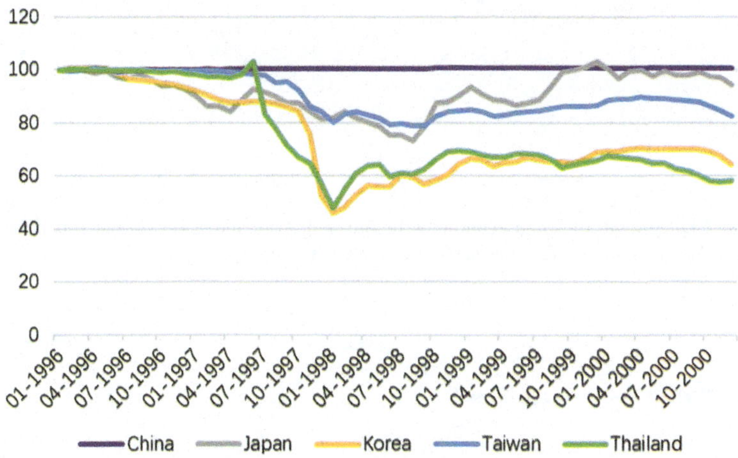

Chart 6 Exchange rate fluctuations in some economies during the Asian Financial Crisis (exchange rate of 1 unit of home currency against the US dollar in January 1996 is used as base number). *Source* CEIC database

triggered by bad loans from its banks during the Asian financial crisis, Asia would have lost its most important stabilizer and the financial crisis would have become exacerbated, potentially evolving into a global financial crisis (Chart 5, 6, 7, 8, 9 and 10).[4]

[4]For specific measures taken by the Chinese government, refer to 1 (4) of Part II of this Article.

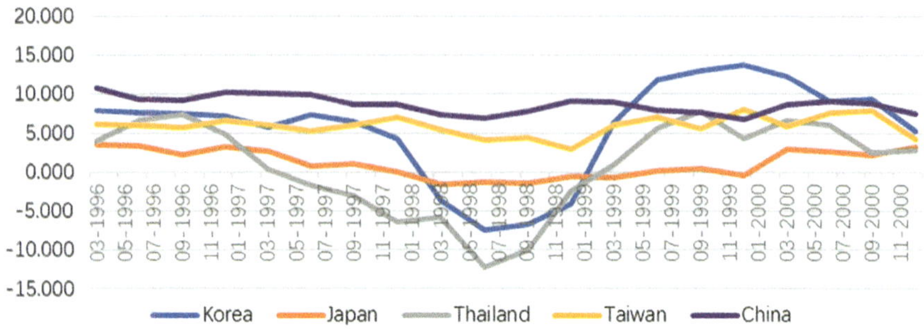

Chart 7 GDP growth of some economies during the 1998 Asian Financial Crisis (quarterly). *Source* CEIC database

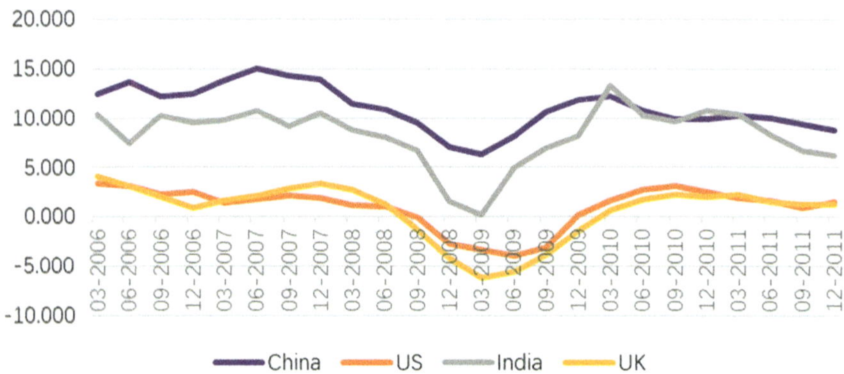

Chart 8 GDP growth of some economies before and After the 2008 Global Financial Crisis (quarterly comparison on a YoY basis, %). *Source* CEIC database

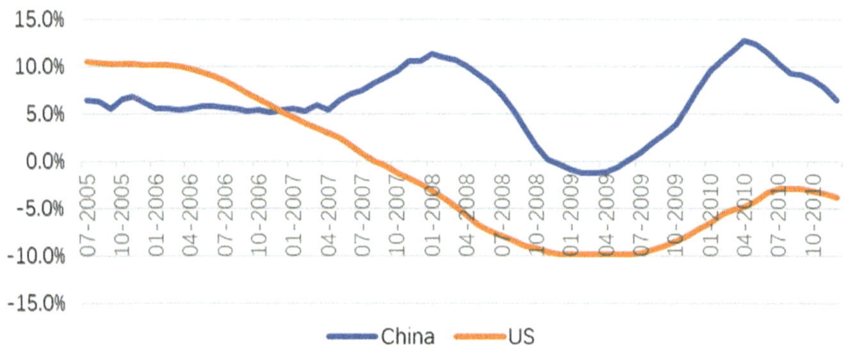

Chart 9 Comparison between housing price fluctuations in China and the US before and after the 2008 financial crisis (monthly comparison on a YoY basis, %). *Source* Zillow, CEIC database

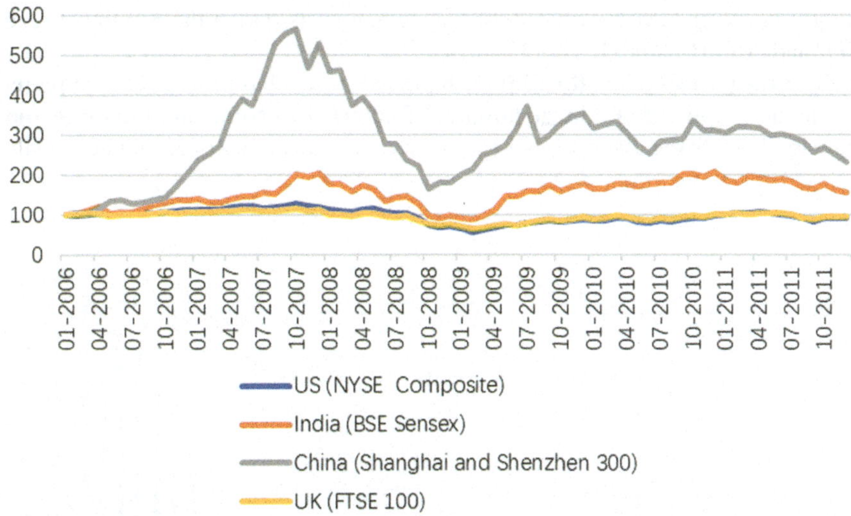

Chart 10 The trend of stock indexes in major markets before and after the 2008 Financial Crisis (January 2006 = 100). *Source* Wind database

1.2 Achievement 2: The Financial System Has Been Supporting the Development of the Real Economy

The financial market played a significant part in the rise of powers like the UK, the Netherlands, the United States, and Germany. Karl Marx knew the importance of financial capital in promoting the growth of the real economy. He once said, "if the world had to wait for certain capital to grow big enough to build a railway, the world would have no railways today. But this can be done in an instant centralizing capital through stock companies." In our review of China's development throughout reform and opening-up, it is clear that the financial market has made a great contribution. In particular, the market has played a positive role in enterprise growth, reform of state-owned enterprises (SOEs), real estate development, infrastructure investment, and innovation and entrepreneurship. It has also helped boost the development, transformation, and upgrading of the Chinese economy. **Over the past four decades, the financial market has assumed the role of converting national savings continually accumulated during China's development into investments. Meanwhile, steady local-currency-based financial deepening ensured that the Chinese economy could remain generally stable during its rapid growth.** Aggregate financing represents the financing of the financial system to the real economy. If we use capital formation to indicate the aggregate financing of the real economy, then the ratio of aggregate financing to capital formation can to some extent measure the contribution of the financial system to the real economy. Our estimation shows that the contribution of the financial system to the real economy remained at 50–60%

in most years, and even exceeded 80% in certain years during the period between 2002 and 2017 (Charts 11, 12, 13 and 14).

Over the past 40 years, the Chinese financial system has provided key support for the development of a large number of enterprises from small to large and from weak to strong. Enterprises are the most important drivers of economic growth,

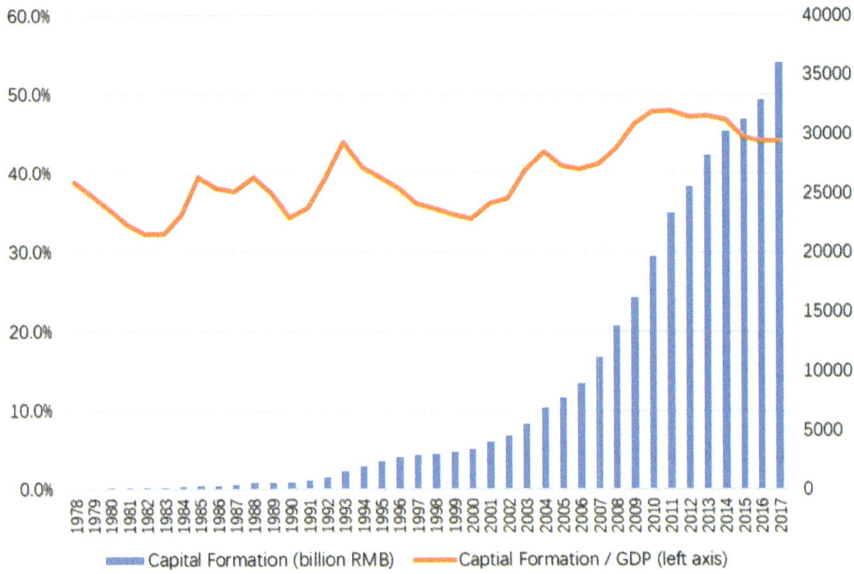

Chart 11 Change in China capital formation and the ratio of China's capital formation to its GDP (1978–2017). *Source* National Bureau of Statistics of China

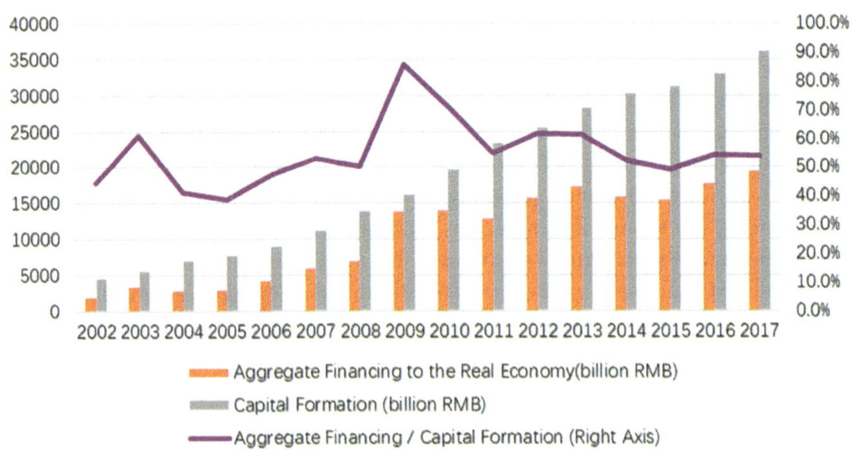

Chart 12 The contribution of aggregate financing to capital formation. *Source* National Bureau of Statistics of China, Authors' calculation

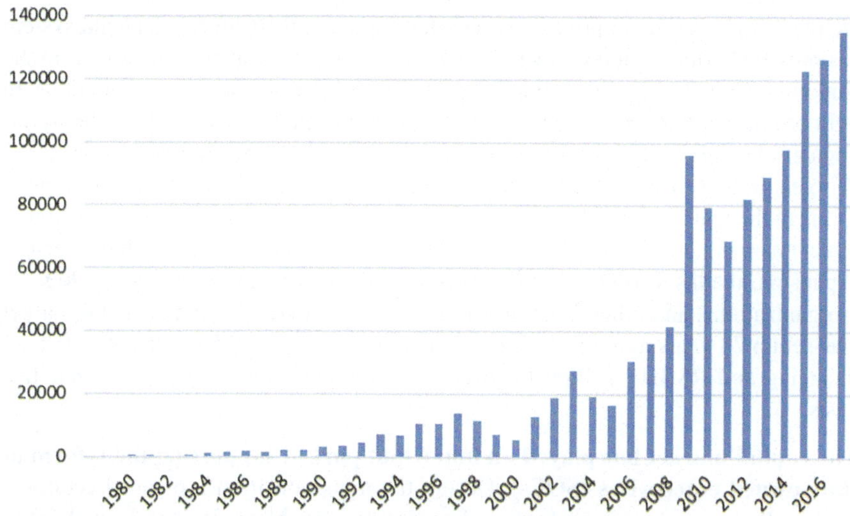

Chart 13 The amount of New RMB loans granted by Banking Financial Institutions to the real economy (Unit: RMB100 million). *Source* People's Bank of China

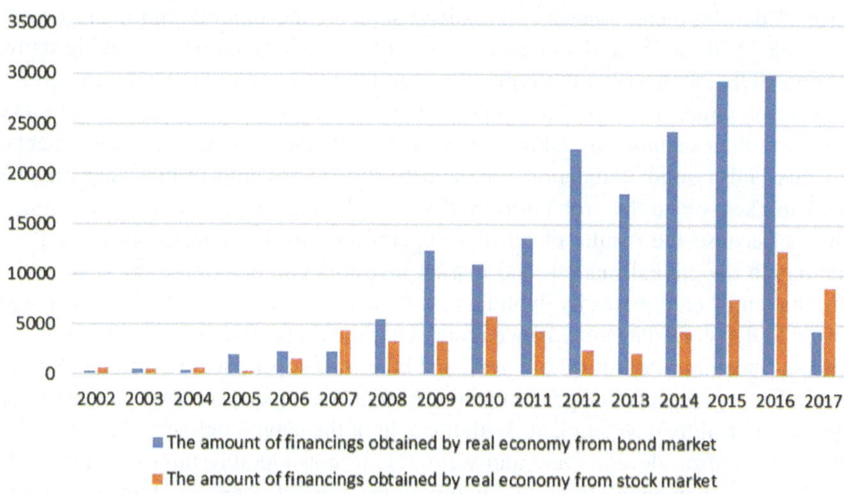

Chart 14 The amount of financing obtained by the real economy from the Stock and bond markets. *Source* People's Bank of China, China Securities Regulatory Commission

and the Chinese economy owes a great deal of its success since reform and opening-up to its various emerging and growing enterprises. The number of Chinese enterprises increased from merely more than 200,000 in 1978 to 140 million in 2017. According to data from the State Administration for Industry and Commerce, the daily average number of newly registered enterprises in 2017 reached 16,600. Over the past 40 years of enterprise entry and development, the Chinese financial system has provided critical support, including not only indirect financing support from the banking system but also direct financing support from the bond and stock markets. In light of indirect financing, credit support from banks played a key role in the development of a large number of high-quality enterprises. According to data from the People's Bank of China, the balance of all loans granted by financial institutions in China to the real economy by the end of June 2018 was RMB125.6 trillion. Through direct financing, many enterprises were able to develop quickly and conduct overseas expansion, thanks to IPOs, additional issuances, mergers and acquisitions (M&A), reorganizations, and other functions of the capital market. Since the capital market was set up 28 years ago, the A-shares market has realized RMB12 trillion of stock financing and RMB17 trillion in M&As and reorganizations on an accumulative basis.

The capital market has played an important part in supporting the reform of state-owned enterprises (SOEs). During the transition from a planned economy to a market economy after reform and opening-up, problems in state-owned enterprises such as intermingling of government and business, blind expansion, low efficiency, and inadequate incentives gradually evolved into serious debt issues in the mid-to-late 1990s. During this time, the stock market, which was still at an early stage of development, conveniently solved some of the funding and management dilemmas of SOEs. First, the stock market reversed the long-term loss-making status of some SOEs. State-owned enterprises secured funding support urgently needed for their development through the capital market, and thus were able to renovate and transform their equipment and hire high-caliber technical and management talents. All this laid a solid foundation for them to turn losses into profits. Second, the stock market solved the problem of SOEs' grossly inadequate incentive structures. This is because the results of business operations can be reflected in price fluctuations in the capital market, and market investors can determine the survival or elimination of enterprises by "voting with their feet." Third, the stock market also solved SOEs' corporate governance issue. After the IPOs of SOEs, they set up shareholders' meetings, boards of directors, and boards of supervisors while maintaining specialized operation management teams, thus providing a systematic guarantee for long-term, healthy development. With the help of the capital market, Chinese SOEs achieved leapfrog development and were able to considerably improve their profitability, management abilities, and international competitiveness. Thus, we can see that the capital market has been an extremely important platform for the reform and development of SOEs. Data shows that by 2017, of 98 central enterprises, 83.7% of them had listed-company platforms and most of them had more than one listed company. The total assets of these central enterprises were RMB54.5 trillion, and 65% of that amount was already injected into listed companies. About 40% of the assets of provincial SOEs were injected into listed companies, and the figure exceeded 50% in cities such as Shanghai, Chongqing, and Anhui. The above-mentioned central enterprises refer to industrial central enterprises under the supervision and administration of the State-owned Assets Supervision and Administration Commission of the

State Council (SASAC). If we further consider the development and strengthening of financial central enterprises—including China's top 4 banks—through corporate governance under listing rules, we can see that the capital market has played an irreplaceable role in China's SOE reform.

The financial system contributed to the development of China's real estate market from scratch. Since the reform of housing commercialization in 1998, the financial system has helped China develop the world's largest real estate market within merely 20 years,[5] which has become its largest wealth carrier with a total market value of RMB280 trillion. At the end of 2017, the balance of individual housing loans of Chinese residents was RMB21.86 trillion and the balance of real estate development loans were RMB8.32 trillion. The combined amount of these two items exceeded RMB30 trillion, which represented nearly 25% of the balance of RMB loans within the same period. It is especially notable that the policy of renovating shantytowns aimed at resolving the problems of dilapidated housing in urban areas and improving the housing conditions of poor households was implemented nationwide on a large scale, thanks to policy-based finance. Since the policy was launched in 2009, China has completed the reconstruction of more than 30 million housing units and thus greatly improved the housing conditions of urban low- and middle-income families. Although there are disputes over whether the financial policy has caused housing prices to rise, there is no doubt that the financial system has played an irreplaceable role in developing China's real estate market and solving the housing problems of Chinese residents in the past two decades. China, a country whose urban population exceeds the total population of Europe, has topped the list of major economies in the world by the proportion of homeownership and overtaken major developed economies like the UK, Japan, and Germany by per capita living space.

The great improvement in China's infrastructure over the past 40 years is also largely attributed to the financial system. Over the past four decades, China has overtaken the world's major economies quickly in terms of infrastructure construction. According to data from the National Bureau of Statistics of China, China's railway operating mileage was only 51,700 km and the average railway speed was less than 40 km/h at the beginning of reform and opening-up. By the end of 2017, 40 years after reform and opening-up, China's total railway operating mileage reached 127,000 km. China's high-speed railway operating mileage also reached 25,200 km, which accounted for 66.3% of the world's total and made China the world's leading country by this measure. China also ranked first in the world for its proportion of electrified railway, which reached 68.2%. At the start of reform and opening-up, China's highways were short and of poor quality, and its total highway mileage was merely 890,200 km. By the end of 2017, China's total highway mileage reached 4,773,500 km with 136,400 km of expressways, placing China at number one in the world in terms of total mileage. In 2017, seven of the world's top 10

[5] According to the latest data from Zillow, the global largest real estate data platform, the total value of the US real estate market was USD31.8 trillion by the end of 2017. Based on our estimation of the real estate sector, the total value of the Chinese real estate market is ~RMB280 trillion.

ports by cargo and container throughput were Chinese. Improved infrastructure not only boosted the scale effect and operating efficiency of the Chinese economy on the whole, but also represented an important component of the country's economic growth. In the case of an economic downturn, infrastructure will also play a prominent role in stabilizing investment and economic growth. Regarding the funding sources of China's infrastructure investment, only a small fraction of the capital[6] comes from budgetary funds, while the vast majority is raised through the financial market, including via loans from policy banks and commercial banks, local government special bonds, and quasi-municipal bonds. It is especially notable that the China Development Bank worked with Wuhu City of Anhui Province in 1998 and adopted the "project entity bundling" model on urban infrastructure loans in China for the first time. **This created a precedent for bank funds supporting local infrastructure construction and cracked the problem of difficulty in financing for urban infrastructure construction.**[7] This model was subsequently popularized across the country and boosted China's urbanization.

The transformation and upgrading as well as the innovation and entrepreneurship of the Chinese economy are also backed up by the financial market. In recent years, the Chinese economy has gradually transitioned from a high-speed growth stage to a high-quality development stage and shifted from a factor-driven, investment-pulling growth pattern to an innovation-driven development pattern. Recently, the transition from old driving forces to new driving forces has accelerated. According to data from the National Bureau of Statistics of China, the proportion of the new economy in China's GDP reached 16% in 2016 and exceeded 30% in cities like Beijing, Shenzhen, and Shanghai. An important factor behind the accelerated growth of the new economy is the rapid development of financial forces including private equity and venture capital funds, which are catalyzing and fostering a large number of innovative start-ups. These enterprises thus no longer depend on

[6]According to Wind's data calculation and estimation, less than 20% of infrastructure investment funds come from financial budget funds and the vast majority of infrastructure investment funds are raised from the capital market.

[7]The particulars of the Wuhu model are as follows: First, subject to the China Development Bank's suggestion, the Wuhu municipal government set up an enterprise named "Wuhu Construction Investment Co., Ltd." ("Wuhu Construction Investment") and used that enterprise as the borrowing entity. Second, the Wuhu municipal government injected a large number of quality assets like land reserves and expressways into Wuhu Construction Investment. Wuhu Construction Investment borrowed loans from the China Development Bank with the foregoing assets as collateral, and the local government just "stood aside" and was not required to provide any guarantee for this process. Third, Wuhu Construction Investment bundled projects with poor financial quality (no loans may be secured through normal approaches) with projects with good financial quality to apply for loans and repay the loan principal and interest together so that projects with good cash flows (e.g., expressways) could make up for projects with poor cash flows (e.g., garbage treatment). This model was known as the "project entity bundling" model. Lastly, China Development Bank further made "land sale revenue" into collateral. In 2002, the Wuhu municipal government authorized Wuhu Construction Investment to apply for RMB1,095 million in loans from China Development Bank "with the pledge of proceeds from land transfer as a major repayment guarantee." With the bank issuing loans first, the government received and invested loan funds in infrastructure construction before selling land and repaying the loans.

bank credit and are less sensitive to traditional economic cycles. This is the very direction and force of China's economic transformation and upgrading. Data shows that 62.5% of 522 enterprises listed on the A-share market since 2017 are backed up by venture capital funds, and that 100% of 98 existing unicorn enterprises in China are supported by venture capital funds.

1.3 Achievement 3: The Chinese Financial Sector Has Become Pretty Comprehensive in the Scope of Its Products and Services

Since reform and opening-up, China's financial system has gradually improved and essentially taken shape with the development of the real economy. Compared with major developed economies, China had a late start but developed fast in terms of the construction of its financial market. Within merely 40 years, China has fostered and developed a basically mature financial system with a full variety of financial products. To understand China's financial system, we must look back on its development over the past four decades. Before 1980, under a highly centralized planned economic system, China's economic activities were marked by fiscal dominance, and the country had no financial market in a strict sense, let alone a financial system. In the early 1980s, the top 4 banks successively spun off from the central bank, which signaled the establishment of a two-tier banking system with the central bank and commercial banks undertaking different functions. In 1988, non-banking financial businesses like trusts, securities, and insurance began to develop, and the People's Bank of China (PBOC) started to implement its supervision function. In 1990, the Shanghai and Shenzhen stock exchanges were set up and the central bank officially proposed securities companies as financial institutions specializing in the securities business, which marked the beginning of separate operations. The China Securities Regulatory Commission (CSRC) and China Insurance Regulatory Commission (CIRC) were set up in 1992 and 1998, respectively. In 1993, separate management as a principle was written into a relevant document of the State Council. In 2003, the founding of the China Banking Regulatory Commission (CBRC) signaled the construction of the Chinese financial system characterized by separate operation and separate regulation. With an increasingly remarkable trend of mixed operation in recent years, the China Banking Regulatory Commission (CBRC) and China Insurance Regulatory Commission (CIRC) were merged into the China Banking and Insurance Regulatory Commission (CBIRC) in 2018.

To further understand China's financial system, we can proceed from various angles including an in-depth look at its institutions, supervision, trading, investment, or financing. Here, we attempt to briefly review China's financial system from the perspective of institutions. **In terms of major categories, the Chinese financial**

system covers fields including banking, trusts, securities, public equity, insurance, futures, asset management, and private equity.[8] Banking, trusts, and insurance are subject to the supervision of the CBIRC, while securities, public funds, futures and private equity are subject to the supervision of the CSRC. Depending on product categories, the bulk of the asset management industry is subject to the supervision of the CBIRC, and a small fraction of that industry is subject to the supervision of the CSRC. In addition to the previously identified institutions, stable operation of the Chinese financial system depends on an array of financial infrastructure, such as venues of stock and equity trading including the Shanghai Stock Exchange, Shenzhen Stock Exchange, and National Equities Exchange as well as quotations and equity exchange centers in different provinces. It also relies on venues of futures trading including the Shanghai Futures Exchange, Dalian Commodity Exchange, Zhengzhou Commodity Exchange, and China Financial Futures Exchange. Transactions in the bond market are carried out in interbank markets and exchange markets, respectively, and registration and clearing institutions for financial products of various types include China Central Depository & Clearing Co., Ltd., China Securities Depository & Clearing Co., Ltd., and Shanghai Clearing House, while payment institutions include China UnionPay. All of the foregoing institutions constitute a basically mature Chinese financial system covering a wide range of fields. Among all of China's financial institutions, the banking system enjoys the largest assets. By the end of 2017, the total size of home and foreign currency assets in all banking financial institutions in China was RMB252 trillion, which represented more than 70% of the total asset size of the financial industry as a whole. Compare this to the asset size of the trust industry, securities industry, insurance industry, public equity industry, and private equity industry in 2017, which were RMB26 trillion, ~RMB6 trillion, nearly RMB17 trillion, RMB11.6 trillion, and RMB11.1 trillion, respectively (Table 1).

Within this review and summary of the development of the Chinese financial system over the past four decades, the following two points deserve our attention. **First, the basically mature financial system gradually developed** on the foundation of the Chinese government's careful guidance and prudent utilization of market forces. **Spontaneous market forces and governmental guidance were indispensable to the development of the financial system.** Take the development of the stock market as an example. In the mid-to-late 1980s, the "old eight stocks" appeared before the Shanghai Stock Exchange or the Shenzhen Stock Exchange were even set up. This was a natural outcome of market forces spurred by the Chinese economy's development at that stage. In response to this historical trend and regarding the experiences of overseas stock markets, the Chinese government set up the Shanghai and Shenzhen stock exchanges in 1990. After that, China established the Securities Commission of the State Council and the China Securities Regulatory Commission, which gradually standardized the buying and selling of stocks.

---

[8]Of course, the financial system also includes financial institutions like rental, microcredit, and finance companies as well as P2P, but those types of financial institutions are smaller and do not have as large of an impact as the types of institutions listed in the body text. Therefore, they are not enumerated here.

Table 1 Comparison among major components of china's financial system by asset size (*Unit* RMB trillion)

Asset in trillion RMB	Banking	Trust	Securities	Insurance	Public equity	Private equity
2012	133.62	7.47	1.72	7.35	3.62	–
2013	151.35	10.91	2.08	8.3	4.22	–
2014	172.34	13.98	4.09	10.2	6.68	2.63
2015	199.35	16.3	6.42	12.4	8.4	5.07
2016	232.25	20.22	5.79	15.12	9.16	10.24
2017	252	26.25	6.14	16.75	11.6	11.1

Source China Banking and Insurance Regulatory Commission, China Trustee Association, Securities Association of China, Insurance Association of China, Asset Management Association of China

Second, the structure of the Chinese financial system differs from that of developed economies. In terms of the completeness of fields covered by the financial system, China has generally caught up with major economies like the United States, the UK, Germany, and Japan. For any type of financial institution existing in developed countries, China has a counterpart, and even has some additional ones. However, the structure of the Chinese financial system is distinct from the structure of financial systems in developed economies. The Chinese financial system differs from the American and British financial systems dominated by direct financing, and yet it is also not fully identical to the German and Japanese financial systems dominated by their banking systems. On one hand, compared with the United States and the UK, the proportion of direct financing in China is still much lower—about 40% in 2016 compared with around 60% in the United States and UK.[9] Structurally speaking, China does not lag far behind the USA and UK in terms of the proportion of its stock market, but the proportion of the bond market in China is too low. The proportions of treasury bonds and corporate bonds are also rather low in the Chinese bond market, the bond market is highly segmented, and the channel between the interbank market and the exchange market has not yet been built. On the other hand, similar to the situation in Germany and Japan, the banking system is the most important funding source for the real economy in China. Nevertheless, China significantly exceeds Germany and Japan by measures such as the activity of its multi-level equity market and the size and growth of private equity and venture capital funds. China also clearly outperforms Germany and Japan and is second only to the United States in terms of the growth and size of innovative start-ups. According to the latest statistics of CB Insights, a leading global venture capital research firm, China is second only to the United States in terms of its number of unicorn companies, which account for

[9]The calculation of direct financing may adopt the inventory method and the incremental method. The incremental method is largely subject to fluctuations in annual financings, so the data in this article is estimated according to the inventory method.

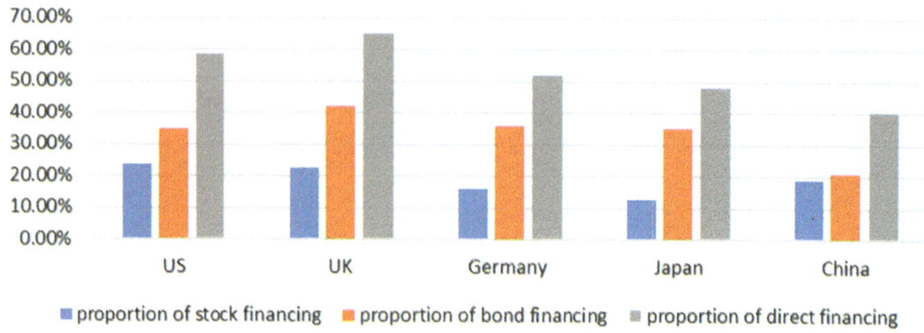

Chart 15 Comparison Among China and Major Developed Economies by Proportion of Direct Financing (According to the calculation method in mainstream literature, the proportion of direct financing is defined as (market capitalization of stock market + market capitalization of bond market)/(market capitalization of stock market + market capitalization of bond market + balance of bank credit). Based on this definition, the proportion of direct financing = proportion of stock market + proportion of bond market. Considering large fluctuations in annual data, the mean value of five years' (2012–2016) data is adopted here. Of course, direct financing in this diagram does not include the statistics of the New Third Board, regional equity markets and private equity markets. If the financings of those markets are included in direct financing, China will further surpass Germany and Japan in terms of equity market advantages) (2012–2016 average). *Source* Bank for International Settlements, World Bank, People's Bank of China

25% of the world's total, and far exceeds major developed economies like Japan, Germany, and France in this regard (Chart 15).

1.4 Problem 1: The Chinese Financial System Has not Been Able to Provide Stable and High Returns to Financial Investors as in Mature Market Economies

The Chinese stock market has notoriously low returns and high volatility. The Shanghai Composite Index was 127.61 at the end of December 1990 and increased to 2630.52 by the end of October 2018, multiplying in size nearly 20 times. Similarly, the Shenzhen Component Index was 880.98 at the end of April 1991 and increased to 7482.83 by the end of October 2018, multiplying in size nearly 7.5 times. To illustrate, suppose we bought composite A-shares worth RMB100 according to the tradable market value-weighted price at the end of December 1990 and kept holding those shares until the end of October 2018 (for dividends obtained during this period, we would continue to buy composite A-shares with them according to tradable market value-weighted price). We would be able to get RMB1,880 after about 28 years, which demonstrates growth of less than 18 times. In contrast, the average monthly salary of employees in Shanghai was RMB243 in 1990 and the figure rose to ~RMB6,500 by 2018, which shows growth of nearly 26 times. China's nominal GDP was RMB1.87 trillion in 1990 and rose to RMB82.7 trillion in 2017, which reveals growth of more

Table 2 Stock index returns (1991–2000)

1991–2000	Start	End	# of years	Average annualized holding return (%)
China	100	1624.9	10	**32.20**
US	100	363.9	10	**13.80**
UK	100	290.3	10	**11.20**
Japan	100	57.8	10	**–5.30**
Korea	100	460.1	10	**16.50**
India	100	378.9	10	**14.20**
Germany	100	460.1	10	**16.50**
Singapore	100	203.4	10	**7.40**
Taiwan, China	100	104.6	10	**0.50**
Hong Kong, China	100	499.1	10	**17.40**

Source CEIC database (China Shanghai Stock Exchange Composite Index, US New York Stock Exchange Composite Index, UK FTSE 100, Japan Nikkei 225, Korea KOSPI Index, India BSE Sensex, Germany DAX, Singapore Straits Times Index, Taiwan Stock Exchange Market Capital Weighted Index, HK Hang Seng Composite Index)

than 43 times. **Thus, we may safely claim that stock price growth did not match that of labor income or GDP during this time.**

Specifically, the Chinese stock market was performing rather well in its early stage, especially during its first 10 years (1991–2000). Based on the Shanghai Composite Index, during 1991–2000, stock prices increased dramatically, **with an average annualized holding return exceeding 32%.** The Shanghai and Shenzhen combined A-share markets with dividends reinvested delivered 24% annualized return, which is quite considerable compared to other economies.

However, over the next 18 years (2001–2018), China's stock market provided only limited returns to investors, barely surpassing the inflation rate. During this time, China's stock market was one of the worst-performing markets across the globe, with an annualized return of only 1.3%. Even with dividends reinvestment considered, the returns barely exceeded inflation (Tables 2 and 3).

Moreover, we calculated China's Sharpe Ratio,[10] a measure of "cost-effectiveness" of stock market returns versus risks, and compared it with the corresponding figures of the United States and India. Before 2009, the Sharpe Ratio of China's Shanghai and Shenzhen combined A-share composite markets was quite

[10]Note: The Sharpe Ratio is defined as the difference between mean annualized returns and mean risk-free interest rate divided by the fluctuation ratio of annualized return. China uses the composite A-share index (tradable market value-weighted, data starting from 1991) and adopts a 1-year bank deposit rate as the risk-free interest rate; the United States uses the S&P 500 (data starting from 1991) and adopts a 1-year treasury yield as the risk-free interest rate; India uses Nifty500 (data starting from 1999) and a 1-year treasury yield as the risk-free interest rate. Dividends are considered but tax factor is excluded. The calculations here use monthly data as the basis, and mean annualized returns are equal to mean monthly returns multiplied by 12, while annualized fluctuation is equal to the standard deviation of monthly returns multiplied by $\sqrt{12}$.

Table 3 Stock index returns (2001–2018)

2001-Oct 2018	Start	End	# of years	Average annualized holding return (%)
China	100	125.5	17.8	**1.3**
US	100	175.8	17.8	**3.2**
UK	100	114.6	17.8	**0.8**
Japan	100	159.0	17.8	**2.6**
Korea	100	177.9	17.8	**3.3**
India	100	867.1	17.8	**12.9**
Germany	100	177.9	17.8	**3.3**
Singapore	100	156.7	17.8	**2.5**
Taiwan, China	100	206.8	17.8	**4.2**
Hong Kong, China	100	165.5	17.8	**2.9**

Source CEIC database (China Shanghai Stock Exchange Composite Index, US New York Stock Exchange Composite Index, UK FTSE 100, Japan Nikkei 225, Korea KOSPI Index, India BSE Sensex, Germany DAX, Singapore Straits Times Index, Taiwan Stock Exchange Market

considerable. However, during 2010–2018, the Sharpe Ratio dropped to literally zero, significantly lower than that of the United States and India (Charts 16 and 17).

What is the case for returns of fixed income financial products—for example, bank deposits or treasury bills and bonds? Based on our estimation, if we deposited RMB100 as a 1-year fixed-term deposit at the end of 1990 and re-deposited both the principal and the interests earned annually afterward until the end of October 2018, we would get RMB310.4, which indicates an average annualized return of 4.2%. In terms of time variation, the interest rate was relatively high in 1990–1998 (5–11%), then fell to 3% and further dropped to 1.5% after 2016. Here, we take a 1-year deposit rate as the risk-free interest rate, and compare China with the United States

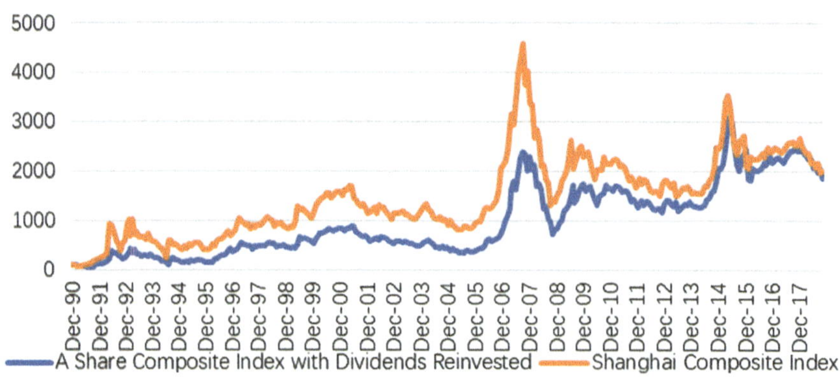

Chart 16 Change in composite A-share index including dividend reinvestment (tradable market value-weighted) (index at the end of 1990 = 100). *Source* CSMAR database, Authors' calculation

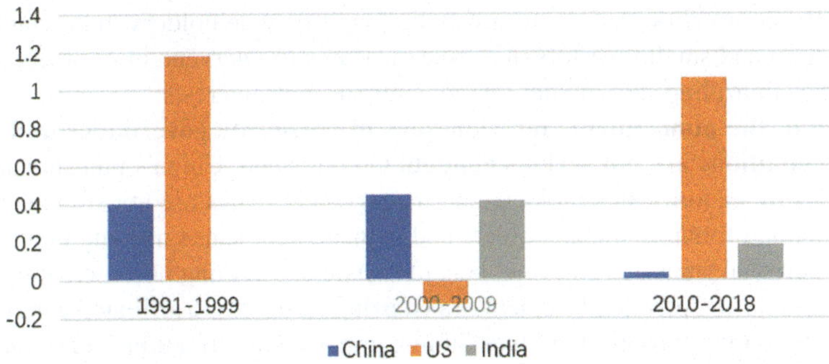

Chart 17 Sharpe ratio among different countries. *Source* CSMAR database, Authors' calculation

and India. The American risk-free interest rate (represented by a 1-year treasury yield) was ~5% in the 1990s, then fell to 1%, and rebounded to 5% in 2006 and 2007. The United States implemented a low-interest rate policy (almost zero) from 2008, and the interest rate gradually rose to 2–3% in subsequent years. For India, the risk-free interest rate was 8–12% in the 1990s and has hovered around 7% since 2000. **Low savings interest rates in China reflect the government's deliberately designed "mild financial repression," i.e., the government's active intervention in bringing down the deposit rates to reduce financing costs of enterprises and governments, and thus support governmental infrastructure construction and corporate investment and expansion. However, the precondition for this delicate equilibrium is that the financial system must remain safe and stable.** If the financial system is unstable with frequent crises, people will demand higher returns or even become reluctant to hold financial assets including stocks and deposits. They will also attempt to move their money overseas to other countries, e.g., the United States, by any means possible.

Additionally, the lawful rights and interests of minority shareholders of listed companies cannot be guaranteed, and the intensity of sanctions against illegal acts are insufficient. The main reasons for this are as follows.

First, the mechanism through which minority shareholders participate in corporate governance is imperfect. The board of directors and board of supervisors are generally regarded as "white elephants" and tend to serve the interests of the management and majority shareholders, while minority shareholders have no say. To protect the rights and interests of minority shareholders and other stakeholders, China began to introduce the independent director system in 2003, but independent directors seldom oppose the management's proposals. According to the findings of Jiang, Wan, and Zhao (2016), less than 6% of independent directors voice their objections. Another related matter is that the corporate information disclosure mechanism is not sound. Many listed companies tend not to disclose their information in a timely, complete, and transparent manner, which is likely to trigger tunneling behavior from controlling shareholders and thus impair the interests of medium and small investors. If a particular company conducts complete information disclosure, especially information disclosure involving majority shareholders' tunneling, then the medium and small investors may take measures to intervene in or object to any act of the controlling shareholder that may impair their interests.

Second, the punishments for violations of corporate governance and securities regulations are not serious enough. On one hand, China's punishments for violations by majority shareholders and management teams are not sufficient. The phenomenon of majority shareholders and management teams abusing their power to seek personal gains and carry out benefit transfers is nothing new—creating price differences during private placement, transferring resources to affiliated enterprises, occupying or misappropriating funds, hiding important information, and so on—but the punishments are far from severe enough. For example, the CSRC imposed the strictest punishment possible in response to Changsheng Bio-Technology's recent improper disclosure of information, even including false disclosures and failure to disclose. However, this punishment only amounted to a fine of RMB600,000 on the company, a warning and fine of RMB300,000 to the personnel directly responsible for the issue, and a lifetime ban from the securities market. Such a punishment is severely insufficient. On the other hand, China's punishments for certain investor violations are also not strict enough. For instance, with respect to punishments for insider trading, China issues the following administrative penalties: "for securities insider trading, if the amount of illegal gains is at least RMB30,000, the amount of the fine shall be at least one time but at most five times the amount of the illegal gains; if no illegal gains are achieved or the amount of illegal gains is less than RMB30,000, the amount of the fine shall be at least RMB30,000 but at most RMB600,000. For futures insider trading, if the amount of illegal gains is at least RMB100,000, the amount of the fine shall be at least one time but at most five times the amount of illegal gains; if no illegal gains are achieved or the amount of illegal gains is less than RMB100,000, the amount of the fine shall be at least RMB100,000 but at most RMB500,000. If a unit is involved in insider trading, the person in charge directly responsible for the case and other persons with direct responsibility shall pay a fine in the amount of at least RMB30,000 but at most RMB300,000," and other administrative supervision measures including a ban from the securities market may also be taken. The rules on criminal punishment are as follows: "if a person commits an insider trading crime, he or she will be sentenced to fixed-term imprisonment of not more than five years of penal servitude, plus alternatively or additionally be forced to pay a fine 1–5 times the amount of the illegal gains. If a unit commits a crime, the unit shall pay a fine and the person in charge directly responsible for the case and other persons with direct responsibility shall serve a fixed-term imprisonment of not more than 5 years or be sentenced to penal servitude. If the crime is especially serious, the person shall be sentenced to fixed-term imprisonment of at least 5 years and at most 10 years and pay a fine in the amount of 1–5 times that of the illegal gains." In contrast, the highest punishment in the United States against an individual guilty of insider trading is fixed-term imprisonment of 20 years and a fine of USD5 million maximum (or USD25 million for the relevant unit).

1.5 Problem 2: The Chinese Financial System Has not Been Able to Effectively Force the Exit of Inefficient Firms

An important measure to determine whether the financial system of a country is mature and efficient is its ability to effectively support the entry of new and good enterprises while also orchestrating the timely dissolution of inefficient firms. Over its 40 years of development, the Chinese financial system has accumulated much experience in supporting the entry of new and good enterprises, but has failed to effectively orchestrate the dissolution of inefficient firms. Dynamic change, including the entry and exit of new and old firms, is an important manifestation of the operating efficiency of an economy—similar to metabolism in the human body. If inefficient enterprises are not eliminated in time, large quantities of element resources like capital, land, and labor will be unduly occupied. Furthermore, the price signals will be also distorted, thus affecting the operating efficiency and quality of the entire economic system. The limited capability of the economic system—including the financial system—to eliminate inefficient enterprises was an important catalyst for China's 2016 supply-side structural reform.

During this reform in 2016, the SASAC's statistics indicate that central enterprises had to conduct special disposal and treatment on a total of 2041 "zombie enterprises" and other extremely problematic enterprises, involving assets worth RMB3 trillion in total. Based on a summary of the estimations of different research teams, zombie enterprises appear to represent 5–10% of industrial enterprises above designated size in China. Since the total assets of industrial enterprises above designated size in 2017 were RMB112.3 trillion, even if calculated according to 5%, we can see that there are assets worth nearly RMB6 trillion that require disposal. Compared with this massive amount, the pace of the Chinese financial system in disposing of non-performing assets are far from satisfactory. According to the exit scale of inefficient enterprise assets estimated by Tsinghua University's CCWE based on listed banks' data on write-offs of non-performing loans (NPLs), ~RMB1.2 trillion inefficient, ineffective assets were eliminated from the Chinese economy in 2017. Even if new inefficient assets are not considered, it takes 5 years for China to eliminate RMB6 trillion of existing inefficient, ineffective assets at the foregoing rate. If we calculate according to the current average loan term of about 3 years, RMB6 trillion of undisposed assets will occupy nearly RMB2 trillion in loans each year—approximately 15% of bank loan resources. On one hand, slow exit of inefficient enterprises exacerbate the problem of costly and difficult financing. Low-quality enterprises being given priority to use financial institutions' credit resources may help banks cover up their problems and reduce their bad loan ratios on the books. However, new and good enterprises will have greater difficulty in securing loans, thus pushing up their financing costs. On the other hand, inefficient enterprises usually have poor technologies and low product quality. They are more willing to carry out price wars and rely on low prices to survive. This drags down the performance of good enterprises and disturbs the market order. More seriously, slow exit of inefficient enterprises also leads to the occupation of production factors like land and labor, and therefore reduces the productivity of the economy. The ability of the capital market to eliminate inefficient enterprises is also inadequate, and the difficulties in de-listing Chinese listed companies are also a prominent problem. In 2001–2017, a total of only 60 listed companies were de-listed from the Chinese A-share market for reasons such as loss, fraudulent issuance, or privatization, and the accumulative de-listing rate was merely 1.83%. On average, there are about 150 IPOs in the American stock market each year, and about 400 companies are eliminated from the stock market annually due to factors like mergers, bankruptcy, and de-listing. As a result, 200–300 listed companies are de-listed each year on average.

2 Historical Overview

2.1 A Brief History of the Banking System

(a) **1978: The People's Bank of China (PBOC) regained independence from the Ministry of Finance**

Before reform and opening-up, China had not established a market-oriented, modern financial system. In terms of organizational structure, the most extreme manifestation of this was when several major commercial banks were merged into the central bank or the Ministry of Finance. Later on, with continued strengthening of the planned economy, the central bank itself was merged into the Ministry of Finance, thus achieving the "mixing" of finance and banking. In 1969, the People's Bank of China was co-located with the Ministry of Finance[11] and retained only nominally.

On November 28, 1977, the State Council issued a document entitled *Requirements on Rectifying and Strengthening Banking Work*, which stated that the PBOC, as a ministry/commission-level institution under the State Council, should be separated from the Ministry of Finance. In March 1978, the First Session of the Fifth National People's Congress approved the proposal to restore the PBOC as a ministry/commission-level institution and set it up separately from the Ministry of Finance. As a national bank, the PBOC was to be in charge of national financial policy, currency issues, credit projects, and fund distribution. At the forum for the first secretaries of the party committees of Chinese provinces, municipalities directly under the central government, and autonomous regions in 1979, Deng Xiaoping clearly pointed out that banks should handle economic affairs. He rejected their limitation to accounting functions at that time and said they did not play the due role of banks. In his speech, Deng illuminated the direction of China's banking system reform, stating that banks shall be used as a lever for economic development and technological innovation, and that China "must truly operate our banks on a commercial basis Hongru [12]."

[11]Qilu Weekly: Central Bank Turned over Its Duty. http://www.sohu.com/a/226397600_351293.

(b) 1980s: The People's Bank of China divested its commercial bank functions

In addition to central banking business, under the "all-in-one" financial system, the PBOC also undertook the role of commercial banks. It not only oversaw currency issues and financial management but also carried out various banking business operations. This unitary, narrow financial model with a highly concentrated management system, which used to work well under the conditions of the planned economy, gradually became unsuitable in the context of reform. In particular, the formation of specialized banks (the Bank of China, Agricultural Bank of China, and China Construction Bank) changed the monopoly of the PBOC, and a competitive landscape gradually formed. Although the policy at the time expressly required that each specialized bank should operate its main business within its field, the banks were not satisfied with their division of work, and it turned out that the "ABC, BOC, and CCB all operated beyond their original business scopes." The central bank's act of "playing the dual role as the referee and the athlete" triggered the dissatisfaction of other banks—each specialized bank refused to obey the management of the PBOC, asserting that it was also a national bank instead of a specialized bank. They all claimed that they were on equal footing with the PBOC and did not recognize the leader/follower relationship. In this environment, the PBOC had no effective measures to regulate and supervise the other banks.

In the face of this situation, academia and related fields generally formed the following three opinions concerning the establishment of a central banking system: (1) China should maintain the status quo; (2) China should return to the all-in-one People's Bank; or (3) China should establish a complete central banking system. In response, a "banking institutional reform group" was formed to conduct a number of research studies domestically and abroad, and ultimately, the third opinion was adopted. With respect to feedback from the PBOC that it could not effectively regulate and supervise specialized banks, Yao Yilin, then vice premier of the State Council, was quoted as saying, "… if you fear that specialized banks will become tigers, then you'd better try to make yourself a lion." This reflected the "chaos" of the banking system and the country's stance on the PBOC's use of its functions as central bank at that time.

In May 1982, the State Council approved the following main functions of the PBOC: carrying out the Party and state's plans, principles, and policies on economic work; drawing up the guidelines, policies, regulations, and basic systems on financial work; taking charge of financial administration and management as well as the issuance of national currency; and managing industrial and commercial credit and urban savings business. In September 1983, the State Council issued the *Decision on the People's Bank of China to Specially Exercise the Functions of a Central Bank* (the "Decision"). According to the Decision, the PBOC was to specially exercise the functions of a central bank and no longer operate industrial and commercial credit and savings business. As the bank of issue, bank of the government, and banker's bank, the PBOC was to be a state organ that leads and manages national financial work and generally takes economic measures to manage various financial institutions. To be specific, the Decision required that the PBOC must control 40–50% of all credit funds in order to adjust and balance national credit receipts and payments. In other words, controlling the total amount of funds became the most effective way for the PBOC to exercise the functions of a central bank. Meanwhile, the Decision set up the Industrial and Commercial Bank of China to take over all industrial and commercial credit business and urban savings business previously carried out by the PBOC. This decision liberated the PBOC from specific credit and savings business and enabled it to exercise the particular functions of a central bank. The Decision also defined the PBOC as a state organ that leads and manages national financial work, and signaled the formation of the Chinese central banking system. This landmark decision also represented the transition of China's central banking system into the unitary stage.

(c) **1994: Policy banks were split from commercial banks**

Globalization triggered fiercer competition in financial markets, and the overlapping complexity of the financial policy business and operational financial business of specialized banks played an increasingly noticeable role in hindering the deepening of financial system reform. This led to the State Council's reform requirement on "separating policy business and commercial business" in 1994. In the same year, China set up three policy banks including China Development Bank, the Export-Import Bank of China, and the Agricultural Development Bank of China—all directly led by the State Council. In total, the country appropriated the RMB73.38 billion for their founding.

Upon their founding, the three policy banks not only took over the policy business of the four major national specialized banks but also undertook several additional missions, like strengthening macroeconomic regulation, achieving the strategic goals of governmental development, promoting the commercialization reform of national specialized banks, and severing the connection between credit and the monetary base during the transition period from a socialist planned economy to a market economy [13].

With a focus on the national macro situation and strategic deployment, China Development Bank is focused on medium- to long-term investment and financing projects in China and offers great support for key projects on railways, highways, energy, and urban infrastructure. In recent years, China Development Bank has invested heavily in fields such as the housing security of middle- and low-income families, small and micro businesses, healthcare, environmental protection, and "issues of agriculture, farmers and rural areas." It has further supported national strategies to improve people's livelihoods and carry out industrial structural upgrading. The Export-Import Bank of China plays an important role in promoting stable and relatively rapid economic growth and foreign trade growth. Finally, the Agricultural Bank of China plays a supporting role in rural financial development and has established a business development pattern of "focusing on supporting international grain and cotton purchasing, sales, and storage business with equal attention to supporting industrialized operation of agriculture as well as agricultural and rural infrastructure construction."

In the more than two decades since their establishment, the three policy banks have played an important role in the formation and improvement of China's financial system. These three policy banks are involved in: (1) implementing national strategies; (2) supporting the construction of national infrastructure, pillar industries, and key national projects; (3) supporting the development of "issues of agriculture, farmers, and rural areas" as well as small and micro businesses; (4) improving people's livelihoods; (5) supporting enterprises "going global"; and (6) promoting economic transition and social development. They have become an indispensable financial force[12] in China's national economic development that sets China apart from other major economies.

(d) **Late 1990s: State-owned banks were stripped of their bad loans with the help of the Ministry of Finance and the People's Bank of China**

After Deng Xiaoping's southern tour speech in 1992, China's reform and opening-up accelerated and the economy developed rapidly. The loan size of commercial banks continued to expand, and there was more administrative intervention in banks from local governments. The non-performing loan (NPL) ratio of the four major state-owned banks reached 25% in June 1996, and the statutory capital of the banking sector was seriously inadequate. In 1997, when the Asian financial crisis broke out, Southeast Asia and Hong Kong, Macau, and Taiwan were hit hard. Domestic and overseas economic situations began to impact the banking industry, prompting the central government to hold the first National Financial Work Conference at the end of the year.

The National Financial Work Conference focused on topics such as stripping the four major state-owned banks of their NPLs and optimizing the PBOC's structure. Provincial branches of the PBOC were shut down after the conference in order to better centralize financial regulation power. In order to solve the NPL problem, the central government set up four asset management companies (AMCs) in 1999, including Huarong, Great Wall, Orient, and Cinda, which were designed to work with the four major banks one-on-one to dispose of non-performing assets.

At that time, the country granted the following preferential policies to the four AMCs: first, they could take over the non-performing assets of the four major banks (BOC, ABC, ICBC, and CCB) with their original prices and have the losses on the disposal of such assets compensated by the Ministry of Finance; second, they received funding sources from the Ministry of Finance; third, they were entitled to tax and capital policy support, e.g., AMCs would be exempt from taxes incurred by the acquisition, disposal, and management of non-performing assets.

As far as funding sources are concerned, the Ministry of Finance provided RMB10 billion in statutory capital for each of the four AMCs, and the central bank granted re-loans of RMB570 billion in addition to financial bonds worth about RMB800 billion. Through the disposal process, a total of RMB1.4 trillion in non-performing assets were eliminated according to book value (principal + on-balance-sheet interest).

[12]Financial Times: *Where is the road for the transformation of policy banks?* http://bank.hexun.com/2013-12-23/160819764.html.

Of this figure, about ~RMB1 trillion in NPLs were stripped from the four major state-owned commercial banks. Besides the disposal process also included RMB100 billion from China Development Bank, over RMB100 billion of on-balance-sheet interest, and over RMB100 billion of loans on debt-for-equity divestiture policies.

Among the total eliminated NPLs, 29% were disposed of through debt-for-equity swaps. At the end of 1999, the State Economic and Trade Commission recommended 601 debt-for-equity enterprises to the four major AMCs, including 365 enterprises with a total amount of RMB28.2 billion in losses on the books. The total size of NPLs was RMB459.6 billion, and the size of banks' on-book NPLs was RMB383.4 billion, or 83% of the total size. In 2000, a total of 580 enterprises concluded agreements on debt-for-equity swaps with the four major AMCs at an aggregate agreed amount of RMB405.1 billion—equal to 29% of the RMB1.4 trillion of all NPLs stripped from the four major banks (ICBC, ABC, BOC, and CCB) and transferred to the four major AMCs. The total amount of NPLs transferred to the four major AMCs—Huarong, Orient, Cinda, and Great Wall—amounted to RMB109.5 billion, RMB60.3 billion, RMB175.9 billion, and RMB11.7 billion, respectively Ran [14].

As China's fifth-largest state-owned commercial bank, the Bank of Communications (BOCOM) also faced similar problems to the four major banks during this time, including an excessively high proportion of non-performing assets and a seriously insufficient capital adequacy ratio. However, unlike the four major banks, BOCOM received no cost-free capital injection but did receive strong support from its shareholders, including the Ministry of Finance. BOCOM sold RMB41.4 billion in questionable loans according to the market principle and brought in PricewaterhouseCoopers to appraise NPLs during this process, thus making BOCOM the first domestic commercial bank to cite international accounting principles. BOCOM's financial restructuring could be summarized as "Doing the work on its own with the help of market forces."

Directly following the elimination process, the NPL ratio of the five major state-owned banks began to decline, but after their initial descent, NPL ratios remained at a relatively high level until 2004. By the end of 2003, the NPL ratios of ICBC (Industrial and Commercial Bank of China), ABC (Agricultural Bank of China), BOC (Bank of China), and CCB (China Construction Bank) were 22%, 30%, 18%, and 12%, respectively. As a result, China decided to carry out a second elimination of NPLs in 2004. In this process, CCB divested and transferred RMB185.8 billion of NPLs to Cinda, and BOC divested and transferred RMB253.9 billion of NPLs to Cinda and Orient. In the same year, China injected USD22.5 billion each in foreign exchange reserves to BOC and CCB. As a result, BOC's and CCB's NPL ratios fell quickly to 4.62% and 3.8% by the end of 2004, making both banks qualified for listing. These two banks went public within the following two years. At the end of 2004, ICBC's NPL ratio still hovered at 14%. After the State Council approved ICBC's share reform plan in April 2005, Central Huijin Investment Ltd. (Central Huijin) injected USD15.0 billion into ICBC. As a result, ICBC's NPL ratio dropped to 2.5% at the end of 2005 and the bank went public in both the A-share and H-share markets in 2006. At the end of 2007, ABC's NPL ratio stood at 23.6%. Central Huijin injected USD19.0 billion into ABC in 2008, after which Central Huijin and the Ministry of Finance each held 50% equity in ABC. The bank's NPL ratio dropped to 4.32% by the end of 2008 and 2.91% by the end of 2009, after which the NPL ratios of all four major state-owned banks were reduced to a reasonable range.

In the context of the 1997 Asian financial crisis, the Chinese government's timely disposal of non-performing assets in banks successfully prevented a national financial crisis, which would have further threatened the economic well-being of the region. This not only improved the overall credibility of banks but also reinvigorated banks and enabled them to continually support the real economy while playing a key role in maintaining the smooth operation of the macroeconomy. The reforms to eliminate non-performing assets of state-owned banks via the establishment of the four major asset management companies were particularly successful in the following four aspects: first, they steadily eliminated the historical burden of non-performing assets; second, they strengthened market restraints on state-owned banks; third, they safeguarded and boosted domestic and international confidence in Chinese state-owned banks; and fourth, they activated the financial system.[13]

In recent years, China has remained especially prudent in the supervision of its banking system. In 2010, the China Banking Regulatory Commission (CBRC) issued a document requiring banks to adhere to a provision coverage ratio of 150%. China maintained this level of provision coverage until February 2018, when the ratio was adjusted from 150% to 120–150%. In contrast, the international requirement for NPL provision rate is generally only 100%. Liu Mingkang, a former CBRC chairman, explained this phenomenon in an interview by mentioning certain deviations between financial statements released by banks and their actual financial conditions. At that time, the CBRC commissioned four major accounting firms to examine the NPLs of the four major state-owned banks according to the "five-class loan classification" standards. The degree of deviation was found to be 20%, i.e., with an actual value of 120% of the reported value. In response, the CBRC organized forces to conduct a field investigation that audited and detected a further 20% deviation from the audited version of the four major accounting firms. Therefore, considering $1.2 \times 1.2 = 1.44$ plus unknown macroeconomic risks, the provision coverage ratio was determined to be 150%. Overall, this initiative objectively reserved space for the development of banks—by the end of 2017, the provision coverage ratio was around 181%.

Today, China's four major banks (i.e., BOC, ABC, ICBC, CCB) have become systematically important global financial institutions, and the Chinese banking industry is a world leader in low non-performing assets ratio, high capital adequacy ratio, and profitability.

(e) 2005–2010: State-owned commercial banks undertook IPOs and listed in the stock market with injections of funds by the central bank

In 2003, China decided to initiate the shareholding reform of large commercial banks through a financial restructuring "four-step" plan involving the use of the national foreign exchange reserves to inject capital into large commercial banks. This process included the write-off of actual lost capital, the divestiture, and elimination

[13] Li Yiqi: A Talk on Non-Performing Loans at That Time. *Mongoose Report*.

of non-performing assets, foreign exchange reserve capital injection, and domestic and overseas issuance and listing [15].

From 2005 onwards, four major banks began their listing efforts. CCB went public in the H-share market in 2005 and the A-share market in 2007. Both ICBC and BOC were listed in the A-share and H-share markets in 2006, while ABC was listed in the A-share and H-share markets in 2010. Through listing, China gradually established a modern commercial banking system in which commercial banks could better utilize market resources. Commercial banks, which formerly relied heavily on fiscal appropriation, could conduct independent financing after listing.

Like the four major banks, BOCOM was encumbered with the heavy burden of NPLs, and thus China paid great attention to its restructuring. However, unlike the four major banks, the main support offered to BOCOM was not direct capital support, but policy support. "Doing the work on its own with the help of market forces" was the theme of BOCOM's financial restructuring. In 1999, BOCOM submitted a *Request for Initial Public Offering and Listing* to the PBOC, and in August 2003, it submitted its *General Plan on Deepening the Shareholding Reform* to the State Council. BOCOM successfully issued its H-shares in 2005 and went public in the A-share market in 2007.

Since the 1970s, numerous urban and rural credit cooperatives have been set up in China to fill the market gap left by traditional large banks. The formation of these credit cooperatives in different regions has effectively activated idle social funds and supported the development of medium, small, and micro-businesses as well as farmers. In July 1995, the State Council issued the *Notice on Establishing Urban Cooperative Banks,* prompting different cities in China to begin setting them up. In March 1998, urban cooperative banks were uniformly renamed as city commercial banks.

(f) **2010–2018: Interest rates (deposit and lending) were gradually liberalized and deposit insurance was introduced**

Over the years, interest rates were gradually liberalized. In 1996 and 1997, the interbank rate and bond repurchase rate were successively liberalized. In 2004, the upper limits of RMB saving and lending rates for financial institutions were lifted. Moreover, in 2013, the lending rate was fully liberalized, and in 2015, the saving rate followed suit. Also in 2015, a key milestone was reached when the deposit insurance system was officially introduced after 22 years of effort. The system pledged to cover 99.7% of all depositors.

The government has also been working hard to further improve the multi-tiered banking system, which now includes 12 national joint-stock commercial banks.[14] Shenzhen Development Bank (now Ping An Bank after its merger with Ping An Bank), which was set up on December 22, 1987, was the first joint-stock commercial

[14]The 12 national joint-stock commercial banks are: China Merchants Bank, China CITIC Bank, China Minsheng Bank, Industrial Bank, Huaxia Bank, China Everbright Bank, Ping An Bank, Shanghai Pudong Development Bank, China Guangfa Bank, China Zheshang Bank, China Bohai Bank, and Hengfeng Bank.

bank in China to be listed. Since then, the vast majority of joint-stock commercial banks have gone public one after the other. Postal Savings Bank of China, a state-owned commercial bank established on the basis of the reformed postal savings management system, received approval for its USD8.0 billion Hong Kong IPO plan on August 27, 2016, and was listed on the HKEx Main Board on September 28 of the same year.

In recent years, Chinese urban and rural commercial banks have been growing in size, and as such, relevant supervision measures have been gradually strengthened. China has further defined the positioning of small and medium-sized banks by requiring them to focus on improving their ability to provide financial services for small-town construction and taking restrictive measures against cross-regional operation. China now has approximately 1,200 rural and urban commercial banks.

Since 2016, China has approved business operations of private banks on a batch-by-batch basis. At present, the number of private banks established or under construction with CBRC's approval has reached 17. Many of those private banks have already entered the profit stage.

Following the tide of the Internet, China conducted pilot projects on the construction of private Internet banks. In 2014, Tencent led the market by setting up WeBank. In 2015, MYBank was established with Ant Financial as the majority shareholder, targeting customer groups such as small and micro businesses, individual consumers, and rural users. Later on, XWBank was co-founded by New Hope, Xiaomi, and Hongqi Chain to provide customized financial services for small and micro businesses.

After many years of development, China has gradually formed a multi-tiered banking system comprising five major state-owned banks, three major policy banks, 12 joint-stock commercial banks, one postal savings bank, hundreds of urban and rural commercial banks, credit cooperatives, and village banks, and several private Internet banks were established with the rise of the Internet economy.

2.2 Development Course of the Capital Market

(a) **1981–1990: The bond market was established** [16]

After the founding of the PRC, in order to restore the national economy ravaged by war, the Ministry of Finance issued a series of treasury bonds. Later on, due to political reasons and an incorrect understanding of treasury bonds, their issuance stopped. After reform and opening-up, the country delegated power to enterprises and the central government delegated power to local governments. SOEs' profit retention increased sharply and residents' income levels considerably improved. However, this also led to a drop in governmental fiscal revenue growth. Meanwhile, large-scale economic construction contributed to a significant increase in the central government's fiscal expenditure. As a result, central budget deficits continued for several consecutive years, amounting to RMB27.0 billion by 1981.

To balance fiscal revenue and expenditure, China began to issue bonds again in 1981. Due to the large influence of the planning mechanism, administrative allocation was adopted at the initial stage of treasury bond issuance, and treasury bonds could not be circulated or transferred after they were issued. Treasury rates also adopted differential treatment: the interest rate of treasury bonds sold to enterprises and public institutions was 4%, while the interest rate of treasury bonds sold to individuals was 8%. Both treasury rates were below the savings deposit rate for the same period. Treasury bonds were redeemed by drawing lots and were redeemed in batches year-by-year. In a sense, 1981–1984 treasury bonds issued under the above-mentioned mechanism were designed more as a tool for fiscal financing with traditional planned economic methods than a type of financial instrument. This shows that the treasury bond market and secondary market could not be established under the conditions at that time. Nevertheless, **resumed issuance of treasury bonds created the basic conditions for the growth and development of the treasury bond market in the following years.**

In the meantime, with the development of the mixed-ownership economy, China's enterprise bonds were budding. In 1984, some enterprises in China began to raise funds spontaneously by issuing different forms of negotiable securities to the general public or internal staff. In May 1985, Shenyang Real Estate Development Co., Ltd. issued a 5-year enterprise bond to the general public, which was the first recorded enterprise bond issued after reform and opening-up. By the end of 1986, China had issued RMB10.0 billion of negotiable securities similar to enterprise bonds.

With the shift of the focus of Chinese economic reform from rural areas to urban areas, the level of retained profits of SOEs further improved, but government expenditure also further increased. Government budget deficits grew, and it became apparent that it was too difficult to mobilize enterprises and residents to subscribe to long-term treasury bonds in large numbers solely through administrative power. In order to maintain the reputation of treasury bonds, the government realized it had to issue treasury bonds according to market-oriented requirements. **In 1985, China began to introduce the market mechanism to the issuance of treasury bonds.** The yield of the treasury bonds issued in that year was 0.7% above the bank deposit rate for the same period, and the redemption period of the bonds was explicitly stipulated. Meanwhile, the Ministry of Finance began to try out circulation work to improve the liquidity of treasury bonds. Due to the introduction of a market-based issuance mode, the degree of administrative allocation in treasury bonds issued in 1985 was weakened, and distorted economic relationships were reduced during bond issuance. **This provided the necessary conditions for the rapid expansion of treasury bond issuance in the following years.**

Before 1987, Chinese treasury bonds had only a primary issue market without a secondary circulation market. On January 5, 1987, the Shanghai Branch of the People's Bank of China published the *Interim Provisions on Over-the-Counter Trading of Securities*, which expressly stated that over-the-counter (OTC) trading of certified government bonds, financial bonds, and enterprise bonds could be conducted at approved financial institutions. **This symbolized the entry of the Chinese treasury bond market into its formation stage.**

In 1988, the issuance of Chinese treasury bonds faced a very serious situation. On one hand, serious inflation and growing government investment greatly heightened government budget deficits. Judging from the financial system and the relationship between fiscal revenue and expenditure at the time, it is clear that the continued increase in the issuance size of treasury bonds became a basic measure to maintain fiscal balance. On the other hand, following the trajectory of treasury bond maturation, the peak in bond redemption was to hit in the 1990s. The source of funds for redemption of treasury bonds was undoubtedly the very funds received from the increased issuance of such bonds. Against this backdrop, if the treasury bond trading market was not built to promote the circulation of treasury bonds, this would not only greatly increase the government's bond issuance cost, but also further exacerbate the black market trading of treasury bonds and affect their reputation, which would eventually lead to difficulty further issuing treasury bonds. Therefore, in April 1988, the State Council approved pilot reform on the treasury bond circulation and transfer market in 10 cities with good basic conditions, including Shenzhen, Guangzhou, Wuhan, Chongqing, Shenyang, and Harbin. In June of the same year, on the basis of these cities' experiences, China approved the implementation of pilot reform on treasury bond circulation and transfer in 61 large and medium-sized cities. **On-the-spot bond transactions began to appear at bank counters—the prototype of the OTC bond market. China's secondary bond market grew from this initial stage**. In 1990, the treasury bond circulation and transfer market further expanded the variety of treasury bond transactions permitted, from the very first bonds issued in 1985 and 1986 to all treasury bills and notes previously issued by the Ministry of Finance.

At the beginning of China's treasury bond circulation market, the main mode of trade for treasury bonds was OTC. The majority of intermediary agencies initially featured treasury bond service departments and financial securities companies set up by the financial sector, and later featured securities companies established by banks and other financial institutions. In the era when OTC trading prevailed, transaction prices of treasury bonds varied greatly in different cities because the national treasury bond market was segmented. In particular, trading desks of various intermediary agencies across the country lacked clearing and supervision mechanisms, so short selling occurred frequently. In order to contain the shortcomings of the treasury bond OTC trading market, the Shanghai Stock Exchange, Shenzhen Stock Exchange, and some urban stock trading centers were successively established after December 1990. These centralized trading markets accepted the escrow of physical bonds and switched to trading book-entry bonds on the basis of escrow vouchers. **On December 19, 1990, the People's Bank of China and the Ministry of Finance issued a notice which permitted the listing and transfer of all unmatured treasury bills and notes issued to individuals.** As a result, **centralized matchmaking treasury bond trading markets emerged in China and a market pattern characterized by the co-existence of floor and OTC trading was formed.** Within about one year, the treasury bond market pricing mechanism emerged, under which floor transaction prices of treasury bonds in the Shanghai Stock Exchange guide OTC transaction prices.

(b) 1990–1991: The Shanghai Stock Exchange and Shenzhen Stock Exchange were established

After reform and opening-up, China began to break away from the bondage of the planned economy system and explore the path to market-oriented resource allocation. **In 1984, the Third Plenary Session of the Twelfth Central Committee of the CPC adopted the decision to reform the economic system. Next, the State Council set up the financial system reform research group led by Liu Hongru. The preliminary scheme for financial system reform put forth the establishment of stock exchanges for the first time and also proposed permitting enterprises to conduct direct financing by issuing shares and bonds.** With strong government support, China's shareholding economy emerged and the size of stock issuance continually expanded. According to statistics from the *Almanac of China's Finance and Banking* (1993), by the end of 1990, China had raised RMB4.59 billion in funds through stocks. The issuing size peaked in 1988, which was attributed to the decision of Chinese central leadership to expand and deepen pilot projects on shareholding reform.[15] In terms of stock trading, the pattern of OTC trading in private was generally adopted before 1986. With an increasing number of stocks issued each year, the PBOC approved the construction of the Shanghai and Shenzhen stock trading desks in 1986 and 1987, respectively. By 1990, Shanghai had a total of 16 stock trading desks and Shenzhen had 10.

The expansion of stock issuance and trading size in the 1980s laid a foundation for the establishment of stock exchanges in 1990, but objective conditions were not ripe at that time. The main problem was that "there [were] a very limited number of companies qualified for listing." For optimal conditions, "it is best that there are 100–200 companies qualified for listing, including 50–100 companies that are able to get listed. The creation of a stock exchange will happen without effort by that time."[16] After the political turbulence at the end of spring and beginning of summer in 1989, foreign countries became skeptical and even resisted China's reform and opening-up. The Group of Seven also imposed economic sanctions on China, which led to a massive withdrawal of foreign capital. The sources of funds required for maintaining production and operation of SOEs shrunk greatly, and banks had difficulty providing required funds due to high risks.[17] Under these circumstances, the possibility of trying direct financing and setting up stock exchanges was put on the agenda (Chart 18).

In order to raise funds for the development of SOEs, promote SOE management system reform, and notify the world that China's reform and opening-up was still in progress, Zhu Rongji, the then secretary of the CPC Shanghai Municipal Committee and mayor of Shanghai, presided over an enlarged meeting of the Standing Committee of the CPC Shanghai Municipal Committee on December 9, 1989. The meeting

[15]Data is quoted from *Research on the 30 Years of China's Financial Reform and Opening-up*, authored by Li Yang and Wang Guogang.

[16]Oral history by Gong Haocheng and Wei Wenyuan: How Shanghai Stock Exchange was Created. http://finance.jrj.com.cn/2018/06/27063224731717.shtml.

[17]Xie Baisan: Chinese Stock Market was Meant to Serve State-run Enterprises. http://finance.eastmoney.com/news/1370,20120528208058219.html.

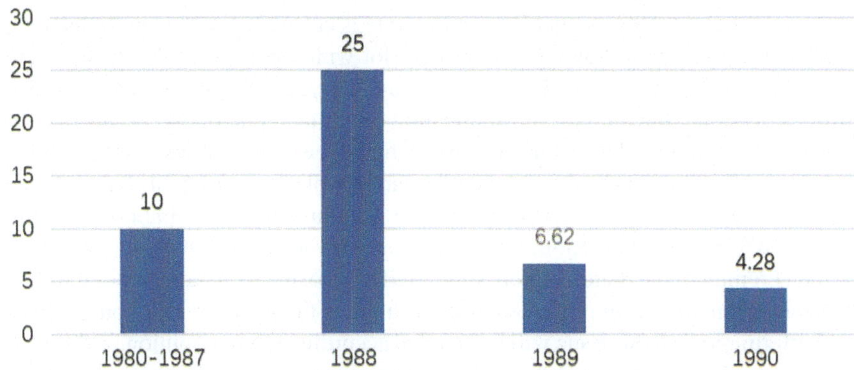

Chart 18 China's fundraising via stock issuance before 1990 (Unit: RMB 100 million). *Source* Qingquan MA, A History of Securities in China 1978–1998 [M]. CITIC Press, 2003

also included experts to help guide the creation of the Shanghai Stock Exchange, including Liu Hongru, the then deputy governor of the People's Bank of China, Gong Haocheng, president of the PBOC Shanghai Branch, Li Xiangrui, chairman of the Bank of Communications, and financial expert Prof. Biaoru [17]. At the meeting, Zhu Rongji was quoted as saying, "enterprises are in financial strain and heavily burdened. This year's contract base can be hardly fulfilled, and things will be more difficult next year," therefore "Shanghai shall accelerate the pace of financial reform and regain its past glory as an international financial hub. The top priorities are to open the market for foreign banks and establish a stock exchange, which are two most pressing issues in the reform…we must be bold enough to set up a stock exchange and develop the stock market." In the end, the meeting established a three-person task force comprising Li Xiangrui, He Gaosheng, and Gong Haocheng, which was responsible for preparing to develop the Shanghai Stock Exchange. Meanwhile, the "Beijing Joint Office on Stock Exchange Research and Design," led by returned scholars like Wang Boming and Gao Xiqing, provided additional advice on the preparation process. The Shanghai Stock Exchange opened for business at the end of 1990, and the Shenzhen Stock Exchange commenced operations in 1991.

(c) **1992: The China Securities Regulatory Commission (CSRC) was established**

The immediate trigger for the founding of the CSRC was the "8.10 Incident" that broke out in Shenzhen in 1992. After the founding of the Shanghai Stock Exchange and Shenzhen Stock Exchange, the stock market gradually devolved into a frenzy. Because the prices of new stocks tended to rise quickly after their issue, investors developed a mentality of "buying is earning" and quickly fell into stock-buying mania. Due to short supply, Shenzhen municipality decided to issue lot-drawing sheets for new stock applications. The announcement stated that "a total of 5,000,000 application forms for new share offerings will be issued, of which 500,000 effective lot-winning sheets are to be drawn on a one-off basis. The lot-winning rate stands at about 10% (actual lot winning rate is calculated according to the total number of recovered lot-drawing sheets). Each lot-winning sheet entitles the holder to subscribe to 1,000 shares issued by the company." Driven by huge anticipated profits, millions of people lined up for the application sheets at a total of 303 points of sale. However, soon after sales began, the application sheets were already sold out. On suspicions of serious internal fraud, people started violent confrontations and staged demonstrations. In response to this crisis, the government made an announcement, distributed 5,000,000 more lot-drawing sheets and advanced the 1993 quota. Li Peng, the then Premier of the State Council, supported Li Hao, the then secretary of the CPC Shenzhen Municipal Committee, saying, "you are at the frontline and you get first-hand information, so this issue will be handled according to your opinion." Although the crisis was successfully resolved, the event pushed the central government to set up a specialized watchdog for the securities market.

In October 1992, the State Council set up the Securities Commission of the State Council and the China Securities Regulatory Commission (CSRC). In December 1992, the State Council then issued the *Notice on Further Strengthening the Macro-Management of the Securities Market*, which defined the system through which the central government would manage the securities market in a unified manner. This signaled the gradual inclusion of China's securities market in the national unified supervision framework, and the national market began to develop from this point on.

Within the same period, legal construction of the securities market was also advanced. In August 1992, the drafting of the *Securities Law of the People's Republic of China* ("Securities Law") kicked off. However, the drafting process was full of twists and turns—the law was not adopted until December 1998 and was not put into force until July 1999. This was the first economic law since the founding of the PRC which was drafted in accordance with international practice under the organization of China's top legislature rather than a particular government department. The implementation of the *Securities Law* meant that China had established the position of the securities market in the form of law, laid the basic legal framework for China's securities market, and signaled that the legal construction of the Chinese securities market had entered a new stage. From then on, the *Securities Law* went through three amendments and one revision along with the continual development of the securities market.

(d) **1999–2007: Formerly pre-IPO non-tradable shares held by pre-IPO owners were allowed to be sold after collective bargaining between the owners and existing shareholders**

The split-share structure means that A-share listed company shares are divided into tradable and non-tradable categories depending on whether they can be listed for trading on stock exchanges. The shares held by shareholders before the IPO of a listed company, which can be transferred by agreement only, are called non-tradable shares. Conversely, publicly offered shares bought by the general public that can be listed for trading on stock exchanges are called tradable shares. By the end of 2004, the total share capital of listed companies was 714.9 billion shares. Within these shares, the total number of non-tradable ones was 454.3 billion—64% of the total share capital of listed companies. State-owned shares accounted for 74% of all non-tradable shares [18].

The root cause of the split-share structure is a concern for privatization. If all shares were listed for circulation and could be bought by anyone, it would be difficult to ensure the basic principle of public ownership as the mainstay, and the stock market could not have been established and allowed to develop. Additionally, shareholding reform and the listing of SOEs were chiefly aimed at exploring new management mechanisms and raising incremental capital. However, **the transfer of state-owned assets often adopted the method of administrative allocation, and state-owned stocks lacked internal demand for listing and circulation.**

As an institutional defect left over by history, **the split-share structure restricts healthy development of the Chinese capital market in many respects.** First, due to the limited size of tradable shares, share prices of listed companies are easily manipulated and tend to fluctuate greatly. Second, the holders of non-tradable shares pay more attention to changes in the net value of assets, and they are not greatly impacted by fluctuations in share prices. Share prices can hardly serve as effective incentives and restraints on majority shareholders and management. Third, capital circulation of listed companies is divided into two markets—negotiating transfer and listed trading—and two prices thus exist. As a result, market-based capital operations of listed companies including mergers and acquisitions (M&A) and restructuring lack a pricing basis. Fourth, the process of negotiating transfer market prices is not transparent and price discovery is not adequate, which adversely affects smooth circulation and market-based valuation of state-owned assets.

Before split-share structure reform, there were two unsuccessful experiments on shareholding reduction of state-owned shares. In September 1999, the Fourth Plenary Session of the Fifteenth CPC Central Committee issued the *Decisions on Several Significant Problems Concerning the Reform and Development of State-owned Enterprises*, which stated, "we may select some reputable state-controlled listed companies with great development potential and appropriately reduce our holding of state-owned shares without prejudice to state control. Funds thus obtained will be used by the country for the reform and development of SOEs." In December 1999, the China Securities Regulatory Commission announced plans for 10 listed companies to reduce holdings of state-owned shares via allotment. However, due to the inappropriate selection of pilot companies and allotment pricing, the pilot project was stopped.

On June 12, 2001, the State Council promulgated the *Interim Measures on the Management of Reducing the Holding of State-owned Shares for Raising Social Security Funds*, which prompted the exploration of the possibility to reduce holdings of state-owned shares through secondary offerings on the securities market. After the implementation of the *Interim Management Measures*, 13 listed companies reduced their state-owned shareholdings as required during their IPOs, while three listed companies also did so when issuing additional shares. However, the market failed to respond actively to the *Measures,* and large fluctuations occurred. The main reason for this was that shareholding reduction was conducted according to a price-to-earnings ratio of about 20, but the original subscription cost for state-owned shareholders was generally around RMB1 or further reduced through repeated allotment. The act of forcing public investors to buy shares transferred by state-owned shareholders with market premiums of tradable shares thus raised suspicions and attracted criticism. On June 23, 2002, the State Council announced that for domestic listed companies, China would no longer exercise the requirements of the *Interim Management Measures* to reduce the holding of state-owned shares through the securities market.

These two failed pilot projects on shareholding reduction of state-owned shares indicated that there would be no silver bullet for resolving the split-share structure problem. The *Several Opinions of the State Council on Promoting the Reform and opening-up and Stable Development of the Capital Market* issued by the State Council on January 31, 2004 expressly stated that relevant departments "should actively and appropriately solve the split-share structure problem" and put forth the general requirement that "as we solve this problem, we shall respect market laws and do everything to promote market stability and development as well as practically protect lawful rights and interests of investors, especially small and medium-sized public investors." **The essential difference between this solution and the previous shareholding reduction of state-owned shares was that the core objective of this time around was not cash realization and fundraising, but rather eliminating the capital market's institutional defect.** After the release of the *Several Opinions*, such departments as the CSRC, SASAC, and Ministry of Finance jointly established a trans-department task force, which completed research and put forth the "theory of consideration." This theory changed the pricing expectation that "shares held by shareholders of a listed company shall not be listed for circulation before the public offering of its shares" **by allowing the listing and circulation of non-tradable shares and determining the "consideration" through market-based approaches depending on the actual conditions of listed companies.**

On April 29, 2005, the China Securities Regulatory Commission issued the *Notice on Issues Concerning the Pilot Program on Split-Share Structure Reform of Listed Companies*, which initiated the pilot program on split-share structure reform. The split-share structure reform was carried out step-by-step according to the principle of "launching a pilot company only when its conditions are ripe." On May 24, China CAMC Engineering Co., Ltd. issued a prospectus and thus realized the first IPO after the "separation of new and old stocks," which signaled the full recovery of the market financing function. By the end of 2006, the total market capitalization of listed companies that completed or entered into the split-share structure reform procedure accounted for 98% of the total market capitalization of all listed companies in need of reform. This demonstrated that the task of split-share structure reform had been essentially completed.

The smooth implementation of split-share structure reform ruled out the problems of interest splitting and price splitting of state-owned shares, corporate shares, and tradable shares. As a result, shareholders of various types enjoyed the same rights of share listing and circulation as well as equal rights to earnings in share prices. Shares of various types were priced under the unified market mechanism and became the basis for the common interest of shareholders of various types. The basic fulfillment of split-share structure reform and a series of policy measures combining split-share structure reform with market stability and development eliminated the biggest uncertainties that could affect the market. **The split-share structure reform is of historical significance, as it laid a market foundation for the enhanced role of the Chinese capital market in optimizing resource allocation and eliminated the essential difference between the Chinese capital market and international markets at the basic level of the market system.**

(e) **2004–2007: Tightening regulations of investment banks and fighting crises of investment banks abusing their clients' funds**

In September 1987, China set up the Shenzhen Special Zone Securities Company, the first specialized securities company in China. In 1988, the PBOC allocated special funds and set up 33 more securities companies in different provinces. Additionally, the finance system established a number of securities companies whose main business was trading treasury bonds. After 1992, securities intermediaries mushroomed in large numbers with the formation of a national securities market. The shareholders of those securities companies were mostly banks, local governments, and relevant ministries. By the end of 2017, China had a total of 131 securities companies.

Due to defects in relevant systems and mechanisms, numerous contradictions and problems arose during the development of securities companies, including frequent illegal or irregular acts such as securities companies arbitrarily misappropriating customers' trading settlement funds and securities, companies conducting financial activities against relevant regulations, and shareholders and affiliates occupying funds. Between the end of 2003 and the first half of 2004, risks lurking in the operations of many securities companies—which had accumulated over several years—simultaneously erupted, and the whole industry was faced with the most serious crisis since its birth. For example, Southern Securities, the then China's biggest securities company, began to manipulate Hafei Aviation and Harbin Pharmaceutical around 2000. When share prices declined and external funds were not enough to sustain its operations, Southern Securities misappropriated customer margins to repay invested principals. In January 2004, due to misappropriated customer margins in the aggregate amount of RMB8.0 billion and huge losses to proprietary trading business, Southern Securities was hit by a payment crisis. Later on, the China Securities Regulatory Commission and Shenzhen Municipal Government announced an administrative takeover of the company.

To fundamentally solve the problems revealed by this incident, the China Securities Regulatory Commission carried out comprehensive regulation of securities companies under the State Council's deployment in three aspects including risk disposal, daily supervision, and development promotion for the industry. Concrete measures included: (1) getting a clear picture of all risks existing in securities companies and forcefully supervising and urging securities companies to make rectifications; (2) treating high-risk companies timely and reliably, setting up securities investor protection funds, and establishing a long-standing risk disposal mechanism; (3) encouraging relevant sides to restructure risky companies without prejudice to the laws, regulations, and regulatory requirements to make sure that they can attain the standards for sustained compliance operation; (4) reforming and perfecting basic systems including the depositing and management of customer funds, repurchasing of treasury bonds, asset management, and proprietary securities trading, and establishing the system of public disclosure of financial information by securities companies; (5) conducting classified supervision of securities companies, and establishing a new mechanism of linking companies' business scopes and sizes to dynamic changes in their net capital; (6) encouraging highly qualified companies to develop innovatively and supporting excellent companies to grow better and stronger; (7) improving the collaboration mechanism among securities regulators, public security officials, and judicial organs, intensifying responsibility investigations, tightening market discipline, severely investigating and punishing illegal and irregular acts, and resolutely containing illegal and irregular activities; (8) devising or revising relevant laws and regulations and perfecting the system of laws and regulations to supervise securities companies [18].

By the end of August 2007, all major regulation goals had been fulfilled and the work on comprehensive regulation of securities companies was concluded. By this point, China had basically solved the problems that had materially affected the industry's healthy development (including false financial information, off-balance-sheet operations, misappropriation of customer assets, and occupation of customer funds by shareholders and affiliates), initially established the long-standing risk prevention mechanism, and reformed and perfected various basic systems. Since 2006, the previous trend of securities companies suffering losses for four consecutive years (2002–2005) has been reversed. By the end of 2007, the aggregate assets and net assets of 106 companies in the industry were RMB1,731.3 billion and RMB3,447.4 billion, respectively—354% and 283% of the corresponding figures at the end of 2000, just before the commencement of comprehensive regulation. In 2007, the whole industry recorded a total operating revenue of RMB284.7 billion and a net profit of RMB132.0 billion, and 104 companies made a profit. All key financial indicators reached or exceeded historical highs [19].

(f) **2003–2018: Allowing limited capital flow between the Mainland and Hong Kong markets; dealing with the stock market crash of 2015**

China's securities market adopted limited and paced opening-up. In 1992, the B-share stock market was launched. Though denominated only in US dollars and HK dollars, it allowed foreign investors to enter China's stock market for the first time. In June 2002, Zhou Xiaochuan, the then President of the CSRC, indicated the possibility of setting up a Qualified Foreign Institutional Investors (QFII) program in an international conference, which would allow foreign institutional investors to invest in China's A-share stock market with RMB. In July 2003, the first QFII order, sent by UBS for the purchase of four stocks, was confirmed and executed, symbolizing the official launch of QFII (Chart 19).

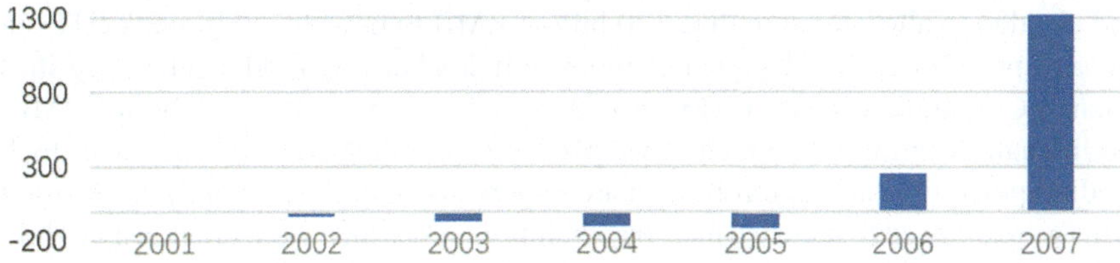

Chart 19 Net profit of securities Companies in 2001–2007 (RMB 100 million). *Source* China Securities Regulatory Commission

To further expand the opening-up of China's capital market, support Hong Kong as an international financial center, and promote the development of the offshore RMB market in Hong Kong, a pilot program of RMB-QFII (RQFII) was jointly announced by the CSRC, PBOC, and SAFE. This program allowed qualified mutual funds and Hong Kong-based sub-companies of securities companies to invest directly with RMB raised in offshore markets. Further reforms of QFII and RQFII were implemented in 2016 and 2018, which comprehensively relaxed investment requirements. By the end of May 2018, 287 QFII investors had been granted USD99.5 billion in quotas, and 196 RQFII investors had been granted RMB615.9 billion in quotas.

In 2014 and 2016, "Shanghai-Hong Kong Connect" and "Shenzhen-Hong Kong Connect" were launched in addition to the QFII/RQFII programs. They were designed to allow international investors and Chinese investors to trade securities with local settlement facilities. By the end of August 2018, traded volume under "Shanghai-Hong Kong Connect" was about RMB10 trillion, and that of "Shenzhen-Hong Kong Connect" was about RMB3.5 trillion. In July 2017, "Bond Connect" was launched, allowing investors in Hong Kong to purchase bonds issued in the Mainland market. By May 2018, foreign investors held more than RMB 1.4 trillion in bonds, 1.7 times the volume before the launch of "Bond Connect."

In 2015, the stock markets in both Shanghai and Shenzhen crashed in the short term. The Shanghai Composite Index dropped by 45% in less than three months and the Second-board Market Index dropped by 56%.

The government intervened with a series of measures. On June 28, 2015, the central bank decreased the deposit reserve rate by 25 base points, but this did not manage to stop the market drop. The China Securities Regulatory Commission reacted by announcing a sequence of measures to boost the market. First, restrictions were placed on the number and size of new IPOs. In early June, only 10 new stocks were scheduled to be listed. Second, efforts were made to attract foreign long-term-oriented funds, nearly doubling the QFII investment quota from 80 billion USD to 150 billion USD. Third, the registered capital of China Securities Finance Corporation was increased from 24 billion RMB to 100 billion RMB and it enlarged its funding support for securities firms' trading operations. Fourth, severe punishments were introduced for those who spread misinformation about the market.

The government coordinated and supported securities firms as they increased their investments in the market. On June 4, 2015, 21 securities firms met with the CSRC and decided to allocate more than 120 billion RMB to buy blue-chip stock ETFs in an attempt to boost the Shanghai Composite Index back to 4200. China Securities Finance Corporation and the CSRC provided funding support up to 520 billion RMB. Additionally, central-government-owned firms were instructed to increase their stock holding portfolios, and controlling shareholders and high-level managers of listed firms were allowed to increase their ownership shares, which were previously tightly regulated. Furthermore, the government put the brakes on stock selling pressures. For example, the CSI 500 futures short-selling margin was raised to 30%. On July 8, the CSRC announced that shareholders of listed firms with more than 5% ownership were not allowed to underweight their shares for 6 months. Thanks to these efforts, the stock market gradually improved.

The government also made efforts to establish and improve the multi-tier capital market. The *Decision of the CPC Central Committee on Several Issues concerning Improvement of the Socialist Market Economy System* adopted at the Third Plenary Session of the Sixteenth CPC Central Committee in October 2003 mentioned the establishment of a multi-tier capital market for the first time. This *Decision* expressly called for "establishing a multi-tier capital market system, improving capital market structure, and diversifying capital market products." Specifically, the *Decision* declared, "we shall regulate and develop the main board market and promote the construction of venture capital and growth enterprise markets."

At that time, the growth enterprise board was not launched for various reasons. As a transitional substitute, a relatively independent small and medium-sized enterprises (SME) board was set up within the main board of the Shenzhen Stock Exchange in May 2004. The SME board was created to serve as an independent board within the Shenzhen Stock Exchange to facilitate the issuance and listed transactions of shares of small and medium-sized enterprises. It is a separate board with independent operation, supervision, codes, and indexes, and it lacks prejudice to existing laws and standards for issuance and listing of mainboard enterprises.

In October 2007, the Report to the Seventeenth National Congress of the Communist Party of China deepened relevant statements by emphasizing that "China shall develop various types of financial markets and an efficient, secure modern financial system with various types of ownership and diverse modes of operation and with a reasonable structure and all sound functions," especially working to "optimize the capital market structure and increase the proportion of direct financing through multiple channels."

On October 30, 2009, the growth enterprise market board was officially launched at the Shenzhen Stock Exchange. According to the data, the average PE of the first batch of 28 GEM listed companies was 56.7X, and the highest PE was recorded by Bode Energy at 81.67X, well above the average PE of all A-shares and that of the SME boards.[18]

In November 2012, the Report to the Eighteenth National Congress of the Communist Party of China further emphasized the importance of "accelerating the development of the multi-tier capital market." The multi-tier capital market included

[18]https://zh.wikipedia.org/wiki/Shenzhen Stock Exchange's Growth Enterprise Market Board.

advanced floor trading markets like the Shanghai and Shenzhen stock exchanges as well as the OTC trading New Third Board and New Fourth Board markets.

In November 2013, the Third Plenary Session of the Eighteenth CPC Central Committee adopted the *Decision of CPC Central Committee on Some Major Issues Concerning Comprehensively Deepening the Reform.* This decision furthered the understanding of the multi-tier capital market by emphasizing that "we shall improve the multi-tier capital market system, promote the reform of the stock issue registration system, advance equity financing through diverse channels, develop and regulate the bond market, and raise the proportion of direct financing. We shall encourage financial innovation and enrich financial market levels and products." At this time, it was clear that China needed to establish a more diverse multi-tier capital market, including floor and OTC markets, publicly offered and privately offered funds, stock and bond markets, and domestic and international markets.

At the end of 2013, the State Council issued a decision on setting up a New Third Board. The New Third Board became the third national stock exchange following the Shanghai and Shenzhen Stock Exchanges, and it was mainly intended to provide services for innovative, entrepreneurial, growing micro, small, and medium-sized enterprises. In the past five years, the New Third Board has become the largest global stock exchange by number of listed enterprises. Furthermore, the number of listed enterprises has increased from less than 200 to "more than 10,000"; the total market capitalization of listed enterprises has increased from less than RMB30.0 billion to RMB5.15 trillion, and the annual financing amount has increased from less than RMB1.0 billion to nearly RMB140.0 billion.

In January 2017, the General Office of the State Council issued the *Notice on Regulating the Development of Regional Equity Markets.* According to the notice, the fourth board market shall be positioned as a private market chiefly serving micro, small, and medium-sized enterprises within their relevant provincial administrative regions. The market is to be an important component of the multi-tier capital market system, and shall be a platform for local people's governments to comprehensively utilize policy measures to serve micro, small, and medium-sized enterprises. So far, China has 40 regional equity markets serving over 80,000 micro, small, and medium-sized enterprises. Regional equity markets in different provinces, autonomous regions, and municipalities directly under the central government explore unique ways to provide precise services for local enterprises.

On November 5, 2018, Chinese President Xi Jinping announced at the opening ceremony of the First China International Import Expo that China would set up a science and technology innovation board and test the registration system at the Shanghai Stock Exchange in order to support the construction of Shanghai as both an international financial hub and a science and technology innovation hub to help continually improve basic systems of capital market (Chart 20).

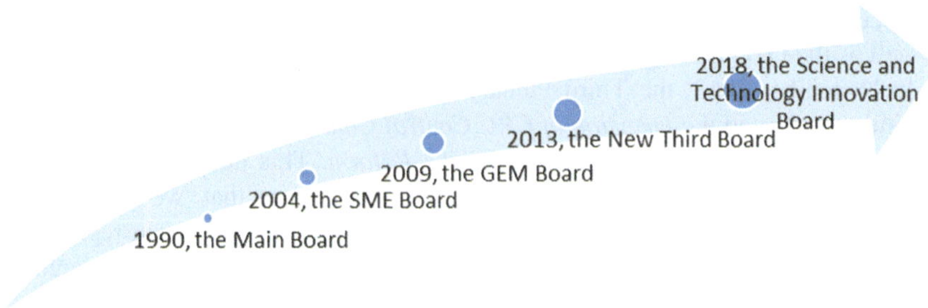

Chart 20 Establishment and improvement of the Multi-Tier Capital Market *Source* Authors' analysis

3 Economic Analysis

3.1 The Development of the Financial System Cannot Be Accomplished Without Governmental Regulation and Support

China's 40-year development of its financial system clearly demonstrates that autonomous adjustment of the financial system alone can hardly guarantee efficient, stable operations. Therefore, the government must participate in fostering and regulating the financial system. On one hand, because of the complexity and importance of the financial system, its distortion or failure will cause more serious damage than that of other markets. On the other hand, because the smooth operation of the financial system has much to do with the development of individuals, enterprises, and the economy, it is a public good and has huge externalities.

On the micro-level, the financial market behavior of microeconomic subjects needs to be regulated by the government. Due to capital's tendency to pursue profits, autonomous adjustment, and correction of financial subjects alone tend to lead to distortion and chaos. For example, before the founding of the CSRC in the early 1990s, a "stock craze" swept the whole country. Autonomous, arbitrary stock issuance by enterprises, both small and large, and securities markets spread unchecked in different cities. People even developed the misconception that "buying is earning." In this crazy atmosphere, people struggled for stock subscription sheets. In 1992, the notorious "8.10 Incident" shocked the whole nation. This incident showed that with the deepening of shareholding reform and the issuance of negotiable securities of various types, especially considering the rapid development of the stock market, it was imperative to establish a centralized, unified supervision agency to streamline regulations, systems, and supervision. It was in this context that the State Council set up the China Securities Regulatory Commission (CSRC).

In terms of industry development, government regulation is an effective force for driving industry reform. In the 1990s, state-owned commercial banks accumulated many risks, which attracted much attention and alarm from the international community. Some international media organizations even asserted that Chinese solely state-owned commercial banks were "technically bankrupt." In order to resolve the massive amount of non-performing assets of solely state-owned commercial banks, the government invested large quantities of resources. For instance, the government issued RMB270.0 billion of special bonds in 1998 to supplement the statutory capital of the four solely state-owned commercial banks. In 1999, China stripped RMB1.4 trillion of NPLs from the four banks[19] and transferred those loans to four specially established financial asset management companies for disposal. After 2003, China implemented shareholding reform and listed the state-owned commercial banks. It can be seen that without government intervention and support, the banks alone could not have safely resolved their crises at that time.

On the macro level, the resolution of systematic crises requires government intervention. Take the 2008 economic crisis as an example. Before that, the core idea of neo-liberalism prevalent in Western societies was that restricting governmental activities and maintaining an unregulated market was superior. The outbreak of the crisis indicated that market self-correction alone could not control risks, restore confidence, re-create balance sheets, or restart economic growth. Only national guidance via government agencies could provide a "life raft" for the financial system at critical periods to prevent collapse, create direct incentives for the real economy to make up for a drastic decline in private demand, and design national and global supervision mechanisms to prevent the reoccurrence of similar crises. Indeed, for systematic financial risks and crises, there is so far no other alternative private financial market solution comparable with strong government intervention [20].

3.2 A Steady Process of Local-Currency-Based Financial Deepening Is Essential for Fast Investment in the Real Economy and Channeling Savings into Investments

Financial deepening is mainly reflected in the expanding varieties and quantity of financial products and services as well as the increasing number of people who have access to these financial products and services.

Academia often uses the ratio of broad money supply (M2) to GDP to measure the degree of "financial deepening." Broad money M2 has been expanding since the start of reform and opening-up. At the end of 1990, M2 stock amounted to RMB1.5 trillion and the M2/GDP ratio was only 0.78. By the end of 2017, M2 stock reached

[19] According to "Several Issues Concerning the Reform of State-owned Commercial Banks"—a speech delivered by Tang Shuangning on March 25, 2005, at the 2005 Academic Conference of China Society for Finance and Banking, the RMB 1,393.9 billion of assets stripped at that time included approximately RMB1 trillion of NPLs from the four major state-owned banks, RMB100.0 billion from China Development Bank, over RMB100.0 billion of on-balance-sheet interest, and over RMB100.0 billion of normal loans stripped via debt for equity swaps.

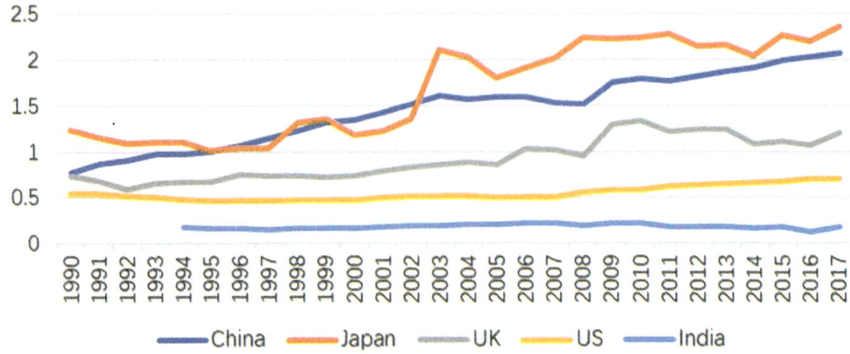

Chart 21 M2/GDP ratio in different countries. *Source* CEIC database

RMB167.7 trillion and the M2/GDP ratio rose to 2.07. Another indicator frequently used to measure the degree of financial deepening is the proportion of the financial industry's added value in GDP. This figure was 5.45% in 1992, but rose to 7.95% in 2017. As a comparison, in 2017, the added value of the finance and insurance industries in the United States accounted for around 7.5% of GDP.

In terms of financial product varieties and quantity, financial assets held by residents were chiefly savings deposits before the reform and opening-up. Since 1990, the bond and stock markets have grown and developed from scratch. By the end of December 1992, China's balance of bonds (government bonds and corporate bonds) was merely RMB210.5 billion and the total stock market capitalization was only RMB104.8 billion. By the end of September 2018, the balance of bonds (government bonds and corporate bonds) reached RMB52.2 trillion, about 248 times that of 1992; the total stock market capitalization reached RMB48.7 trillion, about 464 times that of 1992. Additionally, the balance of financial products of various types was estimated to be nearly RMB30 trillion by the end of 2016 (Charts 21 and 22).

The venture capital (VC) industry has also developed quickly, and China has become one of the world's largest VC markets. According to statistics from Zero2IPO Research, China's VC investment size totaled USD30.0 billion and the ratio of VC investment to GDP reached 0.25% (5 times the 2006 figure) in 2017. In terms of VC investment magnitude and quantity of VC institutions, China may be the world's second-largest VC market.[20] In terms of financing, VC financing size in China reached USD51.0 billion in 2017, surpassing the corresponding US figure for two consecutive years and making China the world's number one VC financing market. The ratio of VC financing amount to GDP in China also reached 0.4%, while the US figure generally ranged between 0.2 and 0.3%. Since new funds raised outnumbered

[20] According to data from FactSet, of total global VC investment in 2017, the US ranked first with a 55% share and China ranked second with a 17% share. According to data from Preqin, measured by the number of VC institutions, the United States now ranks first among the world's major markets with 1,199 VC institutions and China ranks second with 368.

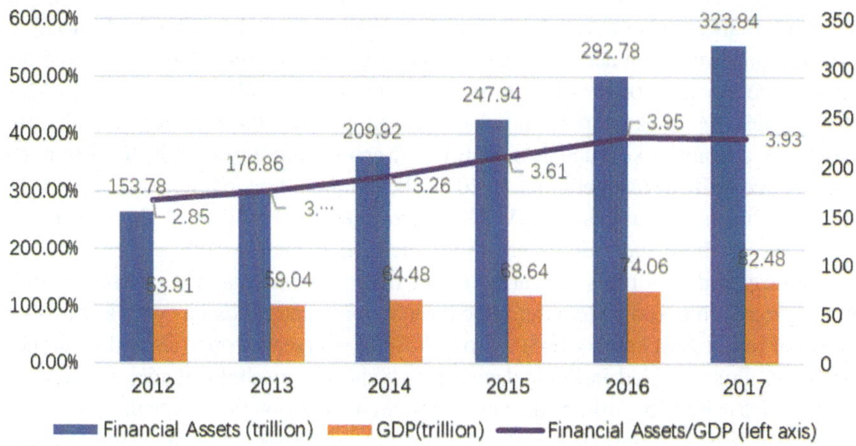

Chart 22 China's financial deepening over recent years. *Source* National Bureau of Statistics of China, CBIRC, China Trustee Association, Securities Association of China, Insurance Association of China, Asset Management Association of China, estimations of the Institute for China's Economic Practice and Thinking, Tsinghua University

investments, the amount of existing investable capital in China continued to rise and has now reached USD114.0 billion, close to the US level.[21]

In addition to these phenomena, it is also notable that new financial products featuring Internet-based FinTech have been growing rapidly in recent years. According to iResearch's survey report, the transaction size of general online credit products exceeded RMB10 trillion and the size of the Internet-based asset management industry reached RMB3.5 trillion in 2017.

Based on the above analyses of various financial assets and the foregoing different categories of statistics on asset size, we have calculated the changes in the value of China's financial assets in recent years as well as the ratio of financial assets value to GDP. China's financial assets have been expanding quickly in recent years. The size of China's financial assets rose from RMB54 trillion in 2012 to RMB324 trillion in 2017, and the ratio of financial assets value to GDP rose from 285% to 393% during the same period. This reflects China's continual financial deepening.[22]

Residents holding huge amounts of financial assets are one side of the coin. The other side is the robust growth of investments in infrastructure, equipment, and land in the past 40 years of the reform and opening-up. According to the National Bureau of Statistics of China, cumulative completed social investments totaled RMB490 trillion during 1981–2017, which showed a CAGR of 20.2%.[23]

Participants in the financial market generally exhibit the following two characteristics. First, they account for a large share of the total population. Take

[21] https://36kr.com/p/5147457.html.

[22] It is noted that there are still omissions in the statistics of financial assets and the data of some small-sized categories like futures and options is not included here.

[23] http://www.stats.gov.cn/ztjc/ztfx/ggkf40n/201809/t20180906_1621360.html.

the stock market as an example: in October 2018, the stock market had a total of 140 million investment accounts. Even if calculated according to two accounts per person, the stock market would have approximately 70 million investors. In May 2015, when the stock market "advanced triumphantly," the number of both SSE and SZSE accounts exceeded 100 million.[24] **Second, participants in the financial market are quite heterogeneous.** In 2017, the number of people with at least RMB6 million of investable assets ("HNWIs") approached 1.90 million.[25] The investment objectives of these individuals are more inclined toward wealth security, wealth inheritance, and children's education rather than pure value appreciation, and they attach greater importance to asset allocation at home and abroad as well as the allocation of investment categories (e.g., purchase of overseas properties and insurance products). For qualified individual investors "whose household financial assets are worth at least RMB5 million, or whose annual average income over the past three years is at least RMB400,000 and who have at least two years' investment experience,"[26] they may invest in privately offered funds. In 2017, the total size of all privately offered funds in China exceeded RMB11 trillion, and the number of these funds issued exceeded 24,000.[27] As for ordinary individual investors, they generally invest in bank deposits, bank financial products, and publicly offered funds. Within this category, following the increasing popularity of products like Yu E Bao, money market funds have substantially squeezed the share of bank deposits. At the end of September 2018, the total size of money market funds reached RMB8.92 trillion,[28] while the total size of publicly offered funds was RMB11.6 trillion. Banks depended on wealth management products to retain investors and improve profits. At the end of 2017, the value of existing wealth management products aimed at ordinary individual investors was RMB14.6 trillion, which indicated an annual growth of nearly 1/4 and accounted for nearly 1/2 of the total size of wealth management products.

Since reform and opening-up, China's financial deepening has been robust and based on local currency, and has been guided by the government in two major ways. First, the government closely controls and supervises the innovation and development of financial products. For example, in March 2018, the government issued the *Guiding Opinions on Regulating the Asset Management Business of Financial Institutions*. This document adjusted the investment threshold of privately offered funds from "any unit and individual whose amount invested in a single privately-offered fund is not below RMB1 million and complies with relevant standards, has individual financial assets not below RMB3 million, or whose annual average income over the past three years was not below RMB500,000" to "any individual whose household financial assets are worth at least RMB5 million, or whose annual average income over the past three years was at least RMB400,000 and who has at least two years' investment experience, or any corporate unit whose net assets

[24]http://data.eastmoney.com/cjsj/yzgptj/2015-05-25%5E2015-05-29.html.

[25]https://baijiahao.baidu.com/s?id=1603692687261408251&wfr=spider&for=pc.

[26]https://finance.sina.com.cn/stock/y/2017-11-17/doc-ifynwnty4270779.shtml.

[27]http://funds.hexun.com/2018-03-21/192673561.html.

[28]https://baijiahao.baidu.com/s?id=1616015285883827077&wfr=spider&for=pc.

by the end of most recent year were not below RMB10 million." This adjustment actually demonstrated a tightening of the requirements for investors. Second, the government restricts residents' purchase of overseas financial assets. This is done by setting an individual annual foreign exchange quota (USD50,000), setting an overseas withdrawal limit (RMB100,000), and requiring investments in overseas capital markets to be conducted through approved qualified domestic institutions' investors (QDII) to restrict "capital flight."

This robust and local-currency-based financial deepening process has promoted economic development. First, it has allowed more investors to access the financial market and enjoy capital gains, and has given more enterprises and individuals the chance to secure funding support from the financial market. Second, the expansion in the variety and quantity of financial products has absorbed large amounts of money, which has enabled the central bank to have greater leeway for its monetary policy while maintaining stable inflation and thus lessened the pressure on fiscal policy.

3.3 The Government Needs to Proactively Monitor and Mitigate Financial Risk

The Chinese government has always attached great importance to proactively resolving financial risks while also underscoring the importance of maintaining social stability. Despite the occurrence of several financial risk incidents, each time, the government has been able to intervene and effectively resolve the problems at hand, successfully avoiding systematic financial crises and large-scale social unrest.

To achieve similar results, countries' core decision-makers must give priority to the prevention and resolution of financial risks. After 1997, China began holding a National Financial Work Conference every five years to have in-depth discussions on such topics as the prevention of systematic financial risks and the perfection of the financial supervision system. During the 2008 financial crisis, the State Council set up an international financial crisis response group led by Wang Qishan. During this time, Wang also formed the system of holding one regular meeting on financial work every 10 days to further strengthen the coordination and cooperation among the "Commission of the Central Bank and Three Regulatory Bodies" and to closely monitor and respond to the international financial crisis. In 2017, the State Council set up a "Financial Stability and Development Commission" chaired by deputy premier of the State Council. This commission had a higher administrative level than the "Commission of the Central Bank and Three Regulatory Bodies." Its main task was to coordinate matters concerning financial stability, reform, and development.

Second, the government must play an important role in preventing a systematic crisis. Compared with other countries, China took particularly active and resolute measures to address the Asian financial crisis and the 2008 global financial crisis, successfully maintaining the basic stability of China's financial system. During the

Asian financial crisis, China strengthened macroeconomic regulation over the money market. In 1998, the PBOC also made two required reserve ratio (RRR) cuts and six interest rate cuts while also issuing RMB150.0 billion in additional treasury bonds, thus maintaining successful control over macroeconomic stability. During the global financial crisis, the PBOC made four RRR cuts and five interest rate cuts while also implementing a large-scale package plan to further stimulate the domestic market, increase domestic demand, and invest in fields important to people's livelihoods, thus promoting a smooth economic transition.

Lastly, the government should properly handle issues concerning social stability while resolving financial risks. Social stability is the foundation for sustained economic development, and therefore the intensity of China's reform has had to reside within the tolerance range of social stability in China as a socially diverse, populous developing nation. The Chinese government's concrete practices can be broken down into the following three aspects: First, when circumstances leave no other choice, the government distinguishes between the fund security of domestic public investors and that of overseas institutional investors. For instance, in the Southern Securities bankruptcy case of 2004, the PBOC specially provided RMB8.7 billion in re-loans to help Southern Securities repay all the margins of investors previously misappropriated. In contrast, institutional investors involved in the 1998 Guangdong International Trust bankruptcy case were not so lucky. In this case, while the RMB700 million of principal deposits of domestic natural persons[29] were fully repaid by the Bank of China, the remaining RMB38.8 billion of domestic and foreign debts (including RMB32.0 billion of debts attributable to overseas creditors) were treated equally, with a final settlement rate of less than 20%.[30] Second, different regulatory agencies have different levels of organization and staffing. That of the PBOC goes down to the county level, the CBRC goes down to the city level, and the CSRC goes down to the provincial level. Furthermore, staffing size of the banking regulatory agency far exceeds that of the securities' regulatory agency, which reflects the government's emphasis on protecting residents' deposit security and maintaining social stability. Third, the government imposes different degrees of punishment on different types of illegal financial acts. For example, a crime of fraud in financing carries the maximum punishment of the death penalty, but the intensity of punishment against illegal acts in the securities market is relatively weak. The difference between these two transgressions lies in the fact that they have different impacts on social stability.

[29]It included RMB132 million of investors' margins misappropriated by 9 securities sales departments, with data coming from the *Actual Record of Court Trial of the Bankruptcy Case of Former Guangdong International Trust & Investment Co., Ltd.* http://www.chinanews.com/n/2003-03-01/26/277482.html.

[30]The figure is the amount of declared claims, with data coming from the Gazette of the Supreme People's Court of the People's Republic of China http://gongbao.court.gov.cn/details/bba0bd0d46cb19999c24e15b160713.html.

References

1. Claessens, M. S., & Ayhan Kose, M. A. (2013). *Financial crises explanations, types, and implications..*
2. Reinhart, C. M., & Rogoff, K. S. (2009). *This time is different: Eight centuries of financial folly.* Princeton University Press.
3. Eichengreen, B., & Bordo, M. (2003). Crises now and then: what lessons from the last era of financial globalization?. Edited by P. Mizen, 52–91.
4. Frankel, J. A., & Rose, A. K. (1996). Currency crashes in emerging markets: An empirical treatment. *Journal of international Economics, 41*(3-4), 351–366.
5. Forbes, K. J., & Warnock, F. E. (2012). Capital flow waves: Surges, stops, flight, and retrenchment. *Journal of International Economics, 88*(2), 235–251.
6. Friedman, M., & Schwartz, A. J. (2008). *A monetary history of the United States.* Princeton University Press, pp. 1867–1960
7. Bluedorn, M. J. C., Decressin, M. J., & Terrones, M. M. (2013). *Do asset price drops foreshadow recessions?.* International Monetary Fund.
8. Schwartz, A., Capie, F., & Wood, G. (1986). *Real and pseudo financial crises.*
9. Kindleberger, C. P., & Aliber, R. Z. (2011). *Manias, panics and crashes: a history of financial crises.* Palgrave Macmillan.
10. Barro, R. J., & Ursúa, J. F. (2009). *Stock-market crashes and depressions.* No. w14760. *National Bureau of Economic Research.*
11. Wang, Y., Wu, L., & Yang, Y. (2009). Does the stock market affect firm investment in china? A price informativeness perspective. *Journal of Banking & Finance, 33*(1), 53–62.
12. Liu, H. (2009). A review of China's financial system reform. *Hundred Year Tide, 13(5)*, 22–28.
13. Zheng, J. (2017). Comparison between governance models of policy banks in China and other countries. *The Chinese Banker* (4), 96–99.
14. Ran, Z. (2017). A study on chinese commercial banks resolving non-performing assets through the approach of debt-for-equity swap. A doctoral dissertation from the University of International Business and Economics.
15. Zhou, X. (2012). Retrospect and prospect of the reform of large commercial banks. *West China Finance*, (5), 4–7.
16. Yang, L., & Guogang, W. (2008). Research on the 30 Years of China's financial reform and opening-up. Economic & Management Publishing House.
17. Xie, B. (2003). International comparison of securities markets [M]. Tsinghua University Press.
18. Liu, H. (2009). The change: The 60-Year development of China's financial system [M]. China Financial Publishing House.
19. Wu, X. (2008). Retrospect and prospect of China's 30 -Year reform of financial system [M]. People's Daily Press.
20. Ma, Y., Chen, Y. (2014). Government-market relationship in financial development: National endowments and efficient frontier. *Finance & Trade Economics*, 03.
21. Samuelson, P. A. (1966). A summing up. *The Quarterly Journal of Economics, 80*(4), 568–583.

Learning Through Opening Up

David Daokui Li, Chi Zhang, Lin Fu, Meixin Guo, and Di Zhou

Abstract This section analyzes China's process of opening up in the past four decades. It argues that the Chinese economy has been integrated into the global economic system and achieved economic upgrading in the process while mitigated the shocks of globalization and revived "Chinese Detroits," which benefited not only China but also the world economy. We summarize two economic lessons from China's experience of opening up in the past four decades. First, learning from advanced market economies through entrepreneurs, laborers, and government officials is essential for economic upgrading. Second, to achieve effective and sustainable learning, the process of opening up must be carefully managed and paced. In other words, opening up in one fell swoop will not bring long-term growth and prosperity to an economy.

Keywords Opening up · Global economic system · Industrial upgrading

D. D. Li (✉) · M. Guo
Academic Center for Chinese Economic Practice and Thinking (ACCEPT), Tsinghua University, Beijing, China
e-mail: daviddaokuili@126.com

M. Guo
e-mail: mxguomx@126.com

C. Zhang
New Development Bank, Shanghai, China
e-mail: zhang.chi@ndb.int

L. Fu
Central University of Finance and Economics, Beijing, China
e-mail: fulinthu@126.com

D. Zhou
School of Social Sciences, Qinghua University, Beijing, China
e-mail: zhoudidkc@gmail.com

D. D. Li (eds.), *Economic Lessons from China's Forty Years of Reform and Opening-up*, https://doi.org/10.1007/978-981-33-4520-1_5

1 Stylized Facts

In the past 40 years of reform and opening up, China has made efforts to enhance the opening up of its economy through the continuous deepening of reforms and has embarked on a smooth, orderly, and well-managed journey to opening up. During this process, Chinese entrepreneurs, laborers, and government officials at multiple levels have successfully responded to the tremendous impact caused by opening up and have achieved structural upgrading, established and improved the market economy, and successfully integrated the Chinese economy into the wider world. As the world's largest developing country and largest transitional economy, China promotes both reform through opening up and opening up through reform, reliance on borrowing, absorption and innovation, achieving synergy via low labor cost, scale advantage, and combining local land and other resources with international capital and technology. Through these means, China has rapidly developed a massive production capacity and spurred economic growth.

Through the process of opening up, the Chinese economy has also made important contributions to the development of the world economy. After 40 years of reform and opening up, China has become the world's largest consumer market. Foreign enterprises have shared the great opportunities associated with China's development through cross-border investment and entry into the Chinese market. China's opening up has thus played an important role in stimulating global economic growth and promoting economic structural upgrading. At the same time, with the deepening of globalization and the prevalence of international production, the scale advantage of China's manufacturing industry has gradually become prominent, showing strong supporting capacity for parts processing, production, and assembly, which has also driven down the costs of global manufacturing. The continuous reduction of costs has promoted competition within industries and improved the economic welfare of consumers around the world.

1. **The Chinese economy has been integrated into the world and has achieved industrial upgrading in the process of opening up**

(a) **The Chinese economy has been integrated into the global economic system**

In the great historical process of China's reform and opening up, foreign trade and foreign direct investment (FDI) have played an important role. Over the past 40 years, China has worked hard to promote the reform of the foreign trade system, actively integrate into the global economy, achieve historical growth of the scale of international trade and FDI, and become the world's largest country in terms of goods traded as well as the second largest destination for foreign direct investment, creating a miracle in the history of world economic development.

The total volume of trade has soared. In the 40 years of reform and opening up, the total import and export volume of China's goods has increased from USD20.64 billion in 1978 to USD4.1 trillion in 2017, an increase of 197 times. The average annual growth rate has reached 14.5%, nearly doubling every five years. China

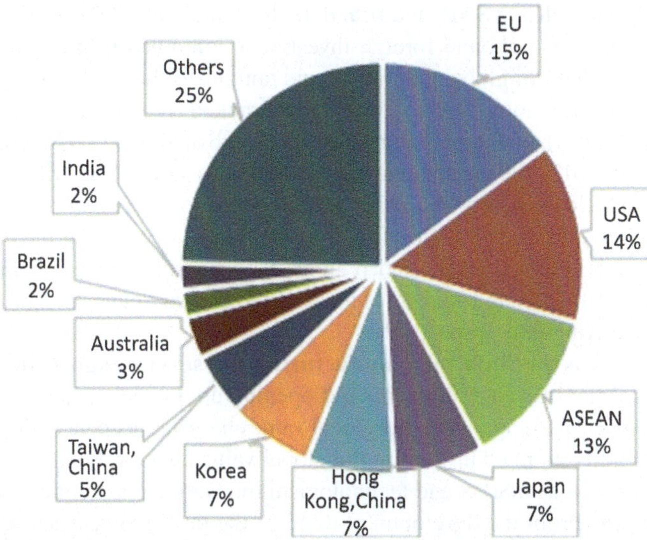

Chart 1 China's Share of Imports and Exports with Major Trading Partners in 2017. *Source* CEIC database

has therefore become the world's largest trading nation. In 1978, China's exports accounted for <1% of the world market. By 2017, this share had grown staggeringly to 12.8%, making China the world's largest exporter. Regarding imports, China's accounted for 10.2% of the world market share in 2017, second only to the United States.[1]

The market covers the whole world. Based on data from 2017, after 40 years of reform and opening up, China's trading partners have grown from 45 in the late 1970s to 31.[2] From the perspective of market distribution, the EU, the United States, ASEAN, Japan, and BRICS countries are currently China's main trading partners. Of these countries, imports and exports to the EU and the United States account for 29.3%[3] of China's total import and export volume. From the perspective of development trends of various markets, China and emerging market countries (particularly "Belt and Road" countries) have seen continual rapid trade growth in recent years. For example, ASEAN's share of China's export market increased from 7.0% in 2000 to 12.5% in 2017, and Africa's share increased from 2.0% in 2000 to 4.1%[4] in 2017 (Chart 1).

China is the largest developing country attracting foreign capital. The top four countries or regions in terms of global FDI inflows in 2017 were the United

[1]The above import and export data are from the World Trade Organization (WTO). China's exports of goods exceeded Germany for the first time in 2009, making China the world's largest exporter.

[2]The data source is IMF Direction of Trade Statistics.

[3]General Administration of Customs data of 2017.

[4]The source of data is the National Bureau of Statistics.

States, China, Hong Kong SAR, and Brazil. In the context of a 23% decline in global FDI in 2017, China's inbound foreign investment continued to grow nonetheless, accounting for 9.53% of global FDI inflow and ranking as the world's second largest FDI destination once more—surpassing the third-ranked Hong Kong SAR by USD32 billion (or 1.3 times), and surpassing fourth-ranked Brazil by USD76.3 billion (2.2 times).[5] As of 2017, the cumulative global FDI was USD31.52 trillion, and the cumulative FDI flowing into China was USD1.49 trillion, accounting for 4.73% of global cumulative FDI and ranking fourth in the world. Comparing the cumulative FDI with the top four countries and regions, China's cumulative inbound FDI is equivalent to 19.1, 75.8, and 95.4%[6] of those of the United States, Hong Kong SAR, and the United Kingdom, respectively.

China serves as the "hub" of manufacturing and service exports in the global value chain. After 40 years of reform and opening up, China's manufacturing and service industries' participation in the global value chain has deepened. Furthermore, China has steadily climbed upward in the global value chain, relying on supporting capabilities as well as market and technological innovation capabilities to serve the global economy. From the development trend of the past two decades, we can see that the international competitive advantage of China's labor-intensive industries has begun to gradually decline, while the international competitiveness of capital and technology-intensive manufacturing has increased significantly. China has become the world's largest supplier of intermediate goods, playing a key role of "hub"[7] in the global value chain.

Chinese multinational companies have stood out in global competition. By the end of 2016, a total of 24,000 Chinese-invested enterprises had established 37,000 foreign direct investment enterprises abroad. At the end of the year, the total number of employees working for these overseas enterprises was 2.865 million, of which 1.343 million were foreigners. The total amount of taxes paid by Chinese companies invested in domestic and overseas countries and regions was nearly USD30 billion.[8] In terms of industry distribution, the manufacturing, wholesale, and retail industries are the most developed industries for foreign direct investment in China, accounting for about 60% of the total enterprises taking part in such investment. From the perspective of traffic, state-owned enterprises directly under the central government are no longer the main force for foreign direct investment, accounting for only 0.7% of the total. Geographically, enterprises established in Asia account for 55.8% of the total number of foreign-invested enterprises, followed by those established in North America and Europe, accounting for 15.2% and 11.3%, respectively.

[5]United Nations Organization for Trade and Development (UNCATD) [1]; Ministry of Commerce, National Statistics of the People's Republic of China Bureau, State Administration of Foreign Exchange [2], Ministry of Commerce, National Bureau of Statistics, State Administration of Foreign Exchange [3].

[6]United Nations Organization for Trade and Development (UNCATD) [1]; the People's Republic of China.

[7]Zhang and Zhai [4].

[8]Ministry of Commerce of the People's Republic of China [5].

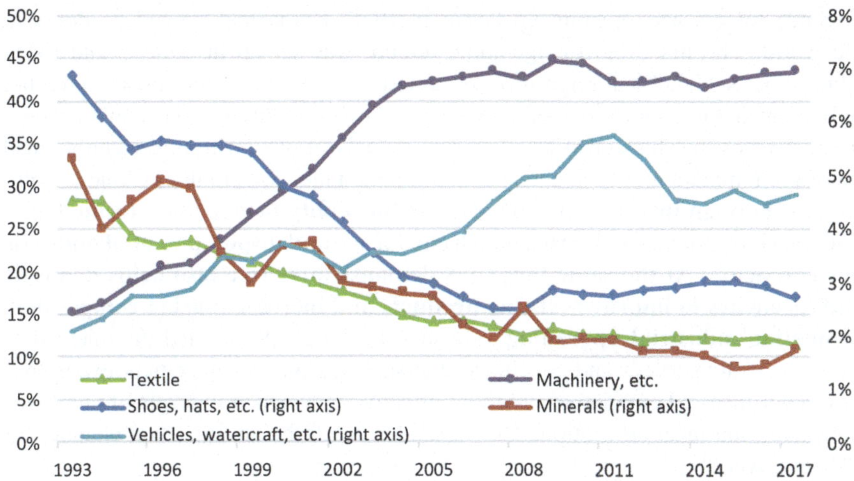

Chart 2 Major products' shares of Chinese exports. *Source* CEIC database, authors' calculation

(b) China has achieved industrial upgrading in the process of opening up

The literature on FDI spillover effects indicates that the technology brought by foreign companies may bring about negative extrusion effects[9] as well as positive upgrade effects. In the case of China, per capita GDP in 2017 was only 27%[10] of that of the United States. In the past 40 years, especially during the early stages of reform and opening up, there was a huge technological gap between China and developed countries such as the United States. In the process of trade and cooperative management with developed countries, there has been a significant spillover effect of technology.

In just four decades, the structures of the Chinese economy have undergone profound changes. In the 1980s, the structure of China's export goods transformed from predominantly primary products to industrially manufactured products. In the 1990s, there was another transformation from light textile products to mechanical and electrical products. **Since the beginning of the 21st century, the percentage of high-tech products represented by electronics and information technology has continued to grow. From 1985 to 2017, China's exports of mechanical and electrical products increased from USD1.68 billion to USD1.32 trillion—an increase of 785 times or an average annual growth rate of 23.2%—and the share of these exports within the global market increased from negligible to more than 17%**, while they came to account for 58.4% of the country's total exports. In the same period, the proportion of high-tech products in China's exports increased from 2 to 28.8% (Chart 2).[11]

[9] Javorcik [6].

[10] Calculated according to purchasing power parity.

[11] The data source is the CEIC database.

Since reform and opening up began in 1978, China has opened its doors to the world. The first Sino-foreign joint venture was set up in 1980,[12] and today China boasts 505,000 foreign-invested enterprises.[13] These enterprises have not only created value and provided employment in China through their own production activities, but have also acted as role models in demonstrating technological innovation, market management, and institutional innovation to their Chinese counterparts. **Foreign-invested enterprises have the ability to bring new technologies and novel organizational forms which encourage and inspire potential domestic entrepreneurs. At the same time, this demonstrative role also helps domestic entrepreneurs to improve existing products and increase market competition, promoting industrial upgrading.**[14] In fact, Liu et al. [9] studied the micro-data from corporate surveys and concluded that start-ups with management experience in foreign-invested enterprises are more effectively designed in terms of employee incentives and legal arbitration. They consider this to be an important channel for FDI spillovers.[15]

For example, Chinese construction machinery is an industry that has flourished during opening up and has thus achieved production upgrades. After years of study, borrowing, absorption, and independent innovation, China's construction machinery has achieved a dominant position, an improved rate of self-sufficiency, and advanced global service capabilities. By 2016, China's construction machinery industry exported goods worth USD17 billion. Ten engineering machinery enterprises have made their way onto the list of the world's top 50 strongest in engineering machinery, and their technological innovation capabilities are improving every day.[16]

In addition to their demonstrative role, foreign-invested enterprises in China have also driven the country's related supporting enterprises to grow through supply chain expansion. They have also promoted enterprise development and industrial upgrading through the process of joining the global industrial chain and integrating into the global market. For example, Fuyao Glass, Yanfeng Decoration, and Shanghai Changhui have all invested and built factories in the United States under the leadership of GM and Volkswagen. They have also provided R&D and production of supporting

[12]On May 3, 1980, Beijing Aviation Food Co., Ltd. was established. This is the first joint venture in China. The registration number of the State Administration for Industry and Commerce is "001", and people aptly called it "Tianzi No. 1". For details, please refer to: Li [7].

[13]Data are from the National Bureau of Statistics data for "number of foreign-invested enterprises (households)" as of the end of 2016.

[14]Li and Liu [8].

[15]Liu et al. [9].

[16]From 2001 to 2016, China's construction machinery industry won one first prize of National Science and Technology Progress Award, four second prizes; two second prizes of National Technology Invention Award; one top prize for industrial science and technology, 25 first prizes, 101 second prizes, and 174 third prizes. For details, please refer to the Ministry of Commerce of the People's Republic of China [5].

components for their own customers in the United States.[17] China's parts and components companies have followed the investment of foreign-invested manufacturers into mature markets, providing favorable conditions for further in-depth participation in vehicle design and development while also strengthening supply efficiency and market service capabilities. Chinese component companies have also improved themselves through this process. The competitiveness of Chinese enterprises has gradually advanced—they have built brand influence and achieved industrial upgrading.

In the process of opening up, Chinese enterprises have entered high value-added industries and improved their international competitiveness by acquiring high-quality assets in developed countries while learning their advanced management models. In this process, Chinese investment has also injected momentum into the economic development of host countries and created a substantial number of jobs. For example, Northern Heavy Industries successfully acquired Germany's Wirth Holding/France's NFM, which enabled the company to gain huge technological advantages in TBM manufacturing and help China's TBM industry achieve industrial upgrading.[18] In another example, the acquisition of Australian architectural firm John Holland by China Communications Construction Co., Ltd. significantly improved the latter's competitiveness in infrastructure upstream design.[19] Furthermore, COFCO acquired the equity of international food trading giant Nidera to enhance its position in the international food trade value chain.[20]

At the same time, over the past four decades, Chinese government officials, entrepreneurs, students, and workers have continued to study and absorb knowledge from around the world. Beginning with the four high-level delegations of the Central Committee of the Communist Party of China in 1978, batches of official delegations and students began to go abroad, bringing back advanced concepts of economic and social development from around the world when they returned. In combination with China's actual national conditions, this spurred economic development and social reform. **From the beginning of reform and opening up to the end of 2017, a total of 5,194,900 persons have gone abroad to study, of which 3,740,800 have completed their studies, and 3,132,000 have opted to return to China afterward—a return rate of 83.73%[21] for graduates**. In this process of learning, borrowing, absorbing, and innovating, the Chinese people have devoted themselves to the tide of economic globalization and have continuously moved forward.

---

[17] After the integration of the interior business of Yanfeng's and Johnson Controls' interior business, it became the world's largest supplier of interior parts, with plants in Kansas and Tennessee, USA, providing interior products for some models of GM and Volkswagen.

[18] Jiang [10].

[19] Smith and Mi [11].

[20] China Securities Network [12].

[21] Zhang [13].

2. **China's process of opening up has also benefited the world economy**

Since reform and opening up, China's low-cost, scale-based production factors have combined with international capital and technology to rapidly form a strong production capacity, become deeply integrated into the global industrial and value chains, and promote world economic growth. China has been an important contributor to the world's economic development. The opened Chinese market has not only grown into the world's largest consumer market, but also the second largest FDI destination country in the world after the United States. The companies which have invested in China have shared huge growth dividends as China's economy has rapidly grown. **Statistics indicate that in the 16 years after China's accession to the WTO alone, the total cumulative profits of foreign-invested enterprises plus enterprises invested in by businessmen from Hong Kong, Macao, and Taiwan exceeded RMB15.57 trillion (close to the GDP of the UK in 2017, denominated in RMB).**[22] At the same time, with the deepening of economic globalization and value chain internationalization, **the scale advantage of China's basic manufacturing industries has gradually become prominent, demonstrating strong supporting capabilities and competitiveness in parts processing, production, and assembly. These capabilities have consistently driven down the production costs of the world's manufacturing industries, promoted competition, and improved the economic welfare of consumers around the world**.

(a) **Direct contributions to economic and trade cooperation**

From the perspective of trade, the developing Chinese economy has become the world's largest sales market for goods. In 2017, China's total imports and exports of goods reached USD4.1 trillion, ranking first in the world. Furthermore, China's total imports and exports of services reached USD695.68 billion, ranking second in the world.[23] In the 40 years of reform and opening up, China imported a total of RMB21.78 trillion worth of goods from abroad[24]—it has become the largest trading partner of more than 120 countries and regions in the world. During the 20 years since accession to the WTO, China has continuously widened its opening up to the outside world and actively integrated itself into economic globalization, becoming an important engine for world economic growth (Charts 3 and 4).

The opening of the Chinese market has created the largest single market in the world. In recent years, with the adjustment of China's economic structure and industrial upgrading, the demand of the Chinese economy within the world market has gradually migrated upstream. Regarding the categories of China's imported products, the proportion of mechanical and electrical products and high-tech products has steadily increased, which has brought growth momentum in particular to developed countries in the high-end industrial chains complementary to China's industries.

[22]Referring to the 16 years from 2001 to 2016, and the total profit data come from the National Bureau of Statistics of China.

[23]Data from the World Trade Organization (WTO).

[24]Data from the National Bureau of Statistics of China.

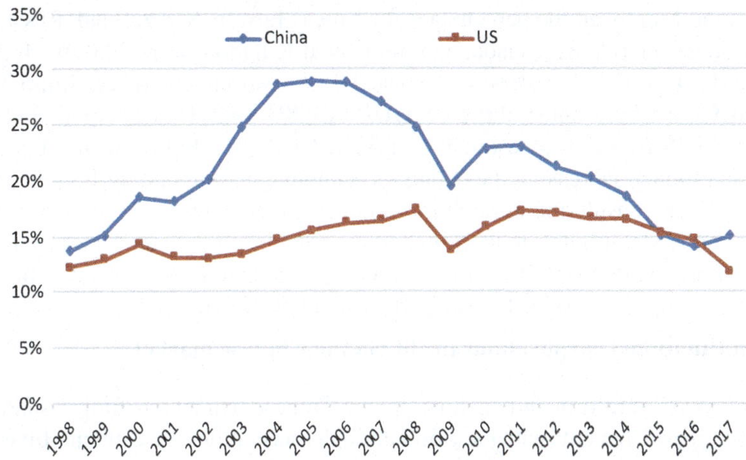

Chart 3 Imports as a percentage of GDP: the US vs. China. *Source* CEIC database, authors' calculations

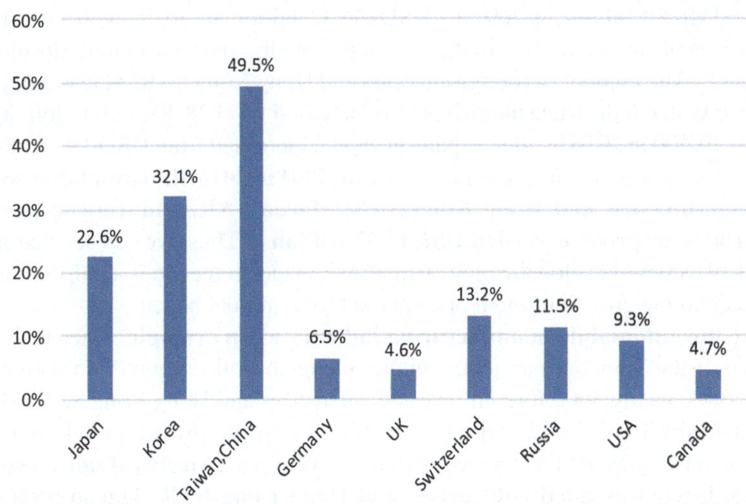

Chart 4 Exports to China as a percentage of total exports. *Source* CEIC database, authors' calculations

Regarding the regional distribution of imported products, China imports the most from Asian countries, followed by the European Union and North America.

In the 40 years of reform and opening up, the developing Chinese economy has driven the export markets of its trading partners, who have shared the benefits of China's economic growth through trade. Take the data from 2016, for example: the products sold to China accounted for 22.59% of Japan's total exports for the year. Moreover, the percentages for Korea, Taiwan, Switzerland, Russia, the United States, Germany, Canada, and the United Kingdom were 32.09%, 49.53%, 12.15%, 11.45%, 9.27%, 6.45%, 4.7%, and 4.57%, respectively. **It is estimated that imports from China boosted the US GDP by 0.8% in 2015.** US exports to China and China/US two-way investment contributed USD216 billion to the US gross domestic product, increasing the country's economic growth rate by 1.2 percentage points.[25] Even considering agricultural products alone, China is a top-five trading partner of 46 federal states in the United States, and on average, an American farmer exports more than USD10,000 of agricultural products to China annually. In 2016, China was a top-five service trading partner of all 50 US states.[26]

(b) **Multinational corporations profit via the Chinese market**

In the 40 years of reform and opening up, the Chinese market has further shared its economic growth benefits with the world through transnational investment. **Investors from abroad, Hong Kong SAR, Macao SAR, and Taiwan have gained access to a huge market and reaped rich profits from the "growth miracle" of the Chinese economy**. Since reform and opening up, foreign direct investment (FDI) in China has continued to expand. Especially after joining the WTO, the scale of FDI has increased from USD46.88 billion in 2001 to USD136.32 billion in 2017, with an average annual growth rate of 6.9%—ranked second globally and first among developing countries.[27] The number of foreign-invested and Hong Kong SAR, Macao SAR, and Taiwan-invested industrial enterprises also increased from 28,400 before joining the WTO to 59,600 in 2016, while the paid-in capital increased from USD0.91 trillion to USD5.23 trillion in the same time period. **From 2001 to 2016, the cumulative profits of foreign-invested and Hong Kong SAR, Macao SAR, and Taiwan-invested industrial enterprises exceeded USD15.57 trillion.**[28] Thus, we can see that in the context of economic globalization, China has made tremendous contributions to global economic growth through open markets and mutual benefit.

Take the automobile manufacturing industry as an example. Since the establishment of the Sino-German joint venture Shanghai Volkswagen Automotive Co., Ltd. in 1984, nearly 3000 foreign-invested enterprises and Hong Kong SAR, Macao SAR, and Taiwan-invested enterprises have been established by automobile manufacturers including GM, BMW, Mercedes-Benz, and Toyota. **In terms of sales revenues in 2015, foreign-invested enterprises and Hong Kong SAR, Macao SAR, and Taiwan-invested enterprises accounted for 47.50% of the whole industry—nearly half of the total.**[29] **In terms of sales volume, the sales of joint venture**

---

[25] Press Office of the People's Republic of China [14].

[26] US China Business Council [15].

[27] Data from the Ministry of Commerce of China.

[28] Referring to the 16 years from 2001 to 2016, and the total profit data come from the National Bureau of Statistics of China.

[29] According to the data of China Association of Automobile Manufacturers in 2015, there were 13,431 enterprises in China's automobile manufacturing industry, including 131 Chinese enterprises, 78 collective enterprises, 53 contractual stock enterprises, 334 joint-stock enterprises, 6790

vehicles accounted for more than 60% of the market share (in 2017, more than 24 million vehicles were sold in China, of which the sales of German, Japanese, American, Korean, and French brands were 5.4 million, 4.55 million, 3.06 million, 1.2 million, and 485,000, respectively). The top three automakers in the United States made a total profit of USD7.44 billion through joint ventures in China in 2015.[30] General Motors alone has 10 joint ventures in China, and in 2017, its production in China accounted for 40% of its global production. In the same year, BMW sold 594,400 vehicles in China, accounting for 24.13% of its global sales. BMW Brilliance, a joint venture set up by BMW in China, sold 366,500 vehicles in 2017 and realized profits of RMB10.475 billion for the year. Since its establishment 15 years ago, BMW Brilliance has sold an aggregate of more than 1,956,800 vehicles in China.[31] In contrast, although some in the United States believe that foreign brand vehicles strongly impact the domestic market, the market share of GM, Chrysler, and Ford in the domestic market reached 68% in 2000 and stood at 45% in 2014.[32]

In recent years, as China's automobile consumer market has upgraded and the domestic business environment has improved, multinational automakers with favorable profits have increased their investments in China. Take BMW (China) for example: in May 2018, the company announced that it would cooperate with Great Wall Motor and invest RMB5.1 billion to build a pure electric MINI car in Jiangsu. In October, BMW (China) further announced that it would continue cooperating with Brilliance Auto and invest RMB30 billion in Shenyang Tiexi to build the Phase III Project of the Tiexi Plant.

Over the 40 years of reform and opening up, China has developed into an important market and profit growth point for high-tech enterprises and service firms in developed countries. On this topic, the Ministry of Commerce issued *The Facts and China's Position on China–US Trade Friction*,[33] which provides a detailed account of this phenomenon: "Qualcomm's income from chip sales and patent royalties in China accounted for 57% of its total revenue. Intel's revenues in China (including the Hong Kong region) accounted for 23.6% of its total revenue. In FY 2017, revenues from Greater China accounted for 19.5% of the Apple Inc. total. By January 2017, 13 American banks had subsidiaries or branches and 10 American insurance companies had insurance firms in China. Goldman Sachs, American Express, Bank of America, MetLife, and other American financial institutions have reaped handsome returns from their strategic investment in Chinese financial institutions. According to the China Securities Regulatory Commission, American investment banks were lead underwriters or co-lead underwriters on 70% of the

---

private enterprises, and 2888 enterprises invested in by foreign businessmen and businessmen from Hong Kong, Macao, and Taiwan.

[30]Press Office of the People's Republic of China [16].

[31]The above includes sales data for BMW, MINI, and Rolls Royce. The data comes from the BMW Group and Brilliance Group Annual Report. BMW Brilliance set up production in Shenyang, Liaoning, China in 2003. Currently, it has two factories in Tiexi and Dadong in Shenyang. BMW Brilliance has 50% investment in both the Brilliance Group and BMW (China).

[32]Kim [17].

[33]Press Office of the People's Republic of China [14].

funds raised by Chinese companies in their overseas IPOs and refinancing. US law firms have set up about 120 offices in China. Trade and economic cooperation have also created a large number of jobs in the US. According to a US–China Business Council estimate, in 2015, US exports to China and US–China two-way investment supported 2.6 million jobs in America. Specifically, Chinese investment covered 46 states of the US, generating more than 140,000 jobs for US citizens, most of them in manufacturing."

(c) **Reducing manufacturing costs and promoting market competition**

In the process of opening up and integrating into the world economy, the Chinese economy has demonstrated tremendous competitiveness. **Part of this competitiveness comes from the cost advantage of production factors such as labor and land, and more importantly, from economies of scale in Chinese manufacturing**. Take smart phone parts as an example: a smart phone needs more than 30 micro-screws, and the manufacturers of these precision parts are mainly concentrated in the Pearl River Delta and Yangtze River Delta. The industry is mainly comprised of three to four large Tier 1 suppliers and more than 100 smaller Tier 2 suppliers. One of them is Shanghai Dedao Heshou Precision Machinery Manufacturing Co., Ltd., which is a secondary supplier of collaborative production, and thus its production costs cannot be sufficiently reduced to achieve profitability unless daily output reaches the scale of 2 million micro-screws (on the premise of assured production accuracy and non-magnetic specifications). In another example, the production costs of disposable lighters[34] and perfume bottle nozzles have been reduced precisely because Chinese companies, relying on economies of scale, have joined the world market. Suzhou producers supply 90% of all the world's stable and low-priced perfumes bottle nozzles—perfume bottle nozzles for Dior, Chanel, and other famous brands are purchased there. In the field of basic manufacturing, economies of scale in China have greatly enhanced the manufacturing capacity of parts and components, thereby significantly reducing production costs, promoting market competition, and further entrenching the advantages of China's manufacturing industry.

In economic and trade cooperation with China, multinational firms from developed countries have enhanced their international competitiveness by integrating the advantages of both countries. For example, Apple designs and develops mobile phones in the United States, has them assembled and manufactured in China, and sells them in the global market. **Although some mercantilist leaders, represented by President Trump, want manufacturing to return to the United States, it is estimated that if all the assembled production were to be done in the United States, the production cost of Apple's mobile phones would increase by 37%.**[35] As the theory of international trade posits, as a whole, developed countries have suffered no loss in the division of labor with China. **China relies on strong supporting capabilities to undertake production links in the global industrial chain, enabling developed countries (especially the United States) to focus on design, market research,**

[34]A disposable lighter sold at RMB1 consists of 6–7 parts.

[35]Goldman Sachs Equity Research, 2017, *Made in the USA…or China?* March 26, 2017.

and other fields. Meanwhile, China continuously upgrades in high value-added fields such as manufacturing and service industries to further improve national strength.

China's opening has promoted global competition and industrial upgrading in developed countries. Since fulfilling its commitment to join the World Trade Organization in 2001, China has taken the initiative to expand market opening and promote market competition through unilateral tax reduction. Upon joining the World Trade Organization, the Chinese government began making great efforts to promote China's full integration into the international economic system. Since 2001, the Chinese central government has cleared more than 2300 laws and regulations to facilitate this, while local governments have cleared more than 190,000 relevant local policies and regulations. The overall tariff level dropped from 15.3% in 2001 to 9.8% in 2015, the same year that the trade-weighted average tariff rate fell to 4.4%—significantly lower than emerging economies and developing countries including South Korea, India, and Indonesia, and close to the rates of the United States (2.4%) and the European Union (3%). Among the 160 service sub-sectors defined by the WTO, China has promised to open 100 of them, falling slightly short of 108, the average number of opened sub-sectors by developed country members. Today, China has improved its business environment and services through 12 free trade zones, which can be regarded as further efforts to draw upon foreign experience and expertise.[36]

(d) Contributing to an increase in global consumer welfare

China's opening up has brought tangible benefits to consumers around the world. International trade has enriched consumer choices, reduced the cost of living, and enhanced the actual purchasing power of people around the world, especially low- and middle-income groups. **In fact, the US–China Business Council and the Oxford Research Institute jointly found that without trade with China, the average annual household expenditure of American families would increase by USD850, or 1.5% of the average annual household income.**[37]

China's opening up has not only promoted global economic growth and improved consumer welfare but also reduced global inflation. As is stated in *The Facts and China's Position on China–US Trade Friction*,[38] estimates from a joint study by the US–China Trade National Committee and the Oxford Research Institute show that "Value-for-money products from China drove down prices for American consumers, and in 2015 for example, reduced the consumer price index by 1–1.5% points. A low inflation environment has created much room for expansionary macroeconomic policies in the US."

[36]Based on the Press Office of the People's Republic of China [14, 18].

[37]Oxford Economics and US–China Business Council [19].

[38]Press Office of the People's Republic of China [14].

(e) Protectionism in the process of industrialization in the United Kingdom, the United States, and Germany: A comparison

In recent times, there have been some doubts and even accusations voiced against China in the international arena. Some from major developed countries such as the United States believe that China's opening process has been slow and has taken "advantage" of the world, especially developed countries. **However, if we survey the development history of major world powers, it is clear that this accusation is unfair. The United Kingdom, the United States, Germany, and other major countries all experienced long periods of "protectionism" during their industrialization**. This point is explained in detail by Li et al. [20].[39]

The United Kingdom strictly protected its industries before the 1850s. Until the repeal of the Corn Laws in 1846, import tariffs on agricultural products were very high. Before the Navigation Acts were laid to rest in 1849, shipping of colonial goods was restricted to ships owned and made by the United Kingdom or its colonies. Furthermore, trade and tariff restrictions were not abolished until around 1860. Even Adam Smith agreed with the high tariffs in industries such as ship building and national defense in *The Wealth of Nations*.[40] Moreover, Britain's foreign trade also included a significant amount of colonial trade—its plundering of the colonies is all too well-known.[41]

The United States had a more closed market prior to World War II. In the first 20 years of the 20th century, exports accounted for only 6–7% of the total national income of the United States, far lower than the level of 20–30% in Europe during the same period. In 1861, the average tariff rate on imported goods was increased to 47% and remained above 40% until World War I.[42] In 1930, the Smoot-Hawley Tariff Act passed, which provoked a trade war between the United States and Europe, causing losses on both sides. The US import and export volume plummeted by more than 50%, aggravating the economic disaster of the Great Depression.

Germany also had a strong protectionist tendency before World War I. In June 1879, Germany introduced a new tariff law which imposed import duties on leather, paper, and other products. The German government further adjusted tariffs twice in 1885 and 1887—the tariff rate of agricultural products in 1887 was five times that of 1879.[43]

As a big country with a population of 1.3 billion, China has gone from a poor country to a key player in the world economy in just 40 years. Through its deepening reforms, China has continuously promoted the process of opening up to the outside world. While integrating into the world economy, China has also shared with the

---

[39] Li et al. [20].

[40] For details, see Chap. 2 of Book 4 of *The Wealth of Nations*, "Of Restraints upon the Importation from Foreign Countries of such Goods as can be Produced at Home."

[41] According to Maddison [21], the total population of the British Empire was 412 million, ten times the population of the British islands. Maddison [21].

[42] Hughes and Cain [22].

[43] Guo and Guo [23].

world the historic opportunities associated with its economic development to stimulate global growth and improve global consumer welfare. In the process, China has also managed to avoid exporting an economic crisis to the world as others have done. The sharp contrast between China's sharing nature and "win-win" approach to opening up versus the "beggar-thy-neighbor" approach adopted by traditional powers in their developmental history is certainly thought-provoking.

3. **The Chinese government has mitigated the shocks of globalization by helping revive "Chinese Detroits"**

Since the regional and industrial distributions of the benefits and costs of opening up are often extremely uneven, damaged industries and regions frequently suffer enormous pain. As such, the government should coordinate various policy tools to help relevant economic subjects survive these difficulties. **In the process of opening up, many regions and industries in China have been greatly affected. Fortunately, the Chinese government has played an important role in helping related industries, regional enterprises, and workers transform, allowing them to cope with the negative effects of opening up**.

The developmental history of Shenyang—the Chinese Detroit—since the 1990s is a good case in point. After the establishment of the PRC in 1945, Shenyang became the vanguard of China's industrial economy. It boasted an industrial base built during Japanese occupation, followed by Soviet aid. **In 1981, the total output value of heavy industry in Liaoning Province ranked first in the country, accounting for 11.5% of the national total. The total industrial output value ranked third in the country, behind only Shanghai and Jiangsu.[44] The area was also a hotbed for innovation—37 large enterprises in Tiexi District of Shenyang created 350 "firsts of the country"** including the first transformer, the first air compressor, the first automatic electrical switch, the first metal cutting lathe, the first cable steel core aluminum stranded wire, the first industrial valves, the first aircraft tire, and more.[45] The three major machine tool factories in Shenyang (First Machine Tool, Third Machine Tool, and the Sino-Czech Friendship) were selected as members of the elite 18 expert factories of the machine tool industry and won the National Quality Gold Award three times in the 1980s.[46] According to a former leader of Shenyang, the city boasted a complete industrial system, hosting 146 industries out of a total of 165 in the country. Together with Beijing, Tianjin, and Shanghai, Shenyang was a barometer of China's economy. These cities were collectively dubbed "Beijing–Tianjin–Shanghai–Shenyang." In the context of unified purchasing and marketing, Shenyang's large-scale enterprise products sold well in China. According to one employee, "unable to buy [the products], certain enterprises were anxious to find people with more power in order to buy through the backdoor. Sometimes we would squeeze one out from the production line."[47]

---

44 China Bureau of Statistics [24].

45 Shenyang Tourism Commission [25].

46 Shenyang Machine Tool (Group) Co., Ltd. [26].

47 Wang [27].

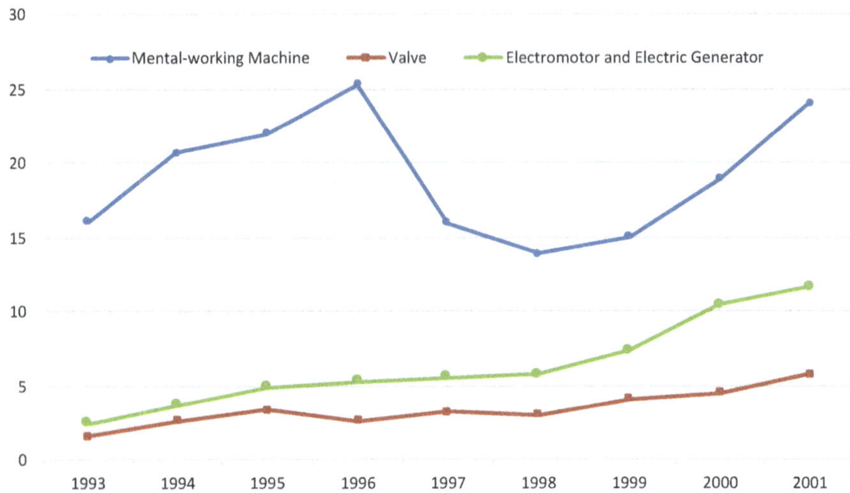

Chart 5 Imports in the equipment manufacturing industry (USD100 million). *Source* CEIC database

As China opened in the 1990s, import tariffs on machine tools fell to 9.7% in 1994 (ahead of schedule) and tariffs on CNC systems fell to 5%.[48] **With the gradual reduction of tariff barriers in the field of equipment manufacturing, imported equipment began to increase substantially in quantity. In 1996, the value of imported metal processing machine tools, valves, motors, and generators were 1.57, 1.58, and 2.08 times of those in 1993, respectively**.[49] The imported products ushered in by China's opening have strongly impacted the industrial enterprises in Shenyang. A former employee of Shenyang Machine Tool Plant indicated in our survey that large domestic enterprises began to use imported machine tools in large quantities after opening up, severely squeezing the market. At the same time, with the deepening of "loans in lieu of grants" reforms, the financial costs of these enterprises surged. **Under the combined effects of these factors, Shenyang industrial enterprises suffered extensive losses**. The Sino-Czech Friendship Factory, formerly one of the top 18 machine tool factories, only had RMB5,000 available for disposal in 1997 and was unable to pay wages for half a year.[50] Wang Tiefeng, former Chairman of Shenyang Heavy Machinery Group, said that at that time, corporate debt was heavy—the sum of financial debts, operating debts, and corporate bonds reached RMB1.5 billion, and wages and debts of employees exceeded RMB100 million. In 1997–2001, it was basically impossible to pay full wages to employees. During the most difficult years, actual paid wages were as low as RMB200 per month (Chart 5).[51]

[48]Customs Tariff Commission of the State Council of the People's Republic of China [28], State Council Tariff Commission of the State Council [29].

[49]Data are from the CEIC China Economic Database, ACCEPT calculation.

[50]Wang [27].

[51]Yan [30].

In addition to the business difficulties brought by opening up, there were also a series of social problems. At the end of 1996, 2.06 million people were employed by state-owned and collective enterprises in Shenyang. By 2000, this figure had fallen to 1.46 million, with nearly 600,000 workers laid off.[52] The Tiexi District, an area of 700,000 residents where industrial enterprises were the most concentrated, became a "vacation resort" as residents were left without jobs. As previously mentioned, under the traditional system, employees of state-owned enterprises earned lower wages and had less savings, as pensions, medical care, and housing were covered by the employers. At that time, there was no mature social insurance system like those in Western countries, and employees were not well prepared to withstand risks. According to a government official then in charge of social securities in the Municipal Bureau of Finance, many senior workers were bought out of office at a rate of RMB800 per person per year of employment. Meanwhile, laid-off workers blocked the government almost every day, and sometimes even blocked the city's railways.

In order to effectively alleviate the enormous social and economic impact of reform and opening up, the Shenyang local government persevered through many challenges and made every effort to achieve a smooth transition for the economy and provide relief to the people. One initiative was to allocate funds from China's already depleted finances to cover the basic security of laid-off workers. In 1990, municipal insurance welfare costs in Shenyang were RMB709 million—increasing to RMB1.87 billion by 1996 and RMB4.47 billion by 2000—while the municipal budgetary income for the year 2000 was merely RMB6.11 billion.[53] During this time, the Shenyang government was also working hard to solve the problem of unemployment through means such as hiring laid-off workers in the government's public welfare departments and providing VAT discounts for laid-off workers to set up individual enterprises.[54] **Another local government initiative was the "Moving to the East, Constructing the West" Program in Tiexi District, which organized the collective relocation of large-scale enterprises to the suburbs in order to vacate land in the heart of the city for the development of the service industry**. This program both created employment and enabled enterprises to use gains from land appreciation for technological transformation and upgrading. In our survey, we learned that the income from land swaps alone reached RMB26 billion. Today, Tiexi District clean and tidy, bustling with high-rise buildings and bright lights.

Compared to the rise and fall of Detroit—an industrial city in the United States—the impact of opening up on China's old industrial areas like Shenyang has been less severe. According to the US Bureau of Labor Statistics (BLS), the

[52]Shenyang Municipal Bureau of Statistics [31].

[53]Shenyang Municipal Bureau of Statistics [31].

[54]According to the document *Shen-Guo-Shui-Fa [2003] No. 63:* the starting point for sales of goods is raised from 800 yuan for non-preferential to 5000 yuan; the starting point for sales of taxable services is raised from 200 yuan for non-preferential to 3000 yuan; The threshold for paying taxes on a per-time basis is raised from 50 yuan per non-preferential (day) sales to 200 yuan.

highest number of unemployed people in the Detroit metropolitan area during the financial crisis (2009) was 323,000, and the increase in unemployment over the four-year period of 2005–2009 was 174,000. This figure is only 1/4 of the increase in the number of unemployed people in Shenyang in 1996–2000. However, Shenyang was able to avoid devolving into a "ghost town," thanks in large part to government initiatives. For more details, see the first part of this report.

The Chinese film industry is another example of an industry that experienced pressure from foreign products during reform and opening up. At the beginning of opening up, China's film industry had achieved a relatively good foundation. There were seven film factories, including Xiamen Fuda, Shantou Gongyuan, Wuxi Aermei, Shanghai Ganguang, Tianjin Ganguang, Liaoyuan Film, and Baoding Lucky, in addition to some Kodak and Fujifilm production lines, which were introduced at a huge expense. While Chinese companies were busy with technological transformation, Kodak and Fujifilm easily took the lead in the market. During this time, **Fujifilm's price in China was about 50% of its price in Japan, and Kodak's price in China was 30% of its price in the United States. The market share of Fujifilm in China was up to 48% at its highest, while that of the domestic film leader, Lucky, was only 20%**. Eventually, the Chinese government approved Kodak's acquisition of the entire Chinese film industry. Under the "98 Agreement," the seven companies of China's film industry all established joint ventures with Kodak.[55]

In addition to the direct impact of imported goods, the impact of trade friction was also enormous. In the 1980s, the textile industry developed rapidly, causing the export quantity to rise accordingly. For a time, countries all over the world were investing in the construction of textile factories. **However, in the mid-1990s, the United States and Europe introduced protectionist policies to restrict Chinese textile imports**. In his negotiations with the United States, Premier Zhu Rongji said, "in the past few years, due to the discriminatory attitude of the United States, such a large textile exporting country as China has fallen behind Mexico and Canada, and can hardly hold the third place in the world. We had to destroy 10 million spindles and 1.2 million people lost their jobs, which caused us great difficulties. Now, the greatest challenge for state-owned enterprises is how to deal with textile enterprises…the spindles are destroyed, the factories are closed, and we have managed to resettle 1.2 million laid-off workers, but the government has spent a great deal of money on it."[56]

Corroborating Zhu Rongji's speech, data indicates that **the United States imposed sanctions on the textile industry three times from 1994 to 1996**. In 1996, the United States applied the "triple penalties" clause for the first time and cut its quota by USD19 million.[57] **During this year, the rapid growth of China's textile exports began to slow down markedly, with the growth rate falling from 35% in 1994 to −17% in 1996.**[58] In 1995, the number of loss-making enterprises in the textile industry reached 8728, an increase of 37% from 1994. Total profits

---

[55] Wang [32], Fu and Yuan [33].

[56] Zhu [34].

[57] Anonymous [35].

[58] Data from CEIC database.

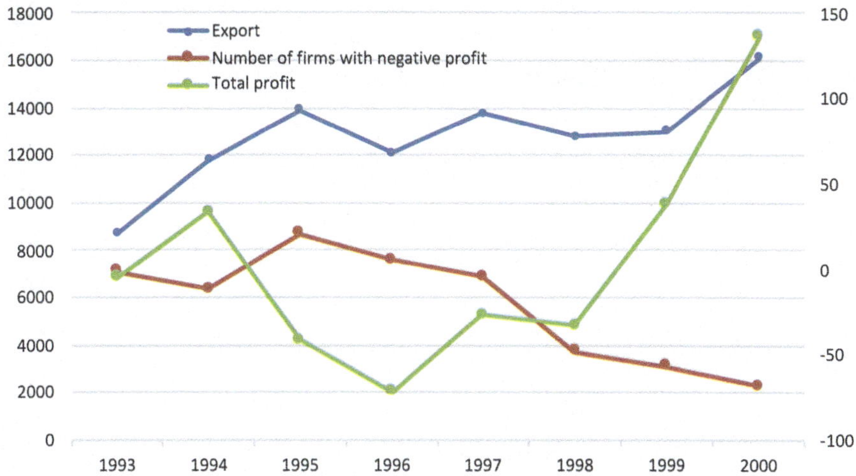

Chart 6 Textile industry exports (USD million), loss-making enterprises (number), total profit (RMB100 million, right axis). *Data Source* CEIC, authors' calculation

also plummeted from RMB3.4 billion in 1994 to RMB −7.1 billion in 1996. Despite many other objective disadvantages such as aging equipment and low production efficiency, trade restrictions were undoubtedly an important factor leading to the further collapse of the textile industry.

Facing such adversities, the central government was determined to dispose of a number of inefficient enterprises, and thus began to carry out the "destruction of spindles" operation. The number of textile enterprises decreased from 25,700 in 1995 to 11,300 in 1998, and the number of employees in the textile industry decreased from 9.14 million in 1994 to 5.11 million in 1999.[59] Meanwhile, local governments worked hard to help laid-off textile workers find new jobs. For example, relevant departments of the Shanghai government negotiated with the city's airlines to recruit aircraft attendants from textile factories.[60] Subsequently, the government set about restructuring the remaining companies and revitalizing stock assets. In 2004, the deputy director of the State-owned Assets Supervision and Administration Commission was appointed Chairman and Party Secretary of Shanghai Textile Group, which issued *The Overall Plan for Adjustment, Reform and Development of Shanghai Textile Holdings (Group) Company*. The operating income of Shanghai Textile Group reached RMB51.4 billion in 2016 (Charts 6 and 7).[61]

4. **Since 2008, the opening up process has slowed down in several industries due to various factors**

[59] Data from CEIC database.

[60] Shanghai Local Records Office [36].

[61] Global Textile Network [37], Shanghai Textile Group [38].

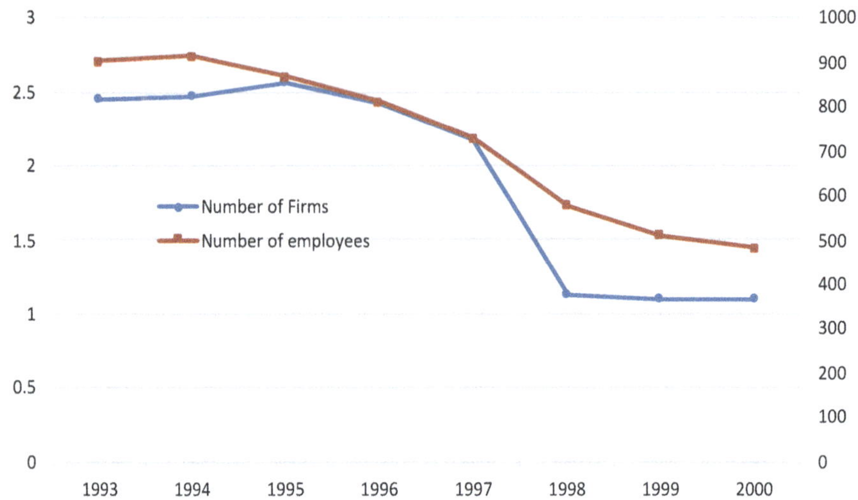

Chart 7 Number of enterprises in the textile industry (thousands), number of employees (10,000 people, right axis). *Data Source* CEIC

As is described in detail in the next section, the Chinese economy underwent substantial adjustment after China joined the WTO, and most of the country's commitments were fulfilled before 2007 (China announced officially that all commitments had been fulfilled in 2010). **However, during the global financial crisis, China faced large external shocks related to exports and capital outflow. This, combined with the vested interests of diversified economic participants, slowed down China's opening up process**. In the automobile industry, both tariffs and the share ceiling for foreign investors in joint ventures were not lowered until April 2018. Similar patterns can be seen in the financial service industry. Foreign banks' share of newly issued loans exhibited a downward sloping trend from 2010 to 2016. Foreign-invested financial institutions, including banks, insurance companies, and securities companies were limited to "small steps forward" during this time, and restrictions were not substantially modified.

However, following the 19th National Congress of the Chinese Communist Party, the pace of opening up accelerated once more. The top leadership of China, including President Xi Jinping, heavily emphasized the importance of continuously opening up. As is detailed in the next section, trade and investment barriers in many industries, including the automobile industry and financial service industry, have been reduced substantially. Many measures originally implemented in the 12 free trade zones to promote and support business activities were later adopted nationwide.

2 Historical Overview

China's opening up to the outside world has not been instant, but has been a process of continuous experimentation, exploration, and deepening. This process has lasted for more than 40 years and continues today, leading China into a more developed future. In this section, we briefly review China's basic course of opening up and further discuss the characteristics of this process.

We are of the view that China's opening up process has passed five milestones. The implementation of the opening up policy in 1979, the opening up of the coastal areas in 1984, the development of a firm socialist market economy in 1992, accession to the World Trade Organization in 2001, and attending the G20 summit following the international financial crisis in 2008.

The process of opening up to the outside world since the 1970s can therefore be divided into the following six stages: (1) importation of whole sets of equipment from 1970 to 1978; (2) exploration of opening up policy from 1979 to 1983; (3) opening up the coastal areas in 1984–1991 to optimize business environment for foreign investors; (4) expanding and deepening of opening up from 1992 to 2000 with the establishment of a market economy system; (5) comprehensive deepening of opening up and integration into the global economic system from 2001 to 2007; (6) participation in global economic governance following the financial crisis to support economic globalization with practical actions.

In the following sections, we will review China's opening up process through data, policies, and leaders' speeches, in conjunction with a large number of case studies. Throughout China's opening, it is clear that the study of the world's advanced institutions, knowledge, and ideas played an important role.

1. **Purchasing whole sets of equipment from 1970 to 1978**

Prior to the official introduction of the reform and opening up policy, the Chinese government had tried to learn advanced production technology by introducing equipment from abroad, and targeted the most developed countries—headed by the United States—from the very beginning. A prime example of this is the "Four Three Program." On February 5, 1972, the Central Committee of the Communist Party of China and the State Council approved the State Development Planning Commission's *Report on the Importation of Complete Sets of Equipment of Chemical Fiber and Fertilizer Technology*. In November 1972 and January 1973, the State Planning Commission again proposed to the State Council to step up the scheme and eventually decided to import USD4.3 billion worth of complete sets of industrial equipment and stand-alone equipment from abroad.[62] Through the "Four Three Program," 26 complete sets of project equipment were imported from developed Western countries such as the United States, the Federal Republic of Germany, France, Japan, the Netherlands, Switzerland, and Italy. The sets were included: 4 sets of large chemical fiber projects with a cumulative investment of RMB6.251

[62] People's Daily Online [39].

billion, located in Tianjin, Shenyang (Liaoning), Shanghai, Changshou (Sichuan), etc.; 3 sets of petrochemical projects, with a total investment of RMB2.718 billion, located in Beijing, Jilin, etc.; 13 large chemical fertilizer projects, with an accumulated investment of RMB3.536 billion, located in Hebei, Liaoning, Heilongjiang, Hubei, Hunan, Sichuan, Guizhou, Yunnan, Jiangsu, Anhui, Guangdong, and Shandong; 3 sets of large-scale power station projects, with an accumulated investment of RMB1.372 billion, located in Tianjin, Hebei, and Inner Mongolia; and 3 sets of steel projects with a total investment of RMB4.21 billion, located in Hubei, Jiangsu, etc.

During this period, China's industrial production increased from USD33.971 billion in 1970 to USD63.787 billion in 1975, with an average annual growth rate of 13.43%.[63] **However, the importation of complete sets of equipment did not change the overall backwardness of China's industrial capabilities.**

2. **Initial Exploration of opening up from 1979 to 1983**

In 1978, the Third Plenary Session of the 11th Central Committee of the Communist Party of China turned the focus of the whole party's work to economic construction. The sporadic import of the aforementioned equipment had not been able to meet the requirements of rapid economic development. **Beginning in 1979, China began to explore the policy of opening up to the outside world through means such as setting up special economic zones, starting to borrow foreign debts, and establishing joint ventures. This serves as the first milestone of China's opening up process.**

Borrowing foreign debts. In 1979, China began to receive foreign loans, beginning with a loan from the Japanese government. On December 5, 1979, the then Japanese Prime Minister Masayoshi Ōhira visited China and pledged to provide China with the first government loan.[64] For 40 years that followed, the Japanese government provided China with a total of about USD45 billion in low-interest and interest-free loans.[65] Meanwhile, **China resumed its representation and membership status in the International Monetary Fund (IMF) and the World Bank (WB)** on April 17, 1980 and May 15, 1980, respectively, allowing the country to begin receiving loans from both organizations.

Setting up joint ventures. On July 1, 1979, the Second Session of the Fifth National People's Congress passed the PRC Sino-Foreign Equity Joint Ventures Law, which provided legal support for the establishment of foreign-invested enterprises. On May 1, 1980, the Foreign Investment Management Committee of the People's Republic of China issued *Foreign Capital Approval No.* 1, approving the establishment of China's first joint venture, Beijing Aviation Food Co., Ltd. The Beijing Administration Bureau of the Civil Aviation Administration of China contributed

---

[63] Source: CEIC database, ACCEPT calculation.

[64] People's Daily Online [40].

[65] Phoenix.com [41], Sohu.com [42].

RMB3 million to the company as capital, holding 51% of the equity, and China Aviation Food Limited, represented by Mr. James Tak Wu of Hong Kong, contributed RMB2.88 million, holding 49% of the equity.[66]

Establishment of special economic zones. On July 15, 1979, the Central Committee of the Communist Party of China and the State Council approved the *Report on the Promotion of Foreign Trade and the Acceleration of Economic Development by Leveraging the Advantageous Conditions of Guangdong* as well as the *Report on the Development of Foreign Trade and the Acceleration of the Socialism Construction in Fujian by Using Capital from Overseas Chinese and Foreign Investors* reports submitted by the Guangdong Provincial Committee of the CPC and the Fujian Provincial Committee of the CPC, respectively. **The reports approved a pilot scheme of special export zones in Shenzhen, Zhuhai, and Shantou of Guangdong Province and Xiamen of Fujian Province**. On August 13, 1979, the State Council issued *Regulations on Vigorously Developing Foreign Trade to Increase Foreign Exchange Income*.[67] **Its main aims were to expand the foreign trade authority of local governments and enterprises, encourage increased exports, and effectively manage export zones, with the primary goal of expanding foreign trade and exports**. On August 23 of the same year, the Central Committee of the Communist Party of China and the State Council formally established **the State Import and Export Management Committee and the State Administration of Foreign Investment**, both headed by Gu Mu, the then Vice Premier of the State Council. On August 26, 1980, the Central Committee of the Communist Party of China and the State Council **decided to rename the four special export zones of Shenzhen, Zhuhai, Shantou, and Xiamen as special economic zones**. Special economic zones enjoy preferential treatment in terms of investment project approval, foreign trade, and business operations. They also benefit from **preferential policies and flexible measures on taxation, land use, and immigration for foreign investors**. In 1983, in order to promote the development of Hainan, the Central Committee of the Communist Party of China approved the *Summary of the Issues Concerning Accelerating the Development and Construction of Hainan Island,* and decided to open up Hainan as well.

Learning from advanced countries to develop China was identified as a primary goal from the very beginning of opening up. As the chief architect of China's economic reforms, Deng Xiaoping directly pointed out in his speeches that: "it is necessary to learn from the advanced in order to catch up with advanced…learn the advanced science and technology of others. **We not only need to work hard to learn from foreign countries because of the backwardness of our science and technology today—even if our science and technology catch up with the world's advanced level, we must also learn from the strengths of others**."[68] He also said, "Now, if you are building, you have to be more resourceful. You can use foreign capital and technology, and overseas Chinese and ethnic Chinese can come back

---

[66] Xinhuanet [43].

[67] Zhang et al. [44].

[68] Deng [45].

to set up factories."[69] We can see from these excerpts that at this stage, Chinese leaders were most concerned with learning about science and technology through opening up. In fact, 10 of Deng Xiaoping's speeches from 1978 to 1979 were related to opening up to the outside world, during which "technology" was mentioned eight times, "funds" four times, "joint ventures" four times, and "export foreign exchange earnings" twice.[70]

However, opinions on the correct course for opening up were not always unified—voices of opposition and controversy were unceasing. Additionally, due to a lack of management experience, there were also omissions in the government's policies. Some exploited policy loopholes to make profits, such as in the *Hainan Automobile Smuggling Case* of 1984. As previously mentioned, in 1983, the Central Committee of the CPC allowed the Hainan Administrative Region to import goods in short supply according to production needs. However, due to a lack of management, the situation quickly spiraled out of control. In the first half of 1984, Hainan imported more than 2000 vehicles, but this figure suddenly rose to 13,000 in July. In the following six months, Hainan issued a total of 89,000 automobile import approvals, which gradually escalated into car dealing and smuggling. In just half a year, 872 companies sprang into existence on the island of Hainan. Even the military played a role in transporting vehicles off of the island. Under the pretext of relocating defense arrangements, the navy used warships to transport vehicles. They changed vehicle names and replaced their license plates with military ones. After unloading the cars from ships in Zhanjiang, the plates were removed and taken back to Hainan, only to be used for the next batch. In the face of such a chaotic situation, the central government had to take serious corrective measures. According to investigation data, within the year, **Hainan illegally purchased overpriced foreign exchanges totaling USD570 million from 21 provinces and cities and 15 units in the central government. The aggregate amount of loans used by various companies for imports was RMB4.21 billion—RMB1 billion more than the total industrial and agricultural production in Hainan in 1984.**[71] **For a time, this caused strong public backlash against special economic zones and opening up, slowing down related foreign exchanges.**

3. **Expanding the areas and fields of opening up from 1984 to 1992**

It is precisely in the context of the aforementioned difficulties with opening up that Deng Xiaoping first traveled south to Shenzhen, resolutely promoting

---

[69]Deng [46].

[70]Deng Xiaoping, 1994: "Speech at the Opening Ceremony of the National Science Conference," Implementing the Four Modernizations, Never Seeking Hegemony, Highly Raising the Self-ideological Banner, Adhering to the Principle of Seeking Truth from Facts, Renovating Enterprises with Advanced Technologies and Management Methods, Implementing an open policy, learning the world's advanced science and technology, liberating the mind, seeking truth from facts, uniting and looking forward, building the role of using foreign capital and playing the role of the original business and industry, adhering to the four basic principles, Opinions on Economic Work, Socialism can also engage in market economy, etc., *Selected Works of Deng Xiaoping (Volume II).*

[71]Hexun News [47].

adherence to the opening up policy and ushering in a new wave of opening up in the coastal areas. On January 24, 1984, Deng Xiaoping inspected three special economic zones in Shenzhen, Zhuhai, and Xiamen. While writing about the Shenzhen Special Zone, he remarked, "Shenzhen's development and experience prove that China's policy of establishing a special economic zone is correct." Deng Xiaoping's inspections soothed tumultuous public debates and promoted the continuation of opening up while exploring new paths. At this stage, phrases such as "persistence in opening up" and "opening up is imperative" were frequently repeated in Deng Xiaoping's speeches. In a speech at the Third Plenary Meeting of the Central Advisory Commission, he commented, "Historical experience and lessons show that opening up is an imperative. Opening up can't hurt us."[72] Furthermore, Deng believed that "closed-door construction can't be successful. China's development cannot be separated from the world...It is also necessary to open up to the outside world and absorb foreign capital and technology to help us develop...China will also make more contributions to the international economy."[73] On this basis, China's opening to the outside world accelerated in 1984. In the following five years, China's opened areas continued to expand, and slogans such as "foreign-oriented economy" and "export-oriented" were proposed. The business environment became even friendlier to foreign investments.

From the opening of special economic zones to the opening up of coastal areas. Before 1984, China's opening up was mainly concentrated in the four special economic zones of Shenzhen, Zhuhai, Shantou, and Xiamen, as well as Hainan Island. In 1984, the central government decided to set up economic and technological development zones in 14 cities along the coast. The policies enjoyed by these cities were basically the same as those of the special economic zones. In 1985, the central government decided to establish opened up areas along the Yangtze River Delta, the Pearl River Delta, and the Xiamen- Zhangzhou-Quanzhou Triangle Area. In this way, opened up areas were expanded from individual points to two-dimensional areas. According to the State Council's documents, we found that in 1985, a large number of approvals for the opening up of various regions appeared. Furthermore, documents of this type run through the process of opening up to the outside world.

Firmly developing manufacturing and a foreign-oriented economy. In 1988, the central government approved and forwarded the Reply from the State Council on Deepening Reform, Expanding Opening up, and Accelerating Economic Development Requests in Guangdong Province, and proposed the development of an "export-oriented economy" for the first time. Comrade Gu Mu, who was in charge of the work of special economic zones, recalled that during the period of 1985–1986, the central government held several meetings to encourage special economic zones to raise exports. In a speech about the Shanghai Pudong New Area, Jiang Zemin remarked, "opened-up cities should focus on developing an export-oriented economy and give

[72]Deng [48].

[73]Deng [49].

full play to their role as bases and windows in opening up."[74] Beginning in 1986, the export levels of special economic zones began to make considerable progress. In 1986, the foreign trade exports of the four special zones reached USD1.03 billion, an increase of 27% over the previous year, of which Shenzhen was responsible for USD725 million.[75]

Vigorously attracting foreign investment and optimizing the business environment. With the continuous expansion of opened up areas, Chinese leaders began to further improve the foreign investment environment, and China ushered in its first peak foreign investment attraction. Gu Mu recalled: "After the opening up in 1984, the momentum of progress was unprecedented. **In 1984 and 1985, 4925 new foreign-invested enterprises were approved, foreign investment reached USD8.22 billion, and actual foreign investment reached USD1.91 billion—3.6 times, 1.3 times, and 1.9 times, respectively, that of the previous five years.**"[76] To further improve the situation, the 10th executive meeting of the State Council passed the *Regulations on Encouraging Foreign Investment*[77] in 1988, which contained 22 rules to further improve the foreign business environment. Data shows that from 1984 to 1988, China's actual use of foreign capital increased from USD2.866 billion to USD10.226 billion—from 1988 to 1993, it soared even higher to USD38.96 billion.[78]

Toward the end of the 1980s, along with the political turmoil of the time, the process of opening up slowed down once more. In the spring and summer of 1989, political turmoil in Beijing and other cities led to a resurfacing of skepticism and arguments against opening up. Coupled with the attacks and sanctions imposed on China by US-led Western forces, China's opening up to the outside world fell into a period of stagnation during 1989–1992.

4. **Deepening opening up with the aim of constructing a market economy from 1992 to 2000**

At a time when China's opening was almost stagnant, Deng Xiaoping once again traveled to the South and strengthened the country's determination to open up to the outside world. From January 18 to February 21, 1992, Deng Xiaoping, who had officially bid farewell to the central leadership position by that point, visited Wuchang, Shenzhen, Zhuhai, and Shanghai to assess their situations and deliver important speeches. "It is not an essential difference between socialism and capitalism whether there is more planning or more market," he said. "We must grasp favorable opportunities, develop ourselves, and the key is to develop the economy." Indeed, Deng remarked, "development is the hard truth."[79] Through these talks, Deng revitalized reform and opening up. In 1992, the 14th National Congress of the CPC officially

---

[74] Jiang [50].

[75] Gu [51].

[76] Gu [52].

[77] Ministry of Commerce of the People's Republic of China [53].

[78] CEIC database.

[79] Phoenix.com [54].

decided to build a "socialist market economy," determining the direction for China's future economic system reform.

In this atmosphere, China's opening up to the outside world accelerated, open regions were further expanded, the industry sector grew, trade barriers were further reduced, and relevant systems began to undergo profound changes. **At this stage, China's foreign economic exchanges underwent two major shifts. First, there was a massive influx of foreign capital. In 1992 and 1993, the actual utilization of foreign capital increased by 152.1% and 150.0%, respectively. Second, exports began to grow, accumulating a substantial amount of foreign exchange reserves. Since 1994, China's trade surplus has been in the black, and foreign exchange reserves have continued to grow steadily since 1993** (Charts 8, 9 and 10).

At this stage, China's opening up to the outside world was further deepened. The country continued to learn through opening up, with the market economy system as a reference. As such, the pace of reform in some areas accelerated, including investment and financing, market access, foreign exchange, and capital flows. This was achieved through six main avenues. **First, trade barriers were systematically reduced beginning in 1992**. China's weighted tariff rate was more than halved between 1992 and 2000—it dropped from around 32% to around 15% (Chart 11).

Second, the financial and foreign exchange sectors were further opened. On January 1, 1994, the official exchange rate of the RMB and the foreign exchange adjustment price were formally unified. China began to implement a single, managed floating exchange rate system based on market supply and demand. Additionally, the financial service industry launched pilot programs to encourage further opening up. After 1995, the pilot city for opening up in the insurance industry gradually expanded from Shanghai to cities such as Guangzhou and Shenzhen.

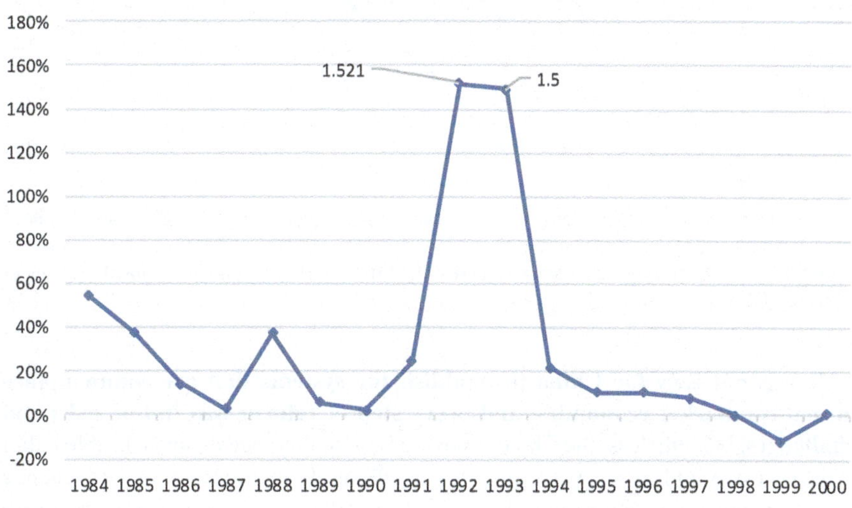

Chart 8 Growth of actual utilization of foreign capital. *Source* National Bureau of Statistics, CEIC database, authors' calculation

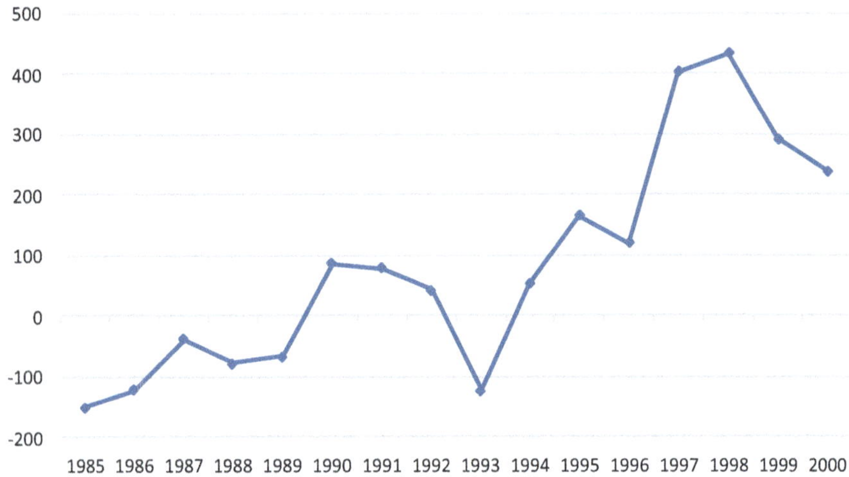

Chart 9 China's trade surplus (USD100 million). *Source* National Bureau of Statistics, CEIC database

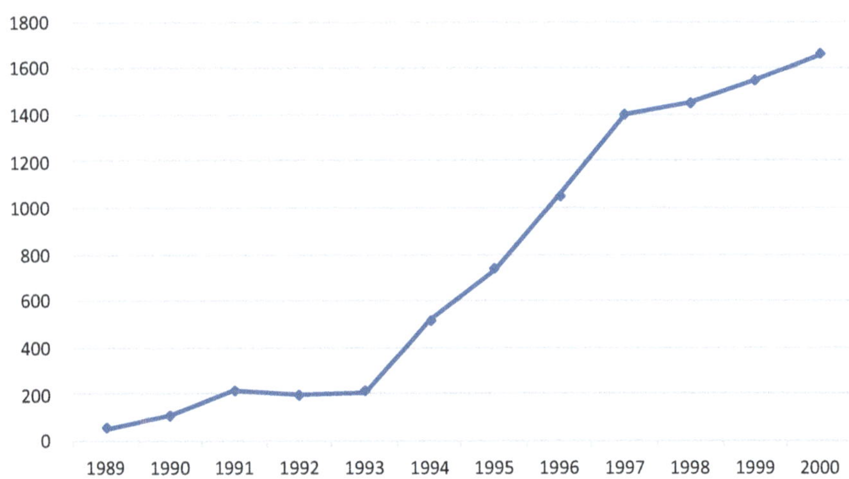

Chart 10 China's foreign exchange reserves (USD100 million). *Source* National Bureau of Statistics, CEIC database

It was not easy for China to establish the systems that are commonplace in mature market economies, and every step of reform was full of risks and challenges. Nonetheless, the Chinese government maintained an unshakeable belief in the necessity and promise of reform. When talking about the reform of the exchange rate system in 1994, Zhu Rongji stressed, "The unification of exchange rates is very

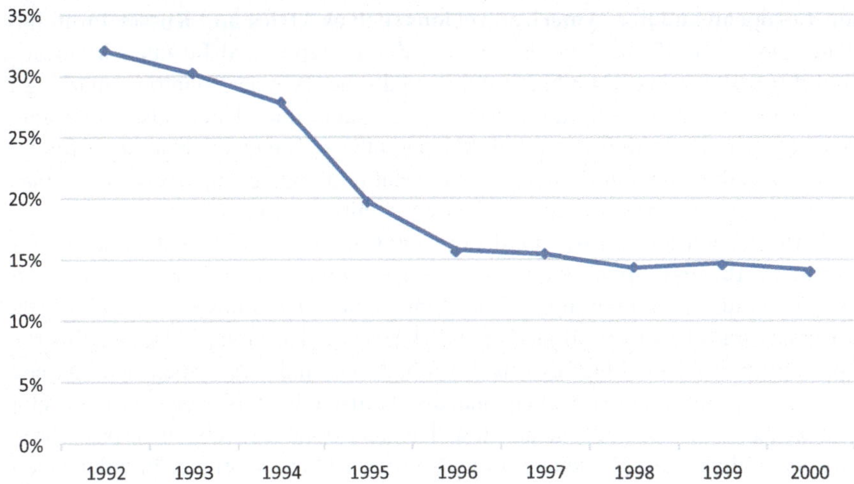

Chart 11 Weighted average tariff rate. *Source* National Bureau of Statistics, CEIC database, authors' calculation

risky, but it must be done…I hope that the relevant leading comrades here will attach great importance to the exchange rate, and we must do a good job in this regard."[80]

Third, opening up was further extended from coastal to inland areas. A number of inland cities, such as Nanjing, Wuhan, Chongqing, etc. began to appear in State Council documents on opening up. This stage included the opening of the Xinjiang Uyghur Autonomous Region as early as March 14, 1994, when the Central Committee of the Communist Party of China and the State Council issued the *Reply of the State Council on Approving the Opening up of Five Border Ports Such as Bhaktu in Xinjiang*.[81] The five border ports were Bhaktu, Jeminay, Ahetubieke, Dulata, and Muzart. The opening of these border ports and the participation of local ethnic groups in the process demonstrated the determination of the Chinese government to carry out reforms nationwide.

Fourth, China began to place more emphasis on the research, mastery, and use of international rules, which in turn was reflected in a focus on and eagerness for international talent. Zhu Rongji once said that in order to attract international talent, "you need to pay as much as you think you should pay. Without this, talent will not come. Especially in banking, securities, insurance, and other related sectors, business personnel unfamiliar with established international rules will be at a disadvantage. Without a cohort of internationally competent top-level talents, we will have no foothold in the international community."[82]

Fifth, China became cognizant of the diversity and three-dimensionality of opening up, and the country began to pay more attention to cooperation with

[80]Zhu [55].

[81]Central People's Government of the People's Republic of China [56].

[82]Zhu [57].

non-European and non-American regions such as Africa and Russia. From July 19 to August 4, 1995, the then Vice Premier Zhu Rongji visited Tanzania, Mauritius, Zimbabwe, Botswana, Namibia, Zambia, and other African countries, marking a new chapter in China–Africa relations. At the same time, China also established closer cooperation with Russia, ASEAN, and others. The diversification of foreign economic and trade relations to a certain extent promoted the upgrading of China's industry, giving Chinese enterprises the opportunity to "go out."

Sixth, more attention was paid to promoting economic transformation and upgrading through opening up. At this stage, China was no longer satisfied with the "three-plus-one trading-mix." Zhu Rongji summarized this issue, stating, "the processing trade has many shortcomings. There are at least five…" He said this was especially true for clothing, as it is not a high-tech industry. "Shenzhen has now stopped the processing trade. Dongguan also realized that it is necessary to develop high-tech and build new advantages. It will not be workable to rely on the past 'three-plus-one trading-mix.'"[83] Jiang Zemin also stressed the importance of independent innovation on the basis of studying international advanced technology. It was his belief that "it is necessary to handle the relationship of opening up to the outside world and upholding self-reliance, actively promoting regional economic cooperation and extensive international economic and trade exchanges on the basis of self-reliance, and combining the introduction of advanced technologies with development and innovation to form our own technological advantages. While using foreign capital, we should pay attention to our own accumulation to accelerate the closing of the gap between developed countries and developing countries."[84]

At this stage, China's learning from abroad was also changing significantly. While referring to "technology" and "equipment," leaders began to emphasize "learning all achievements of advanced civilizations." **Jiang Zemin once said that we should "expand and draw on all the achievements of advanced civilizations created by the countries around the world, including developed capitalist countries, and actively participate in international economic and technological cooperation and competition**."[85] At the turn of the century, he once again stressed, "whether it can continue to learn all the advanced things in the world, whether it can keep up with the trend of world development, is a big issue that affects the success or failure of a country or a nation."[86] On April 18, August 10, August 13, and September 26 of 1992, within a span of less than half a year, the then Vice Premier Zhu Rongji emphasized the importance of learning on four separate occasions. He pointed out that in every industry, be it urban construction, tourism development, or the financial supervision system, we should learn to absorb the experience of developed countries.[87] It can thus be seen that at this stage, China's national leaders viewed learning as central to the rise and fall of the nation.

[83]Zhu [58].

[84]Jiang [59].

[85]Jiang [60].

[86]Jiang [61].

[87]Zhu [62].

5. Fully integrating into the global economic system from 2001 to 2007

On November 10, 2001, the Fourth Ministerial Conference of the WTO reviewed and approved China's accession, and China's opening up embarked upon a new stage. This accomplishment was the result of tremendous efforts over numerous years. In 1986, China applied to restore its founding member status of the GATT. From this point, the process of China's re-entry and accession to the WTO dragged on for 15 years. China repeatedly made concessions on agricultural products, non-agricultural products, and trade in services, but nevertheless failed to reach a re-examination agreement due to the extortionate terms demanded by some parties. After the establishment of the WTO in 1995, China became an observer on June 3 of the same year and continued to unswervingly push forward various reforms as part of its efforts to join.

Chinese leaders pushed for their country to join the World Trade Organization with great political courage and firm will. At that time, China's accession to the WTO was not unanimously accepted—dismissive voices and opposing views poured in from home and abroad. In the years before and after China's accession, many "theories of China's collapse" circulated internationally. In 2001, Chinese American Gordon Chang published his book *The Coming Collapse of China*,[88] predicting that China would collapse within 5–10 years. Chang even attributed part of this collapse to the WTO, stating in an interview that "before joining the World Trade Organization, the Chinese government was able to control trade exchanges; but after joining the WTO, Beijing no longer has the authority to control commercial transactions outside the country."[89] In addition, other figures including Lee Teng-hui, the former leader of Taiwan, and Mineo Nakajima, former president of Tokyo University of Foreign Studies, publicly expressed similar views. In addition to these voices, there was also panic in Mainland China. For a time, there was a popular saying that "the wolf is coming,"[90] meaning that the entry of foreign companies would lead to the closure of domestic enterprises and large numbers of layoffs.

Despite many difficulties and uncertainties, the Chinese government fully recognized the importance of learning through opening up to promote economic upgrading, and continued to initiate a series of changes following its accession to the WTO. The first of these initiatives was to revise a number of domestic laws and regulations. According to statistics from the *Overview of Adjustments to China's Economic Law After Joining the WTO*,[91] the State Council comprehensively cleared 756 administrative regulations by the end of 2000. On the basis of the 1992 price regulations, the State Planning Commission cleared 341 documents, revised 51 documents, and abolished 124 ministerial price regulations and other normative documents. The State Economic and Trade Commission also cleared 113 ministerial regulations, of which 19 were abolished and 38 were revised. The Ministry

[88]Gordon Chang [63].

[89]Wikipedia [64].

[90]People's Forum [65].

[91]Zhang [66].

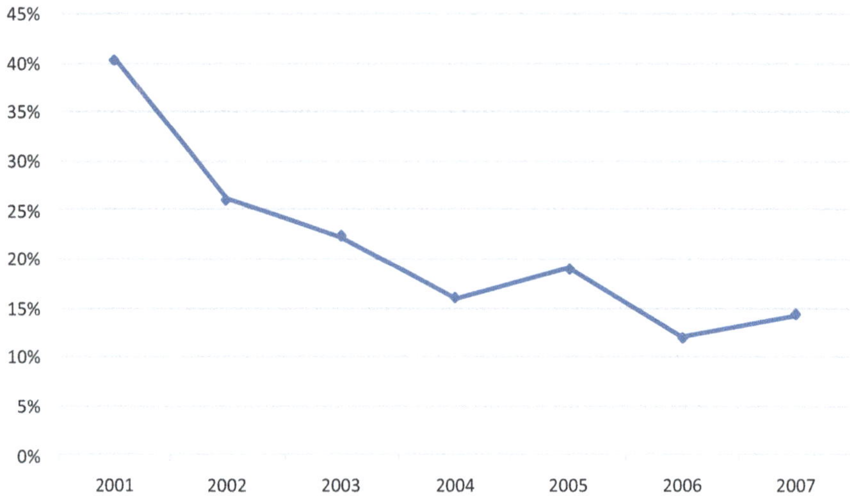

Chart 12 Proportion of tariffs reaching the highest international tariff rate. *Source* National Bureau of Statistics, CEIC database, authors' calculation

of Foreign Trade and Economic Cooperation cleared 1413 documents, including 6 foreign trade laws, 164 administrative regulations, 887 ministerial regulations, 191 bilateral economic and trade agreements, 72 bilateral investment protection agreements, and 93 double taxation agreements. Such intensive and efficient document adjustments reflected the government's determination to enter the WTO as a historical opportunity (Chart 11).

Second, China continued to reduce tariffs and began to remove non-tariff barriers. Chart 12 shows that in the detailed catalog of China's tariffs, the proportion of those reaching the highest international tariff rates has dropped from around 40% to around 15%. Chart 13 depicts that China's weighted average tariff rate has dropped from around 14% to around 5%. In addition, as one of its four major commitments for joining the WTO, China canceled all import quotas for ordinary commodities in January 2005 (Chart 14).[92]

Finally, China further opened up areas such as finance and capital. Reforms on capital flow management and the exchange rate system were relaxed. Since 2003, China's financial opening up and financial reforms have made breakthroughs, mainly in the reforms of the shareholding system of state-owned banks and the exchange rate formation mechanism. At 19:00 on July 21, 2005, the People's Bank of China announced the adjustment of the official exchange rate of USD/RMB from 8.27 to 8.11, raising the RMB by about 2.1%. At the same time, the central bank announced the abolition of the monetary policy that was originally pegged to a single dollar, and implemented a managed floating exchange rate system based on market supply and demand with reference to a basket of currencies. From July 2005 to July 2008,

[92]NetEase [67].

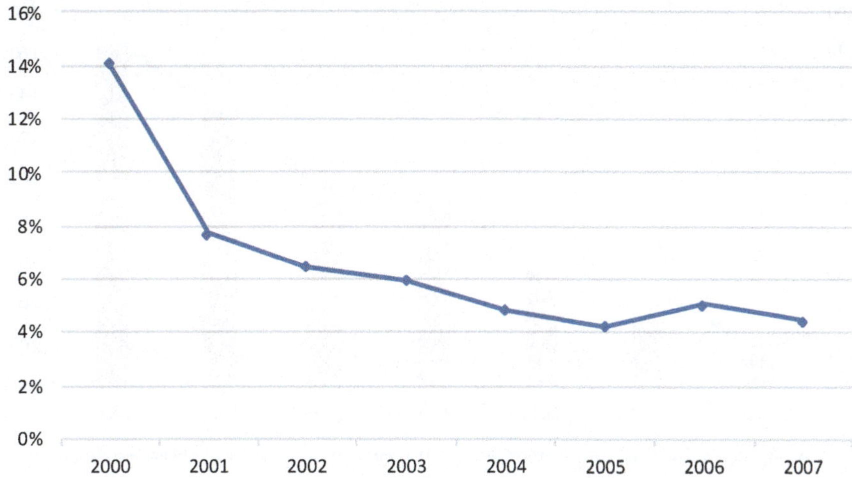

Chart 13 Weighted average tariff rate. *Source* National Bureau of Statistics, CEIC database

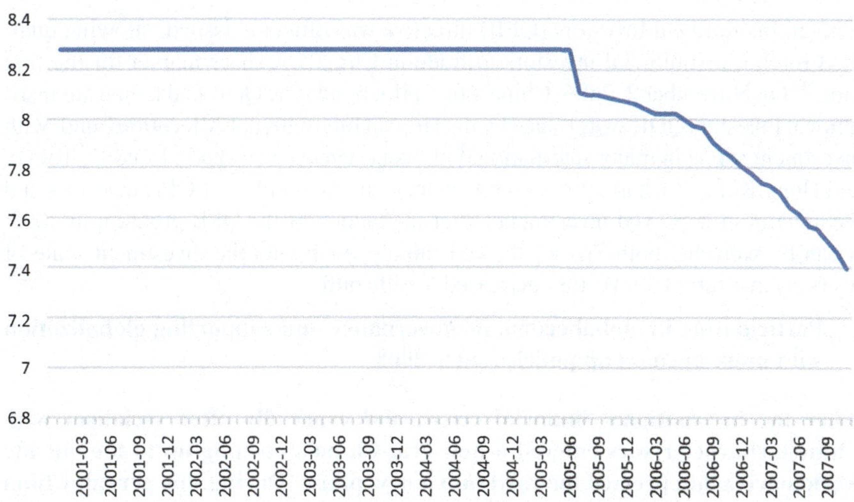

Chart 14 RMB to USD exchange rate. *Source* National Bureau of Statistics, CEIC database

the RMB appreciated by 21% against the US dollar, and the exchange rate volatility improved significantly. At the same time, the regulation of financial accounts entered a preliminary stage of relaxation, and relevant regulations became more standardized, providing a more convenient environment for domestic and foreign institutional investors to conduct foreign business. On July 9, 2003, China's first Qualified

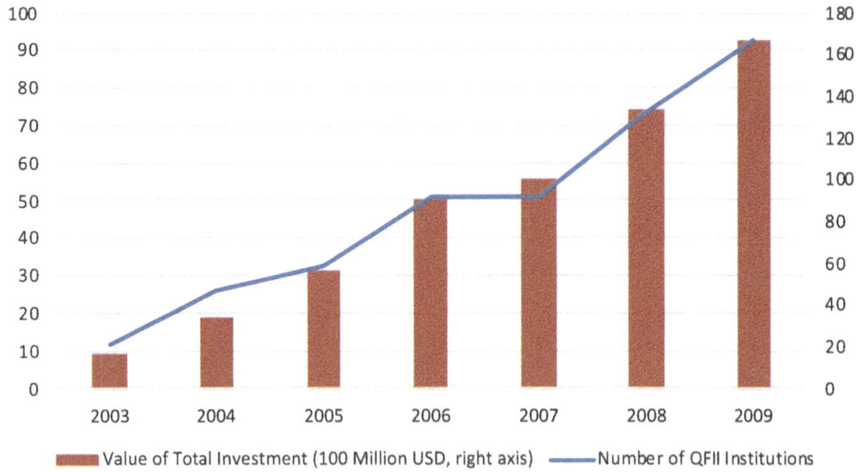

Chart 15 Change of QFII quantity and investment amount. *Source* National Bureau of Statistics, CEIC database

Foreign Institutional Investors (QFII) directive was officially issued, allowing qualified foreign institutional investors to trade in China's A-share market for the first time.[93] On November 2, 2006, China's first pilot bond type Qualified Domestic Institutional Investor (QDII) was issued by the Hua'an International Allocation Fund, with investment scope in major international markets such as New York, London, Tokyo, and Hong Kong.[94] Chart 15 shows the changes in the number of QFII investors and the amount of approved investments after the launch of the QFII program in 2003. It can be seen that both factors showed rapid growth, and the investment scale of overseas institutional investors increased significantly.

6. **Participating in global economic governance and supporting globalization with more opening up policies since 2008**

After the international financial crisis, and especially after socialism with Chinese characteristics entered a new era, China's opening up to the outside world once again pressed forward into a new phase. During this period, China has actively participated in global economic governance while studying the advanced achievements of foreign countries and supporting economic globalization through practical actions. On November 15, 2008, the first G20 summit was held in Washington, DC. China attended the summit as a founding member and officially assumed the chairmanship of the G20 on December 1, 2015. This was an affirmation of China's influence on the global economy, and it also marks the beginning of China's increased acquisition of international responsibilities. Since then, China has proposed the "New Silk Road Economic Belt" and "21st Century

[93]Sohu.com [68].

[94]Sina.com [69].

Maritime Silk Road" cooperation initiatives, initiated the establishment of the Asian Infrastructure Investment Bank, increased its voting rights ratio in the IMF to 6.39% (changing its ranking from #6 to #3, after only the United States and Japan), and gotten the RMB officially accepted as part of the SDR currency basket. This series of landmark events together reflect the substantial enhancement of China's global economic status.

Simultaneously, the pace of opening up in China has further accelerated. On September 29, 2013, the China (Shanghai) Free Trade Zone was formally launched. At present, many experimental policies that were first tested in this free trade zone, such as the negative investment list, have been gradually extended to the whole country. In 2018, China lowered its shareholding ratio requirements in finance and automobiles, continued to cut tariffs, further protected intellectual property rights, and held the world's first import exhibition. The country also announced that it would further reduce tariffs, improve customs clearance, and reduce systematic costs upon importation. There were additional promises to accelerate the development of new modes and formats of trade such as cross-border e-commerce and to accelerate the opening up of telecommunications, education, medical care, and culture, especially in the areas of education and medical care where foreign investors are concerned and the domestic market demand is significant, through relaxed shareholding ratios.[95] These new initiatives reflect China's determination to continue opening up.

Protectionist forces have gained steam internationally since 2016, and voices advocating anti-globalization have become increasingly loud. However, Chinese leaders' belief in the benefits of exchange and integration of people from around the world remains unchanged. **At the 2017 Davos Forum, President Xi Jinping declared, "It is impossible, and against historical trends, to artificially cut off the capital flow, technology flow, product flow, industrial flow, and personnel flow between countries or to let the sea of the world economy relapse to small lakes and rivers in isolation**."[96] At the Bo'ao Forum for Asia in 2018, President Xi Jinping once again stressed, "in today's world, the tide of peaceful cooperation is rolling forward, the trend of opening up and integration is rolling forward, and the trend of change and innovation is rolling forward. People of all countries should work together and forge ahead, hand in hand, to build the community of shared human destiny, to create a peaceful, tranquil, prosperous, open, and beautiful Asia and world."[97] Based on this conviction, China continues to promote opening up in-depth and has written a vision of building a community of shared human destiny as a program of action into its Constitution. China has become a bulwark against unilateralism.

China's opening up has experienced a magnificent journey. Despite short-term ups and downs, it has never reversed. At the same time, China has regarded learning from advanced countries as an important goal from the very beginning of its opening up process, and has improved itself through learning from other's strengths. It is

[95] Xinhuanet [70].

[96] People.com [71].

[97] Xinhuanet [72].

precisely for this purpose that the government carefully guides and manages the pace of opening up and monitors the stability and sustainability of economic development. Chinese leaders share a deep conviction to push for continued opening up with great political courage and responsibility.

3 Economic Analysis

Based on these stylized facts and the history of the Chinese opening up process, we propose the following two economic conclusions.

First, learning from advanced economies through entrepreneurs, laborers, and government officials is essential for economic upgrading. Opening up accelerates this learning process by pushing economic subjects in China to study the most advanced knowledge, institutions, and ideas from around the world and to put them into practice in light of China's reality. In the process of opening up, Chinese local enterprises, laborers, and governments have interacted with international advanced enterprises and markets in import and export trade and joint ventures, gone abroad to study and practice, and come to actively study, know, and understand the market economy. In this process, China has gradually established a market economy system and promoted continuous upgrading.

We argue that in the process of opening up, comparative advantage is not as essential as learning. While comparative advantage has contributed to China's development, its benefits have been limited. Much of China's successful industrial upgrading has violated the principles of comparative advantage but resulted in valuable learning. Of course, learning does not depend on trade, which has been true for many cases of industrialization in history besides China's, such as in the United States and Germany in the late 19th century. It is also true that opening up has brought additional benefits such as technology and funds, employment creation, and tax generation. However, from a macro perspective, the impact of learning has been more far-reaching.

Second, to achieve effective and sustainable learning, the process of opening up must be carefully managed and paced. Opening up "in one fell swoop" will not bring long-term growth and prosperity to an economy. The Chinese government's management of the opening up process is mainly reflected in three aspects. **First**, the government has always focused on cultivating the endogenous growth capacity and self-sufficiency of the Chinese economy. The Chinese government (especially the central government) has attentively guided the transformation and upgrading of the real economy while fully recognizing the far-reaching impact of learning on opening up. In this vein, the central government has issued a series of policies to encourage investment and maintain a dynamic balance between moderate protection of domestic enterprises and the introduction of external competition. **Second**, the Chinese government has worked hard to absorb the shocks of opening up. **Third**, the government abides by the tenet that borrowing in foreign exchange and capital flows must be subtly guided and constrained. Since the initial influx of foreign capital, the Chinese government has attached great importance to the repayment of foreign debts. The foreign exchange has been carefully allocated as a strategic resource, and the exchange rate policy has been carefully formulated to avoid a balance of payment crisis.

1. **Learning is the most fundamental benefit of opening up**

Opening up pushes domestic economic agents to study the most advanced knowledge, institutions, and ideas from around the world. In fact, this is the most fundamental benefit of the opening up process—it allows entrepreneurs, laborers, and government agencies to learn. This continuous path of learning has helped China outgrow previous mindsets of the planned economy, promote the market economy system, and accelerate economic upgrading.

In the process of reform and opening up, China's economic subjects have embraced the opportunity to learn through every situation, from **overseas inspections, to training at famous universities, to hands-on experiences such as importing equipment, engaging in export trade, and running joint ventures.** Participants in these learning processes include not only entrepreneurs and laborers, but government officials as well. In fact, the government has gone beyond striving to change its own role through opening up—it has also mobilized its resources to promote the transformation of entrepreneurs and workers. **In the process of learning, Chinese entrepreneurs, laborers, and governments have escaped the inertia of the planned economy and come to understand, recognize, and adapt to their roles and tasks under the market economy. These economic actors have jointly promoted the market economy system and allowed it to take root in China. With their support, the market economy system has continued to strengthen, promoting China's economic transformation and upgrading.**

(a) **A discussion of learning and comparative advantage**

Before detailing China's learning process, we begin with the assertion that comparative advantage is not as essential as learning. Although comparative advantage did contribute to China's development, its benefits have been limited. Much of China's successful industrial upgrading, such as in the automobile industry and electronics industry, has violated the principle of comparative advantage. Industrial distribution in China also violates this principle. More importantly, many cases of industrialization in world history do not support comparative advantage as a strategy.

First, the decline in the proportion of textile, shoe, and hat exports from China in the early 1990s is inconsistent with the theory of comparative advantage. Calculations of the proportion of China's labor income to GDP (i.e., the share of labor income) show a decline from 1995 to 2007, indicating a significant amount of low-cost labor. Furthermore, the share of labor income did not drop below the "Lewis turning point." According to comparative advantage theory, China should focus on exporting labor-intensive goods. However, the proportion of labor-intensive product exports such as textiles, shoes, and hats compared to total exports has steadily declined, and the share of exported machinery, vehicles, and ships, which require

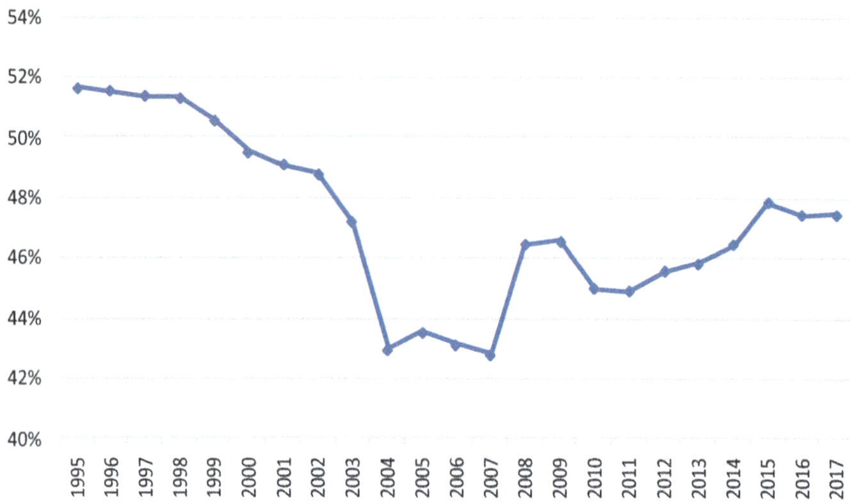

Chart 16 China's labor income share. *Source* CEIC database

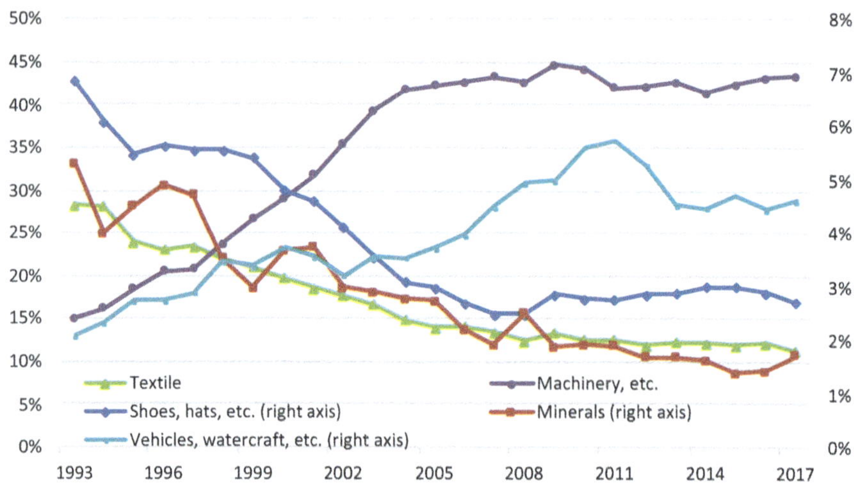

Chart 17 Percentages of China's major exports. *Source* CEIC database, ACCEPT calculation

more capital and technology, has steadily increased. Furthermore, quota sanctions on textiles cannot explain the downward trend because absolute textile exports have grown steadily since China's accession to the WTO, and China's share of global textile exports has also steadily increased. Even when the global textile integration agreement came into effect in 2002/2005, export share did not increase significantly due to reduced trade barriers (Charts 16 and 17).[98]

[98]Ministry of Commerce of the People's Republic of China [73].

Second, much of China's successful industrial upgrading has violated the principle of comparative advantage. According to the theory of comparative advantage, China should have focused on the price advantages of labor and land at the beginning of reform and opening up, and should not have rushed to engage in complex and technically demanding industries. **However, China planned the development of many capital and technology-intensive industries in advance—for example, the automobile industry.** In 1979, when China first opened up to the outside world, central government officials and representatives of Beijing automobile manufacturing plants began communicating with the American Automobile Corporation (AMC) to discuss the establishment of joint ventures. In 1983, the two sides officially signed a contract to begin cooperation.[99] According to World Bank WDI data, China's per capita GDP was only USD225.4 at the time, ranked 181 globally—1.45% that of the United States, 2.59% that of the United Kingdom, 2.16% that of Japan, 2.26% that of France, and 2.29% that of Germany. Even under such conditions, Rao Bin, the then Minister of the First Machinery Ministry, stressed, "it should be no more than three years until the joint venture launches its second-generation vehicles. The yardstick of performance for joint ventures is not the number of cars made or amount of money earned, but the time when new cars can be launched." Today, beyond the BAIC Group, China's whole automobile industry has been rejuvenated. There are six Fortune 500 companies in the industry, which has produced excellent private enterprises such as Geely and BYD.[100]

Electronics is another industry to which China has attached great importance for development, ever since Jiang Zemin proposed in 1984 that "the electronics industry should be developed."[101] From 1984 to 1990, various local governments, state-owned enterprises, and universities in China imported a total of 33 wafer production lines from abroad at an estimated cost of USD150 million. Subsequently, the state formulated a number of special projects such as "Project 908" and "Project 909." In June 2000, in its *Several Policies to Encourage the Development of the Software Industry and Integrated Circuit Industry*, the State Council proposed strong support to the electronics and information industries.[102] After 40 years of development, although many companies have experienced failure and elimination, some have grown formidable in international competition. Huawei, ZTE, Lenovo, Xiaomi, and others have a firm foothold not only in the domestic market but also in overseas markets such as Africa and India, and are gradually moving toward the forefront of independent innovation. In 2016, Polar Code, which was developed primarily by Huawei, was selected as the 5G short code signaling standard. This was the first time that a Chinese company entered an international basic communication framework agreement and signaled international recognition of the innovation capability within China's electronics industry.

[99] Liu [74].

[100] China Economic Net [75].

[101] Jiang [76].

[102] Fa [77].

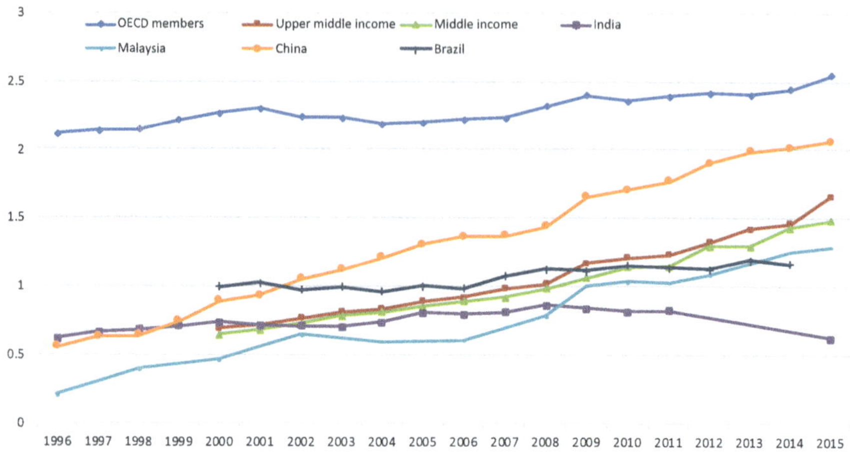

Chart 18 National R&D investment as a percentage of GDP (%). *Source* World Bank WDI database

Third, China attaches great importance to R&D investment and has made remarkable achievements in scientific research and innovation. According to the traditional theory of comparative advantage, developing high technology is a subpar choice for latecomer countries. However, the Chinese government has always focused on R&D investment in high-tech projects. In March 1986, four famous Chinese scientists wrote to the national leaders and proposed to formulate a high-tech development plan. In November of that year, China formulated and implemented the *National High-Tech Research and Development Plan* (863 Program) and approved RMB10 billion in funding—50 times the amount recommended by the four scientists.[103]

The proportion of China's R&D investment in GDP exceeded that of India in 1999, Brazil in 2002, and the UK in 2010. It is consistently higher than the average of middle-income countries and even the average of middle- and high-income countries. In 2015, the figure (2.07%) was only 0.5% points below the average of OECD countries.[104] Such investments have generated significant results. According to the World Intellectual Property Organization (WIPO), in 2017, the number of international patent applications from China was 48,900, ranking second in the world after only the United States (56,600, or 13.4% higher). There are also three Chinese companies among the top 10 applicants for international patents. Huawei ranked first in the world with 4024 applications, surpassing established technology companies such as Intel and Qualcomm (Chart 18).[105]

In addition, comparative advantage theory can hardly explain the development of some micro-enterprises. In the following paragraphs, we will detail the developmental history of two manufacturing companies—Jiangnan Mould & Plastic Technology Co., LTD (JNMPT) and Chengxing Group. JNMPT generated almost no

[103] Ma and Hu [78].

[104] Data from the World Bank WDI database.

[105] World Intellectual Property Organization [79].

profit when producing low-end products such as plastic toys and Christmas candles in the 1980s. Rather, it found success making automobile bumpers with higher production technology and stricter capital requirements. Similarly, the production requirements of Chengxing Group food-grade phosphoric acid products involve significant R&D investment, but the company has still been able to succeed. Clearly, comparative advantage theory is too narrow to fully explain the rapid upgrading and development of the Chinese economy. By learning from advanced enterprises, Chinese enterprises have been able to break through the limitations of narrow comparative advantage and realize their own development. China's current achievements in high-tech fields such as electric vehicles, high-speed railways, and electronic chips lend further evidence to our claims.

Looking back at China in the 1980s, given the macrotraits of cheap labor, land, and other factors, the comparative advantage of primary manufacturing in the Northeast seems straightforward. Shenyang had a complete industrial system, a large number of skilled workers, and entire supporting enterprises. Furthermore, Liaoning had ports such as Yingkou and Dalian, and the road and rail transportation was very convenient (the Shenyang-Dalian Expressway was the first expressway built in the PRC). Dalian set up its economic and technological development zone in 1984, enjoying the same preferential policies as the Shenzhen Special Economic Zone. However, in our field interviews, we learned that a large number of entrepreneurs and workers in Liaoning opted to go south to Shenzhen, where they established their own new businesses. After reform and opening up, a large number of outstanding industrial enterprises also appeared in Guangdong, Jiangsu, and Zhejiang rather than the Northeast. This demonstrates that comparative advantage alone cannot fully explain the significance of opening up to China.

More importantly, this phenomenon also holds true in many examples from world history when industrialization did not abide by the principle of comparative advantage. As mentioned in the first section, Germany and the United States adopted protectionist policies in the late 19th and early 20th centuries when they were catching up to Great Britain. Without free international trade, it was impossible to rely on comparative advantage to develop. However, before WWI, both countries acquired the most advanced machines and business institutions, perfected them, and surpassed Britain in terms of industrial output.

In 1791, Alexander Hamilton, the finance minister and one of the founding fathers of the United States, and Cox, who supported increased tariffs and trade protection, jointly submitted the *Report on Manufactures* to Congress and openly encouraged the plagiarism and introduction of foreign technology. However, their path to these goals was not smooth. In fact, Britain set strict rules protecting what it invented. For instance, textile workers were banned from entering the United States. **It was Samuel Slater, an apprentice in a British textile factory, who memorized the machine designs and brought them to the new continent. To US President Andrew Jackson, Slater was the Father of the Industrial Revolution, while to Britain, he was a traitor**.[106]

[106]Summarized from BBC News [80].

The UK also adopted similar methods when developing its tea industry. In 1851, Robert Fortune, head of the Chelsea Royal Botanic Gardens in London, stole 17,000 types of tea and 23,892 tea trees from China. He even took home an experienced team of tea planters and a complete set of tea making equipment. In 1858, he was hired by the US Patent Office to travel to China to "learn" tea planting at an annual salary of 500 pounds.[107]

This was a classic model of learning in history. Learning, the most fundamental component of opening up, does not necessarily require international trade. In this regard, China has indeed been a polite student. Through joint ventures and gradually opening up its domestic market, China has shared the fruits of its learning with the world. Although as a less developed country China did enjoy comparative advantage due to the low cost of land and labor while opening up, many successful practices in the Chinese economy cannot be explained by comparative advantage alone.

(b) **Enterprises have gradually upgraded through learning from abroad**

Enterprises are the source of vitality for the market economy. Conversely, under the planned economic system, state-owned enterprises received instructions from their superiors, conducted administrative management of their subordinates, and produced according to state plans. Raw materials and products were allocated and distributed by the state, and the profits and losses were also borne by the government. Under the planned economy in China, almost all enterprises lacked a modern governance structure.

We believe that joining the supporting system of international advanced enterprises has been the first important channel for Chinese enterprises and entrepreneurs to learn from and understand the commercial thinking and management experience of the market economy and gradually achieve transformation and upgrading. Two township enterprises in Jiangyin City, Jiangsu Province, illustrate this point.

Chengxing Group. Chengxing Group is a chemical enterprise which produces fine phosphorus chemicals. Its products are sold in more than 70 countries and regions around the world. In 2017, the company's operating income reached RMB72.3 billion. It has more than 50 wholly owned and controlled subsidiaries and more than 10,000 employees, placing it among the top 300 Chinese companies within the China Top 500 for many years. At the same time, **Chengxing Group is also a township enterprise which was founded in 1984 (as a village-run enterprise in Chengnan Village, Yaosai Town, Jiangyin City). The company's initial capital was only RMB38,000 and its original product was phosphorus pentoxide. In its first year, the enterprise only made a profit of RMB80,000**.

---

[107] Dai [81]. The article also gives many similar cases, including references to *For All the Tea in China,* Sarah Rose, 2015; *Green Gold: Tea Empire*, McFarlane, 2016; *Letters with Jefferson and others,* National Archives, 1788; *Trade Secrets: Intellectual piracy and the origins of American industrial power*, Doron S. Ben-Atar, 2004; *Smuggler Nation: How Illicit Trade Made America,* Peter Andreas, 2014; *Industry and Empire: From 1750 to the Present Day,* Eric Hobsbawm, 2016.

Mr. Li Xing, Founder and Chairman of Chengxing Group, said in the survey that the secret to Chengxing's success was "to be closely tied to the train of major international companies and to become a part of their industrial chain." The turning point of the company from "small workshop" to "big business" was when it began to supply phosphoric acid additives to the joint ventures of Coca-Cola and Colgate in China in the mid-1990s. However, making one's way into the industry chains of major companies is very difficult, and orders cannot be obtained simply by low cost. **Colgate's product quality requirements at the time included a list of 21 specifications, while domestic lists were no longer than 10. To this end, the company spent more than RMB1 million on patents and RMB1.6 million on improving technical equipment, and it took four years before they were able to reach the standard requirements. Technological improvements to meet Coca-Cola's supply requirements also took three years. By 1998, Colgate awarded Chengxing Group the title of "Excellent Supplier," and most of the hydrogen peroxide products for toothpaste required by the 36 Colgate subsidiaries around the world were purchased from Chengxing.**[108]

It should be noted that interaction with international advanced enterprises not only brings "hard" knowledge of equipment and technology to Chinese enterprises but also introduces changes in thinking and management methods. Colgate has strict requirements on product quality, and has detailed regulations on business processes such as production, order taking, billing, and transportation. Suppliers and employees must receive training and assessment from Colgate.[109] When preparing to meet Colgate's requirements, Chengxing Group attached great importance to these standards. Mr. Li Xing personally supervised their implementation, and the company finally passed the certification. Meanwhile, Chengxing Group's management also experienced a qualitative leap. During the survey, Mr. Li Xing shared with us another interesting anecdote. Chengxing Group's production workshop set up access control, and the swiping of an access card was normally required to enter. When he was receiving foreign business partners, Mr. Li Xing opened the door in advance according to Chinese customs to show respect. However, the foreign visitors believed that this was not in compliance with the management regulations and therefore not worth practicing. We can see that the changes in thinking and ideas brought by foreign enterprises have been profound and meticulous.

Jiangnan Mould & Plastic Technology Co., Ltd. (JNMPT). JNMPT is a high-quality equipment manufacturing enterprise. It is the largest automobile bumper manufacturer in China—a supplier of BMW and Jaguar Land Rover. In 2015, its operating income was RMB3.1 billion and its net profit was RMB295 million, and the company now has factories in the United States and Mexico. **Its predecessor was a small-town-owned-and-operated firm founded by Mr. Cao Mingfang in Zhouzhuang Town, Jiangyin City in 1984. In the first five years since after its formation, the company produced export products like toys and Christmas candles.**

[108] Relevant information compiled from Yu and Zhu [82], Yang [83].

[109] Yang [84].

In 1988, Volkswagen's Santana car project was launched in Shanghai, and they needed to purchase car bumpers in the Yangtze River Delta region to meet the required localization rate. **After learning of this, Mr. Cao Mingfang managed to contact Shanghai Volkswagen, and with the support and guarantee of the Jiangyin Municipal Government, he borrowed USD2.53 million to import German equipment and hire German experts to guide production.** Within one year, the company was able to produce bumpers up to VW's technical requirements, and it successfully won the orders for Santana sedans. Since then, bumpers have become the calling card of this township enterprise—it has subsequently supplied supporting goods to well-known enterprises such as BMW, GM, and Mercedes-Benz, and was listed in 1997. By the year 2000, the company's net assets reached RMB260. With the support of the Jiangyin Municipal Government, it was privatized and renamed JNMPT.[110]

From a small firm that could merely produce plastic toys to a high-value-added manufacturing enterprise doing business around the world, JNMPT has undergone profound changes by learning advanced management and commercial concepts through participation in the supporting system of foreign enterprises. Every time JNMPT has expanded its factory or set up new factories elsewhere, the company has engaged German companies as general contractors for proper quality control. JNMPT has recently tried to build its own factory, but still chose to work with German companies for the overall design. Additionally, following the trends of foreign enterprises, JNMPT has begun to sell its products globally. In fact, JNMPT even built an overseas factory to complement BMW's project in Mexico. It is situated directly opposite the BMW Mexico factory, signaling JNMPT's entry to the North American market.

Through joining the supporting system of advanced international enterprises, many Chinese "small workshops" have been transformed into "big enterprises." While bringing in profits, technology, and equipment, advanced international enterprises have also brought advanced management methods, business ideas, and brand awareness to China. We believe that the impact of opening up in this regard has been profound and extensive, and the two examples detailed above are no exception. In fact, Liu et al. [9],[111] relying on micro-data from corporate surveys, found that start-ups with management experience in foreign enterprises have better mechanism design in terms of employee incentives and legal arbitration. They believe that this is an important channel for FDI spillover.

While interacting with advanced international enterprises, a large number of entrepreneurs have begun to go abroad and learn through government training, inspection projects, and self-funded training programs. In 1985, the Foreign Experts Bureau launched the Business Foreign Language Test (BFT) to determine the English level of those from governments, businesses, and finance sectors going to receive overseas training. As of 2011, the total number of candidates for the exam exceeded 200,000.[112] Mr. Li Xing of Chengxing Group attended a training at the

[110]Based on survey.

[111]Liu et al. [9].

[112]Sina Education [85].

University of California Business School in 1992, where he first learned about the "shareholding system" and was exposed to the argument that "[the shareholding system] is an effective form of economic organization to divide social wealth equitably, resolve labor-management disputes, and promote social progress." He was so persuaded by this argument that he has since been determined to have the company listed in order to build a modern corporate structure and raise funds for development. To this end, Mr. Li Xing tried to list Chengxing Group company on the NASDAQ in the mid-1990s and had a roadshow in New York. However, the 1997–1998 financial crisis intervened, and he had to change course and list the company domestically.[113]

(c) **A large number of state-owned enterprise laborers have formed market economy thinking through engaging with foreign enterprises**

Along with the entry of foreign-invested enterprises, a large number of state-owned enterprise employees in China began to break through the barriers of planning and to understand and accept the market economy mindset. In the era of the planned economy, most of China's urban laborers worked in state-owned enterprises. In Shenyang, for example, in 1990 there were a total of 2.3 million employees, of which 1.46 million worked in state-owned enterprises and 750,000 worked in collective enterprises.[114]

Before the reforms at the end of the 20th century, state-owned enterprises not only provided jobs but also assumed social responsibility for their employees. **Although the wages paid by state-owned enterprises were low, employees' housing (rental housing provided by their employers), medical treatment (hospitals affiliated to state-owned enterprises), children's education (schools affiliated with state-owned enterprises), welfare (distribution of fruits, fish, meat, etc.), and pensions (paid upon retirement) all came from SOEs**. It can thus be said that state-owned enterprises at the time were literally "units"—that is to say, units upon which people were dependent, rather than enterprises in the modern sense. **Therefore, many employees of state-owned enterprises were afraid of being "laid off,"** and there was even a case wherein a state-owned enterprise employee publicly killed the manager who had fired him.[115]

It was the entry of foreign-invested enterprises that allowed many employees of state-owned enterprises to realize that they could still live decently and respectably after leaving the government system and its SOEs. Foreign-invested companies provided new choices for workers with their generous pay and benefits. According to an old leader, the joint venture of BMW Brilliance not only paid well but also provided attractive benefits. Many sought employment at the joint venture, and people were proud if their children were able to enter BMW Brilliance.[116] This is not an isolated case. As a matter of fact, even by 2013, when private enterprises were flourishing and state-owned enterprise reforms were progressing, the average salary of

[113]Based on Yu and Zhu [82].

[114]Shenyang Municipal Bureau of Statistics [31].

[115]Based on survey.

[116]Based on survey.

foreign-invested enterprises (RMB62,000) was still significantly higher than that of joint-stock companies (RMB52,000) and state-owned enterprises (RMB56,000).[117]

With changing ideas of employment, employees began to obey management and value efficiency, and official-centered thinking began to crumble. There was no strict efficiency incentive during the era of large state-owned enterprises. Many employees "passed a day with a newspaper and a cup of tea." Mr. Wei Haijun, Chairman of Northeastern Pharmaceutical Co., Ltd, another state-owned enterprise in Shenyang, shared a vivid case with us. When he first came to Northeastern Pharmaceuticals, which was on the verge of bankruptcy, he proposed the slogan of, "No room for bad work, even if slightly bad!" However, several employees reported him to the municipal party committee and the municipal government, alleging that such a request demonstrated "idealism" because it was not possible to achieve 100% accuracy in work. Although the report was dismissed, it still demonstrates that some employees' ideas were incompatible with the market economy.[118] However, the generous salary of foreign-invested enterprises gradually altered people's ideas. BMW Brilliance provided no "iron rice bowls," employees were recruited through strict examinations, and unsatisfactory performance would lead to job loss—even the mayor could not intervene.[119] These facts made people realize that they had to rely on their own ability to find work and earn better pay rather than relying on powerful connections.

(d) **The government has transformed its role by interacting with foreign-invested companies**

Under the planned economy system, the government plays a central role as the coordinator of economic activities and controls the entire national economy through the formulation of production plans, the allocation of raw materials, and the distribution of manufactured goods. **What role should the government play in a market economy? In the face of this extremely complex issue, the initial approach of Chinese government officials was relatively simple**. After the central government proposed the strategy of "grasping the large and letting go of the small" in 1995,[120] Shenyang (a major industrial city in Northeast China) altered the ownership of a large number of enterprises, delegated the management of municipal enterprises to the district government, and then privatized them. According to statistics, there were 789 local state-owned industrial enterprises in Shenyang in 1995. By 2000, the number of state-owned enterprises decreased to 391. In the same period, the number of collective enterprises decreased from 6453 to 2787, while the number of private enterprises increased from 11 to 1127. Meanwhile, the number of municipal state-owned enterprises decreased from 522 in 1995 to 27 in 2017.[121] In our research, we learned that many of these privatized "small" enterprises were in fact

[117] Data from the annual database of the National Bureau of Statistics.

[118] Based on survey.

[119] Based on survey.

[120] National People's Congress [86].

[121] Shenyang Municipal Bureau of Statistics [31].

profitable, including more than 460 "invisible champions" in niche fields. However, the majority of these enterprises now cease to exist because of suspended bank loans or management withdrawal.

Clearly, simply "letting things go" is no solution. Practice results in real knowledge, and interactions between the government and advanced foreign enterprises have become an important way for the government to learn the ideas and institutions of the market economy. We believe that through interaction with foreign-invested companies, the Chinese government (especially local governments) has altered its economic practices in the following ways.

First, the government refrains from interfering with the day-to-day operations of companies and works to provide quality public services. In this regard, joint ventures have provided a vivid lesson to Chinese government officials. This is illustrated by the remarks of Gu Mu, the then Vice Premier of the State Council. He stressed the need for improvement of the operating environment for foreign-invested enterprises, pointing out that "foreign investors are mostly put off by the way of managing foreign-invested enterprises in the same way of managing state-owned enterprises and the imposition of arbitrary administrative interventions, for example, the replacement of a Chinese senior officer of a joint venture without deliberation on the board meeting."[122]

The Shenyang government's transformation provides a case in point of this principle within the Chinese government. In 2003, Shenyang invited BMW and a local automobile company, Brilliance, to establish a joint venture to produce complete vehicles. In our research, we learned that BMW was very strict with corporate management, the company's supporting procurement was controlled by BMW, and employees were hired via standardized tests. An old leader told us that "even a note from the mayor wouldn't help you get a job in BMW!" At the same time, BMW put forward detailed and strict requirements for the construction of its facilities. The Shenyang government made a great deal of effort to level hills, replace the original soil with new soil, build roads, and install traffic lights as required.[123] Under the planned economy, it would have been unthinkable for the government to provide such nuanced service to a non-state-owned factory.

Second, the success of joint ventures has strengthened the government's determination to work toward further reform. Shenyang has made many efforts and attempts to reform state-owned enterprises, including their contracting, tax-for-profits system, and shareholding system. In fact, China's first bankruptcy case of a state-owned enterprise even took place in Shenyang (the Shenyang Anti-Explosion Equipment Factory went bankrupt in 1984). Nevertheless, these measures were not able to fundamentally change the face of state-owned enterprises. In our survey, we learned that important state-owned enterprises such as Shenyang Machine Tool and Northeast Pharmaceutical also had the opportunity to carry out joint ventures during that period, but were not able to for various reasons. **In contrast, the success of BMW Brilliance prompted the government to realize that the introduction of**

[122]Gu [87].

[123]Based on survey.

advanced business partners was the right direction for state-owned enterprise reform. Recently, the Shenyang government has promoted 27 state-owned enterprises to carry out mixed ownership reforms. Among them, the reform of Northeast Pharmaceuticals has been completed. Meanwhile, companies such as Northern Heavy Industries are actively inviting strategic investors.

Third, the government respects and values entrepreneurship. As the economy has developed, government officials have become increasingly aware of the important role of entrepreneurs in business development. **Zhu Rongji once pointed out that "it is easy to buy equipment, and it is also possible to introduce technology, so long as there is money, but it is not so easy to train real corporate executives."**[124] When talking about efforts to open up the international market, he also stressed that " **as long as we have real entrepreneurs, we can break into their markets to make big money**."[125] In 2018, the United Front Work Department of the CPC Central Committee and the National Federation of Industry and Commerce jointly issued a list of "100 Outstanding Private Entrepreneurs in the 40 Years of Reform and Opening Up," which they intended "as a showcase of the development of China's private economy and the major achievements of entrepreneurs as builders of socialism with Chinese characteristics."[126] We can therefore see that the government's reliance on and respect for entrepreneurs has reached new heights.

Local governments have followed the trends of the central government. The change in Shenyang's former leadership's view of Yang Rong, the then head of Brilliance, illustrates this point. Yang Rong was the founder and head of Brilliance—he introduced Japanese technology to produce Jinbei Auto and then initiated cooperation with BMW. Around 2002, however, he found himself in conflict arising from equity rights with a provincial leader and had to move to Hong Kong. **Over time, many people came to praise Yang Rong's strategic vision and assert that if his leadership had been allowed to continue, Brilliance would have developed more favorably**.

Fourth, the government recognizes that the development of the national economy cannot rely solely on state-owned enterprises. Since the mid-1990s, Chinese leaders have tried to open up new markets and reduce excessive dependence on exports to Europe and the United States. In this regard, non-public enterprises have taken the lead. **Zhu Rongji repeatedly commended Huawei, Haier, and other enterprises for successfully entering the Russian market**:

> **There is something wrong with our existing enterprise system. We cannot solely rely on state-owned enterprises. This also shows that there is no future for state-owned enterprises without reform...**More and more problems with our state-owned enterprise system have been exposed...I heard that Huawei has entered the telecom market here, with sales of USD100 million last year. This is a private enterprise. Haier is also developing in Russia. Sichuan Changhong also wants to enter the Russian market, and is prepared to invest

[124] Zhu [88].
[125] Zhu [89].
[126] Xinhuanet [90].

USD30 million to build a factory with an annual output of 1 million TV sets. I think they have a vision.[127]

While learning from foreign-invested enterprises, Chinese government officials have also attached great importance to studying the systems and experiences of foreign governments, international organizations, and scholars under the market economy system. At the early stage of reform and opening up, the government sent a large number of delegations abroad to observe and learn from other countries. In fact, the 1978 delegation led by Gu Mu—the then Vice Premier of the State Council—to visit five European countries was the prelude to reform and opening up. After returning, Gu Mu delivered a report of nearly 10 h to the Politburo, which ultimately played an important role in Chinese leaders' determination to carry out reform and opening up.[128] Into the 1990s, the Chinese government began to cooperate with famous foreign universities and dispatched officials from all levels to receive training. Between 1992 and 2005, there were 42 bilateral training programs authorized by the National School of Administration alone, including 8 in collaboration with the United States—the country with the largest number. In 2010, about 70,000 people from the national party, government, enterprises, and institutions were sent abroad to receive training.[129]

The Kennedy School of Government of Harvard University and the Chinese government have three high-level projects, among which the "New World Harvard Senior Civil Servants Training Program" was the first to launch. Interviews were conducted in English by senior leadership of the Kennedy School, and the program admission rate was under 50%. Li Yuanchao (former member of the Political Bureau of the CPC Central Committee, former Vice President of China, and then Secretary of the Nanjing Municipal Party Committee) and Ma Jiantang (Party Secretary of the Development Research Center of the State Council, former Director of the National Bureau of Statistics, and then Deputy Governor of Qinghai Province) both participated.

In the process of advancing reforms, the Chinese government has also paid great attention to understanding and drawing on the experiences of advanced countries. In 1991, the then Vice Premier of the State Council, Zhu Rongji, spoke at a meeting with Alan Greenspan, the then Chairman of the Federal Reserve: "China pays attention to the US experience and practices in banking reform. We have changed the pattern of the central bank's original provincial branch and established nine major branches, with a view of strengthening the supervision of the central bank and eliminating improper administrative interference from local governments."[130] When he met with US Treasury Secretary Lloyd Bentsen in 1994, he also stated, "[in order to unify the exchange rate, China has] adopted the proposals of The International Monetary Fund and, for now, the situation is good and there is no problem…"[131]

[127]Zhu [91].

[128]Gu [92].

[129]Wang and Yu [93].

[130]Zhu [94].

[131]Zhu [95].

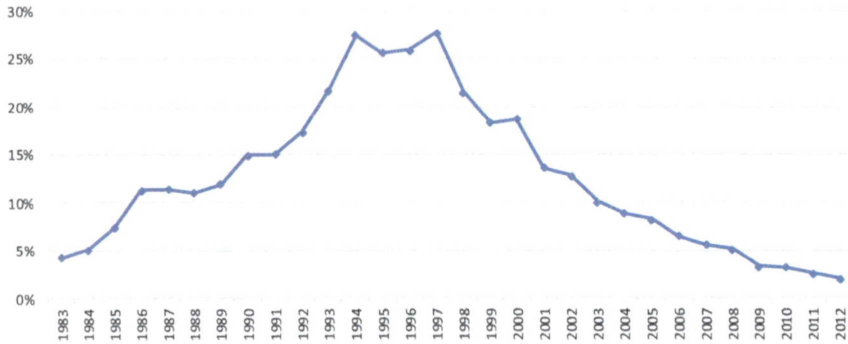

Chart 19 Actual utilization of foreign capital as a percentage of fixed-asset investment. *Source* National Bureau of Statistics, CEIC database

Since this time, China has more fully drawn on the experience of other countries in the process of establishing stock markets and reforming the banking system, as previously detailed. In fact, the pace of learning has still neither slowed nor stopped. When we conducted our survey in the Shenyang Area of the Liaoning Free Trade Zone, we learned that relevant leaders repeatedly mentioned the World Bank's *Business Environment Report* in their speeches, striving to align with the world's advanced benchmarks, simplifying the business registration process, and achieving the goal of efficiency exemplified by "business licenses being issued on the same day, the official seal being delivered within four hours, and tax registration being completed on the same day."

(e) **Discussions on capital, technology, tax creation, employment, etc.**

It is admittedly true that opening up has brought more funds, technology, and equipment to China, created taxation and employment, and enabled China to integrate into the international economic system via its comparative advantages. However, we believe that the impact of these benefits has been far less significant than that of learning advanced knowledge, institutions, and ideas through opening up.

As a country with a high savings rate, China does not lack funds in the general sense. From 1983 to 1986, the proportion of China's actual use of foreign capital in fixed-assets investment was consistently less than 10%. Even in the 1990s, when the inflow of foreign capital was at its greatest, the highest proportion only reached 28% (1994, 1997), followed by yearly decline. Overall, the scale of investment generated by foreign investment has been limited (Chart 19).

The introduction of technical equipment was an important reason for China's reform and opening up. Chinese enterprises have indeed introduced and learned many advanced technologies through foreign-invested enterprises, which has promoted China's productivity and improved welfare. Holmes et al. [96] **gave a detailed explanation of this issue**[132] (but we disagree with the view that China gains

[132] Holmeset al. [96].

at a loss to other countries, as thoroughly explained in the first part of this chapter). **However, we believe that the impact of narrow technical equipment has been limited.**

First, China imports technical equipment to learn from its use rather than to simply use it for production. In the survey, a previous leader of the State Planning Commission mentioned that before 1980, the tolerance standards of the Chinese manufacturing machinery industry were designed according to Soviet Union standards until reform and opening up. Through imports of Western parts, China realized the need for updating and therefore established the current system of tolerance of form and position standards. This shows that even imported parts can inspire significant learning.

Second, the improvements made by purchased equipment alone are limited and should not be overstated. As mentioned above, as early as the 1970s, Zhou Enlai presided over the introduction of Western fertilizer, chemical fiber, large rolling mills, and other equipment through the "Four Three Program," but this did not fundamentally change the face of the relevant industries. In a similar example, Brilliance Auto, a joint venture partner of BMW, created its own brand: "04 Chinese Car." Although this car was produced on the same line as the BMW "3 Series" and "5 Series" before and after 2004, the Chinese car still has not been recognized by the market.[133] One researcher who has attempted to explain such situations is **Huang Yasheng (2003)**, who conducted an in-depth study on the issue of foreign investment in China. He explored the case of clothing and other industries, and concluded that the knowledge transfer caused due to export-oriented FDI has been very limited. At the same time, he also stressed the benefits that FDI has brought to the Chinese economy at the institutional level. Huang believes that foreign investment can help Chinese companies break through old institutional obstacles and promote China's economic development while introducing new technology.[134]

Third, Chinese companies have paid a huge cost to introduce technical equipment. As mentioned earlier, JNMPT imported equipment from Germany at the price of USD2.53 million—undoubtedly a huge amount for a township enterprise with a registered capital of only USD320,000 a few years ago.[135] Huang et al. (2003) points out that most SOEs similarly acquired by foreign-invested enterprises have been able to accumulate many excellent assets in their early stages despite poor profitability.[136]

Finally, core advanced technologies are also difficult to obtain through joint ventures or purchases. In 2005, Shenyang Machine Tool Group acquired the famous German machine tool company Heath Group, which was on the verge of bankruptcy, and obtained the complete set of technology for its 17 products. However, due to

---

[133]Su [97].

[134]Huang [98], Introduction and Chap. 9.

[135]Xu [99].

[136]Huang et al. [98], Chap. 9.

the restrictions of the German Federal Economic and Export Administration, the relevant documents could not be shipped to China for domestic use.[137]

From a macro perspective, the tax contribution of foreign-invested enterprises to the government is also limited. In the first 30 years of reform and opening up, in order to attract foreign investment, the Chinese government introduced a series of tax incentives. According to Lin [101],[138] foreign-invested enterprises enjoyed an income tax policy of "exempt for 2 years and reduced for 3 years"—that is to say, the first two years of profit were exempt from tax, and the tax for the next three years was halved. Furthermore, equipment and necessary materials imported by a joint venture according to the contract were exempt from customs duties and uniform import business taxes, and non-restricted export goods were exempt from customs duties and uniform business taxes. Foreign-invested enterprises enjoyed the most preferential tax policies in the four special economic zones, fourteen coastal urban economic and technological development zones, and the Yangtze River Delta, Pearl River Delta, and Xiamen-Zhangzhou-Quanzhou Triangle Area, e.g., corporate income tax levied at 15% (versus 33% for domestic companies). This "super-national treatment" of foreign capital in taxation did not end until the "Enterprise Income Tax Law" was officially implemented in 2008. According to data from the *China Foreign Investment Report*, the tax contribution rate of foreign-invested enterprises in 2002–2007 was consistently around 20%.[139] In 2016, foreign-invested enterprises contributed 20% of the tax revenue, while non-financial state-owned enterprises contributed 30%.[140] Tianliang [104]. Therefore, from the perspective of taxation, although foreign-invested enterprises are very important, their importance should not be overstated.

From the perspective of employment, the macro impact of foreign-invested enterprises is still more limited. According to employment data from 1998 to 2015, even before the rapid development of China's non-public ownership economy in 1992, the employment of urban foreign-invested enterprises (the sum of Hong Kong, Macao, and Taiwanese investment enterprises plus foreign-invested enterprises) was consistently smaller than that of urban private enterprises. When compared to the employment of rural township enterprises, that of foreign-invested enterprises was even more insignificant (Charts 20 and 21).

2. **Opening up requires proactive government management**

Opening up is a complex process involving all aspects of a country's economic activities. In order to guide the economy to develop healthily, the government (especially the central government) should actively manage and guide the process of opening up to the outside world, and must not "release it." Surveying China's development over the past four decades, we believe that a sound and sustainable process of opening up requires the government to carefully manage at least the following

---

[137] Based on survey, cf He [100].

[138] Lin [101].

[139] Xing [102].

[140] Chen [103].

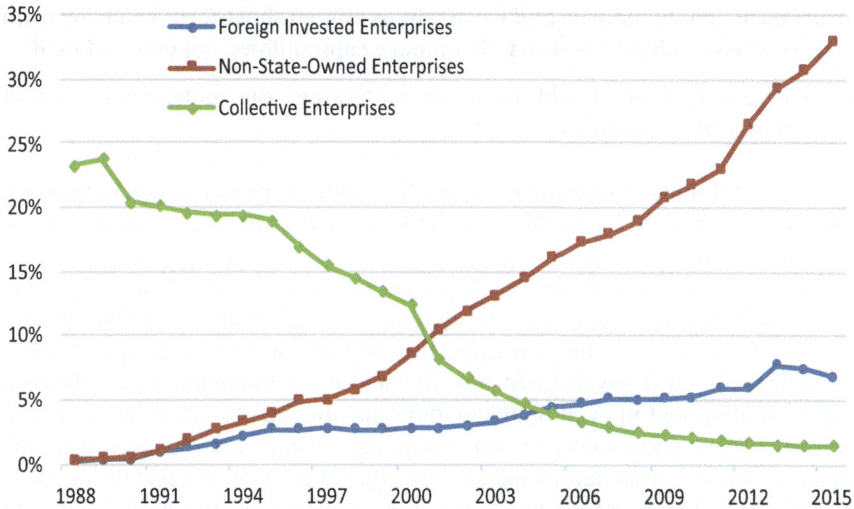

Chart 20 Proportion of foreign, private, and collective employment in urban employment. *Source* National Bureau of Statistics, CEIC database

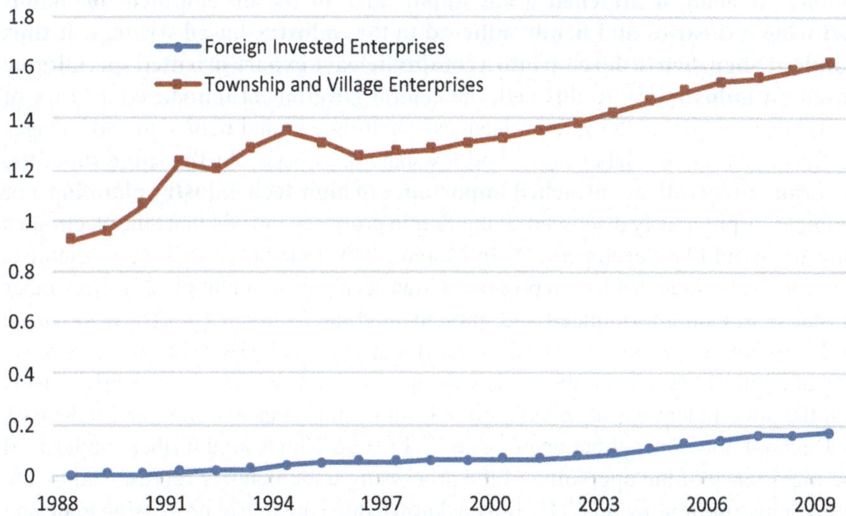

Chart 21 Employment of foreign and township enterprises (100 million). *Source* National Bureau of Statistics, CEIC database

three aspects: **first, the government should focus on cultivating the endogenous growth capacity of its economy; second, the government should help microeconomic subjects alleviate the negative impact of opening up; and third, the**

government should manage and constrain irrational short-term behavior from microeconomic subjects and strictly manage capital flows and external debt.

(a) **The government should focus on cultivating the endogenous growth capacity of its economy**

Since the beginning of opening up, Chinese leaders have focused on cultivating and activating the vitality of the economy through the opening up process. Deng Xiaoping repeatedly emphasized that opening up is to "develop productive forces" and "lead domestic enterprises."[141] As we examine the course of China's opening up, we find that many policies were meant to serve the self-sufficiency of the Chinese economy. Four aspects of this self-sufficiency building process are detailed below.

First, the central government has attached great importance to industrial transformation and upgrading throughout opening up. As mentioned above, in the early 1980s, many foreign businessmen and some experts believed that "the conditions for industrial development in Shenzhen were poor, and that the products were mainly exported and contrary to the purpose of investors (the products entered the mainland market), and proposed to build Shenzhen into a center of finance, commerce, foreign trade, and tourism."[142] **However, the central government was not satisfied with the development of tertiary industries such as tourism and finance. Instead, it attached great importance to the development of manufacturing industries and firmly adhered to the industry-based strategy. It thus required Shenzhen to develop into a comprehensive export-oriented special zone based on industry.**[143] To this end, the central government introduced a series of measures to optimize the foreign business environment and realize the advantages of "low taxation, low labor costs, and low land use costs." **At the same time, the government has always attached importance to high-tech industry planning.** For example, as previously discussed, Jiang Zemin proposed in 1984 that "the electronics industry should be developed."[144] In March 1986, four famous Chinese scientists wrote to the national leaders to propose a high-tech development plan. In November of that year, China formulated and implemented the *National High-Tech Research and Development Program* (863 Program) and granted RMB10 billion in funding (50 times the amount recommended by the four scientists). This event clearly reflects that the government has attached a great level of importance to high-end industries and technologies throughout opening up.[145] In 1996, Zhu Rongji further emphasized the importance of the upgrading of the processing trade industry represented by the "three-plus-one trading mix." He fully acknowledged the role of processing trade and encouraged enterprises to build their own factories through the introduction of new technology and equipment. He urged: "it is necessary to develop toward high-tech

[141] Deng [105, 106].

[142] Gu [107].

[143] ibid.

[144] Jiang [76].

[145] Ma and Hu [78].

and increase new advantages. It is not possible to rely on the past 'three-plus-one trading mix.'"[146]

Second, the government (especially the central government) attaches great importance to the learning brought about by opening up. In his 1978 speech, Deng Xiaoping clearly stated that it was imperative to learn through opening up.[147] He believed it was important to "inherit and learn the science and technology developed and all kinds of useful knowledge and experience accumulated by the people of all countries under the capitalist system."[148] As previously mentioned, leaders such as Jiang Zemin and Zhu Rongji also placed significant emphasis on the role of learning. Jiang Zemin emphasized, "whether it can continue to learn all the advanced things in the world, whether it can keep up with the trend of world development, is a big issue that affects the success or failure of a country or a nation."[149] Zhu Rongji once said that "without competition, there will be no progress. Without opening up, how can advanced management experience, business methods, and technical means come in?" He then placed this concept specifically in the context of the insurance agency industry in China: "AIG introduced the practice of insurance agencies in Shanghai, and it has developed very rapidly. PICC Shanghai Branch immediately adopted this method…but however smart the Shanghainese are, if AIG had not come in, there would be no model, and it would not have led to the existence of insurance agencies."[150]

In view of the above, it is not difficult to appreciate why China's top leaders have continued to open up to the outside world with great political courage and determination. As mentioned before, on the issue of joining the World Trade Organization, there were many different opinions at home and abroad, questioning and even dismissing China's decision to join the WTO. Since joining the World Trade Organization, the Chinese government has made great efforts to promote China's full integration into the international economic system. Since 2001, the Chinese central government has cleared more than 2300 laws, regulations, and ministerial regulations, and local governments have cleared more than 190,000 local policies and regulations. The overall tariff rate dropped from 15.3% in 2001 to 9.8% in 2015, and the trade-weighted average tariff rate fell to 4.4%—significantly lower than emerging economies (such as South Korea, India, and Indonesia) and developing countries, but close to the United States (2.4%) and the EU (3%). Among the 160 service sub-sectors defined by the WTO, China has promised to open 100 of them, close to the average of developed country members (108). Today, China has improved its business environment and service quality through 12 free trade zones. These efforts can all be regarded as upgrading and developing through learning from abroad.[151]

---

[146]Zhu [108].

[147]Deng [109].

[148]ibid., 168.

[149]Jiang [110].

[150]Zhu [111].

[151]Based on the Press Office of the People's Republic of China [14, 18].

Third, Chinese leaders have attached great importance to attracting foreign investment because they recognize that interaction with advanced foreign economies can bring about tremendous learning effects. From 1986 to 1987, the then Vice Premier of the State Council, Gu Mu, personally coordinated the introduction of documents to optimize the foreign business environment. In order to prevent the policy from being warped during implementation, he also presided over the formulation of 22 implementation rules. From October to December 1986, Gu Mu personally hosted 12 meetings to evaluate and oversee the implementation process.[152] Zhu Rongji also emphasized the importance of attracting foreign investment several times. When talking about the development of Shanghai, he once said, "the land in Pudong should not be too expensive in order to attract foreign investment and speed up development…[in order to attract major foreign investment projects] it is necessary to strengthen the confidence of investors, and things must be done quickly or time will run out."[153] At the same time, the central government regarded attracting foreign investment as an important indicator for assessing local officials and guided local governments to do their utmost to provide services for foreign-invested enterprises. As mentioned previously, the Shenyang government even "leveled the hills and replaced the soil" to win the BMW project. In our survey, Jiangyin City's deputy mayor in charge of industry told us that in the 1990s, every time he went to Beijing or Shanghai for business trips, he organized companies to translate materials, such as recent catalogs, into English and Japanese. He would then bring these materials and speak in person with the representatives of foreign enterprises.

Fourth, the Chinese government aims to coordinate the pace of opening up in different fields, give domestic firms opportunities to develop while continuously opening up, introduce competition, and promote learning. To protect and improve the endogenous growth capacity of the domestic economy, imported goods were introduced gradually. Otherwise, the domestic market would have been flooded with foreign products overnight, and it would have been difficult for domestic enterprises to survive. However, if the protection had been excessive, enterprises would not have learned from advanced foreign enterprises, they would not have faced the pressure of competition, and they would not have been likely to grow in strength and size. As the ancient Chinese proverb says, "a country is doomed to perish if there are neither capable officials within nor enemy threats without."

When Zhu Rongji spoke on the opening up of the financial industry in 1994, he stressed, "China's banks are far from the standards of commercial banks. If a large number of foreign banks are approved to do RMB business at this time, Chinese banks will be forced to compete with them on an unequal footing."[154] **This kind of protection by the Chinese government should not be seen as "spoiling" domestic enterprises. Rather, pressures were applied to domestic enterprises through measured opening up to promote their growth. Zhu Rongji said on the same occasion that "we must adopt a gradual approach. The protection from**

[152] *Gu Mu Memoirs*, Chap. VI.
[153] March 25, 1992.
[154] Zhu [112].

the Chinese government is not unconditional and permanent."[155] In fact, since 1994, China's financial services industry has gradually opened up, and tariffs in the automotive sector have gradually declined. In 2018, **against the backdrop of rising trade protectionism, China further relaxed or even removed the restrictions on the shareholding ratio of joint ventures in the financial and automobile sectors on the basis of the WTO commitments, and drastically reduced automobile import tariffs. These facts once again show that the protection of the Chinese government is temporary and conditional**.

(b) **The government has worked hard to absorb the shocks of opening up**

As previously mentioned, although the learning brought by opening up has greatly promoted economic transformation and development, it has still had a major impact on some industries, regions, and economic subjects. Imported machine tools and other mechanical equipment hit enterprises in Shenyang, causing nearly one million people to be laid off. China's local film industry was also swept by foreign companies such as Fujifilm and Kodak and eventually acquired as a whole. The export restrictions on Chinese textile products in Europe and the United States were further aggravated, causing the industry to decline with even more intensity. In the face of such shocks, the central government and local governments shouldered the responsibility for recovery. On one hand, they guaranteed the basic welfare of laid-off workers through fiscal expenditures and supported the re-employment of laid-off workers through taxation and employment guidance (the "textile air hostess" program is the epitome of this). On the other hand, the government has made efforts to help industries adjust. For example, the Shenyang government organized the "Moving East Construction West" program, and the State Council promoted the "Destroying Textile Spindles" initiative to achieve liquidation as soon as possible and help the industry return to the right track.

(c) **Guiding and constraining debts in foreign exchange and capital flows**

In the process of opening up, the government should carefully manage capital flows and strictly limit the tendency of companies to over-borrow foreign debt to prevent a balance of payments crisis.

The Chinese government had drawn on the development experience of Latin America and other regions and dialectically understands the advantages and disadvantages of borrowing foreign debt. When China began to borrow foreign debts in 1979, Deng Xiaoping emphasized the issue of "solvency."[156] In 1986, he further emphasized that **"external debt should be moderate and should not be borrowed excessively. Pay attention to the experience of these two aspects. The borrowing of foreign debt is not worrying, but it should mainly be used for developing production and it is not good if it is used to solve the fiscal deficit."**[157] In 1997, Zhu Rongji also concluded that "our inflow of foreign capital is

---

[155] ibid.

[156] Deng [113].

[157] ibid., 192–193.

foreign investment in the form of equipment investment and borrowings are basically medium- and long-term foreign debts…so we can basically avoid a financial crisis throughout Asian countries."[158] At the same time, the Chinese government regards foreign exchange reserves as a strategic resource and carefully allocates their use in the early stages of development. For example, Zhu Rongji repeatedly stressed that **"the precious foreign exchange cannot be used for importing consumer goods, including cars. The limited foreign exchange should be mainly used for the introduction of advanced technology, transforming weak sectors of the national economy, and accelerating industrial restructuring."**[159]

In fact, even in the field of direct investment, the government pays great attention to the issue of foreign exchange payments. A former leader of the State Planning Commission spoke to us about the formation of the "foreign exchange balance" policy in the early stage of reform and opening up. The fundamental purpose behind the development of this policy was to ensure that, in the context of foreign exchange shortages, there would be sufficient foreign exchange to ensure remittance of profits required by foreign investors. To this end, the State requires that a joint venture must have the ability to provide the foreign exchange required for the foreign investor's profit remittance, otherwise the project will not be approved. **A typical case is that of the Daya Bay nuclear power plant project, which was originally shelved because the foreign exchange balance problem could not be solved. In response, Jieke Lin, the general manager of the US International Nuclear Energy Corporation, proposed to sell part of the electricity to Hong Kong to earn foreign exchange and solve the foreign exchange balance problem. In this way, the joint venture project was finally implemented.**[160] Although foreign exchange restrictions have limited consumer demand to a certain extent, they have also helped the Chinese economy to achieve steady and sustainable development.

At the same time, the Chinese government has carefully formulated exchange rate policies, considering factors such as inflation, exports, and confidence to ensure a stable currency. In practice, the exchange rate is linked to the real economy and financial markets, and there is no way to calculate the equilibrium exchange rate in the academic sense. Therefore, the government must consider the price signals of foreign exchange market transactions, but also the affordability of the real economy, and seize key moments to implement reforms. Zhu Rongji once stressed:

> [A sharp change in exchange rate] not only brings greater risks and uncertainties to import and export enterprises, but also increases the pressure of domestic inflation and affects the confidence of overseas investors. Some people say that the value of the depreciated RMB is beneficial to future exports, but I disagree. The experiences of various countries prove that excessive depreciation of the domestic currency does not promote exports. Whether exports are increased is not entirely determined by the exchange rate, but mainly by the variety, quality, and service of the products. It is not necessarily a useful tool to restrict

[158]Zhu [114].
[159]Zhu [115].
[160]Wen [116].

imports. Even if USD1 is equivalent to RMB15, as expected by some people, certain areas or departments will still import Mercedes-Benz cars.[161]

Economic practice is the fountainhead of economic theory. Summarizing China's opening up process, we believe that learning is the most fundamental benefit of opening up. Furthermore, a stable and sustainable process of economic opening up requires careful management by the government. We believe that these two conclusions can serve as a guide to other countries and are a useful complement to mainstream open economics and international trade theory.

References

1. United Nations Organization for Trade and Development (UNCATD). (2018). World Investment Report 2018. Retrieved November 15, 2018, from https://unctad.org/en/PublicationsLibrary/wir2018_overview_ch.pdf.
2. Ministry of Commerce, National Statistics of the People's Republic of China Bureau, State Administration of Foreign Exchange. (2017). 2016 China foreign direct investment statistics bulletin. Retrieved November 15, 2018, from http://www.mofcom.gov.cn/article/tongjiziliao/dgzz/201803/20180302722851.shtml.
3. Ministry of Commerce, National Bureau of Statistics, State Administration of Foreign Exchange. (2018). 2017 China foreign direct investment statistics bulletin. Retrieved November 15, 2018, from http://www.mofcom.gov.cn/article/tongjiziliao/dgzz/201809/20180902791492.shtml.
4. Zhang, H., & Zhai, X. (2018). Characteristics and insights of China's participation in global value chains. *Quantitative Economics and Technology Economics* (1), 3–22.
5. Ministry of Commerce of the People's Republic of China. (2017). China Foreign Investment Cooperation Development Report 2017. Retrieved November 15, 2018, from http://fec.mofcom.gov.cn/article/tzhzcj/tzhz/upload/zgdwtzhzfzbg2017.pdf.
6. Javorcik, B. S. (2004). Does foreign direct investment increase the productivity of domestic firms? In search of spillovers through backward linkages. *American Economic Review, 94*(3), 605–627.
7. Li, J. (2018). Beijing air food: "No. 001" Joint Venture, Unforgettable "Fresh Air", Xinhuanet reprinted from People's Daily Overseas Edition. Retrieved November 15, 2018, from http://www.xinhuanet.com/Fortune/2018-08/14/c_1123264464.htm.
8. Li, Y., & Liu, S. (2018). Opening up and industrial upgrading in the context of global value chains—An empirical study based on quasi-nature experiments. *China Soft Science* (8), 165–174.
9. Liu, Q., Lu, R., & Zhang, C. (2017). Entrepreneurship and spillovers from multinationals: Evidence from Chinese private firms. *China Economic Review, 29*, 95–106.
10. Jiang, M. (2007). *North heavy industry acquired*. German Wirth Holding Company/French NFM Company. Retrieved November 15, 2018, from http://finance.people.com.cn/GB/6181939.html.
11. Smith, J., & Mi, Q. (2014). China communications group acquires Australian builders for A$1.15 billion. *Financial Times Chinese*. Retrieved November 15, 2018, from http://www.ftchinese.com/story/001059633?full=y&archive.
12. China Securities Network. (2016). COFCO acquires the entire equity of Nidera. Retrieved November 15, 2018, from http://news.cnstock.com/news,bwkx-201608-3881870.htm.

[161] Zhu [117].

13. Zhang, S. (2018, March 31). *Number of Chinese students studying abroad last year broke 600,000* (2th ed.). People's Daily Overseas Edition.
14. Press Office of the People's Republic of China. (2018). Facts and China's position on China–US economic and trade friction. Retrieved November 14, 2018, from http://www.xinhuanet.com/politics/2018-09/24/c_1123475272.htm.
15. US China Business Council. (2018). US–China business council state export report. Retrieved November 15, 2018, from https://www.uschina.org/sites/default/files/final_uscbc_state_report_2018_1.pdf.
16. Press Office of the People's Republic of China. (2018). Facts and China's position on Sino-US trade friction. Retrieved November 14, 2018, from http://www.xinhuanet.com/politics/2018-09/24/c_1123475272.htm.
17. Kim, P. (2014). The big three aren't so big anymore. *CBS News* Website cites data from IHS. Retrieved November 18, 2018, from https://www.cbsnews.com/news/the-big-three-arent-so-big-anymore/.
18. Press Office of the People's Republic of China. (2018). White paper on china and the world trade organization. Retrieved November 14, 2018, from http://www.mofcom.gov.cn/article/i/jyjl/l/201808/20180802773208.shtml.
19. Oxford Economics and US–China Business Council. (2017). Understanding the US–China trade relationship. Retrieved November 15, 2018, from https://www.uschina.org/reports/understanding-us-china-trade-relationship.
20. Li, D., Li, Y., & Zhang, C. (2018). How does the great practice of China's economy make important economic contributions?—Analysis and reflection based on the history of economic history and economic thought. *Journal of Economics, 2018*(5), 1–16.
21. Maddison, A. (2007). *The world economy volume 1: "A millennial perspective*"(pp. 96, 97, 100). Academic Foundation.
22. Hughes, J., & Cain, L. P. (2011). *American economic history*. Pearson.
23. Guo, X., & Guo, H. (2014). *Characteristics and insights of "The German Road in 1914"—Historical experience of germany in dealing with the "Government-Industry" relationship*. People's Forum, Pre-Academic.
24. China Bureau of Statistics. (1982). *China statistical yearbook 1981*. China Statistics Press.
25. Shenyang Tourism Commission. (2018). Fuyun Shenyang|The birth of the eldest son of the republic, a place where there are the most "firsts" of new China's industry. Retrieved November 14, 2018, from http://www.sohu.com/a/223124363_349299.
26. Shenyang Machine Tool (Group) Co., Ltd. *Our history*. Retrieved November 14, 2018, from http://www.symg.cn/channels/33.html.
27. Wang, B. (2016). The once Golden Rice Bowl now in a quagmire, Shenyang machine tool is bailing itself out. *Chinese Entrepreneur*. Retrieved November 14, 2018, from https://www.sohu.com/a/71893454_355067.
28. Customs Tariff Commission of the State Council of the People's Republic of China. (1994). *China's import tariff rate adjustment table (part 1)*. International Trade, No. 2, pp. 47–62.
29. State Council Tariff Commission of the State Council. (1994). *China's import tariff rate adjustment table (part 2)*. International Trade, No. 2, pp. 51–62.
30. Yan, K. (2016). Northeast in crisis: Why did the cradle of industry become the hometown of the past? *Chinese Entrepreneur*. Retrieved November 14, 2018, from http://business.sohu.com/20160422/n445482813.shtml.
31. Shenyang Municipal Bureau of Statistics. (2000). *Shenyang statistical yearbook 2000*.
32. Wang, J. (1998). Foreign Films Competing for the Chinese market. *Contemporary Economy* (5), 45–46.
33. Fu, Q., & Yan, W. (2008). 1998: Kodak's billion-dollar 'Gambling' for China. Sina.com reprinting. *First Financial Daily*. Retrieved November 14, 2018, from https://finance.sina.com.cn/roll/20081215/02105634054.shtml.
34. Zhu, R. (2011). *Talks with the US trade representative Barshefsky, the record of Zhu Rongji's speech* (Vol. III, pp. 352–374). People's Publishing House.

35. Anonymous. (1996). The causes and impacts of US sanctions on textiles. *Shandong Foreign Trade and Economics* (11), p. 3.
36. Shanghai Local Records Office. (2018). Open space and Shanghai local history. Website reprinting, *Shanghai Zhi·industry division·textile industry volume*. Retrieved November 14, 2018, from http://www.shtong.gov.cn/Newsite/node2/n189654/n189918/index.html.
37. Global Textile Network. (2009).Textile in 60 years: Shanghai textile industry old branch blooms. Retrieved November 14, 2018, from https://www.tnc.com.cn/info/c-001001-d-131048.html.
38. Shanghai Textile Group. (2018). Group profile—Enterprise achievements. Retrieved November 14, 2018, from http://www.shangtex.biz/default.shtml.
39. People's Daily Online. (1972). The Central Committee of the Communist Party of China and the State Council approve the report of the State Planning Commission on the import of complete sets of chemical fiber and fertilizer technology equipment. Retrieved November 14, 2018, from http://cpc.people.com.cn/GB/64162/64165/77552/77557/index.html.
40. People's Daily Online. (2016). On December 6, 1979, "Deng Xiaoping met with Japanese Prime Minister Masayoshi Ōhira". Retrieved November 14, 2018, from http://cpc.people.com.cn/n1/2016/0603/c69113-28410390.html.
41. Phoenix.com. (2018). A total of 45 billion US dollars: Japan was the country that provided the most assistance to China! Retrieved November 14, 2018, from http://news.ifeng.com/a/20180813/59849110_0.shtml.
42. Sohu.com. (2018). Japan will end its 40-year long government aid to China and China's Ministry of Foreign Affairs comments. Retrieved November 14, 2018, from http://www.sohu.com/a/270787430_115479.
43. Xinhuanet. (2018). Beijing air food: 'No. 001' joint venture, unforgettable 'Fresh Air'. Retrieved November 14, 2018, from http://www.xinhuanet.com/fortune/2018-08/14/c_1123264464.htm.
44. Zhang, J., et al. (1992). *The dictionary of national history of the People's Republic of China*.
45. Deng, X. (1994). Speech at the opening ceremony of the national science conference. In *Selected Works of Deng Xiaoping* (Vol. II, pp. 85–100).
46. Deng, X. (1994). Liberating the mind, seeking truth from facts, seeing unity and forward. In *Selected works of Deng Xiaoping* (Vol. II, pp. 140–153).
47. Hexun News. (2008). Lei Yu and 1984 Hainan automobile smuggling incident. Retrieved November 14, 2018, from http://news.hexun.com/2008-09-08/108638576.html.
48. Deng, X. (1994). Speech at the third plenary meeting of the central advisory commission. In *Selected works of Deng Xiaoping* (Vol. III, pp. 83–93).
49. Deng, X. (1994). Our grand goals and fundamental policies. In *Selected works of Deng Xiaoping* (Vol. III, pp. 77–80).
50. Jiang, Z. (2006). Developing Shanghai Pudong new area. In *Selected works of Jiang Zemin* (Vol. I, pp. 35–36).
51. Gu, M. (2009). A new milestone in the development of special economic zones. In *Gu Mu Memoirs* (pp. 359–370).
52. Gu, M. (2009). Regulations on absorbing foreign investment work. In *Gu Mu Memoirs* (pp. 371–379).
53. Ministry of Commerce of the People's Republic of China. (1986). Regulations on encouraging foreign investment. Retrieved November 14, 2018, from http://www.mofcom.gov.cn/article/swfg/swfgbl/201101/20110107352171.shtml.
54. Phoenix.com. (2011). Deng Xiaoping's southern tour speeches (full text). Retrieved November 14, 2018, from https://finance.ifeng.com/opinion/sjgc/20111231/5389402.shtml.
55. Zhu, R. (2011). Continue to rectify the financial order and strictly control the total amount of credit. In *Records of Zhu Rongji's speeches* (Vol. I, pp. 449–458).
56. Central People's Government of the People's Republic of China. (1994). Reply from the state council on agreeing to open five border ports such as Bhaktu in Xinjiang. Retrieved November 14, 2018, from http://www.gov.cn/zhengce/content/2016-08/31/content_5103947.htm.

57. Zhu, R. (2011). Intensifying the cultivation of scientific and technological talents. In *Records of Zhu Rongji's speeches* (Vol. III, pp. 509–512).
58. Zhu, R. (2011). To adjust and improve the processing trade policy. In *Records of Zhu Rongji's speeches* (Vol. II, pp. 365–270).
59. Jiang, Z. (2006). Building a new historical monument for sino-African friendship. In *Selected works of Jiang Zemin* (Vol. I, pp. 35–36).
60. Jiang, Z. (2006). Speech at comrade Deng Xiaoping's memorial conference. In*Selected works of Jiang Zemin* (Vol. I, pp. 627–640).
61. Jiang, Z. (2006). Continuing to push forward the cause of building socialism with Chinese characteristics in the new century. In *Selected works of Jiang Zemin* (Vol. III, pp. 117–135).
62. Zhu, R. (2011). Speech at the symposium on the pilot work of stock markets in some provinces and cities. In *Records of Zhu Rongji's speeches* (Vol. I, pp. 204–213).
63. Gordon Chang. (2002). *The Coming Collapse of China.*
64. Wikipedia. (2016). China separatism. Retrieved November 14, 2018, from https://zh.wikipedia.org/wiki/China_Separatism.
65. People's Forum. (2018). From joining the WTO to building belt and road initiative. Retrieved November 14, 2018, from http://politics.rmlt.com.cn/2018/0911/528021.shtml.
66. Zhang, D. (2002). *Overview of economic law adjustment upon China's entry into the WTO.*
67. NetEase. (2004). Abolition of all general commodity import quotas. Retrieved November 14, 2018, from http://tech.163.com/04/1217/08/17PR5UPR000915BD.html.
68. Sohu.com. (2003). Historical first order—QFII first entry into the market.
69. Sina.com. (2006). Fund QDII goes out to sea. Retrieved November 14, 2018, from http://finance.sina.com.cn/focus/jjqdiich/index.shtml.
70. Xinhuanet. (2018). Xi Jinping's keynote speech at the opening ceremony of the first China international import expo (full text). Retrieved November 14, 2018, from http://www.xinhuanet.com//2018-11/05/c_1123664692.htm.
71. People.com. (2017). Sharing the responsibility of the age to promote global development. In Keynote Speech at the Opening Ceremony of the 2017 Annual Conference of the World Economic Forum.
72. Xinhuanet. (2018). Xi Jinping attended the opening ceremony of the 2018 Annual Meeting of the Boao Forum for Asia and delivered a keynote speech. Retrieved November 14, 2018, from http://www.xinhuanet.com/2018-04/10/c_1122660064.htm.
73. Ministry of Commerce of the People's Republic of China. (2005). Special topic 1, textile trade integration and China's textile. Retrieved November 20, 2018, from http://zhs.mofcom.gov.cn/aarticle/Nocategory/200504/20050400081560.html.
74. Liu, Y. (2013). The inside story of China's first automobile joint venture. *China Economic Weekly*, No. 37. Retrieved November 20, 2018, from http://paper.people.com.cn/zgjjzk/html/2013-09/23/Content_1303907.htm.
75. China Economic Net. (2018). "2018 World Top 500" list: 6 Chinese auto companies are on the list again, reprinted by Xinhuanet. Retrieved November 20, 2018, from http://www.xinhuanet.com/2018-07/21/c_1123157964.htm.
76. Jiang, Z. (2006). Revitalizing the electronic industry, promoting the construction of the four modernizations. In *Selected works of Jiang Zemin* (Vol. I). People's Publishing House. Retrieved November 14, 2018, from http://cpc.people.com.cn/GB/64184/64185/180137/10818670.html.
77. Fa, C. (2018). *China's Semiconductor industry in the historical process.* Ge Long Hui reprinted the article as "Fa Chai Business Matters". Retrieved November 15, 2018, from https://m.gelonghui.com/p/178262.
78. Ma, Y., & Hu, X. (2009). The '863 Program:' 200 million applied and 10 billion approved. *China Economic Weekly*, No. 2, pp. 61–62.
79. World Intellectual Property Organization. (2017). Patent cooperation treaty yearly review 2018. Retrieved November 20, 2018, from http://www.wipo.int/edocs/pubdocs/en/wipo_pub_901_2018.pdf.

80. Summarized from BBC News. Samuel Slater: American hero or British traitor? Retrieved December 1, 2018, from https://www.bbc.com/news/uk-england-derbyshire-15002318.
81. Dai, B. (2018). A pre-publicized 'curve overtaking'. *The Rice Barrel Financial.*
82. Yu, W., & Zhu, J. (2008, October 28). *The vicissitudes of the life—The legend of the rise of Li Xing and Cheng Xing* (8th ed.). People's Daily (overseas version).
83. Yang, Y. (2014). *Running ten thousand mountains—Talking about the things of Li Xing* (pp. 110–111, 123). Jiangsu People's Publishing House.
84. Yang, Y. (2014). *Running ten thousand mountains—Talking about the things of Li Xing* (p. 115).
85. Sina Education. (2011). National training program for foreigners in foreign countries. Retrieved November 13, 2018, from http://edu.sina.com.cn/yyks/2011-09-21/1657313513.shtml.
86. National People's Congress. (1996). Proposal of the Central Committee of the Communist Party of China on formulating the ninth five-year plan for national economic and social development and the vision of 2010. Retrieved November 13, 2018, from http://www.npc.gov.cn/wxzl/gongbao/2001-01/02/content_5003506.htm.
87. Gu, M. (2009). *Gu Mu Memoirs* (p. 377). Central Literature Publishing House, Chapter 6.
88. Zhu, R. (2011). Strengthening economic and trade cooperation with developing countries. In *Records of Zhu Rongji's speeches* (Vol. 2, pp. 194–201). People's Publishing House.
89. Zhu, R. (2011). Several issues needing attention in the development of Shanghai. In *Records of Zhu Rongji's speeches* (Vol. II, pp. 271–276). People's Publishing House.
90. Xinhuanet. (2018). List of outstanding private entrepreneurs in the 40 years of reform and opening up. Retrieved November 14, 2018, from http://www.xinhuanet.com//finance/2018-10/24/c_129978412.htm.
91. Zhu, R. (2011). Enterprises should enter Russia. In *Records of Zhu Rongji's speeches* (Vol. IV, pp. 230–236). People's Publishing House.
92. Gu, M. (2009). *Gu Mu Memoirs* (p. 305). Central Literature Publishing House, Chapter 6.
93. Wang, D., & Yu, Y. (2011). Full record of overseas training for mainland officials. *Phoenix Weekly Magazine.* Retrieved November 13, 2018, from http://news.ifeng.com/shendu/fhzk/detail_2011_09/08/9041977_0.shtml.
94. Zhu, R. (2011). Talks with chairman of the Federal Reserve Board Alan Greenspan. In *Records of Zhu Rongji's speeches* (Vol. II, pp. 34–41). People's Publishing House.
95. Zhu, R. (2011). Talks with U.S. Treasury Secretary Bentson. In *Records of Zhu Rongji's speeches* (Vol. II, pp. 464–471). People's Publishing House.
96. Holmes, T. J., Mcgrattan, E. R., & Prescott, E. C. (2013). Quid pro quo: Technology capital transfers for market access in China. *Staff Report, 82*(3), 1154–1193.
97. Su, Q. (2003). China and domestic BMW co-production to lay the foundation for quality, reprinted by Sohu Auto, from *Beijing Morning News.* Retrieved November 13, 2018, from http://auto.sohu.com/2003/12/16/01/article216960166.shtml.
98. Huang, Y., Huang, P. Y., & Kirby, W. (2009). *Selling China: Foreign direct investment during the reform era.* Cambridge University Press.
99. Xu, D. (2017). *Cao Mingfang: Blowing up the yellow sands for gold, Jiangyin industrialists* (pp. 289–302). Shanghai People's Publishing House.
100. He, Y. (2007, June 27). Shenyang machine tool buying a ship to the sea. *People's Daily,* 6th ed. Retrieved October 26, 2018, from http://media.163.com/05/0526/11/1KM5FS4P00141E37.html.
101. Lin, Z. (2008). *Historical investigation and theoretical analysis of tax policies for foreign-funded enterprises in China.* Southwestern University of Finance and Economics.
102. Xing, H. (2017). *China foreign investment report* (p. 18). Retrieved November 13, 2018, from http://images.mofcom.gov.cn/wzs/201804/20180416161221341.pdf.
103. Chen, D. (2018). Reform and open witness China's 40 years of intensification and deep impact on global value chains. *International Trade Issues, 1,* 13–16.

104. Tianliang, B. (2017, July 28). These five years, the state-owned enterprises are starting to take off (see changes in the new normal). *People's Daily*, 10th ed. Retrieved November 13, 2018, from http://paper.people.com.cn/Rmrb/html/2017-07/28/nw.D110000renmrb_20170728_1-10.htm.
105. Deng, X. (1994). Implementation of open policy, learning the world's advanced science and technology. In *Selected works of Deng Xiaoping* (Vol. II, pp. 132–133).
106. Deng, X. (1994). Opinions on economic work. In *Selected works of Deng Xiaoping* (Vol. II, pp. 194–202).
107. Gu, M. (2009). *Gu Mu Memoirs* (pp. 359–371). Central Literature Publishing House, Chapter 6.
108. Zhu, R. (2001). To adjust and improve the processing trade policy. In *Selected works of Zhu Rongji* (Vol. II, pp. 265–270). People's Publishing House.
109. Deng, X. (1994). Implementation of an open policy, learning the world's advanced science and technology. In *Selected works of Deng Xiaoping* (Vol. II, pp. 132–133).
110. Jiang, Z. (2006). Continuing to push forward the construction of socialism with Chinese characteristics in the new century. In *Selected works of Jiang Zemin* (Vol. III). People's Publishing House. Retrieved November 14, 2018, from http://cpc.people.com.cn/GB/64184/64185/180139/10818611.html.
111. Zhu, R. (2001). Doing a good job in the opening of the financial insurance market. In *Selected works of Zhu Rongji* (Vol. II, pp. 298–302). People's Publishing House.
112. Zhu, R. (2011). Talks with U.S. Treasury Secretary Bentsen. In *Records of Zhu Rongji's speeches* (Vol. II, pp. 464–471). People's Publishing House.
113. Deng, X. (1994). Several opinions on economic work. In *Selected works of Deng Xiaoping* (Vol. II, pp. 194–202).
114. Zhu, R. (2011). Learn the lessons of the Asian financial crisis seriously. In *Records of Zhu Rongji's speeches* (Vol. II, pp. 505–511). People's Publishing House.
115. Zhu, R. (2011). Opinions on the current economic situation and macroeconomic regulation. In *Records of Zhu Rongji's speeches* (Vol. I, pp. 228–240). People's Publishing House.
116. Wen, X. (2018). Daya Bay nuclear power plant: The birth of China's largest Sino-foreign joint venture in the early days of reform. Retrieved November 14, 2018, from http://www.sohu.com/a/232147417_468637.
117. Zhu, R. (2011). Strengthening foreign exchange management. In *Records of Zhu Rongji's speeches* (Vol. I, pp. 346–351). People's Publishing House.

Proactive Macroeconomic Management

David Daokui Li, Ming Feng, Shaobo Long, Gangming Yuan, Peng Zhou, and Yusha Li

Abstract China has achieved a relatively stable and high-speed economic growth for four decades since 1978. At the same time, China has maintained a significantly lower inflation than that of other emerging economies and transition countries during their respective high growth and transition periods. China managed to avoid a real economic crisis and successfully responded to major external shocks, which has also been a great contribution to world economic stability and the so called "the Great Moderation" in developed economies since the 1980s. In this chapter, we analyze the microeconomic mechanisms why developing countries are prone to high macroeconomic fluctuations, review the history of China's macroeconomic management since 1978, and summarize the "three arrows" used by the Chinese government to implement macroeconomic management. The take home message of this chapter is that the central government of developing countries must manage its macroeconomy proactively during economic take-off.

Keywords Macroeconomic management · Macroeconomic fluctuations · Economic take-off

D. D. Li (✉) · S. Long · G. Yuan · Y. Li
An Academic Center for Chinese Economic Practice and Thinking (ACCEPT), Tsinghua University, Beijing, China
e-mail: daviddaokuili@126.com

S. Long
e-mail: longshbcqu@126.com

G. Yuan
e-mail: yuangm@sina.com

Y. Li
e-mail: liyusha2015@outlook.com

M. Feng
National Academy of Economic Strategy, CASS, Beijing, China
e-mail: fengmingthu@126.com

P. Zhou
China International Capital Corporation Limited, Beijing, China
e-mail: peng3.zhou@cicc.com.cn

D. D. Li (eds.), *Economic Lessons from China's Forty Years of Reform and Opening-up*, https://doi.org/10.1007/978-981-33-4520-1_6

1 Stylized Facts

1.1 Stable High-Speed Economic Growth for 40 Years

China's economy has achieved steady, high-speed growth since 1978. From 1978 to 2017, China's GDP grew from USD294.3 billion to USD10.2 trillion (calculated according to constant 2010 USD), with an average annual real growth rate of over 9.5%. During the same period, the per capita GNP grew from USD307 to USD7,329, with an average annual growth rate of 8.5%.

At the same time, China's real GDP growth volatility is significantly lower than that of other economies. Whether compared with other countries over the same period or other high-growth economies in history, the stability of China's economic growth over the past 40 years is rare and can be called a miracle in human economic history.

The volatility of the real economic growth rate can be divided into two parts: the change of the potential economic growth rate and the change of cyclical factors. We split the economic growth rate of various countries from 1961 to 2017 into two pieces—the trend and the residual—via the Hodrick-Prescott filter. The trend can be used as an estimate of the potential economic growth rate, and the residual corresponds to periodic economic fluctuations. We used the standard deviation of the cyclical fluctuation from 1961 to 2017 from the mean of the potential growth rate to represent the fluctuation of real economic growth and found that the fluctuation of China's economy was significantly less than that of developed countries and other developing countries (Table 1).

If we compare China's high-speed growth period (1978 to 2017) with that of Japan and South Korea (1961 to 1990) via the same approach, we find that the volatility of China's real GDP growth is also relatively low (Table 2). Especially considering that China experienced the Asian financial crisis and the 2008 global financial crisis during this period, this is an even more impressive achievement (Chart 1).

We can also take a longer view and compare China's economic growth since 1978 with that of Britain during the industrial revolution, Germany at the end of the 19th century, the United States from 1890 to 1920, and the Soviet Union from its foundation to its disintegration. Compared with these typical high growth periods in human history, China's economic performance since 1978 is outstanding both in terms of growth rate and stability of growth (Chart 2).

1.2 Successful Suppression of High Inflation

Generally speaking, high growth is often accompanied by high inflation. In the period of rapid economic growth, investment growth rate is high, resulting in high demand for raw materials. To a certain extent, this results in higher inflation pressure. Once inflation is too high, it often means that the real economy growth rate is higher than the potential growth rate, there is an excessive use of production factors, and a recession

Table 1 Real GDP growth fluctuations of typical economies (1961–2017)

Country	Real GDP fluctuations
China	0.19
Middle-income countries	0.25
World	0.34
India	0.36
OECD countries	0.43
Korea	0.44
Europe	0.60
Britain	0.61
Japan	0.67
USA	0.68
Brazil	1.00
Argentina	2.21
Russia(3)	4.54

Note (1) *Source* WDI database of the World Bank, ACCEPT calculation. (2) The numerator of the real GDP fluctuation is the standard deviation of the residual of the real GDP y-on-y growth rate minus the HP filter trend ($\lambda = 6.25$) and the denominator is the average of the trend of the real GDP y-on-y growth rate by the HP filter trend ($\lambda = 6.25$). (3) Russia only includes data from 1991–2017

Table 2 Real GDP growth fluctuations of China, Japan, and Korea during their high-speed growth periods

Country	Real GDP fluctuations
China 1978–2017	0.19
Korea 1961–1990	0.27
Japan 1961–1990	0.37

Note (1) *Source* WDI database of the World Bank, ACCEPT calculation. (2) The numerator of the real GDP fluctuation is the standard deviation of the residual of the real GDP y-on-y growth rate minus the HP filter trend ($\lambda = 6.25$) and the denominator is the average of the trend of the real GDP y-on-y growth rate by the HP filter trend ($\lambda = 6.25$)

of economic growth will follow. As a result, high inflation is often associated with fluctuations in economic growth, and from this perspective, stable economic growth often also means stable inflation.

In China's case, high inflation pressure has come not only from economic growth itself, but also from the unique and complicated economic system during the transition period. Planned economies usually have a supply shortage, the government makes allocations, and either the economy as a whole does not have a price or the

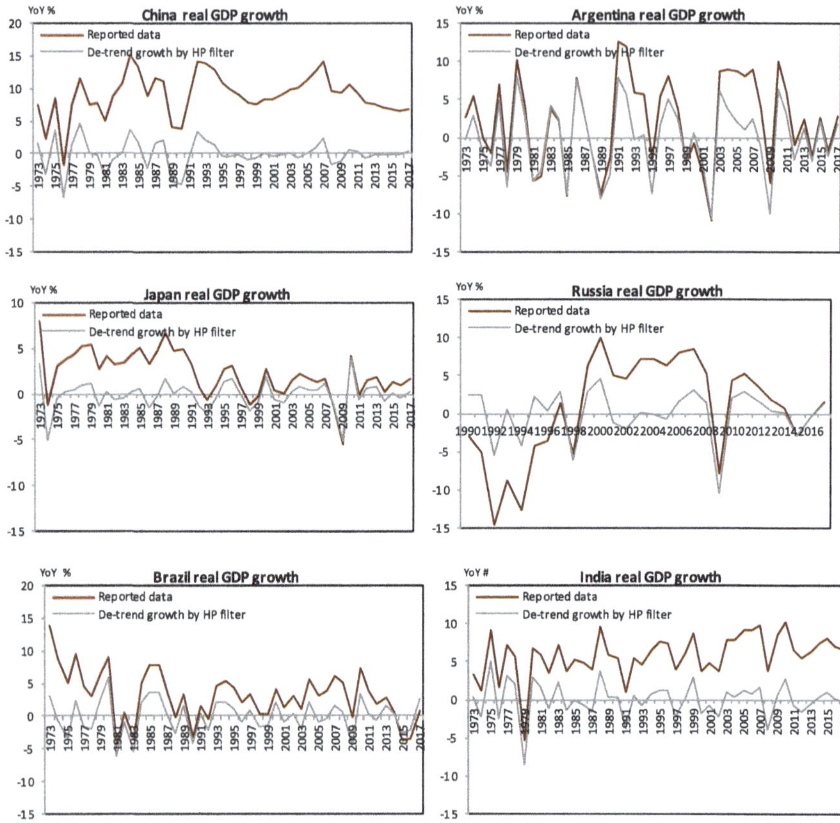

Chart 1 Real GDP Growth Fluctuations of Typical Economies. *Source* WDI database of the World Bank, ACCEPT calculation

price is artificially lowered. When transforming from a planned economy into a market economy, the prices depressed by policies tend to rise rapidly, which often results in high inflation. High inflation then leads to currency instability, which is not conducive to economic growth. The resulting excessive changes in relative prices are likely to cause distortion of social wealth allocation, and can even lead to serious social problems.

Compared to other countries in transition, China was able to more effectively control its inflation. China's average annual CPI growth during 1978–2016 was 5.3%, lower than that of India and Brazil over the same period, and lower than the inflation rates of Japan and South Korea during their respective high growth periods (Table 3). If we compare China with other economies that have experienced price reform, such as Russia and Poland, we can see that China's economy grew at a much faster pace than these economies, while its inflation was significantly lower. Specifically, China's post-price reform CPI y-on-y growth during 1989–1993 was only 18%, 3.1%, 3.4%,

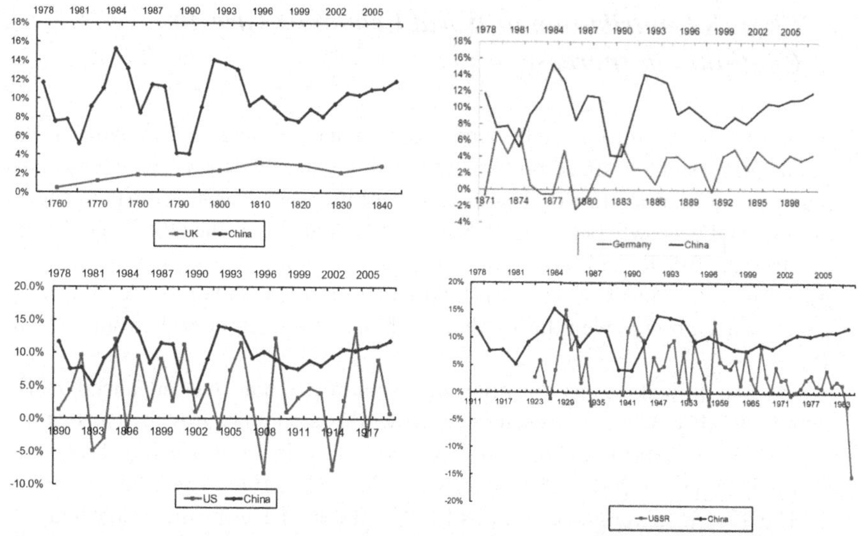

Chart 2 Comparison of Economic Growth Rates of Major Economies During High Growth Periods in History: UK, Germany, USA, and Soviet Union. *Source* World Economy: A Bicentennial Perspective [10]

Table 3 Average annual CPI growth of typical countries

	Average annual CPI growth (geometric average) (%)	Average annual CPI growth (arithmetic average) (%)
USA (1986–2016)	2.60	2.70
China (1978–2017)	4.90	4.90
China (1986–2017)	5.00	5.30
Japan (1960–1980)	7.30	7.20
India (1986–2016)	7.50	7.70
Korea (1967–1990)	11.40	11.60
Russia (1986–2016)	38.00	73.00
Poland (1988–2000)	58.50	87.90
Brazil (1986–2016)	99.40	361.20

Note China's data is from the National Bureau of Statistics, while the data of other countries is from the WDI database of the World Bank

6.4%, and 14.7% for each year, respectively,[1] while that of Russia during the four years after its price reform was over 100%,[2] and that of Poland was also over 30%.[3]

[1] *Source* Haver database.

[2] *Source* Haver database.

[3] *Source* Haver database.

1.3 China's Contribution to World Economic Growth Continues to Increase

Over its 40 years of reform and opening up, China has managed to avoid a real economic crisis and has successfully responded to external shocks, which has also been a great contribution to world economic stability. China has never experienced a negative real GDP growth between 1978 and 2019 (Chart 3). On the other hand, Japan, Korea, Russia, Brazil, and almost all other major countries experienced negative economic growth after war. The real GDPs of Korea and Japan also experienced negative y-on-y growth even during their high-speed growth periods from 1960 to 1980.

In addition to stabilizing the domestic economy, China has advanced world economic stability. China's contribution to world economic growth has steadily increased since its reform and opening up, from 5.11% in 1980–1989, to 12.33% in 1990–1999, 24.83% in 2000–2009, and 28.75% in 2010–2017. Overall, for the period of 1978–2017, China's contribution was 18.35% (Table 4). During the Asian financial crisis and global financial crisis, China's role as a "stabilizer" in the global economy was particularly prominent. During the Asian financial crisis in 1998, China guided the recovery of total domestic demand through active fiscal policy and sound monetary policy, while the RMB did not depreciate with other currencies and made contributions to the stability of the Asian monetary system. After the 2008 global financial crisis, nearly all industrialised economies experienced negative growth. Against this backdrop, China's recovery in 2009 was an important factor in stabilizing the global economy (Charts 4 and 5).

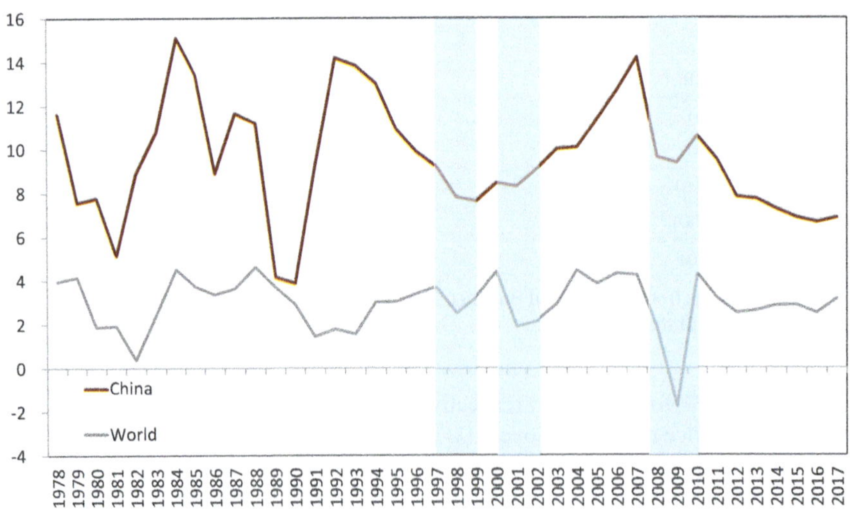

Chart 3 Real GDP Growth of China and the World (%). *Source* WDI database of the World Bank

Table 4 Contributions of the USA, Europe, China, and Japan to world economic growth

	United States (%)	Euro area (%)	China (%)	Japan (%)
1978–2017	20.38	13.07	18.35	6.27
1980–1989	26.43	17.94	5.11	16.37
1990–1999	31.50	18.24	12.33	5.01
2000–2009	14.26	8.82	24.83	0.92
2010–2017	16.58	7.42	28.75	3.23

Source WDI database of the World Bank

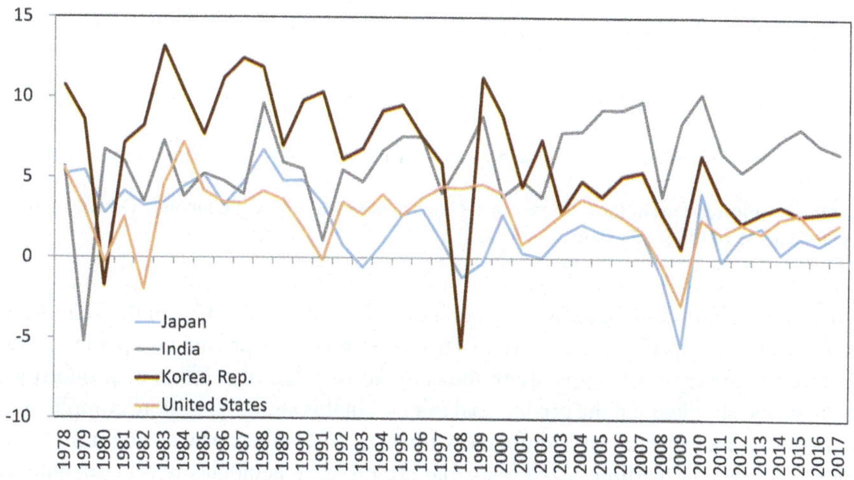

Chart 4 Real GDP Growth of the USA, Japan, India, and South Korea (1978–2017). *Source* WDI database of the World Bank

1.4 Problems: Causing Disproportionate Harm to Private Enterprises During Macroeconomic Management

In proactive macroeconomic management via "the visible hand," the government often treats private companies unfairly, which is reflected in the following two aspects.

First, more burdens of reducing redundant investment and "removing excess capacity" are assumed by private companies. The steel industry is a typical case: in 2016, 140 steel companies assumed the task of removing excess capacity, 88.6% of which were private companies. Furthermore, of the total removed excess capacity, private companies accounted for 65%, while SOEs accounted for only 35%.[4] In Hebei

[4]Beijing Steel Information Network, http://news.steelcn.cn/a/120/20160907/874650DCC8FC2C.html.

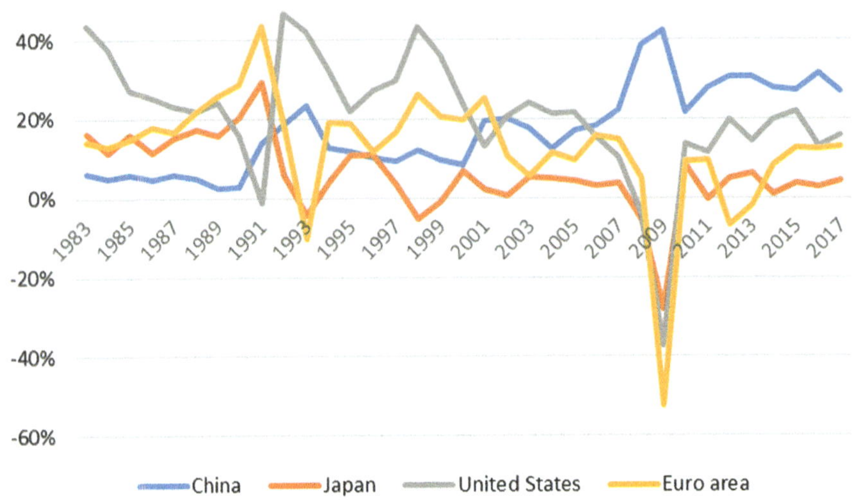

Chart 5 Contributions of the USA, Europe, China, and Japan to World Economic Growth. *Source* WDI database of the World Bank

Province, an important base for the steel industry, for example, 97% of the 16 million tons of excess capacity removal in 2016 was assumed by private companies.[5] The task of removing excess capacity in the coal industry has also fallen disproportionately on the shoulders of the private coal mines, but this situation is more complicated than that of the steel sector. Compared with SOE coal mines, private coal mines are mostly small and medium-sized ones that are prone to accidents and lag behind in complying with environmental protection criteria. The key targets to remove excess coal capacity in 2016 were small and medium-sized coal mines with an annual output at or below 300,000 tons. "Such coal mines accounted for only about 15% of the country's coal production, but more than 50% of coal mine accidents."[6] Due to these specifications, however, mostly private coal mines were affected by the policy.

Second, during an economic downturn, bank loans and other resources mainly flow into SOEs. For example, in the response to the global financial crisis in 2009, SOEs received much support from the "RMB4 trillion" stimulation package. They were therefore able to recover very quickly, whereas private companies received fewer benefits and recovered more slowly (Chart 6). A similar situation occurred during the proactive macroeconomic management of 2015.

[5]Caixin Media, http://hefan.blog.caixin.com/archives/157890.

[6]State Coalchem Network, http://www.coalchem.org.cn/dujia/html/800214/177642.html.

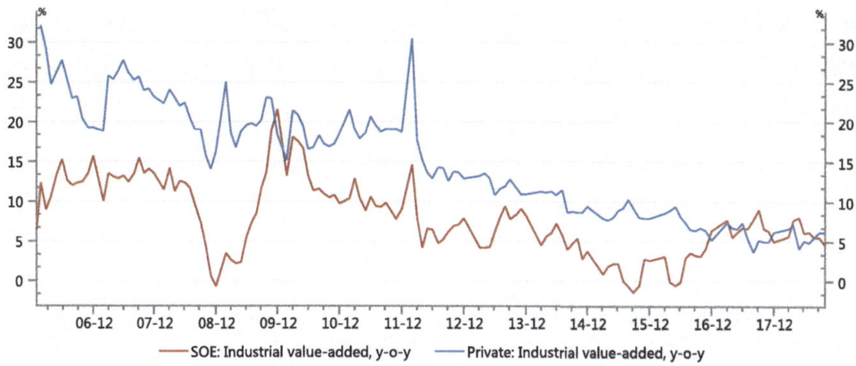

Chart 6 SOEs Recovered Faster than Private Companies During Recession as a Result of Macroeconomic Management. *Source* WIND database

2 Historical Overview

Since the beginning of reform and opening up in 1978, the Chinese economy has experienced many complicated transitions, ups, and downs. These include the transition from a planned economy to a market economy and from a closed economy to an open economy, not to mention the complicated process of transforming from a shortage economy to an economy with basic supply and demand balance, and then to an economy with overcapacity in several sectors. Beyond these transitions, China has also undergone large-scale urbanization involving hundreds of millions of people, the rapid development of infrastructure and real estate construction, and the Asian financial crisis in 1997 and the global financial crisis in 2008. Despite complicated and ever-changing internal and external environments, one of the important reasons why China has been able to maintain stable, high-speed economic growth and secure prices for 40 years is its overall success at proactive macroeconomic management.

In the following section, we will briefly discuss the backgrounds, measures, and effects of proactive macroeconomic management over several typical periods in chronological order. These typical periods include (Chart 7): the economic overheating period in the early days of reform and opening up (1978–1980); the economic overheating period around 1985; the economic overheating period from 1988 to 1989; the economic overheating period after Deng Xiaoping's "southern tour speeches" in 1992; the period after the outbreak of the Asian financial crisis in 1998; the economic overheating period from 2003 to 2007; the period after the outbreak of the global financial crisis in 2008; and the period of continued economic growth slowdown from 2012 to 2016.

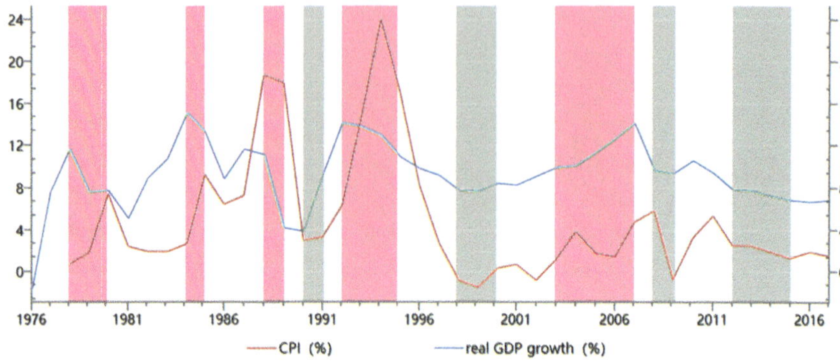

Chart 7 Basic Course of the Chinese government's Proactive Macroeconomic Management. *Note* (1) The pink shadows represent economic "overheating" periods, and the grey shadows represent economic "downturn" periods; (2) The Chart was drawn by the author; and the data is from the WIND database

2.1 The Economic Overheating Period in the Early Days of Reform and Opening Up (1978–1980)

(a) **Macroeconomic Background**

At the end of 1978, China decided to implement the strategy of reform and opening up and speed up the process of modernization. Enthusiasm for economic development—which had been suppressed during the "Cultural Revolution"—was revived and released, and the whole country became excited about economic construction, driving the national economy to experience recovery growth and overheating. The key features were as follows.

First, economic growth accelerated significantly. Real GDP grew by 11.7%, 7.6%, and 7.8% in each year, respectively, from 1978 to 1980. Both investment and consumer demand saw great increases, which led to a supply shortage in the investment and consumer sectors.

Second, investment in fixed-assets expanded dramatically. On one hand, the scale of infrastructure development expanded, and investment repeatedly increased. The number of large and medium-sized projects under construction grew from over 1,400 in 1977 to over 1,700 in 1978, and some products with less demand accumulated large inventory due to uninformed and blind production. In order to speed up economic construction, foreign advanced equipment imports increased on a massive scale. In just a few months after the State Council Theory Discussion Meeting in September 1978, the equipment for nine large chemical projects worth RMB16 billion, plus another 22 projects (including Baosteel) and 100 sets of comprehensive coal mining equipment worth RMB60 billion were imported [15]. This large-scale equipment introduction also stimulated domestic demand for investment in supporting and commentary sectors and accelerated fixed-asset investment growth.

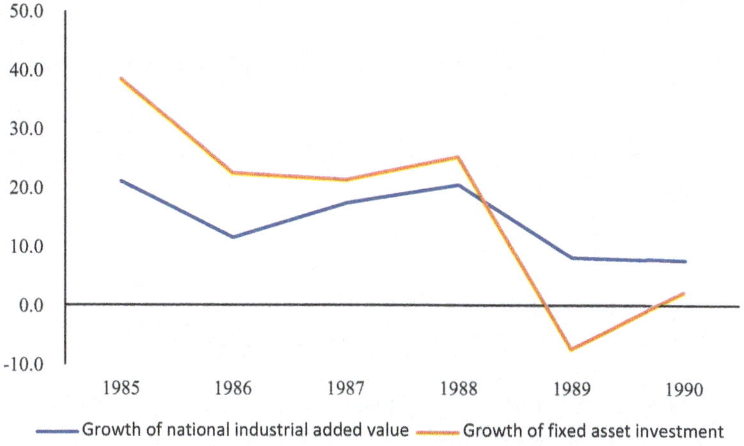

Chart 8 The Real Growth of Industrial Added Value and the Growth of Total Retail Sales During 1978–1982. *Source* CEInet Statistics Database

Industrial production skyrocketed, with the actual growth rate of industrial added value reaching 16.4%, 8.7%, and 12.6%, respectively, from 1978 to 1980 (Chart 8). On the other hand, consumer demand exploded. The increase in wages and welfare for urban workers resulted in an increase in residents' income and purchasing power. From 1978 to 1980, the total retail sales of consumer goods nationwide increased by 8.8%, 15.5%, and 18.9%, respectively.

Third, prices skyrocketed. The unbalanced ratio of light to heavy industry resulted in a shortage of agricultural and light industrial products. However, the sharp increase in residents' income and purchasing power led to increased consumer demand, and the prices, which had been suppressed for a long time in the planned economy, were released. When combined, these factors led to a sharp rise in price. Meanwhile, the increase in investment and consumers led to the expansion of fiscal spending and the fiscal deficit, and the overdraft of fiscal funds within the banking system led to the expansion of the money supply, thus increasing the pressure of inflation. The national budget recorded a deficit of RMB20.6 billion in 1979, down from a surplus of RMB1.01 billion in 1978, with a deficit ratio of 5.2%. From 1978 to 1980, the growth of fiscal revenue and spending both declined significantly. The balance of fiscal revenue and spending went from RMB1.017 billion in surplus in 1978 to RMB13.541 billion and RMB6.890 billion in deficit in 1979 and 1980, respectively (Chart 9). Cash (M0) supply increased sharply by 9.7% in 1978, and up to 24.4% in 1979 and 25.5% in 1980. The credit balance of the banking system increased by 10.2% in 1979 and by 18.3% in 1980. The consumer price index rose by 0.7% in 1978 and was up by 7.5% in 1980, the peak of that period. From 1978 to 1980, the commodity retail price index increased by 0.7% in 1978 and 6% in 1980, once more the highest of that period.

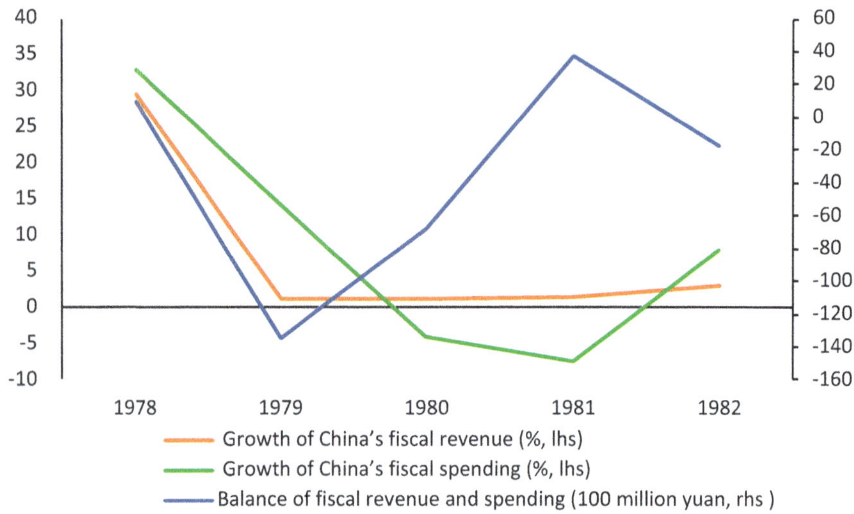

Chart 9 Growth of China's Fiscal Revenue and Spending and its Balance During 1978–1982. *Source* Comprehensive Statistical Data and Materials on 60 Years of New China

(b) **Proactive Macroeconomic Management Measures**

In order to cope with this economic overheating, the government released the "Eight Character Guiding Principles" of "adjustment, reform, rectification, and improvement" in addition to the 12 principles for regulation in 1979 [8]. Since this overheating in the early stage of China's market-oriented reform, the government's proactive macroeconomic management has mainly adopted the philosophy that the "planned economy is the main factor and the market economy is an auxiliary."

The first proactive macroeconomic measure was to curtail fixed-assets investment and reduce investment demand. The government decided that infrastructure development size had to match the country's financial and material resources to avoid the uninformed and blind expansion of infrastructure development. To this end, infrastructure development sizes were reduced, and a number of unqualified construction projects were suspended and postponed. Infrastructure development scales were cut significantly to be compatible with the supply capacity of steel, cement, timber, equipment, and capital.

The second measure was to adjust the structure of the national economy and improve the supply of agricultural and light industrial products. Efforts were made to adjust the structure of the agricultural and industrial sectors, to concentrate on the development of agriculture, and to increase the support and investment directed toward the agricultural sector. Furthermore, the government aimed to better balance light and heavy industries in a coordinated approach, develop the textile industry along with other light industries, increase production and capacity construction within light industry, and reduce investments in steel and other heavy industries.

The government also worked to speed up the production and capacity construction of coal, power, oil, transportation, and building materials to ensure an adequate supply of production materials and infrastructure for other industries.

The third measure was to tighten liquidity and strictly control bank credit. In 1981, the State Council issued the *Decision on Strengthening Credit Management and Strictly Controlling the Issuance of Currency,* which required government authorities to control currency issuance, strictly initiate credit management, and try to realize the balance of credit. All regions and departments were required to strictly implement the credit plan and currency issuance plan approved by the government, with no exceptions. Banks and their branches were instructed to review and grant loans according to the credit policy and use of funds. Additionally, inventories of materials and commodities were downsized to reduce the use of working capital. The principle of basing production and procurement on demand was to be strictly followed, and banks were to refuse loans to companies producing and procuring products and materials without adequate demand.

(c) **Effectiveness of Proactive Macroeconomic Management**

By 1981, the government's proactive macroeconomic management had achieved favorable results and this round of economic overheating was basically under control. The real GDP growth in 1981 slowed down to 5.1%, while the fixed-asset investment of the whole country grew by 5.2%. The rate of price increase was also reined in, with CPI growth back to 2.5% and PPI growth back to 2.4%.

However, although infrastructure investment within the state budget was basically subdued, factors outside the state budget were beyond the scope, and uninformed and redundant construction continued [14].

2.2 The Economic Overheating Period Around 1985

(a) **Macroeconomic background**

In 1982, the *12th CPC National Congress* set the goal of quadrupling the annual industrial and agricultural output by the end of the 20th century. Local governments raced to realize the goal before the deadline or even to surpass it. They began applying to expand their production and investment scales, and thus the blind investment boom resurfaced, resulting in total demand exceeding the total supply. From 1984 to 1985, China's real GDP grew intensely at 15.2% and 13.4%, respectively. The key features of this round of macroeconomic overheating were as follows.

First, the nationwide fixed-asset investment scale increased dramatically under the investment boom. The allowance of more discretion for local governments, companies, and banks released investment constraints, and as a result, blind and redundant investments by various departments and regions led to an excessive number and scale of projects under construction. On one hand, China initiated the reform of "changing the appropriation of funds into granting loans" in 1985, which gave local governments and companies more discretion in making investment and production decisions, resulting in a large number of infrastructure, production, and processing projects under construction. On the other hand, the fund allocation relationship between the central bank and commercial banks shifted from planned allocation to credit granting, and loans granted by commercial banks for the next year were set based on the actual loans granted in the previous year. To some extent, this measure encouraged commercial banks to lend aggressively, providing funds for investment expansion. In 1984 and 1985, China's total fixed-asset investment reached RMB183.3 billion and RMB254.3 billion, respectively, growing at rates of 28.2% and 38.8% (Chart 10). This sharp increase in investment spending caused a fiscal deficit, while the expansion of the credit gap increased the issuance of currency, both of which contributed to the price hike.

Second, the wage system reform released a large amount of consumer demand in a short period of time. The wage system reform promoted by the state from 1984 to 1985 gave more discretion to companies when determining the wages for their workers. Some government agencies, organizations, enterprises, and institutions raised wages and welfare for their staff and increased social purchasing power in a short time. The average wage of employees in urban areas nationwide increased by 14.8% y-on-y in 1984, and national consumer spending grew by 12% and 13.5%, respectively, in 1984 and 1985 (Chart 11). However, during the transition period from planned economy to market economy, production and supply capacities were relatively stable, so the expansion of consumer demand in a short period of time resulted in tight market supply and price increases. The total retail sales of goods increased by 18.5% and

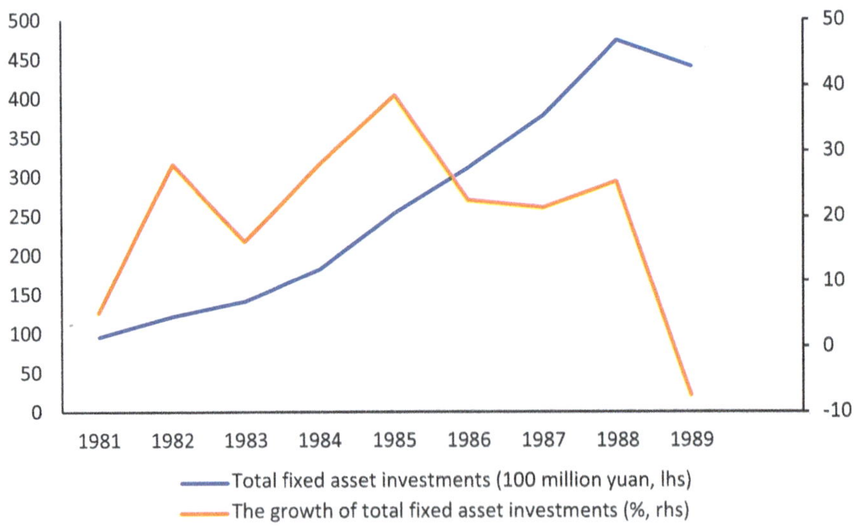

Chart 10 China's Total Fixed-Asset Investments and Their Growth During 1981–1989. *Source* Comprehensive Statistical Data and Materials on 65 Years of New China

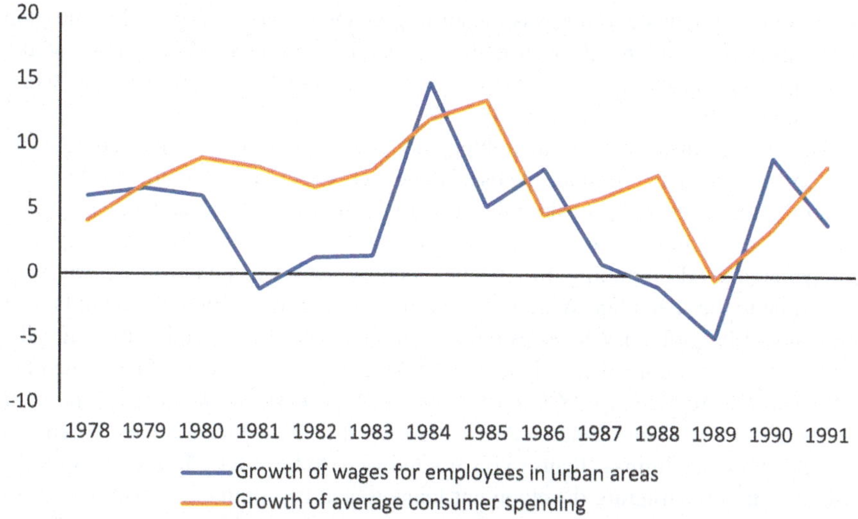

Chart 11 Growth of Wages for Employees in Urban Areas and Growth of Average Consumer Spending from 1978 to 1991. *Source* Comprehensive Statistical Data and Materials on 65 Years of New China

27.5%, respectively, in 1984 and 1985. At the same time, CPI increased from 2.7% to 9.3% and PPI increased from 2.8% to 8.8%. These Charts clearly indicate inflation.

(b) Proactive Macroeconomic Management Measures

In response to the macroeconomic overheating once again promoted by the expansion in investment and consumption, the government mainly adopted administrative orders like investment control, credit tightening, purchasing power restriction, and price supervision to directly control and curtail total domestic demand. Meanwhile, the government also initiated indirect control by using market-oriented measures such as adjusting the reserve requirement ratio (RRR) and the deposit and loan interest rates. At the same time, government authorities wasted no time in promoting the reform of the economic system to release economic vitality and lay the foundation for the full introduction of more market-oriented measures.

The first proactive macroeconomic measure was to control and reduce fixed-asset investment. The government abided by the principle that infrastructure investment should be commensurate with national strength as it initiated stringent control over fixed-asset investments and set out to prevent the blind pursuit of excessively high growth rates. In 1985, the State Council issued the *Notice on Controlling the Scale of Investment in Fixed Assets*, which required fixed-asset investment to be strictly controlled. Chief executives of all departments and regions were to be held accountable for any breaks with this policy, and fixed-asset investments were to be reviewed each quarter, resulting in a review report to the State Council. The *Three Guarantees and Three Restrictions* policy concerning infrastructure development was also promulgated, which was meant to guarantee construction within the plan while restricting unplanned construction, to guarantee productive construction while restricting non-productive construction, and to guarantee key construction while restricting unnecessary construction.[7]

The second measure was to tighten monetary policy and control credit. The government set out to eliminate the fiscal deficit and the credit gap within the banking system, and to achieve a basic balance between fiscal revenue and spending and the balance of credit. The government stipulated that infrastructure development and technological upgrading projects financed by bank loans had to be carried out according to the state plan. Without the approval of the State Council, no unplanned loans could be granted, and investment scale could not be expanded by using the bank loans in the name of self-financing. In April 1985, the State Council issued the *Notice on the Approval and Circulation of the Regulations of the People's Bank of China (PBoC) on Controlling the Scale of Loans* in 1985, which stipulated loan and currency issuance limits—loans to be granted were to be strictly limited to RMB71 billion. The infrastructure development loans issued by commercial banks were to be controlled by projects, all the while observing state plans. In addition, the PBoC also adjusted the interest rates of some deposits and loans, and also conducted credit checks.

The third policy was to curb consumption increase and strengthen price supervision. In February 1985, the State Council issued the *Urgent Notice on Strictly Controlling the Purchasing Power of Companies and Institutions* to limit spending power expansion. The Notice first required appropriate centralized review and approval by the authorities to specifically control commodities, and resolutely reduced the purchasing power of social groups—down by 20% y-on-y. Second, the categories of goods to which companies and institutions were not to have access to were redefined and changed from 31 to 17. Third, the systems and measures for strengthening macro-management of consumption funds were further strengthened so that the growth of consumption funds would be commensurate with the development of production and the increase in national income. In addition, price administration was enhanced, and unauthorized price hikes were restricted. In March 1985, the State Council issued an urgent notice requesting all provinces, regions, and municipalities to strengthen price control, supervision, and inspection to combat unauthorized price hikes.

Meanwhile, efforts were made to vigorously promote economic system reform. Among them, the promotion of the household responsibility system fundamentally changed the old system (which had restricted the development of agricultural productivity) and improved the efficiency and supply of agricultural production. Additionally, enterprise reform was further promoted through the establishment of the enterprise operation mechanism, which combined accountability, authority, and benefits into one. The reform of the financial system also accelerated the market-oriented

[7]*Report on the Work of the Government* (1987), by Premier Zhao Ziyang of the State Council at the fifth session of the Sixth National People's Congress on March 25, 1987.

allocation of financial elements.[8] Furthermore, the reform of enterprises' employment and wage systems helped rationalize distribution and promote the coordinated development of light and heavy industries, while the promotion and improvement of various forms of investment responsibility systems improved investment efficiency.[9] These institutional reforms not only released vitality for China's future economic growth, but also laid a foundation for the government to make better use of market-oriented measures in its future proactive macroeconomic management.

(c) Effectiveness of Proactive Macroeconomic Management

With the implementation of a series of tightening macro policies, this round of economic overheating was brought well under control. China's real GDP growth dropped to 8.9% in 1986, and CPI growth dropped to 6.5%. On one hand, infrastructure development expansion was subdued. Fixed-asset investment grew by 22.7% and 21.5%, respectively, in 1986 and 1987 versus 28.2% and 38.8%, respectively, in 1984 and 1985. In 1986, infrastructure investment by entities owned by the whole people increased by 7.3% y-on-y, much lower than the 44.6% growth rate in 1985. However, the growth of unplanned fixed-asset investment remained out of control. On the other hand, the situation of excessive consumption was alleviated, and the growth of total retail sales of consumer goods dropped to 15%. In addition, credit expansion growth also declined, while the growth of RMB loans from financial institutions dropped from 33.1% in 1984 to 31.4% in 1986 and 20.5% in 1987.

2.3 *The Economic Overheating Period from 1988 to 1989*

(a) Macroeconomic Background

In 1988, China's economy experienced a strong rebound in terms of overheating and inflation. On one hand, economic growth and investment growth bounced back rapidly. In 1988, real GDP growth reached 11.2%, while the real growth of national industrial output reached 20.8%. Meanwhile, China's fixed-asset investment grew by 25.4% in 1988 (Chart 12). On the other hand, prices increased overall by double digits. The CPI grew by 18.8% and 18%, respectively, in 1988 and 1989. The main reasons for this round of economic overheating were as follows.

---

[8]These reforms included the development of various financing instruments; they made financial institutions operate like enterprises on a conditional basis so as to gradually make them operate independently, and thus responsible for their own profits and losses; they reformed the interest rate system of the banks, gradually rationalized the deposit and loan interest rates and implemented different interest rates based on the length of terms and floating interest rates; they improved management approaches, which helped enterprises manage their liquidity and change the practice of banks being responsible for enterprises' supply funds; they gradually implemented centralized and unified management of foreign exchange and foreign debt; and they invigorated foreign exchange funds, developing financing markets at different levels and sizes step-by-step.

[9]Ibid.

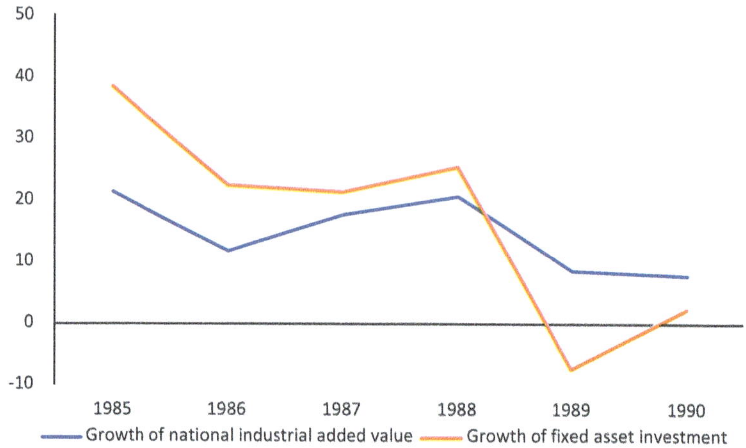

Chart 12 Growth of National Industrial Added Value and Fixed-Asset Investment. *Source* Comprehensive Statistical Data and Materials on 60 Years of New China

First, the loosening of credit eased the constraint on funds for investment. During the previous round of overheating, fixed-asset investments like infrastructure investments occupied a large part of the credit resources, enterprises faced tight liquidity, and production activities were affected by the tightening credit policy. The real growth of industrial added value dropped from 18% in 1985 to 9.6% in 1986. In order to prevent the continued slowdown of the industrial sector, in 1986 the central bank loosened the release of money and credit, which promoted the subsequent investment expansion and rising inflation.

Second, the introduction of the "Price Breakthrough" price and wage reforms intensified rising prices and enhanced inflation expectations. With economic overheating already on the horizon, the 1988 "Price Breakthrough" reforms caused a sharp rise in commodity prices. Prior to the reforms, the planned and controlled prices of products were significantly lower than their prices as freely determined by the market. The sudden liberalization of price control and the merging of the double-track price system into one track lifted the general price level and formed a strong inflation expectation. In 1988, "a wave of panic buying" occurred in which basic consumer goods and inflation-resilient goods were all targeted—TV sets, refrigerators, washing machines, grain and cotton fabrics, etc. were in short supply. The rapid growth of social purchasing power surpassed the growth of commodity supply very quickly. In 1988, the total retail sales of consumer goods across the country grew by 27.8%. Retail prices soared, with the Retail Price Index reaching 18.5% and 17.8% in 1988 and 1989, respectively. An inflationary spike was imminent.

Third, the excessive expansion of investment demand aggravated the bottleneck effect of raw material supply. This problem of too many large fixed-asset investment projects began to emerge in 1986. The expansion of infrastructure investment demand stretched the supply capacity of energy, raw materials, and transportation, and pushed up the price of production materials. Moreover, the failure to get the previous expansion of unbudgeted investment under full control also exerted pressure on the overheating of the economy.

(b) **Proactive Macroeconomic Management Measures**

In order to cope with the strong inflation expectation and excess growth in fixed-asset investment, the government tightened fiscal and credit policies to reduce total demand while also actively expanding effective supply. This was meant to address the problem of total social demand exceeding total supply, and to achieve basic balance in finance, credit, raw materials, and foreign exchange. In this round of proactive macroeconomic management, the government still primarily adopted administrative measures, but also used some market-oriented measures such as interest rates. The government also deepened the reform of the economic system in the regulation process. The specific control measures were as follows.

First, the government set out to drastically reduce the scale of infrastructure development and rectify the economic order. On one hand, in order to reduce the demand expansion resulting from the increase in the number and scale of the investment projects, the central government issued an order to compress, clear, and eventually stop fixed-asset investments so as to be commensurate with the actual basic supply capacity. In 1988, the scale of fixed-asset investments was significantly reduced, and the approval of unplanned construction projects was suspended. From the end of September 1988 to the end of February 1989, 18,000 fixed-asset investment projects were suspended or postponed nationwide, and RMB64.7 billion (12%) was cut from the remaining workload of all projects.[10] On the other hand, in the years after 1988, efforts were made to rectify the budget of those projects, overcome the chaos in the fields of production, construction, circulation, and distribution, and conduct major inspections on tax, financials, and pricing.

The second measure was to strictly control the purchasing power of institutions and companies. In order to control the ability of institutions and companies to purchase popular products and prevent consumer demand from continuing to expand, the government issued administrative orders to control sales of special goods, increasing the categories of special goods controlled by the government from 19 to 32. Furthermore, efforts were made to strictly control the excessive growth of the funds available for consumption so as to adapt to the growth of national income.

The third measure was to tighten credit and increase savings. Tight monetary policy was implemented to strictly control the credit scale and adjust and optimize credit structure. Banks' savings rates were raised, measures like value-preserved savings and savings rewards were offered, and some economic leverage measures were implemented so as to increase savings and reduce consumption.

The fourth measure was to increase effective supply of non-discretionary goods to alleviate their supply and demand imbalance. While taking measures to curtail the

---

[10]"*Resolutely Implementing the Policy of Improvement and Rectification and Deepening Reform*", Report of Premier Li Peng on Government Work at the Second Session of the Seventh National People's Congress on March 20, 1989.

aggregate demand, measures to expand supply to meet basic demand were concurrently implemented. Prudent efforts were made to adjust the industrial structure and product supply from many angles, such as money supply, materials, foreign exchange, and transportation. This was meant to guarantee production and yield increases for grain, cotton, oil, and other agricultural products to support the production and supply of daily use products,[11] thus alleviating the supply shortage relative to their high demand.

The fifth measure was to deepen the reform of the economic system. In 1989, the Fifth Plenary Session of the 13th Central Committee adopted the *Decision of the CPC Central Committee on Further Improvement and Rectification and Deepening Reform*, which required that attention be paid to promoting and deepening economic system reform while making efforts to deal with and rectify the inflation. Such efforts included making and amending the necessary economic laws and regulations and gradually promoting institutional reform concerning planning, investment, materials, finance, and foreign trade. There were also initial measures to strengthen the management of the fiscal, taxation, banking, prices, auditing, customs, industrial, and commercial administration structures.[12]

(c) **Effectiveness of Proactive Macroeconomic Management**

This round of regulation quickly curbed domestic inflation, slowed economic growth, and brought the economic overheating under control. However, due to the high intensity of this round of proactive macroeconomic management, there was a sharp fall in economic growth during 1989–1990. The real GDP growth declined to 4.2% and 3.9%, respectively, in 1989 and 1990, the lowest since reform and opening up. The trend of investment scale expansion was brought under control, while fixed-asset investment was down y-on-y—RMB441 billion in 1989, down by RMB34.4 billion from 1988.

Momentum to curb consumption overheating and inflation was kept under control. The growth of total retail sales of consumer goods came down from 27.8% in 1988 to 8.9% by 1989 and 2.5% in 1990. The increase of consumer demand also cooled down significantly, while "panic buying" subsided. CPI growth declined from 18% in 1988 to 3.1% in 1989 and 3.4% in 1990—inflation trends were markedly curbed.

2.4 The Overheated Economy After Deng Xiaoping's 1992 Southern Tour Speeches

(a) **Macroeconomic background**

After Deng Xiaoping's Southern Tour speeches in 1992 and the confirmation of the establishment of a socialist market economy at the 14th CPC National Congress,

[11] Ibid.

[12] Ibid.

there was an upsurge in development and investment across the country, resulting in economic overheating and serious inflation. In 1992, the real GDP grew by 14.2%, the real industrial added value grew by 21% y-on-y, and CPI rose 6.4%. The next year, the real GDP grew by 13.9%, the real industrial added value grew by 20% y-on-y, and CPI grew by double digits to 14.7%. By 1994, the real GDP growth rate remained as high as 13%, while the CPI rose 24.1%—a historic high since reform and opening up. The features of this round of economic overheating were as follows.

First, the reforms stimulated the enthusiasm of local governments to expand investment in construction. After the Southern Tour Speeches in early 1992, local governments became more confident and strived to "make greater efforts to speed up growth" through increased infrastructure investment. A nationwide investment and construction boom emerged, which also resulted in the problem of regions competing with each other to pursue high-speed growth. Fixed-asset investment started to grow rapidly from 1992, and an excess of projects were launched, resulting in higher follow-up investments. In 1993, a huge amount of investment was put into production sectors and infrastructure development, and nominal growth of fixed-asset investment across the country reached 61.8%, much higher than the 23.9% in 1991 and 44.4% in 1992 (Chart 13). This rapid investment growth made total social demand larger than the total supply, and caused raw materials, capital, and other factors to be in short supply. The price index of fixed-asset investment rose sharply, growing by 15.3% in 1992 and 26.6% in 1994.

Second, companies were highly enthusiastic about making investments, but redundant investments became a prominent issue. On one hand, this investment expansion was caused by government behavior, various irregular administrative interventions, and the motivations of local governments to encourage local enterprises to speed up

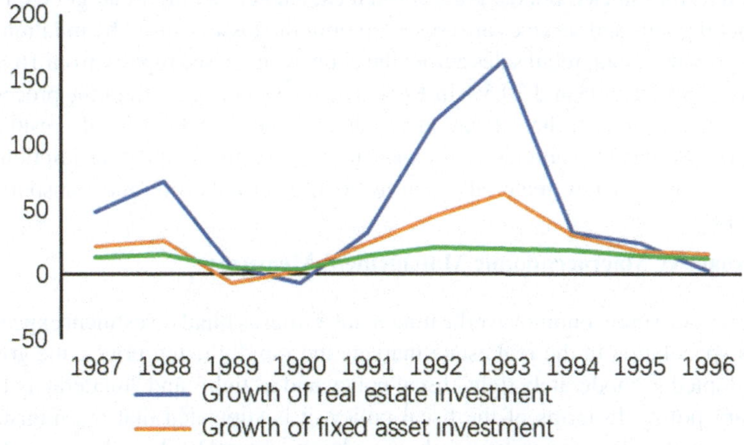

Chart 13 Growth of Real Estate, Fixed-Asset Investment, and Real Industrial Added Value. *Source* CEInet Statistics Database

investment.[13] On the other hand, the soft budget constraints faced by some companies were another important reason for repeated and excessive investment.

For example, during this period, China's textile industry experienced redundant investment, fierce market competition, and a serious inventory backlog. As light industries like the textile industry are often some of the leading industries in a country at the beginning of industrialization, their labor-intensive and relatively low threshold played an important role in boosting local economic growth, increasing tax revenue, and solving employment problems. All regions of the country blindly developed their textile industries, resulting in redundant construction and overstocking inventory. However, even though the total textile products in the country were in oversupply, many companies were reluctant to exit voluntarily, and still some new companies joined the sector and made investments.

Third, a boom of industrial park development and real estate investment swept the country, with a large amount of credit funds flowing into the real estate market in coastal areas (such as Hainan) in pursuit of high profits. Although the loan scale in 1992 was kept under control and did not break the budget limit, tens of billions of loans bypassed the limit, were awarded to coastal areas through fundraising and lending, and were transformed from short-term loans into long-term ones.[14] Funds from financial institutions flew into the real estate market through various channels. In 1992, nationwide real estate development investment grew by 117.5%, and it reached a historical high of 165% in 1993. A large amount of credit funds flooded the real estate market, crowding out funds for key national construction projects and resulting in the steady rise of the overall price level as well as a sharp price rise of raw materials such as cement, steel, electricity, and oil.

Fourth, the sharp expansion of consumer demand pushed prices up and strengthened the inflation expectation. People began to panic and tried to buy everything they could, like stocks, bonds, gold, foreign exchange, and high-end goods. Prices for general goods and services also rose[15] to limit the losses caused by inflation. The y-on-y growth of total retail sales across the country increased rapidly from 16.8% in 1992 to 29.8% in 1993 and 30.5% in 1994. The investment growth of the processing sectors was faster than that of raw materials and energy, which finally resulted in economic overheating with the dual expansion of investment and consumption, and the tight supply of raw materials such as coal, electricity, oil, and transportation (Chart 14).

(b) **Proactive Macroeconomic Management Measures**

In order to curb the economic overheating manifesting as blind investment expansion, serious speculation in the real estate market, and rapidly rising prices, the government adopted a "moderately tight" fiscal policy and a "tight" and "moderately tight" monetary policy. In terms of the fiscal policy, it is stipulated that the ministry of finance would no longer permit overdrawing by the central bank, and the investment

[13]*Zhu Rongji on the Record* (Book 1), Page 291.

[14]Ibid., Page 278.

[15]Ibid., Page 290.

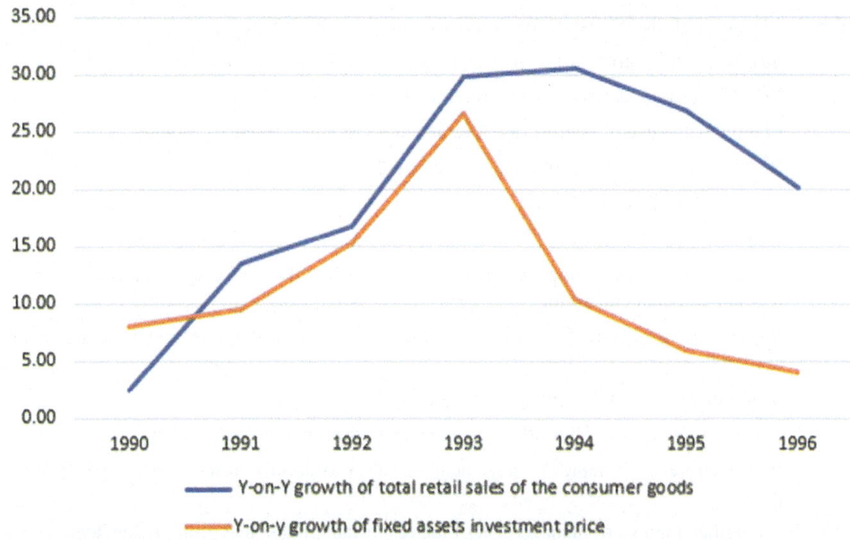

Chart 14 Growth of Total Retail Sales of Consumer Goods. *Source* CEInet Statistics Database

scale would be controlled by selectively tightening infrastructure projects. In terms of the monetary policy, some measures of direct administrative control were used to control the flow of credit. However, as the situation changed and more experience was gained, the government used more and more market-oriented monetary policy tools such as interest rate, the reserve requirement ratio, and open market operations in its proactive macroeconomic management.

In June 1993, the Central Committee of the CPC and the State Council issued the *Opinions on the Current Economic Situation and Strengthening Proactive Macroeconomic Management* [1993] (No. 6), which put forward 16 measures to strengthen proactive macroeconomic management (Table 5). In July of the same year, Vice Premier Zhu Rongji was appointed as the President of the People's Bank of China to help cool the overheated economy. The focus of the 16 measures was on rectifying the financial order to crack down on speculations in the real estate sector and redundant infrastructure project development as well as to control the purchasing power of institutions and companies. In this way, the overheating was finally brought under control.

From the contents of these 16 measures, we can see that this round of proactive macroeconomic management demonstrated the following characteristics.

First, the government cut funding sources for infrastructure construction and real estate investment. Eleven out of the 16 measures were closely related to the rectification of the financial order. In order to control the sources of funds flowing into real estate and infrastructure projects, the government reduced the money supply by strictly controlling currency issuance, tightening the credit scale, raising interest rates, curbing illegal fundraising, and clearing up and collecting previously lent funds that exceeded the requirements of scope and maturity.

Table 5 Measures of the 1993 proactive macroeconomic management

1.	Strictly control currency issuance and stabilize the financial situation
2.	Resolutely crack down on illegal fundraising
3.	Make flexible use of interest rate leverage and vigorously increase savings
4.	Resolutely stop all kinds of unauthorized fundraising activities
6.	Strictly control the total credit
6.	Require commercial banks to ensure any withdrawal from savings accounts
7.	Accelerate the pace of financial reform and strengthen the central bank's power to regulate the financial sector
8.	Implement the reform of the investment system together with the reform of the financial system
9.	Complete treasury bill issuance on schedule
10.	Further improve securities offerings and standardize market management
11.	Improve foreign exchange management measures to stabilize foreign exchange market prices
12.	Strengthen the macro management of the real estate market and promote the healthy development of the real estate industry
13.	Strengthen tax collection and administration and management, and avoid tax revenue losses
14.	Review the projects under construction and sort them by priority, while strictly controlling new projects
15.	Actively and steadily promote price reform and prevent the overall price level from rising too fast
16.	Strictly control the excessive growth of purchasing power of institutions and companies

Source The Opinions of CPC Central Committee and the State Council on Current Economic Situation and Strengthening Proactive Macroeconomic Management issued in June 1993

Second, the measures made simultaneous use of economic and administrative means to tighten the credit policies. They strengthened the role of economic means and used the market mechanism to address the problems at hand. For example, interest rates were used as leverage to attract deposits and increase the cost of borrowing to tighten the money supply. In 1993, the People's Bank of China raised the benchmark deposit rate and lending rate twice: the benchmark interest rate for one-year deposits increased from 7.56% in May 1993 to 10.98% in July 1993, while the benchmark interest rate for one-year loans was increased from 8.64% in May 1993 to 10.98% in July 1993. In addition, administrative means were used to tackle the economic disorder from a different angle. For example, the credit sizes of financial institutions were subject to stringent supervision and review, banks were required to apply for differentiated policies when approving loans for different types of projects, projects under construction were reviewed and sorted by priority, and urgent measures were taken to control various types of land lease projects. In order to cope with inflation and inflation expectation, the government also set a price limit on grains and subjected another 20 kinds of daily necessities to stringent price review. The government also aimed to keep the price of agricultural products stable and ensure an adequate supply of agricultural products for urban residents by paying special attention to the "vegetable basket" program and making it one of the top priorities of party secretaries, governors, and mayors of all provinces and cities.[16] The government required that financial subsidies for grain and other agricultural production be fully delivered, and misappropriation was strictly prohibited so as to safeguard the interests of farmers and help them to stabilize grain production, agricultural supply, and agricultural prices.

In addition, for the issues which could not be resolved via market-oriented measures alone (like the overcapacity of the textile sector), necessary administrative measures were used. Redundant investments were cut through administrative measures such as production restriction, inventory reduction, and suspended production for rectification. Measures were also implemented to speed up the consolidation, reform, upgrading, and restructuring of the textile sector, and some factories switched to other production lines, while others were acquired or relocated.[17] Efforts were made to clear textile projects one by one. For the projects having accepted the arrangements, a liquidation procedure was initiated. The Ministry of the Textile Industry allocated the task of restricting production and reducing spindles to the provinces, autonomous regions, and municipalities. These tasks were then re-allocated to the county level or below, and banks cut their lending based on such indicators. For projects failing to "cut spindles" as required, it was declared that no loans would be granted for their technological upgrading in the future.[18]

The third main characteristic of the measures was to deepen reforms through regulation. Beginning in 1994, a series of reform measures covering fiscal, tax, finance, and foreign exchange were introduced. For example, tax-sharing reform as part of the fiscal system reform rationalized the financial and administrative power of the central and local governments and increased the share of the central government in fiscal revenue, which allowed the fiscal policies to play their functions more effectively in proactive macroeconomic management. The reform of the fiscal system to stop overdrafts from the central bank helped rationalize the relationship between fiscal and monetary policies and subjected the implementation of fiscal policies to some restraints.

In terms of financial system reform, policy finance was separated from commercial finance, three major policy banks were established, and four major specialized banks were restructured into state-owned commercial banks. The reform of the banking system changed the operating system of the specialized banks, enhanced their governance, strengthened the authority of the central bank, and allowed the central bank to establish its own proactive macroeconomic management system.[19] In terms of the

---

[16] *Zhu Rongji on the Record* (Book 1), Page 303.

[17] Ibid., Page 522–523.

[18] "China National Textile Council held a national textile industry working conference in Beijing" [J]. *Textile Herald*, 1994 (1).

[19] *Zhu Rongji on the Record* (Book 1), Page 283.

foreign exchange administration system, the unification of exchange rates was initiated and a managed floating system reform was introduced, which was conducive to the establishment of the formation mechanism in the interest rate market and the transmission mechanism of monetary policy. The central bank cooperated with the Ministry of Finance to issue treasury bonds to cover the deficit. Securities (including treasury bills, fiscal bills, and national long-term development credit bank notes) and pledging and trading businesses were allowed on a pilot basis, which made it possible to indirectly regulate the money supply.[20]

(c) **Effectiveness of Proactive Macroeconomic Management**

With the implementation of the 16 proactive macroeconomic management measures, nationwide investment and credit granting were brought under control. Beginning in 1994, the credit scale saw rapid contraction and the growth of investment, as well as the growth of real estate investment, slowed down dramatically. Investment growth fell from 61.8% in 1993 to 30.4% in 1994, 17.5% 1995, and 14.8% in 1996. Meanwhile, the growth of real estate investment gradually fell from 165% in 1993 to 31.8% in 1994, 23.3% in 1995, and 2.1% in 1996.

Due to a time lag, economic growth and prices did not see any decline until 1995. In 1995, real GDP growth dropped to 11% and CPI growth dropped to 17.1%, down by 7% points from 1994. In 1996, the real GDP growth was 9.9% and CPI growth dropped to 8.3%. After three years of proactive macroeconomic management, China's first economic overheating since the establishment of the market economy system was brought fully under control—the economy's "soft landing" was successfully achieved.

2.5 *Proactive Macroeconomic Management After the Outbreak of the Asian Financial Crisis in 1998*

(a) **Macroeconomic Background**

Impacted by the Asian financial crisis, China's economic growth and price levels dropped significantly after 1998 in the first deflation since reform and opening up. Real GDP growth sank from near 10% in 1996 (Chart 15) down to 7.8% and 7.7%, respectively, in 1998 and 1999. The real y-on-y growth of industrial added value was also down to 8.9% and 8.6%, respectively, in 1998 and 1999. The CPI showed negative growth, at −0.8% in 1998 and −1.4% in 1999. Signs of economic cooling and deflation were clearly visible. This was inevitable because on one hand, external demand decline during the Asian financial crisis resulted in the export decline, while on the other hand, excessive domestic investment in previous years resulted in overcapacity. The specific features of this economic cooling period were as follows.

[20] Ibid.

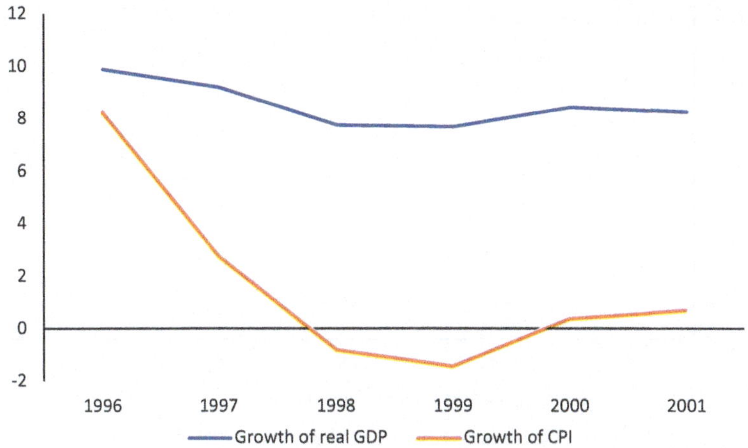

Chart 15 Growth of Real GDP and CPI from 1996 to 2001. *Source* CEInet Statistics Database

First, impacted by the Asian financial crisis, China's export demand dropped significantly. In 1997, the net exports of goods and services contributed 42.6% to GDP, while this contribution dropped to just 6.6% in 1998, and further down to −9.8% in 1999. In 1996, net exports of goods and services contributed 3.9% points to GDP growth, which dropped sharply to 0.4% in 1998 and −0.7% in 1999, effectively dragging down economic growth by 0.7% points (Chart 16).

Second, redundant investment and overcapacity in previous years resulted in insufficient domestic demand during this period. On one hand, the growth of domestic

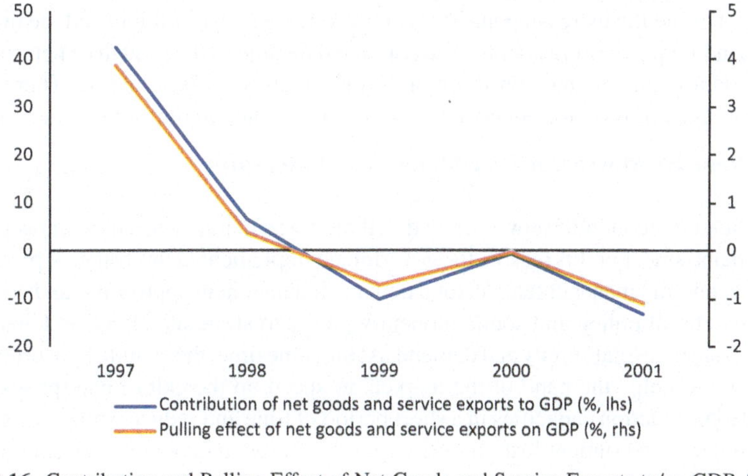

Chart 16 Contribution and Pulling Effect of Net Goods and Service Exports to/on GDP. *Source* CEInet Statistics Database

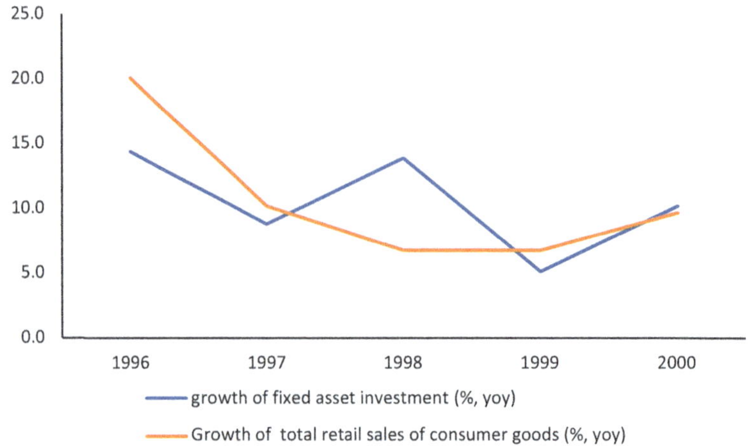

Chart 17 y-on-y Growth of Fixed-Asset Investment and Total Retail Sales of Consumer Goods. *Source* CEInet Statistics Database

fixed-asset investment demand declined significantly. The nominal growth of fixed-asset investment dropped from 14.5% in 1996 to 8.8% in 1997, and further dropped to 5.1% in 1999 after a brief recovery to 13.9% in 1998 (Chart 17). Domestic consumption demand, on the other hand, also showed a continuous and obvious downward trend. The growth of total retail sales of consumer goods dropped from 20.1% in 1996 to 10.2% in 1997 and 6.8% in 1998 and 1999. As the final and direct demand, the main reason for the decline in consumption growth was that people did not fully understand the goals of housing, education, and health care reform, and they opted to save money as a protective measure. At the same time, the poor performances of companies and the increasing numbers of workers being laid-off reduced the income and spending power of residents. The continued decline in the growth of net exports, domestic investment, and consumption further intensified the situation. There were obvious signs of inventory overstock, overcapacity, and continued price decline.

(b) **Proactive Macroeconomic Management Measures**

This round of economic slowdown and deflation was mainly caused by impact from the demand side. For this reason, the government implemented this round of proactive macroeconomic management via total demand management approaches and adopted proactive fiscal policy and sound monetary policy to stimulate effective demand in order to balance total supply and demand. At the same time, the "hand of government" was used to help "the hand of the market" to speed up the exit of enterprises with outdated production capacities in a short period of time and reduce welfare losses. In addition, the government lost no time in pushing forward economic system reforms that considered both short-term regulation and long-term development. The main regulation measures were as follows.

First, the government used proactive fiscal policies to boost economic growth through the multiplier effect. On one hand, the government modestly expanded the fiscal deficit by issuing more treasury bills to provide funds for infrastructure investment. In 1998 and 1999, China's fiscal deficit increased to RMB150 billion and RMB180 billion, respectively. This included RMB100 billion and RMB110 billion in treasury bills issued in 1998 and 1999, respectively. The proceeds of the treasury bills were mainly used for investment in infrastructure projects rather than redundant investment in industrial production so as to avoid aggravating the contradiction between supply and demand. There were six main types of infrastructure projects, including highway construction, rural power grid upgrading, grain depot construction, urban infrastructure construction, water conservation construction, and interest subsidies for technical renovation. On the other hand, the government cut taxes by adjusting tax rates to promote economic growth. The rate of the adjustment tax on fixed-asset investments was cut by 50% and suspended from January 1, 2000. The government also put forth export tax rebates to encourage and promote exports, while also offering tax incentives to attract foreign investors. In January and July 1999, China raised the export tax rebate rate twice, with the comprehensive tax rebate rate reaching 15.51%.

Second, the government adopted a sound monetary policy to stimulate economic growth by increasing the money supply and credit granting. This was done by first lowering the benchmark interest rates on lending and deposits. From March 1998 to June 1999, the central bank lowered the benchmark interest rates four times. The benchmark one-year lending rate was lowered from 8.64% to 5.85%, while the benchmark one-year deposit rate dropped from 5.67% to 2.25%. The government also reduced the reserve requirement ratio (RRR). From March 1998 to November 1999, the central bank drastically reduced the reserve requirement ratio twice, from 13% prior to the adjustment in 1998 to 6% in 1999—7% points in total. As part of these efforts, on March 21, 1998, the mandatory reserve account and provision account were combined into one, and the reserve requirement ratio was reduced by 5% points at a time—the largest decrease of the reserve requirement ratio in history. Meanwhile, the government also lowered the rediscount rate and the refinancing rate. Finally, credit limits imposed on state-owned banks were removed to enhance the loan granting capacity of the specialized banks.

Third, the government used the "hand of government" to help the "hand of the market" speed up the exit of enterprises with outdated technologies and accelerate market clearing. During the previous overheating periods, redundant investment brought about overcapacity, structural imbalance, and poor company performance. Impacted by falling external and domestic demands, the serious shortage of effective demand relative to total supply caused deflation and economic slowdown. It would be a long and painful process to realize market clearing by relying entirely on the market mechanism. For this reason, the government worked to increase supply by reducing redundant construction and providing support to companies in their technological renovation through administrative measures, helping outdated and non-profitable enterprises to exit, and completing business upgrading so as to quickly correct market failure and speed up market clearing.

On one hand, efforts were made to stop low-level redundant production and construction and to reduce low-end supply. Administrative measures like access approval, bank loan approval, land use approval, urban planning approval, environmental evaluation approval, and others were applied in a comprehensive approach to eliminate enterprises with outdated capacities and reduce the production of hard-to-sell the products. In August 1999, the government promulgated the *Catalogues of Restricting Redundant Investment in Industrial and Commercial Sectors*, which required government authorities at all levels concerning land, city planning, environmental protection, fire protection, and others not to grant approval to projects of low-level redundant construction (Table 6). The catalogues specified that relevant personnel accountable for any violations would be subject to penalty. At the same time, loss-making enterprises and those with redundant construction projects had no access to their bank loans cut off in order to force them to close their factories, suspend production, merge with others, and switch fields. The government also required relevant departments and banks to conduct a joint nationwide inspection and stop granting any loans to factories with overstocked inventories so as to prevent them from producing and thus encourage them to close down and exit the market.

On the other hand, the government guided enterprises to implement technical upgrading and improve supply quality, using a market-oriented approach to guide enterprises to increase their investments in technological transformation and upgrading. For example, the government issued RMB60 billion in new government bonds and allocated RMB15 billion in interest subsidies for companies that applied

Table 6 Administrative measures restricting redundant investment in industrial and commercial sectors

<table>
<tr><th>Prohibited catalogue</th><th>Approving authorities</th><th>Approval requirements</th></tr>
<tr><td rowspan="7">(1) Projects explicitly prohibited by relevant laws and regulations
(2) Projects of low-level redundant construction, which would contribute to the current overcapacity and be subject to total amount control
(3) Projects with outdated technologies and knowhow, replaceable by new projects with advanced and established technologies and knowhow
(4) Projects that would cause environmental pollution and resource waste</td><td>Government authorities at all levels responsible for investment approval</td><td>Deny the approval</td></tr>
<tr><td>All banks and financial institutions</td><td>Reject loan application</td></tr>
<tr><td>Land administration authorities</td><td>Reject application</td></tr>
<tr><td>Urban planning authorities</td><td>Reject application</td></tr>
<tr><td>Environmental protection department</td><td>Reject application</td></tr>
<tr><td>Fire protection department</td><td>Reject application</td></tr>
<tr><td>Customs and others</td><td>Reject application</td></tr>
<tr><td>*Including 17 sectors, and 201 items*</td><td></td><td></td></tr>
</table>

Source The Catalogues of Restricting the Redundant Investment in Industrial and Commercial Sectors (Batch 1) drafted by the State Economic and Trade Commission in August 1999

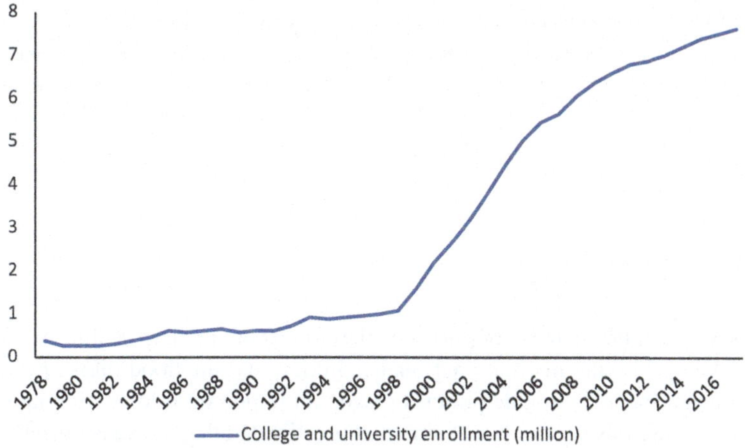

Chart 18 College and University Enrollment. *Source* Wind database

for technology transformation loans, which generated about RMB200 billion in technical transformation investment.[21] Investment projects encouraged by the state and foreign investment projects were exempt from customs duties and import value-added taxes. Beginning in July 1999, technological renovation projects that met national industrial policy standards were eligible for an enterprise income tax exemption based on 40% of the purchase price of their domestic-made equipment.

Fourth, the government took the opportunity to promote economic system reform. For example, housing commercialization and the reform of the urban housing system, which began in 1998, not only helped achieve the proactive macroeconomic management goal of increasing demand in the short term but also released the vitality of economic growth in the long term. In another example, the government further deepened SOE reform to improve the operating efficiency and performance of the textile, coal, petroleum, petrochemical, and metallurgical industries, reduce ineffective supply, and alleviate the contradiction between supply and demand. Furthermore, through the massive "enrollment expansion" reform of colleges and universities in 1999 (Chart 18), employment pressure was eased and, more importantly, the upgrading of human capital was promoted and the endowment for the long-term development of China's economy was enhanced. These reforms further improved the market mechanism, strengthened proactive macroeconomic management, and enhanced the vitality of the Chinese economy for future economic development.

(c) **Effectiveness of Proactive Macroeconomic Management**

This round of proactive macroeconomic management successfully responded to the external adverse impact brought about by the Asian financial crisis. Real GDP growth in 1998 and 1999 was 7.8% and 7.7%, respectively. Although still below 8%, this

[21] *Zhu Rongji on the Record* (Book 1), Page 294.

Table 7 Change of performance in industrial enterprises above designated size

Year	Product sales rate for the industrial enterprises above designated size (%)	Debt to asset ratio of the industrial enterprises above designated size (%)	Growth of total profit of the industrial enterprises above designated size (%)
1998	96.52	63.74	−14.38
1999	97.15	61.83	56.93
2000	97.67	60.81	92.00

Source CEInet Statistics Database

success was significant and hard-earned in the context of the sharp decline in external demand caused by the international financial crisis and the flood disaster in 1998. On one hand, macroeconomic policies played an important role in stimulating the economy during this period. For example, it is estimated that the active fiscal policy adopted by the government boosted economic growth by 1.5% points in 1998 and 2% points in 1999.[22] On the other hand, real GDP growth in 2000 and 2001 reached 8.5% and 8.3%, respectively, and economic growth began to recover. This indicates that proactive macroeconomic management played an important role in China's subsequent economic stability and recovery.

The proactive macroeconomic management on the exit and elimination of outdated capacity by the companies with the help of the government also achieved good results. By the end of 1999, about 31,000 small coal mines had been closed, reducing capacity by about 280 million tons, and the coal industry basically restored the supply and demand balance in 2000. The supply and demand dynamics improved, and the operating efficiency and quality of enterprises enhanced significantly. Many industries went from loss making to turning a profit, and the growth of the total profits of the industrial enterprises above the designated size increased from -14.8% in 1998 to 56.9% in 1999 and 92% in 2000 (Table 7). The overstocked inventories decreased, and the product sales rates for industrial enterprises above the designated size increased significantly, from 96.52% in 1998 to 97.15% in 1999 and 97.63% in 2000. The bank debts owned by companies with poor management and performance were reduced, the debt to asset ratio of the industrial enterprises above designated size dropped from 63.74% in 1998 to 61.83% in 1999 and 60.81% in 2000.

More importantly, the proactive macroeconomic management during this period also contributed to the rapid infrastructure construction and development and laid a good foundation for China's future economic development. Take expressways for example, before the Asian financial crisis in 1997, the total expressway mileage was only 4,700 km, which increased to 24,000 km by the beginning of 2002.[23] The rural power grid renovation project also greatly improved the living standard and production capability of rural residents and expanded rural consumption indirectly.

[22]*Zhu Rongji on the Record* (Book 1), Page 409.

[23]Ibid., Page 446.

2.6 *The Economic Overheating Period from 2003 to 2007*

(a) **Macroeconomic Background**

China's economy started a new round of recovery in 2003, and gradually showed signs of an economic boom. The key characteristics of this period were fast growth of fixed-asset investment, high money and credit supplies, and a large foreign trade surplus, which resulted in an imbalance in which domestic total demand was larger than total supply. From 2003 to 2007, China's real GDP maintained double-digit growth and kept rising from 10% in 2003 to 11.4% in 2005 and 12.7% in 2006, reaching a record high of 14.2% in 2007 (Chart 19). The CPI growth rate fluctuated from 2003 to 2007, but also reached 3.9% and 4.8%, respectively, in 2004 and 2007 (although it was only 1.5% in 2006). House prices also rose by more than 10% [9]. Economic growth occurred at an alarming speed, with inflation glaringly apparent.

On one hand, domestic fixed-assets grew too quickly, and blind investment and low-level redundant construction reappeared. Investment overheating was clearly observed in steel, aluminum, cement, and other industries, and upstream products like coal, electricity, oil, transportation, and infrastructure were in tight supply. From 2003 to 2007, the average growth of fixed-asset investment reached 25.8%. From 2004 to 2007, the average growth of fixed-asset investment in the manufacturing industry reached 32%. Real estate investment grew by 25.5% on average. Growth rates of all kinds of investments were all at an all-time historic high. Meanwhile, the real growth of industrial added value also increased from 11.6% in 2005 to 14.9% in 2007 (Charts 20 and 21).

This long-term economic boom made companies too optimistic about their economic prospects, and a "rush to the top" game appeared, which generated redundant investments. Both SOEs and private companies made blind investments, and

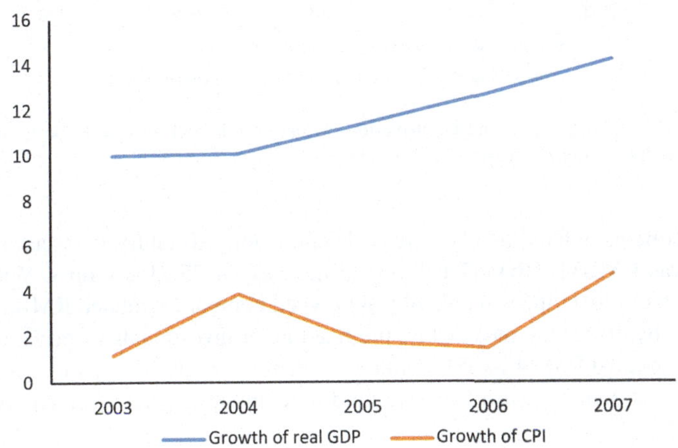

Chart 19 Growth of Real GDP and CPI during 2003–2007. *Source* CEInet Statistics Database

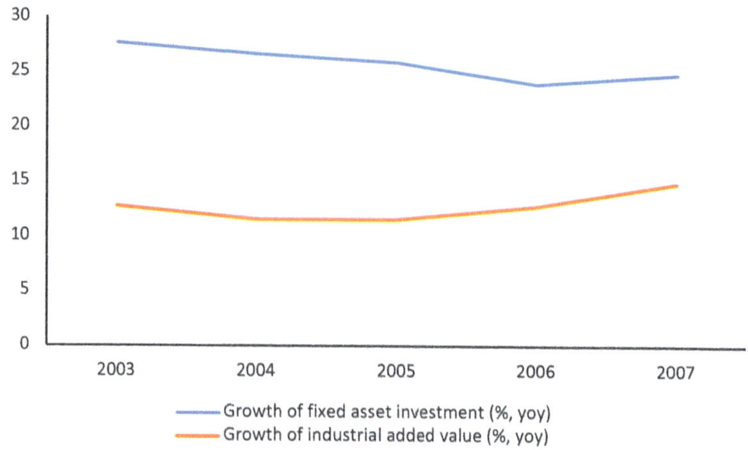

Chart 20 y-on-y Growth of Fixed-Asset Investment and Industrial Added Value During 2003–2007. *Source* CEInet Statistics Database

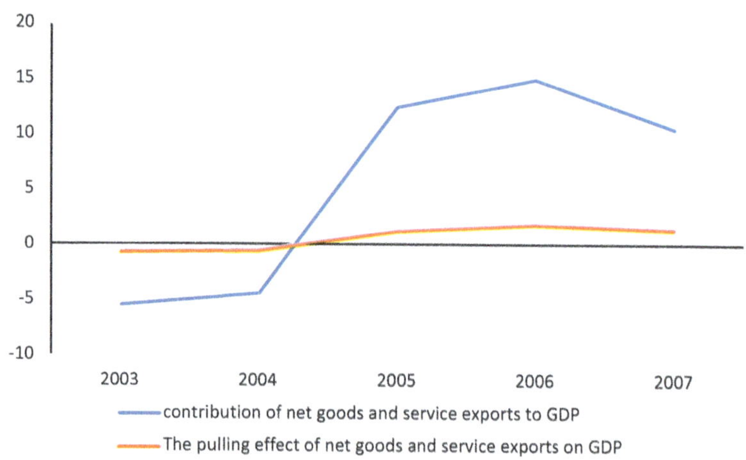

Chart 21 The Pulling Effect and Contribution of Net Goods and Service Exports on/to GDP During 2003–2007. *Source* CEInet Statistics Database

their investments in fixed-assets increased significantly. Total fixed-asset investment in 2007 was RMB11.7464447 trillion, an increase of 25.81% y-on-y. Within this Chart, the fixed-asset investments of state-owned companies totaled RMB5.222939 trillion, up by 16.52% y-on-y, while the fixed-asset investments of private holding companies totaled RMB4.640513 trillion, an increase of 39.03% y-on-y. As we can see, the investment growth of private holding companies was significantly higher than that of state-owned companies.[24] In the manufacturing and mining industries, where redundant investment and overcapacity were more concentrated, the investment growth of private companies was also higher than that of state-owned companies. This rule also held true in the following sub-sectors: non-metallic mineral product manufacturing, non-ferrous metal smelting and rolling processing, metal product manufacturing under the manufacturing industry, coal mining and washing, oil and gas extraction, and non-ferrous metal mining and mineral processing under the metal and mining industry (Table 8).

The fact that private companies were more aggressive in making investments during the economic boom could not be explained by the theories of SOE "soft budget constraints" [11, 16] or the "promotion tournament" of local government officials [16, 17]. During the economic boom, most companies were over-optimistic about the future and made redundant investments, which resulted in a faster expansion of production capacity of the whole industry and accelerated the economy toward overcapacity.

On the other hand, the rapid growth of external demand after China's accession to the WTO made a significant contribution to the rapid growth of China's economy. Especially after 2005, China's net exports showed a sharp upward trend, which was also one of the important reasons why total domestic demand overtook total supply. The contribution of net exports of goods and services to China's GDP reached historic highs of 12.5%, 15.1%, and 10.6% in 2005, 2006, and 2007, respectively. From the perspective of the pulling effect of external demand on the economy, net exports contributed 1.4, 1.9, and 1.5% points to China's economic growth in 2005, 2006, and 2007, respectively.

In addition, the increase in currency issuance resulting from the funds outstanding for foreign exchange pushed the price up. From 2003 to 2007, China's increasing trade surplus resulted in an increase in China's yuan funds outstanding for foreign exchange and domestic money supply, while additional currency issuance exerted pressure on prices in the long term. After China's accession to the WTO in 2001, the yuan funds outstanding for foreign exchange owned by financial institutions in M2 began to show a significant upward trend and reached a historic high during the international financial crisis in 2008. The yuan funds outstanding for foreign exchange owned by financial institutions in M2 rose from 15.8% in 2003 to 31.8% in 2007, or more than doubled. M2 also showed rapid growth during 2004–2007, and grew by 14.7%, 17.6%, 17%, and 16.7% y-on-y in 2004, 2005, 2006, and 2007, respectively. The rapid growth of money supply had a significant impact on economic overheating and inflation (Chart 22).

[24]The growth of fixed-asset investment by private companies in 2007 was also higher than that by SOEs. In 2007, total fixed-asset investment was RMB13.7324 trillion, up by 24.84% y-on-y. Within this Chart, fixed-asset investment by SOEs was RMB3.87066 trillion, up by 17.42% y-on-y. However, the fixed-asset investment by private companies reached RMB2.7056 trillion, up by 40.42% y-on-y (calculated by the author based on data from the CEInet Statistics Database).

Table 8 Investment Growth in 2007: state-owned companies versus private holding companies

Sector	State-owned companies		Private holding companies	
	Fixed-asset investment (RMB000' million)	Growth (%)	Fixed-asset investment (RMB000' million)	Growth (%)
Total investment	52229.39	16.52	46405.13	39.03
Manufacturing	7264.14	26.46	20338.23	46.29
Ferrous metal smelting and rolling processing	1632.71	23.60	737.08	17.22
Nonmetallic mineral product manufacturing	285.67	21.87	2073.44	60.49
Non-ferrous metal smelting and rolling processing	422.98	13.88	630.19	48.57
Metal product manufacturing	96	29.36	1181.18	54.01
Mining	3456.9	18.30	1378.29	44.35
Coal mining and washing	1044.15	10.92	536.25	43.55
Oil and gas extraction	2132.89	20.38	40.26	103.33
Non-ferrous metal mining and mineral processing	108.11	30.54	295.14	77.77
Non-metal mineral mining and processing	54.44	78.84	212.71	46.45
Ferrous metal mining and mineral processing	115.02	22.10	285.85	16.42

Source ACCEPT calculation based on data from the CEInet Statistics Database

(b) **Proactive Macroeconomic Management Measures**

In order to cope with the excessive economic boom during 2003–2007, the government implemented comprehensive policies—including market-oriented demand management measures and stringent administrative measures—and continued to speed up economic reform. In this round of regulation, market-oriented total demand management measures were introduced more frequently, and the areas covered by such measures were more extensive. For example, the central bank significantly increased the use of market-oriented monetary policy measures such as interest rate adjustment, open market operation, and the reserve requirement ratio. The fiscal policy mainly focused on reducing bond issuance, cutting investment spending

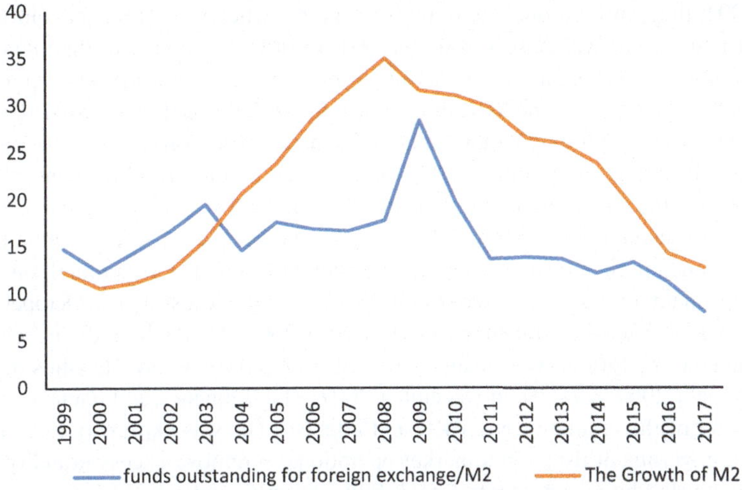

Chart 22 The Yuan Funds Outstanding for Foreign Exchange/M2 and Growth of M2 (%). *Source* CEInet Statistics Database

and adjusting spending structure, and redirecting spending to areas more related to people's well-being, with relatively small multiplier effects. Since such measures did not immediately yield ideal results, the government also adopted administrative measures such as loan approval, land use approval, technical standards, and environmental protection standards to quickly cool down the economy. At the same time, the government continued to deepen and advance reforms in key areas of the economic system while also managing the relationship between the government and the market, economic growth, and social development.

(1) The government adopted a sound fiscal policy and a tight monetary policy to cope with economic overheating and inflation. The government adopted a sound fiscal policy and rationalized the investment structure in a variety of ways. First, policymakers reduced the issuance of government bonds. From 2003 to 2007, long-term state construction bonds were reduced by RMB100 billion in total. Second, the government adjusted the structure of fiscal spending. Investments in projects with larger pulling effects were reduced, while investments in "agriculture, rural areas, and farmers," science and technology, social security, and other public services were increased. From 2003 to 2007, the central government spent RMB1.6 trillion in total on "agriculture, rural areas, and farmers," and significantly increased investment in social security and education. Third, the government canceled or reduced export tax rebates for high energy-consuming, high emission and resource-based products, reducing the pressure from the pulling effect of exports. The government also adopted a tight monetary policy to prevent the fast growth of credit. First, the government raised the reserve requirement ratio (RRR) several times to reduce the money supply. In September 2003, the People's Bank of China raised the RRR by 1% point, and in April

2004, they raised it once more by 0.5% points when no significant contraction of bank credit was observed in 1Q2004. In order to cope with the intensified economic overheating, the government maintained a tight monetary policy in 2006, when it raised the RRR three times. In 2007, the RRR was raised 10 times. The reserve requirement ratio for large financial institutions reached 14.5% after the adjustment in December 200—up from 6% before the adjustment in 2003. Second, the government raised the benchmark deposit and lending interest rates to raise capital costs. From 2004 to 2007, the People's Bank of China raised the benchmark deposit and lending rates eight times. The benchmark one-year deposit interest rate increased from 1.98% before the adjustment in October 2004 to 4.14% after the adjustment in December 2007. Meanwhile, the benchmark interest rate for one-year loans increased from 5.31% before the adjustment in October 2004 to 7.47% in December 2007. The frequency and intensity of this round of the regulation via RRR and interest rates was extremely rare. Third, the government used open market operations to remove excess liquidity from the market by issuing central bank bills and initiating repurchase agreements (repo).

(2) The government made use of all kinds of administrative measures in a comprehensive approach to speed up the exit of outdated and non-profitable companies and reduce redundant investment. In order to control excessive investment and its accompanying overcapacity, as well as low-level redundant construction and illegal construction in steel, cement, aluminum, and other industries, the government adopted administrative measures such as credit, land, and environmental protection to control uninformed market access and redundant construction, thus speeding up market clearing.

First, the government moved to enhance supervision and strictly control the flow of credit. Relevant government authorities issued a series of documents calling for an increase in the capital ratio of the steel and other industries, strengthening credit supervision, strictly controlling the flow of credit to overheated industries (such as real estate, steel, aluminum, and cement), and conducting a special inspection on the flow of credit by the China Banking Regulatory Commission (CBRC).

Second, the government tightened the land supply approval policy. The land for infrastructure construction and industrial investment was brought under control by limiting the new land available for construction projects. In April 2004, a State Council executive meeting was called to discuss the rectification of land market governance, and local departments were ordered to spend one and a half months cleaning up their in-progress and proposed fixed-asset investment projects. The central government also asked local governments to investigate the *Tieben event* and severely punish the people responsible. Following the meeting, the State Council and the Ministry of Land and Resources issued a series of documents strictly controlling the land supply (Table 9) to halt the land supply for steel, cement, aluminum, and other projects that did not comply with the national industrial policy and market access conditions. The policies were also meant to hold local governments accountable for any illegal land use, and to focus on investigating three major types of

Table 9 China's regulations on land use approval during the 2003–2007 proactive macroeconomic management

Time	Meeting or documents	Requirements
April 28, 2004	State Council executive meeting	(1) Discussed the rectification of land market governance (2) Issued the order to investigate the *Tieben event* and had the people responsible for it seriously punished
April 29, 2004	The Urgent Circular of the General Office of the State Council on Deepening the Improvement and Rectification of the Land Market and Exercising Strict Land Administration	(1) Decided to spend about 6 months to make centralized efforts to rectify the land market (2) Cleaned up and inspected land approvals granted since the previous year, especially the land use status of new projects; rectified issues such as violation of national industrial policies, as well as land use approvals beyond planning, beyond the subjects' power, and the land use approval obtained by splitting the land into several pieces
May 30, 2006	Urgent Notice of the Ministry of Land and Resources on Further Intensifying the Land Use Administration	(1) The required that the land use master plan and annual plan be strictly followed (2) Intensified efforts to investigate the cases of unlawful land use and punish those accountable. Focused on investigating and handling typical land use cases not following the planning or beyond the planning, or land use approvals given without complying with the laws
October 21, 2004	Decision of the State Council to Deepen Reform and Intensify Land Administration	(1) Strengthened pre-approval management. No approval was to be granted for projects with no pre-approval opinion or for projects that failed to pass the pre-approval (2) Strictly prohibited evasion of the statutory approval authority to split a single construction project into small pieces and get approval for them one by one

(continued)

Table 9 (continued)

Time	Meeting or documents	Requirements
August 31, 2006	Notice of the State Council Regarding Relevant Matters on Strengthening the Control of Land	Held governors of local government accountable for any serious consequences caused by land use violations in their locality as well as the failure to stop land use violations or the failure to organize investigations into such violations
September 2, 2007	Decision of the Ministry of Land and Resources	Focused on investigating three major kinds of violations, namely "land renting instead of expropriating," expanding industrial land use in violation of the overall land use plan, and "land use prior to approval." Had illegal projects cleared and corrected

Source Summarized by the author based on the related documents

violations, namely "land renting instead of expropriating," expanding industrial land use in violation of the overall land use plan, and "land use prior to approval." Illegal projects were to be cleared and corrected.

Third, the government raised environmental protection standards to limit the redundant construction of outdated production capacity. On one hand, the environmental protection department strictly implemented an environmental impact assessment policy, the principle of "three at the same time," and a total pollutant emission control system for new projects as well as renovation and expansion projects. On the other hand, efforts were made to strengthen the supervision of environmental law enforcement. On June 3, 2007, the State Council issued the *Comprehensive Work Plan for Energy Conservation and Emission Reduction* formulated by the National Development and Reform Commission (NDRC) in conjunction with relevant departments to strengthen energy conservation and emission reduction management as well as supervision and inspection of law enforcement.

Fourth, the government raised the technological bar for market entry. In order to prevent enterprises that lacked technological advantages from continuing to enter the industry with excess capacity and redundant investments, relevant departments formulated technical standards and stringent market access conditions.

3. The government vigorously promoted the reform of the fiscal and taxation system as well as the financial system. In executing these regulations, the government seized the opportunity to promote the joint-stock transformation of state-owned commercial banks and their successful listing, the reform of non-tradable shares of listed companies, the marketization of interest rates, and the reform of the exchange rate formation mechanism. The government conducted value-added tax reform on a pilot basis and also combined the income tax system of

domestic and foreign companies into a single system. These reform measures added new vitality to the Chinese economy and created better conditions for the implementation of fiscal policy and the transmission of monetary policy.

(c) Effectiveness of Proactive Macroeconomic Management

The proactive macroeconomic management from 2003 to 2007 focused on forward-looking policy and the effectiveness of different policy combinations, and thus achieved better results. First, the government grasped the economic trends in a forward-looking manner to achieve timely and flexible policy changes. The basic theme of fiscal policy and monetary policy was changed from "loose" to "tight." For example, in response to signs of overheating, the 2004 *Central Economic Work Conference* promptly decided to adjust the active fiscal policy and prudent monetary policy to a "double-prudent" fiscal and monetary policy. Second, the government realized the effective combination of market-oriented measures and administrative measures. While the fiscal and monetary policies were in force, administrative measures such as land control, project approval, and environmental protection policies were used to strictly limit the investment demand of outdated production capacity and effectively reduce investment growth. The specific effects of these government regulations were as follows.

First, the economy maintained relatively rapid growth and prices remained stable. From 2003 to 2007, the economy grew at a rapid rate, from 10% to 14.2%, while the consumer price index (CPI) grew at a rate of 1.2% to 4.8%. Prices were generally stable and there was no vicious inflation. The momentum of investment overheating was basically under control, and the real and nominal growth of fixed-asset investment in society as a whole showed a downward trend (Chart 23).

Second, the business situation of enterprises was improved. The product sales rate for industrial enterprises above the designated size increased from 98.02% in 2003 to 98.14% in 2007. The growth of the total profit of the industrial enterprises above the designated size recovered to 39.23% in 2007 after experiencing a decline.

Third, excess capacity was significantly reduced. The proactive macroeconomic management during 2003–2007 restrained the output increase in surplus industries and eased the contradiction between supply and demand. The output growth of key surplus industries was curbed, and the output showed a steady downward trend. The year-on-year growth of crude steel production decreased from 27.24% in 2004 to 16.73% in 2007. Meanwhile, the year-on-year growth of cement production dropped from 18.91% in 2003 to 10.06%. The year-on-year growth of raw coal production dropped from 18.39% to 7.39%, and the year-on-year growth of flat glass production decreased from 33.66% to 15.77%. At the same time, a large number of outdated enterprises and capacities were eliminated. From 2003 to 2007, small thermal power stations with an installed capacity of 21.57 million kilowatts and 11.12 million small coal mines were shut down nationwide. In addition, 46.59 million tons of outdated iron smelting capacity, 37.47 million tons of steelmaking capacity, and 87 million tons of cement capacity were also eliminated (Chart 24).[25]

---

[25] Report on the Work of the Government (2008).

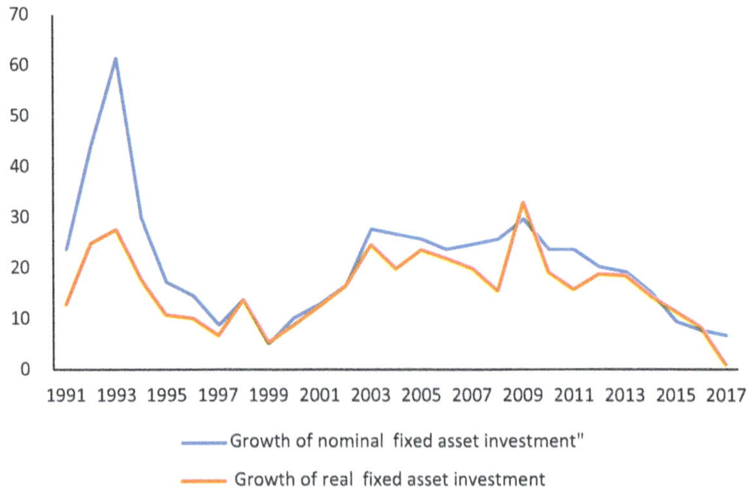

Chart 23 Real and Nominal y-on-y Growth of Fixed-Asset Investment in the Whole Society. *Source* WIND database

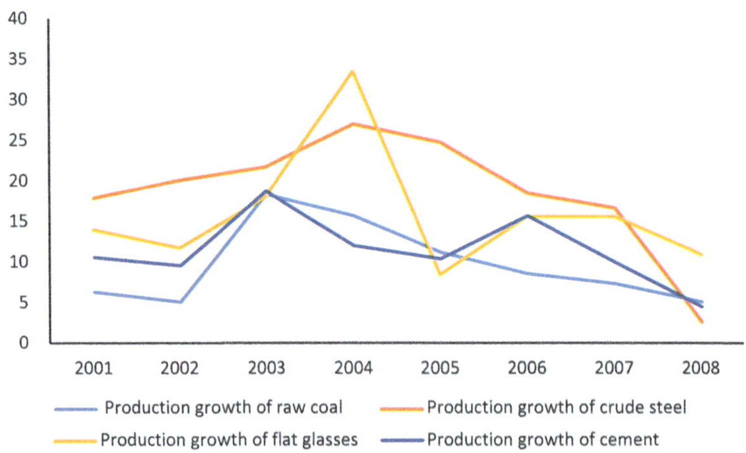

Chart 24 Production Growth of Raw Coal, Crude Steel, Flat Glasses and Cement During 2001–2008. *Source* CEInet Statistics Database

2.7 *The Proactive Macroeconomic Management Period After the Outbreak of the Global Financial Crisis in 2008*

(a) **Macroeconomic Background**

Starting in 2008, the negative impact of the international financial crisis on China's economy began to gradually emerge. China's economy also shifted from overheating in 2007 to a slowdown beginning in 3Q2008. Of the causes, the sharp downward trend of external demand played an important role in the decline of China's economic growth. China's net export growth reached a record high of 40.1% year-on-year in May 2008, only to then gradually decline and slip into the negative in November 2008. In January 2009, the year-on-year growth of net exports fell to a record low of −43.06%. There was obvious evidence that external demand shocks had resulted in the slowdown and cooling of China's macroeconomy:

First, the contribution and pulling effect of external demand to/on China's economic growth changed from positive to negative. The contribution of the net exports of goods and services to GDP dropped sharply from 10.6% in 2007 to 2.6% in 2008 and then to −42.6% in 2009. The pulling effect of exports of goods and services on economic growth dropped from 0.25% in 2008 to −4% in 2009. The dragging effect of external demand on China's economic growth is clearly demonstrated by these dramatic Charts (Charts 25, 26 and 27).

Second, the production growth of domestic industrial enterprises declined. The year-on-year growth of the real industrial added value decreased from 16% in June 2008 to 5.4% in December 2008 and further down to −2.4% in January 2009, reflecting the negative growth of the economy.

Third, deflation was clearly noticeable. The year-on-year growth of the consumer price index fell rapidly from 8.7% in February 2008 to 1.2% in December 2008 before dropping into the negative in February 2009. The negative year-on-year growth of the consumer price index continued until September 2009, during which deflation was apparent.

Chart 25 Year-on-Year Growth of China's Net Exports During 2008–2009. *Source* CEInet Statistics Database

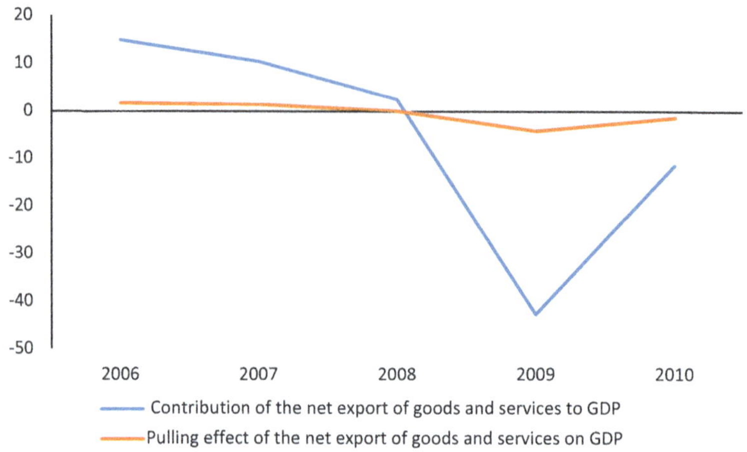

Chart 26 Pulling Effect and Contribution of the Net Export of Goods and Services on/to GDP during 2006–2010. *Source* CEInet Statistics Database

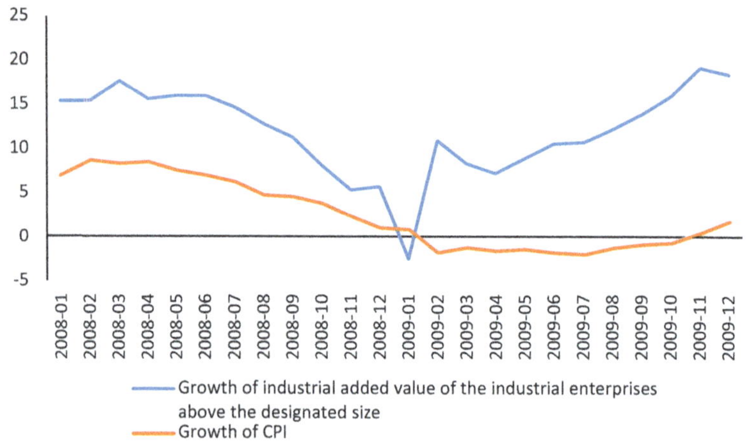

Chart 27 Growth of Industrial Added Value of the Industrial Enterprises Above the Designated Size and Growth of CPI. *Source* CEInet Statistics Database

(b) **Proactive Macroeconomic Management Measures**

In order to cope with the adverse impact of the international financial crisis on China's economy, the government adjusted the basic theme of macro policy in a timely manner. According to the changes in the economic situation and the effects of the regulatory policies, the basic policy theme of "double prevention" (prevention of economic overheating and prevention of obvious inflation) in early 2008 was changed to the basic theme of "one maintenance, one control" (maintaining economic growth and controlling price hikes) in the middle of the year, and then to the basic theme of "one maintenance, one expansion, and one adjustment" (maintaining economic growth, expanding domestic demand, and adjusting structure) in 4Q2008. In terms of the actual implementation of the proactive macroeconomic management policies, the first step was to enact a proactive fiscal policy and a moderately light monetary policy. The second was to formulate and implement an industrial revitalization plan. Part three was to accelerate reform in key areas and crucial fields.

(1) The government implemented a proactive fiscal policy and a moderately light monetary policy

A proactive fiscal policy. The executive meeting of the State Council in November 2008 approved the "RMB4 trillion" stimulus package to increase domestic demand and promote economic growth. The plan also included measures to significantly increase government spending and implement structural tax cuts. In addition to increasing investment in railways, highways, airports, water conservancy, and other infrastructure projects, the plan specified investments in post-disaster reconstruction, affordable housing, rural well-being projects, and public welfare projects. The central government also allocated funds to subsidize home appliances sold in rural areas to promote the growth of rural consumption.

A moderately light monetary policy. On one hand, the benchmark deposit and lending interest rates were lowered several times in a row. From September 2008 to December 2008, the central bank lowered the benchmark deposit and lending interest rates four times in a row in three months. The benchmark interest rate for one-year loans dropped from 7.47% to 5.31%, while the benchmark interest rate for one-year deposits dropped from 4.14% to 2.25%. On the other hand, the reserve requirement ratio (RRR) was also cut several times in a row. From September to December 2008, the RRR for large financial institutions was lowered three times in a row from 17.5% to 15.5%. The RRR for small and medium-sized financial institutions was lowered four times in a row from 17.5% to 13.5%. In addition, credit limits on commercial banks were removed to release liquidity and stimulate the economy.

(2) The government formulated and implemented a plan to revitalize 10 key industries. On one hand, the *Adjustment and Revitalization Plan* for 10 key industries (including steel, automobile, shipbuilding, petrochemical, light industry, textile, non-ferrous metals, equipment manufacturing, electronic information, and logistics) was drafted to stimulate the growth of industries in the upstream and downstream of value chains to revitalize the economy. On the other hand, the promotion of scientific and technological innovation was integrated into industrial revitalization to encourage enterprises to speed up technological upgrading. In 2009, a specialized fund of RMB20 billion was allocated to support 4,441 technological upgrading projects.
(3) The government accelerated the reform of key areas and crucial fields. The response to the international financial crisis was taken as an opportunity to intensify reform efforts. In 2009, VAT transformation was fully implemented, and refined oil prices, taxes, and fees were also smoothly reformed. The process

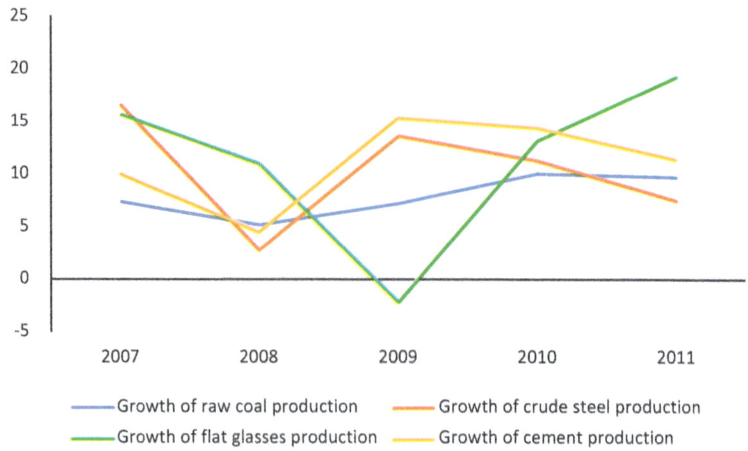

Chart 28 Year-on-Year Growth of Raw Coal, Crude Steel, Flat Glasses, and Cement Production During 2007–2011. *Source* CEInet Statistics Database

of commercializing the National Development Bank and introducing the joint-stock system in the Agricultural Bank of China (ABC) was carried forward. Meanwhile, the RMB cross-border trade settlement was launched on a pilot basis. The ChinNext stock market was launched to open new financing channels for independent innovation companies and other start-ups. The reform of local government departments proceeded, and the reform of the institutions by type on a pilot basis was kicked off.[26] As a whole, these reforms effectively promoted economic and social development and played a positive role in boosting market confidence and expanding domestic demand.

(c) Effectiveness of Proactive Macroeconomic Management

This period of proactive macroeconomic management in response to the international financial crisis was faster and more forceful than its predecessors, and also highly successful. China's economy emerged from the crisis very quickly, taking the lead in recovery and contributing to the rehabilitation of the world economy. In 2008 and 2009, China's real GDP grew at rates as high as 9.7% and 9.4%, respectively. The growth of real industrial added value also reached 10% and 9.1%, respectively, while the growth of fixed-asset investment in the manufacturing industry reached 27.4% and 24.5%, respectively (Chart 28).

The mergers and acquisitions and restructuring of key industries paved the way for new achievements. The government made great efforts to curb the overcapacity of certain industries. For example, 26.17 million kilowatts of small thermal power stations were closed down, as well as outdated facilities with a total production

[26] *Report on the Work of the Government,* delivered by Wen Jiabao, Premier of the State Council at the Third Session of the Eleventh National People's Congress on March 5, 2010.

capacity of 16.91 million tons in the steelmaking industry, 21.13 million tons in the iron-smelting industry, 74.16 million tons in the cement industry, and 18.09 million tons in the coke industry.[27] However, this large-scale stimulus also brought certain negative effects. For example, repeated investment in industries with excess capacity, such as steel, was stimulated and led to overheating and inflation in 2010–2011.

China realized rapid economic growth and the rise of inflation in 2010–2011. Real GDP growth in 2010 and 2011 reached 10.6% and 9.5%, respectively. Consumer price index growth reached 3.3% and 5.4%, respectively, while food prices represented by agricultural products rose even more dramatically. Total fixed-asset investment in society as a whole grew strongly, with the year-on-year growth rate reaching 23.83% and 23.76%, respectively. In order to curb the strong price hikes and prevent the economy from overheating, the government made overall price stabilization its top priority in proactive macroeconomic management. The government also aimed to maintain the relatively fast economic growth that had developed, and emphasized prudent flexibility, moderation, goal-orientation, and proactiveness in its policies.

First, the government changed the direction of its monetary policy in a timely manner. The monetary policy was changed from the basic theme of "moderately loose" to "moderately light," and efforts were made to manage the inflation expectations. Reserve requirement ratio (RRR), benchmark deposit and lending interest rates, open market operations, and other market-oriented monetary policy tools were used in a comprehensive approach to tighten money supply and curb inflation. From January 2010 to November 2011, the central bank raised the RRR for large financial institutions 12 times in a row from 15.5% to 21.5%. From November 2010 to November 2011, the central bank raised the RRR for small and medium-sized financial institutions nine times in a row from 13.5% to 18%. From October 2010 to July 2011, the benchmark deposit and lending interest rates were raised several times. The benchmark interest rates for one-year deposits and loans were raised from 2.5% to 3.5% and from 5.56% to 6.56%, respectively.

Second, the government continued its proactive fiscal policies and focused on the role of fiscal policies in stabilizing growth and adjusting structures. While reducing general spending, the government strengthened local debt management, blocked construction projects without informed studies, and optimized the structure of fiscal spending. Emphasis was given to the implementation of fiscal and monetary policies together with investment, land, trade, and other policies in a coordinated approach. The goal was to form a policy portfolio with economic measures as the primary policies and administrative measures as the complementary policies.

Third, the government accelerated structural adjustment and intensified reforms. It actively promoted the transformation of the economic development mode and attached attention to the quality and efficiency of growth. Inflation was curbed by ensuring the adequate supply of agricultural products, reducing their distribution costs, and strengthening price regulation. At the same time, the government vigorously promoted reforms in the fiscal, tax, financial, and investment systems as well as reforms regarding resources and the environment.

---

[27] Ibid.

Through this round of proactive macroeconomic management via tightening policies, the excessive price hikes were brought fully under control. The consumer price index (CPI) and producer price index (PPI) dropped month-on-month gradually beginning in August 2011.

2.8 The Macroeconomic Management Period of Continuing Economic Growth Slowdown from 2012 to 2016

(a) **Macroeconomic Background**

Starting from 2012, China's economy entered the "new normal." The potential economic growth rate continued to decline, and real economic growth also began to shift from a high-speed growth platform to a medium-high-speed growth platform. China's real GDP growth gradually dropped from 9.5% in 2011 to 7.9% in 2012, 7.8% in 2013, 7.3% in 2014, 6.9% in 2015, and 6.7% in 2016—the momentum of economic growth significantly weakened. The real growth of industrial added value dropped from 10.9% in 2011 to 6% in 2015 and 2016, with a clearly noticeable downward trend (Chart 29).

First, the pulling effect of exports on the economy noticeably weakened. With the rise of labor costs and the gradual disappearance of China's demographic dividend, the low-cost export advantage of labor-intensive products also diminished, and the pulling effect of exports on China's economic growth also showed a downward trend. From 2012 to 2016, the contribution of net exports of goods and services to China's

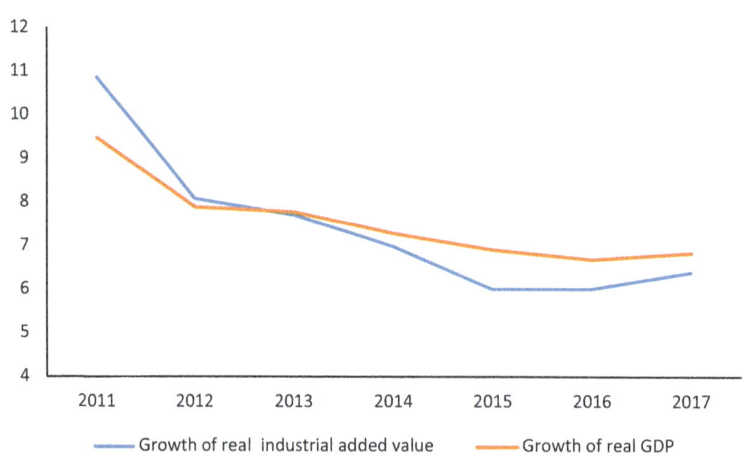

Chart 29 Year-on-Year Growth of Real GDP and Industrial Added Value During 2011–2017. *Source* CEInet Statistics Database

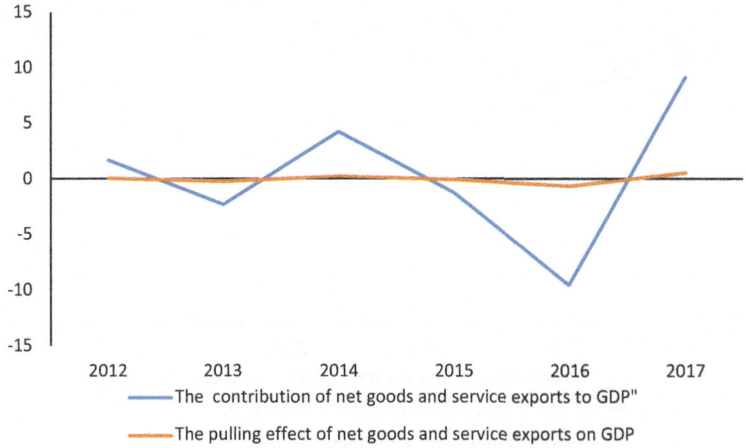

Chart 30 The Pulling Effect and Contribution of Net Goods and Service Exports on/to GDP. *Source* CEInet Statistics Database

GDP hovered between −9.6% and 4.3%, the pulling rate of net exports of goods and services on the GDP hovered around zero, and the pulling effect of net exports on the economy was quite weak.

Second, the growth of fixed-asset investments in all sectors declined sharply. The growth of fixed-asset investments in society as a whole continually declined from 20.2% in 2012 to 5.7% in 2017. The growth of fixed-asset investments in manufacturing decreased from 21.3% in 2012 to 3.1% in 2017, while fixed-asset investments in real estate decreased from 21.4% in 2012 to 2.7% in 2017. It is evident that the growth of investments in all sectors slowed significantly, and growth dropped sharply (Charts 30 and 31).

Third, the oversupply of industrial industries was still very severe. Some industries like the steel, coal, electrolytic aluminum, cement, and chemical industries continued to face a serious overcapacity problem. By the end of 2012, the capacity utilizations of China's steel, cement, aluminum, flat glass, and shipbuilding industries were only 72%, 73.7%, 71.9%, 73.1%, and 75%, respectively—significantly lower than international standards. Serious overcapacity resulted in a sharp decline of profits in steel, aluminum, shipbuilding, and other industries, and the companies in these sectors generally experienced operating difficulties. Even then, there were still some proposed and in-progress projects in these industries with serious overcapacity, further worsening the overall situation.[28]

Fourth, prices in consumption and production areas experienced structural deflation. Deflation occurred in the industrial sector because of oversupply. Under the economic slowdown, overcapacity problems in the upstream industrial sector became more prominent, which was directly reflected in the drop in the ex-factory prices of

[28]"Guiding Opinions of the State Council on Resolving Serious Production Overcapacity" (*Guofa* [2013] No. 41).

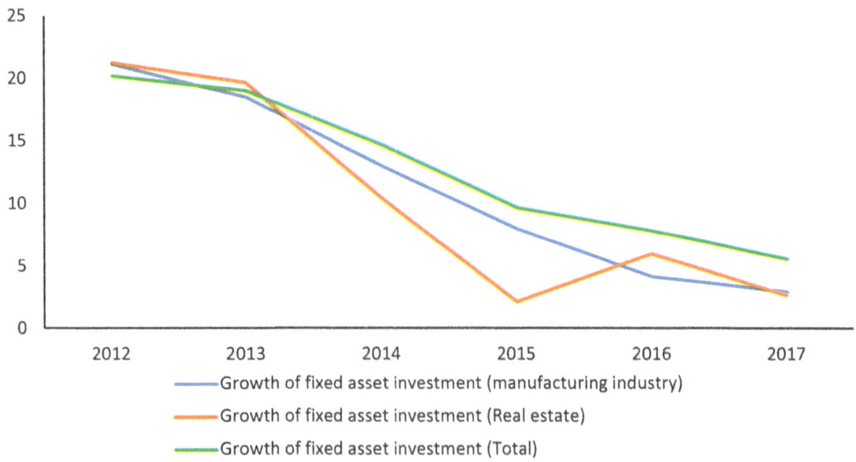

Chart 31 Year-on-Year Growth of Fixed-Asset Investment During 2012–2017. *Source* CEInet Statistics Database

industrial products. From March 2012 to August 2016, the producer price index (PPI) experienced negative growth for 54 consecutive months, indicating that prices in industry had been in deflation for a long time. Although the CPI growth in the consumer sector did not show negative growth year-on-year, the CPI growth once hovered around 1%, indicating that the inflation slowdown was significant, and there would be a risk of deflation in the case of continued decline.

(b) **Proactive Macroeconomic Management Measures**

In response to the declining trend of economic and investment growth, the government did not engage in the "flood irrigation" type of strong stimulation, but instead adapted to the new normal of economic development and initiated macroeconomic management through the combination of structural reforms on the supply side and range-based regulation on the demand side. Focus was placed on the supply side structural reforms when the economy was operating in a reasonable range. When the economy was heading toward the lower end of the range, directional and precise regulations were made via the fiscal and monetary policies to keep the economy in a reasonable range and win time and space for structural reform. Meanwhile, market and administrative measures were used to help ease overcapacity and help companies with outdated technologies exit and speed up market clearing.

(1) The government implemented a proactive fiscal policy and a prudent monetary policy.

A proactive fiscal policy. On one hand, the government moderately increased the fiscal deficit and the government debt, guided the fiscal deficit ratio during 2012–2017 within the upper limit of 3%, and proposed to maintain a larger fiscal deficit at RMB800 billion, RMB1.2 trillion, RMB1.35 trillion, RMB1.62 trillion, RMB2.18

trillion, and RMB2.38 trillion, respectively, in 2012–2017. On the other hand, the government tried to rationalize the fiscal spending structure and increase fiscal spending to plug the gaps and improve people's well-being. In fact, the focus of fiscal spending was shifted to improving people's well-being, and key projects and local governments were allowed local government bonds via the local government bond replacement program. In addition, the business tax was replaced by the VAT, and many taxes and fees were cut to reduce the burden on small and micro enterprises.

A prudent monetary policy. On one hand, the money supply was strictly controlled to slow down the growth of the broad money supply. Beginning in 2012, the growth of broad money supply M2 decreased from 13.6% in 2011 to 12.2% in 2014 and 8.1% in 2017. On the other hand, the government took an innovative approach in its monetary policy through precise regulations. Structural monetary policies were implemented, including targeted RRR cuts and targeted re-lending to strengthen credit support to small and micro enterprises, "agriculture, rural areas, and farmers," and other key and weak areas.

(2) The government made efforts to promote the supply side structural reforms and speed up the rationalization and upgrading of the economic structure. To increase effective supply and cut inefficient capacity, some major supply side structural reforms were actively carried out, including removing capacity, cutting inventory, de-leveraging, cutting costs, and plugging gaps. The government also made efforts to deepen the reform of *Streamlining Administration, Delegating Power, and Strengthening Regulation* and accelerated the transformation of government functions. The supply side structural reforms were designed with both the short-term and long-term in mind. They aimed to enhance efforts to eliminate the outstanding contradictions and deep-rooted institutional obstacles limiting long-term economic and social development, while also maintaining relatively stable economic growth (Charts 32 and 33).

(3) The "hand of the government" was used to help "the hand of the market" to reduce overcapacity and respond to the "war of attrition" among enterprises. As the economy cooled down and overcapacity became apparent, companies were reluctant to exit, instead choosing to engage in the "war of attrition." Although the companies faced excessive competition and even sometimes the loss of the whole industry, they generally believed that as long as they could survive, they would be the final winner when the economy started to recover. In this case, when the market mechanism failed, it would have taken too much time to complete market clearing via the hindered market mechanism. This would have resulted in a waste of social resources and a loss of welfare. Therefore, it was necessary for the government to adopt certain administrative measures and to use the "hand of government" to help the "hand of the market" to force enterprises to exit. This round of the proactive macroeconomic management aimed to help companies exit while also denying entry to outdated companies and removing overcapacity through the market mechanism and the guidance of the central government, strengthening the restraint on and incentives to local governments

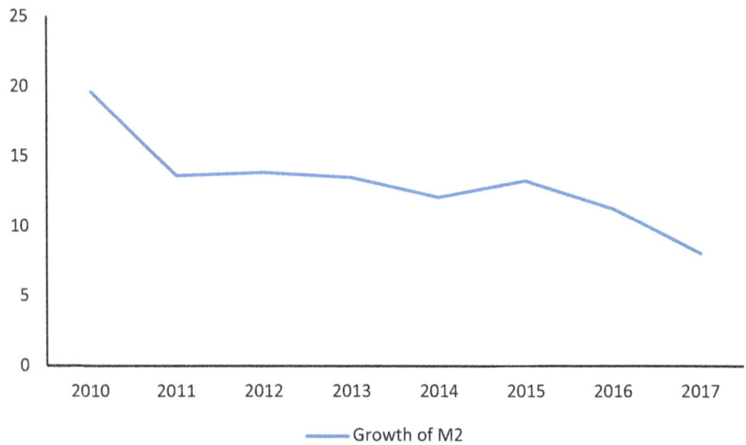

Chart 32 Growth of Broad Money Supply M2 During 2010–2017. *Source* CEInet Statistics Database

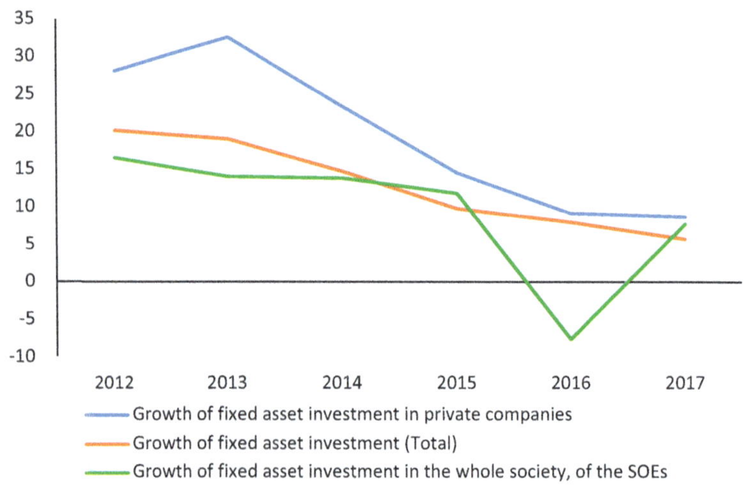

Chart 33 Growth of Fixed-Asset Investment in the Whole Society, of the SOEs and Private Companies. *Source* CEInet Statistics Database

and enterprises. In this process, the central government, local governments, and enterprises played their roles in harmony. Their main responsibilities are detailed below in Table 10.

Table 10 Responsibilities and tasks of each entity in the market clearing process initiated by the "Hand of Market" with the Help of the "Hand of Government"

Entity	Overall responsibilities	Specific tasks
Central gov. and related depts. and commissions	Play the overall decision-making, leading, and regulatory role in helping outdated enterprises and capacities exit	(1) Formulate the standards for the exit of outdated companies and the removal of overcapacity, and specify and allocate the overall task of removing production capacity, including the formulation of industrial standards on technology, environmental protection, and energy consumption for outdated production capacity; force enterprises that do not meet the standards to close; and provide guidance on their expectations to prevent small and outdated enterprises from entering into the market (2) Hold local governments accountable for the exit of outdated companies and the removal of overcapacity; the fulfillment of this task would be reviewed during their performance review process via an incentive and punishment mechanism (3) Assign inspection teams to supervise and review the execution process, and punish those accountable for mistakes (4) Allocate funds to local governments and companies as an incentive, and offer favorable policies

(continued)

Table 10 (continued)

Entity	Overall responsibilities	Specific tasks
Enterprises	Mainly responsible for removing overcapacity	(1) Responsible for its profits and losses, and required to exit from the market based on the price signals of the market (2) Forced to close factories, suspend production, merge with others, and switch into other businesses according to related criteria
Local governments	Responsible for ensuring the exit of outdated companies and removal of overcapacity within the region	(1) Execute the overcapacity removal tasks designated by the central government (2) Protection or doing nothing in handling outdated companies and overcapacity for the sake of local GDP and tax revenue is forbidden (3) Draft detailed execution plans and organize them based on the specific situation, and force the closure or exit of companies

Source Summarized by the author based on related documents

(c) **Effectiveness of Proactive Macroeconomic Management**

Since the economy entered into the state of the new normal, the government has initiated proactive macroeconomic management through the combination of structural reforms on the supply side and range-based regulation on the demand side, using the "hand of government" to help the "hand of the market" to force enterprises to exit and speed up market clearing. Such measures achieved very good results. During 2012–2016, economic growth maintained a reasonable range of over 6.5%. The labor market also performed well, with more than 66 million new jobs created in cities and towns from 2013 to 2017. Overall prices rebounded from rock bottom, and the ex-factory price index of industrial producers ended its 54 consecutive months of negative growth in August 2016, indicating that industrial overcapacity had been alleviated. The risk of deflation in the consumer sector was eliminated, and the growth of CPI was up to more than 2%, indicating that the supply and demand situation in the consumer sector had basically reached equilibrium.

Repeated investment in industries with overcapacity was curbed and investment growth declined. The growth of fixed-asset investment in society as a whole dropped from 20.3% in 2012 to 7.8% in 2017. The growth of investment by SOEs dropped from 16.6% to 7.8% in 2017, with a negative value of −7.6% in 2016.

Operating performance of companies also improved significantly. The profitability of industrial enterprises improved, and the profit growth of industrial enterprises above the designated size rose from a negative value in 2014 and 2015 to a positive value in 2016 and 2017, increasing by 8.7% and 4.2%, respectively. The leverage ratio of industrial enterprises also steadily declined. The debt to asset ratio of industrial enterprises above the designated size decreased from 58% in 2012 to 55.9% in 2016 and 56% in 2017.

The combination of market and administrative measures played an important role in speeding up the exit of outdated and zombie enterprises, resulting in effective market clearing. China removed over 170 million tons of steel capacity and 800 million tons of coal capacity from 2013 to 2017 and reallocated over 1.1 million workers. The steel industry's capacity utilization reached 80% in 2018, compared with 73.6% in 2014 and 71.2% in 2015. At present, steel prices have basically returned to a reasonable range, and the profit margin of steel enterprises has been steadily increasing. In 2017, the coal industry's capacity utilization rate increased by 8.7% points, up to 68.2%. The number of coal mines decreased from 18,000 in 2015 to 7,000 in 2017. The profits of coal enterprises above the designated size in the whole country increased by 290.5% year-on-year in 2017. Therefore, it is evident that steel, coal, and other industries have benefited greatly from this round of proactive macroeconomic management, particularly with regard to overcapacity removal and the exit of enterprises with the help of the government (Chart 34).

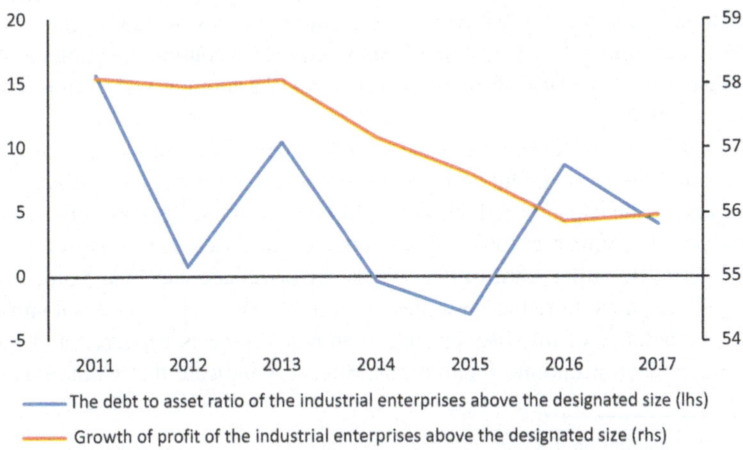

Chart 34 Growth of Profit and Debt to Asset Ratio of the Industrial Enterprises Above the Designated Size During 2011–2017. *Source* CEInet Statistics Database

Feature 1 The "War of Attrition" and its Proactive Macroeconomic Management in the 1990s Chinese Textile Industry

At the end of the 1990s, the Chinese government took diligent measures to address and control overheating in the textile industry, reduce excessive capacity, force out outdated manufacturers, maintain the balance of supply and demand, and speed up market clearing. These measures and their results provide valuable lessons for economic academia to study and reference. Directly after reform and opening up, in an economic environment lacking adequate funds and up-to-date technology, the textile industry became a key industry for investment, thanks to its rapid capital turnover, smaller market exposure, lower requirements for equipment, and broad job offerings. Between 1985 and 1993, the textile industry earned a cumulated tax income of RMB 103 billion and a foreign exchange of USD 110 billion. The industry once accounted for 29.2% of total national exports.[29]

After Deng Xiaoping made his famous southern tour speeches in 1992 and the 14th National Congress of the Chinese Communist Party released its plans to build a socialist market economy, enterprises and companies were greatly incentivized. They rushed to invest in the textile industry and enlarge their capacity to seize the opportunity within the market in a phenomenon called the "rush to the top." The soft budget constraints of state-owned textile enterprises also exacerbated the over-investment, which resulted in overly rapid amassment of capacity, low-level redundant construction, serious inventory backlog, and excessive supply. As a result, the whole textile industry saw a substantial shrinkage of profits or even losses: in 1992, the profit was only RMB1.3 billion, and in 1993 the industry even recorded a loss of RMB500 million. Beginning in 1992, the government started to reform the industry by reducing spindles, requiring a reduction of 1 million outdated spindles per year. In 1993, against the backdrop of rising cotton prices and rapid cost increases in the textile industry, the government unveiled the *Opinions on Resolution of Issues Existing in the Cotton Textile Industry*, which required a continuous implementation of spindle reduction and transformation policies until a cumulative 5 million spindles were cut by 1996.

However, with the deepening of the spindle reduction initiative, a "war of attrition" began in the market. Out of a general expectation that the one who could ultimately survive the capacity reduction would become the biggest beneficiary, more and more textile companies took a "wait-and-see" approach and "attrition" strategy. They preferred to suffer losses rather than exit or reduce capacity. Some companies even "pretended to reduce spindles" to fraudulently obtain financial subsidies. Finally, the balance of microscopic inter-company contests triggered and intensified China's macroeconomic fluctuations. Statistics indicate that China had 41.92

[29]"Notice for Opinions on Resolution of Issues Existing in Cotton Textile Industry Approved and Forwarded by the State Council to State Economic and Trade Commission," *State Development Planning Commission and China National Textile Council*, February 1994.

million knitting spindles in 1991, and still 41.71 million in 1996—only 210,000 less.[30] Meanwhile, the textile industry suffered losses of RMB 4.1 billion in 1995 and 7.1 billion in 1996.

The shock of the financial crisis in Asia further aggravated the conflict between excessive supply and insufficient effective demand. In 1997, the 15th National Congress of the Chinese Communist Party announced that it would take about three years to drag most state-owned large and medium-sized deficit enterprises out of their difficulties by way of reform, reorganization, transformation, and enhanced management. The aim was that by the end of 2000, most state-owned large and medium-sized key enterprises would have an embryo-form modern enterprise organization in place. Thereafter, the textile industry not only became the key to proactive macroeconomic management for de-capacity, but a breakthrough point to advance the state-owned enterprise reforms as well. In November 1997, Premier Zhu Rongji pointed out in a visit to the textile industry in Shanghai that the spindle reduction, lay-offs, and efficiency improvement of the loss-suffering textile industry were to be regarded as the breakthrough point for state-owned enterprises to conduct reforms and overcome difficulties.[31] At the beginning of 1998, the State Council published the *Notice of the State Council on Relevant Issues for Deepening Reforms, Restructuring, and Turning from Deficits to Profits of the Textile Industry*, requiring approximately three years (beginning from 1998) to reduce and eliminate 10 million outdated knitting spindles, settle 1.2 million laid-off workers, turn from deficits to profits for the entire industry by 2000, and pave the way for textile industry upgrading and revitalization. Furthermore, the government pledged to fully implement the policy of encouraging mergers and acquisitions, standardizing bankruptcy, laying-off and resettling workers, and downsizing and increasing efficiency.

We can see that these proactive macroeconomic management measures took the primary form of administrative orders, supported by market approaches, and in the meantime pushed ahead by system reforms—especially the formation of the modern enterprise policies of state-owned enterprises. This round of measures can be summed up as follows.[32]

First, applying administrative measures to persistently reduce and phase out outdated knitting spindles. The State Council required that no region, department, or enterprise could, at any time during the Ninth Five-Year Plan period and for any reason whatsoever, introduce new spindles or relocate outdated knitting spindles. The manufacture and sale of cotton spinning frames and other textile machinery was strictly subject to manufacturing permits and purchasing permits, and the manufacturing of cotton spinning frames without a permit or within China was strictly forbidden. Manufacturers of cotton spinning frames without permits would receive

---

[30] "Why Can't Spindles be Pressed Down?" *People's Daily*, December 4, 1997, 2nd section.

[31] *Zhu Rongji On the Record* (Books 1, 2, 3 and 4) [M]. People's Publishing House, 2011.

[32] *Notice of the State Council on Relevant Issues for Deepening Reforms, Restructuring, and Turning from Deficits to Profits in the Textile Industry*, February 27, 1998.

economic sanctions, and the person in charge would be held responsible. In addition to manufacturing restrictions, the import of cotton spinning frames was also strictly limited pursuant to relevant regulations.

Second, sharing the cost of backward capacity elimination among the central government, local governments, relevant enterprises, and financial institutions. Every thousand spindles reduced was eligible for a subsidy of RMB 3 million (equally shared between the central and local government) and a discount loan of RMB 2 million (borne by the local government). In the meantime, the debt of enterprises was addressed through the process of spindle reduction and capacity limitation. The state reserve for canceling bad debts of banks in 1998 changed its focus to the textile industry, as the local governments were required to allocate a percentage not lower than that of 1997 for canceling bad debts from the textile industry when preparing their 1998 Year Plan. The measures for canceling bad debts of banks were improved in 1999 to further support the exit of enterprises.

Finally, using social security to bolster reforms and help reemploy laid-off workers. The laid-off workers had to be appropriately settled subject to different options. In 1998, the *Merger, Bankruptcy and Staff Re-employment Plan of Chinese Enterprises* was published to actively guide the laid-off workers to re-employment.

By the end of 1999, the textile industry, as the breakthrough point for state-owned enterprises to overcome difficulties (within only three years), had reduced outmoded knitting spindles by 9.06 million in aggregate, realized a full-year revenue of RMB 800 million, and almost hit the three-year spindle reduction target one year earlier than expected. These successes marked the end of the many years' losses suffered by the industry. By 2000, the textile industry successfully accomplished the targets of spindle reduction and staff settlement.[33] In particular, the coastal areas had basically accomplished the spindle reduction target as early as 1998 by phasing out 4.8 million outmoded spindles, settling 600 thousand laid-off workers, and decreasing losses by RMB 3 billion. Other areas basically accomplished the target in 1999 by phasing out 5.2 million spindles.[34] The Charts below show that both the number of enterprises and the number of employees dropped considerably at the end of the 1990s, in particular between 1997 and 1999. Furthermore, fixed-asset investment stock decreased between 1998 and 2000, and the fixed-asset investment increment was lower than asset depreciation, which demonstrates that the trends of over-investment and blind capacity expansion had been effectively contained by 2002 (Chart 35).

[33] "Sharpen the Competitive Edge, Embrace New Challenges after China's Entry to WPO, China's Textile Industry Continues to Speed up Structural Adjustment," March, 2000.

[34] "History is Always Surprisingly Similar: What can State-Owned Enterprise Reform in 1998 and Supply-Side Reform Bring to Us?" *Fixed Income Research of Industrial Securities*.

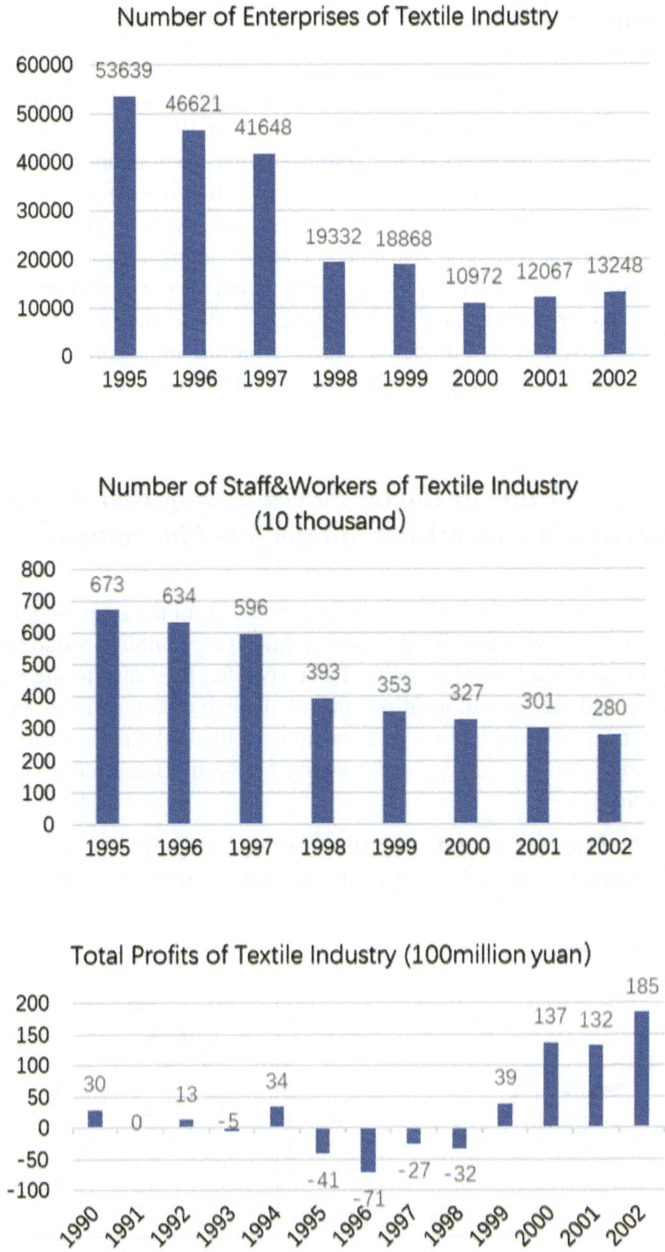

Chart 35 Number of Enterprises, Number of Staff and Workers, and Total Profits of the Textile Industry. *Source* China Statistical Yearbook, China Textile Industry Yearbook of each year

3 Economic Analysis

Looking back at the proactive macroeconomic management conducted by the Chinese government since reform and opening up in 1978, we find it is a unique opportunity for us to understand and rethink major macroeconomic theories. As detailed above, we are convinced that existing mainstream economic textbooks and studies have a deficient understanding of the economic cycle and proactive macroeconomic management. The proactive macroeconomic management experience of the Chinese government since reform and opening up may serve as a beneficial supplement to this deficient understanding. The fundamental economic theories reflected in the Chinese government's proactive macroeconomic management efforts in the past 40 years may be concisely summarized in the following two aspects.

3.1 The Equilibrium of Games Played Among Enterprises Leads to and Exacerbates Macrocycle Fluctuations

The contest between decision makers of enterprises from the microscopic perspective may trigger and intensify the macroeconomic cycle, amplify economic fluctuation, and bring about a loss of benefits. To be specific, the "rush to the top" during market access and the "war of attrition" during the exit of enterprises—both microscopic acts—triggered and intensified economic cyclical fluctuations and caused the macroeconomic situation to repeatedly swing between "overly cold" and "overly hot" (see Chart 36):[35]

(1) When the economy is on the up (the "expansion" period) at the microscopic level, enterprises actively rush to the market, increase their investment, and

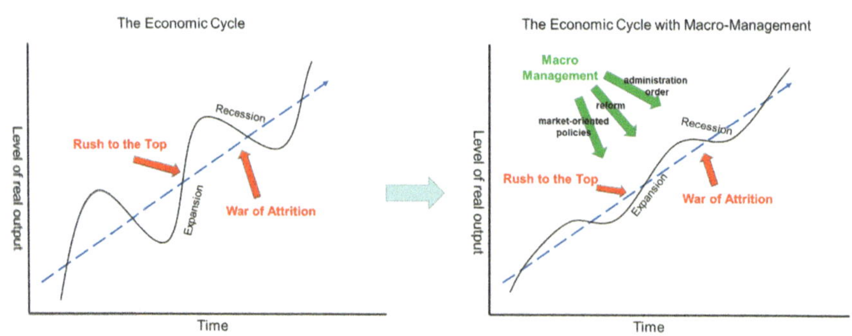

Chart 36 Schematic Diagram of the Economic Cycle and Proactive Macroeconomic Management. *Source* [3]

[35]The following explanation on "rush to the top" and "war of attrition" are expanded on the basis of the section II(1) of [3].

enlarge their capacity, hoping to grab the opportunity within market competition. Though such acts and decisions are rational judging from the perspective of any certain single enterprise, at the macroscopic level an ill balance is formed, **referred to as the "rush to the top"** in this report. On one hand, the "rush to the top" may easily lead to economic "overheating" in the short term and put the macroeconomy under the pressure of inflation. On the other hand, it may also cause the economy to rapidly accumulate capacity and sow the seeds of excessive competition, excessive capacity, and deflation in the subsequent economic downstream cycle.

(2) When the economy is on the downward (the "recession" period), at the microscopic level, enterprises pursue the strategy of attrition, whereby they are not ready to exit the market despite impending losses, but rather believe that their competitors will become bankrupt and they will have the last laugh as long as they keep going. Though such acts and decisions are rational judging from the perspective of any single enterprise, at the macroscopic level an ill balance is also formed, **referred to as the "war of attrition"** in this report. The "war of attrition" will undoubtedly lead to super excessive market capacity, aggravated vicious competition, profitability drop, and loss spreading, which will put the macroeconomy under the pressure of deflation. Microscopic theories have touched on the "war of attrition" [2] but unfortunately failed to draw attention to its macroeconomic applications.

The performance of the Chinese economy after the 1998 Asian financial crisis, the 2008 US subprime crisis, and between 2014 and 2015 provided typical cases for an on-the-downward economic cycle, while its performance in the periods of 1985–1986, 1988–1989, 1993–1994, and 2003–2007 provided typical cases for an on-the-up economic cycle (see Table 11). Generally speaking, developing countries may experience more intense hot/cold fluctuation in their economies compared with mature developed countries. China, being a developing country in the transition from planned economy to market economy, may exhibit even more intense macroeconomic cyclical fluctuations due to its particular situation. First, as a state-owned economy is subject to "soft budget restraint" (Kornai, 1986, 1998), it tends to make excessive investments when the economy is on-the-up, which may intensify the "overheating." On the other hand, economic actors may be reluctant to exit the market voluntarily when the economy is on-the-downward, causing the economy to face excessive capacity and suffer loss, which may prolong the process of capacity clearing [7, 13]. Second, the contest between local governments and the "promotion championship" of local officials are some of the most striking characteristics of China's economic development (Zhou Li'an, 2004, 2007). Local officials and governments are inclined to increase investment and protect local outdated capacity in exchange for GDP and tax income. Such practices can also intensify economic cyclical fluctuations.

However, it should be stressed that such regime-related reasons are by no means the root causes of macroeconomic cyclical fluctuations. Instead, the root cause lies in the universal phenomenon of the market economy—the loss of benefits caused by the "rush to the top" and the "war of attrition." This loss of benefits tilts the

Table 11 The Economic principles of proactive macroeconomic management by the Chinese government

	Macro-Economic performance	Micro-mechanism	Main measures for proactive macroeconomic management	Typical period
Economic up cycle	Investors are optimistic and the production capacity is expanding rapidly Redundant construction High inflation Rapid expansion of production capacity may accelerate the economy toward overcapacity	Rush to the Top	Limit redundant construction and control the blind expansion of production capacity Control the scale of infrastructure construction Tighten monetary and fiscal policies Curb inflation Raise nominal interest rates, protect the interests of depositors, and ensure financial stability	1984–1985 1988–1989 1993–1994 2003–2007
Economic down cycle	Overcapacity Deflation Declining profitability of enterprises Backward production capacity unwilling to withdraw, which makes the market difficult to clear	War of Attrition	Accelerate the exit of low-quality production capacity and promote market clearing Active fiscal policy, expansionary monetary policy Expand infrastructure building, boost aggregate demand, and help the economy escape from deflation Reform, release vitality, cultivate the market and expand domestic demand	1998–1999 2008–2009 2012–2016

Source Prepared by the author

macroeconomy into an ill balance. It has been shown in the past experience of the Chinese economy that SOEs are not the only participants of the "rush to the top" and "war of attrition"—so too are a large number of private businesses. In fact, private businesses were among the causes that gave rise to severely excessive capacity in such sectors as cement, steel, coal, sheet glass, and photovoltaic in 2014 and 2015. In fact, even in those economies that are widely recognized as having a higher level of marketization, it is also common for the "rush to the top" and "war of attrition" to cause economic cyclical fluctuations and loss of overall social welfare. The rise and fall of the "Internet Bubble" between 1995 and 2001 may be taken as a typical case of the "rush to the top," and the long-term excessive competition and resource consumption of the US airline industry can serve as an example of both the "rush to the top" and the "war of attrition" (see details in Feature 2).

3.2 The Government Must Utilize Market, Reform, and Administrative Means (The "Three Arrows") to Stabilize the Macroeconomy

The "visible hand" of the government should help the "invisible hand" of the market to stabilize cyclical fluctuations via proactive macroeconomic management. This will help avoid the "loss of overall welfare due to individual rational behavior." When the economy is too "hot," the government should leverage proactive macroeconomic management to limit excessive investment and repetitive construction, control the size of infrastructure construction, and put a lid on inflation. When the economy is too "cold," the government should also leverage proactive macroeconomic management to accelerate the exit of outdated capacity, drive capacity clearing, and at the same time expand infrastructure construction, stimulate total demand, and help the economy emerge from deflation.

Looking back at the past 40 years, one of the key reasons the Chinese economy was able to realize long-term, steady, and rapid economic growth from a low-income economy to a medium- and high-income economy is that the government properly utilized proactive macroeconomic management measures to resolve the challenges of economic "overly-cold" and "overheated" periods, avoiding great shocks in the economy.

The Chinese government fired "three arrows at the same time" in its proactive macroeconomic management through the application of market approaches, administrative orders, and system reforms. In this way, the government was able to cool the market when the macroeconomy was too "hot" and warm the market when the economy was too "cold," so as to stabilize economic development in the short run and to promote the optimized allocation of resources and improve social welfare in the long run. The "three arrows" are summarized as follows[36] (Table 11).

[36]The following three paragraphs of the "three arrows" are expanded in detail on the basis of the section II(3) of [3].

Market Approaches: (1) Utilizing such monetary policy tools as the adjustment of deposit and lending benchmark rates and RRR to indirectly influence the investment and financing behavior of enterprises and the saving and consumption decision making of households; (2) utilizing tax rate adjustments (enterprise income tax rate, export rebate rate, VAT rate, tax incentives for car purchase), fiscal expenditure subsidies for supporting consumption (subsidy for rural appliance purchases), fiscal expenditure subsidies for supporting enterprise equipment upgrading, and other fiscal expenditure tools to expand or tighten the overall demand.

Administrative Orders: (1) to strictly control the approval of newly added investment projects and prevent redundant construction in the overheating period (Typical case: In the 1990s, administrative orders were taken to strictly control new projects and address overheated admissions to the industries of TV sets, washing machines, and refrigerators[37]); (2) to force outdated capacity out of the market via administrative orders in the economic overly-cold period (Typical cases: "Spindle reduction and capacity limitation" in the textile industry in the 1990s, and compulsory de-capacity by directly setting specific quantitative targets for the sectors of steel, cement, electrolytic aluminum, sheet glass, etc. after 2015.[38] For instance, the *Opinions on Dissolving Excess Capacity and Realizing Profitable Development of the Steel Industry* distributed by the State Council in February 2016 clearly set targets to reduce crude steel capacity by 100 to 150 million tons in the five years' period from 2016, and to demand compulsory exit of the enterprises that failed to reach the standard requirements in aspects of environmental protection, energy consumption, quality, safety, and technology (see Table 12). Such targets were communicated from the central government down to each province, city, and county); (3) to expand infrastructure construction and directly and indirectly enlarge overall demand in the economic overly-cold period (Typical case: In order to address the shock of the Asian financial crisis, the central government additionally issued RMB100 billion in national bonds in 1998, and put in place RMB100 billion in loans solely for expanding infrastructure construction, including rural power grid upgrading, irrigation project construction, highway construction, granary construction, urban infrastructure construction, interest subsidies for technical transformation, etc.); (4) by reducing land approvals, tightening credit granting, and raising the threshold through administrative orders to "restrict house purchases" on the real property market of key cities.

System reform: To set free economic vitality by pushing ahead economic system reforms and tactfully utilizing the turning point between an economic "overly-cold" period and an "overheated" period. The typical case of realizing proactive macroeconomic management purposes through reform measures is exemplified by the Chinese government's response to the outbreak of Asian financial crisis: (1) drove housing system reform by seizing the appropriate opportunity after the Asian financial crisis,

---

[37] *Zhu Rongji On the Record* (Book II), Pages 374 and 498.

[38] See details in the "Opinions on Dissolving Excess Capacity and Realizing Profitable Development of the Steel Industry" (*Guo Fa* [2016] No. 6) distributed by the State Council on February 1, 2016.

Table 12 De-capacity rules of administrative orders in the steel industry

Overall principles: to strictly abide by the laws, regulations, and industrial policies relating to environmental protection, energy consumption, quality, safety, and technology, and to force out capacity that fails to reach the standard requirements	
Categorized metrics	Measures
Environmental Protection	Those whose pollutant discharge rate fails to satisfy the requirements under the *Emission Standard of Water Pollutants for the Iron and Steel Industry*, the *Emission Standard of Air Pollutants for the Sintering and Pelletizing of Iron and Steel Industry*, the *Emission Standard of Air Pollutants for the Iron Smelt Industry*, the *Emission Standard of Air Pollutants for the Steel Smelt Industry*, and the *Emission Standard of Air Pollutants for the Steel Rolling Industry* shall receive continuous daily penalties and, in cases of grave violation, shall be ordered to shut down or close after approval by the competent People's Government
Energy consumption	Those who fail to satisfy the statutory standard requirements under the *Norm of Energy Consumption Per Unit Product of Major Individual Process of Crude Steel Manufacturing Process* shall make the rectification within 6 months, and may file an application for no more than 3 months' extension if necessary. Failure to make the rectification within the timeframe or failure to satisfy the requirements for such rectification will cause the capacity to be closed, shut down, or forced to exit the market pursuant to relevant law
Quality	Those whose steel products fail to satisfy the statutory quality requirements shall be penalized and ordered to stop production for rectification, and those who fail to make the rectification within the timeframe or fail to satisfy the requirements for such rectification will be closed, shut down, or forced to exit the market pursuant to law
Safety	Those who fail to reach the third grade under the enterprise manufacturing safety standards, or whose safety conditions fail to satisfy the standard requirements under the *Safety Regulations for Ironmaking*, the *Safety Regulations for Steelmaking*, or the *Gas Safety Regulations for Industrial Enterprises*, shall immediately stop production for rectification, and shall be closed, shut down, or forced to exit the market pursuant to the law if they fail to make the rectification within 6 months or still fail to reach the standard after rectification
Technology	To immediately close, shut down, and demolish 400-cubic meter and below iron-making blast furnaces, 30-ton and below steelmaking converters, and 30-ton and below steelmaking electric furnaces and other such outdated manufacturing equipment in accordance with the *Catalogue for Guiding Industry Restructuring (2011 Version) (Amendment)*. Those who manufacture substandard steel shall be immediately closed, shut down, demolished, and penalized according to the law

Source Opinions on Dissolving Excess Capacity and Realizing Profitable Development of the Steel Industry issued by the State Council, February, 2016

and turned the original welfare-oriented public housing distribution system into a market-oriented purchasing system, which not only achieved the effect of short-term proactive macroeconomic management, but also added new momentum to marketization reforms and long-term economic growth; (2) the "expansion of college enrollment" initiative started in 1999 expanded domestic demand and relieved short-term employment pressure on the one hand, and also built up a rich talent reserve for long-term economic development; (3) seized the opportunity to speed up WTO entry negotiations so that China could successfully join the WTO in 2001, further opening the economy; (4) the four asset management companies were established to spin off the bad assets of the four state-owned commercial banks, which marked the start of the joint-stock reform of state-owned commercial banks. In another example, the government seized the overheating opportunity between 1993 and 1994 to drive the "tax distribution system" reform, which substantially transformed the basic framework of China's financial and fiscal systems. In conclusion, the Chinese government's proactive macroeconomic management mission statement is: **to drive system reform by tactfully utilizing the opportunity of proactive macroeconomic management so as to use reform as a means to stabilize economic fluctuation, release new vitality, and add new momentum to long-term economic development.**

Finally, we must emphasize that **it is costly to digest cyclical economic fluctuations purely by relying on the "invisible hand" of the market**. Some believe that the power of the "invisible hand" will clear the market no matter what. While this is true, in practice, it often takes a long time to clear the market purely by means of market power, which may result in a significant waste of social resources. Taking the US airline industry as an example, we can see that the market clearing process has lasted over 30 years, from the 1980s to the 2010s. Such a long waiting period and huge waste of resources are unaffordable for a developing country like China. For a developed country, sitting back and waiting for the "invisible hand" to take effect could just result in back and forth economic fluctuations or a sporadic economic crisis, while for a developing country like China, the abovementioned "rush to the top" and "war of attrition" could mean interruption or even suspension of economic development, social turbulence, and the "middle-income trap." This has been proven by the experience of many Latin-American and Sub-Saharan African countries.

Feature 2 "Dream of an Empire" of Airline Companies and Excessive Competition in the US Civil Aviation Industry

In 1978, the *US Airline Deregulation Act* was enacted to loosen the US government's grip on air ticket prices, air routes, and market access. Following the act's passage, the supervisory power of the Civil Aeronautics Board also began to withdraw. As a result, airline companies became freely able to enter and exit the aviation industry and set their own air routes and ticket prices.

Initially, deregulation worked as expected, as the average ticket price actually paid by passengers dropped 30% after considering the actual inflation rate between 1976 and 1990.[39] Between 1979 and 1988, the number of domestic airports for which American Airlines provided services grew from 50 to 173, and the same Chart for United Airlines grew from 80 to 169.[40]

With new players flocking into the market, existing airline companies were not willing to give up their established positions, and therefore tried every means to expand their size and improve capacity in pursuit of an economy of scale. At the same time, they restricted the development of their competitors, hoping to win the "rush to the top" and realize the "dream of an empire." Eventually, the balance of microscopic inter-company contests triggered and intensified macroeconomic fluctuations. The "rush to the top" in aviation prompted enterprises to blindly expand and rapidly accumulate capacity, which led to a vicious price war, illegal booking services, and other acts of unfair competition.

Since the 1980s, in a fight for market share, airline companies have established a special network of hub-and-spoke routes, which, compared with "fully connected" routes, may adjust prices more flexibly. Research shows that when new entrants attempt to access the market of hub-and-spoke routes, existing companies will have sufficient motive to engage in a price war [6].

Unfair competition also lurked in other areas. In the competitive environment of the aviation industry, companies with many integrated services like booking and air transport were able to use technical tools to control the direction of cross-product externalities, and thus adversely impact their competitors with no integration of services. For example, at the early stage of the online booking system, the airline company owning this system intentionally placed its own flights ahead of those of competitors. Given agency costs, travel agencies had no incentive to compare and screen all the flights even if they knew the flights that ranked in the top were not necessarily the best ones. Fisher and Neels (1997) estimated that in 1984 alone, this ranking priority translated into an impact of USD58 million [4].

Faced with fierce competition, airline companies adopted an attrition strategy, and were unwilling to exit the market despite the losses suffered. Rather, they pinned their hopes on the possibility that their competitors would exit or go bankrupt before them. The balance of inter-company "rush to the top" interactions also intensified economic fluctuations at the macroscopic level and resulted in excessive capacity and heavy losses within the industry as a whole. The aviation industry suffered losses for as many as 14 years out of the 28 years between 1980 and 2008.[41] Under the intense competition pressure, many airline companies went bankrupt or were acquired, such as Pan American's acquisition of National Airline in 1980, People Express's acquisition of Frontier Airline in 1985, and Northwest Airlines' acquisition

---

[39] Alfred Kahn, "Airline Deregulation," see details at http://www.econlib.org/library/Enc1/AirlineDeregulation.html.

[40] Ibid.

[41] "China Merchants Securities, Invisible Supply-Side Reform, 9-Year Secular Bull Ten-Baggar – Deep Probe into Mega Bull Market of U.S. Aviation Industry," March 12, 2018.

of Republic Airlines in 1986. The number of large airline companies dropped from 11 prior to the deregulation to 8 in 1996, and the domestic market share of the three major airline companies grew from 31% in 1981 to 55% [1]. On the other hand, most surviving companies suffered long-term severe losses or even bankruptcy. American Airlines filed for bankruptcy protection twice in 2002 and 2004, respectively, United Airlines filed in 2002, and Delta Airlines and Northwest Airlines filed in 2005.

After American Airlines merged with Western Airlines in 2005, Delta Airlines acquired Northwest Airlines in 2008, United Airlines merged with Continental Airlines in 2010, Southwest Airlines acquired AirTran Airways in 2012, and American Airlines merged with US Airways in 2013, forming the biggest airline company in the world. At that point, an oligopoly was finally formed in the US aviation industry, which marked the end of over 30 years' excessive competition. As a result, compared with the net loss of USD51.8 billion suffered between 1979 and 2010, the US aviation industry recorded aggregate earnings of USD59.4 billion between 2011 and 2016—nearly equal to the aggregate loss of the past 30 years.[42]

We can see from the development history of the US aviation industry that it is extremely costly to rely solely on the power of the market to address economic cyclical fluctuations. It took the US aviation industry more than 30 years—from its deregulation at the end of the 1970s to the financial crisis in 2008—to weather its fluctuations. In this long process, overcapacity and excessive competition caused long-term loss and unfair competition in the industry. This serves as a valuable lesson regarding the role of the government in a market economy system.

References

1. Button, K. (2002).*Transport Economics*, translated by Feng Zongxian, The Commercial Press.
2. Bulow J. I., & Paul, K. (1999). The generalized war of attrition. *American Economic Review, 89*(1), 175–189.
3. Feng, M. & Li, D. D. & Wu, S. (2021). How did China maintain macroeconomic stability 1978–2018? *China & World Economy*, forthcoming.
4. Fisher, F., & Neels, K. (1997). Estimating the effects of display bias in computer reservations systems. In *Microeconomics: Essays in Theory and Applications* edited by Maarten-Pieter Schinkel, Massachusetts: Cambridge University Press, 450–483.
5. Fudenberg, D., & Tirole, J. (1986). A theory of exit in duopoly. *Econometrica, 54*(4), 943–960.
6. Hendricks, K., Piccione, M., & Tan, G. (1997). Entry and exit in hub-spoke networks. *RAND Journal of Economics, 28*, 291–303.
7. Li, D. D., & Liang, M. (1998). Causes of the soft budget constraint: evidence on three explanations. *Journal of Comparative Economics, 26*(1), 104–116.
8. Li, X. (1979). Speech at the Central Government Work Conference, April 5, 1979.
9. Lu, F. (2016). *Logic of proactive macroeconomic management* [M].
10. Maddison, A. (1997). *World economy: a bicentennial perspective* [M], translated by Li Dewei and Gai Jianling, Reform Press.
11. Kornai, J. (1986). The soft budget constraint. *Kyklos*, 39(1), 3–30.

[42]Da Cheng International Asset Management Company Limited, "Will the Aviation Industry have Opportunities for Investment in 2018?".

12. Kornai, J. (1998). The place of the soft budget constraint syndrome in economic theory. *Journal of Comparative Economics, 26*(1), 11–17.
13. Qian, Y., & Roland, G. (1999). Federalism and the soft budget constraint. *The American Economic Review, 88*(5), 1143–1162.
14. Wang, T. (2005). All previous proactive macroeconomic management since the reform and opening up and their take-aways. *New Finance*, (07), 9–13.
15. Wei, J. (2008). The course of proactive macroeconomic management in china since reform and opening up, (I)[J]. *Tide of the Century*, (5), 8–14.
16. Zhou, L. (2004). Incentivizing and cooperation among government officials in promotion contest—reasons for chronic existence of China's local protectionism and redundant construction. *Economic Research Journal*, (6), 33–40.
17. Zhou, L. (2007). A study on the mode of promotion championship among chinese local officials. *Economic Research Journal*, (7), 36–50.

The manufacturer's authorised representative in the EU is Springer Nature Customer Service Centre GmbH, Europaplatz 3, 69115 Heidelberg, Germany. If you have any concerns regarding our products, please contact ProductSafety@springernature.com

Printed and bound by CPI Group (UK) Ltd, Croydon, CR0 4YY
30/09/2026
02225251-0006